THEORY OF
PSYCHOANALYTICAL PRACTICE

PSYCHOANALYTIC IDEAS AND APPLICATIONS SERIES

IPA Publications Committee

Gennaro Saragnano (Rome), Chair; Leticia Glocer Fiorini (Buenos Aires), Consultant; Samuel Arbiser (Buenos Aires); Catalina Bronstein (London); Paulo Cesar Sandler (São Paulo); Christian Seulin (Lyon); Mary Kay O'Neil (Montreal); Gail S. Reed (New York); Rhoda Bawdekar (London), Ex-officio as Publications Officer

Other titles in the Series

THEORY OF PSYCHOANALYTICAL PRACTICE

A Relational Process Approach

Juan Tubert-Oklander

General Editor

Gennaro Saragnano

Psychoanalytic Ideas and Applications Series

KARNAC

First published in 2013 by
Karnac Books Ltd
118 Finchley Road, London NW3 5HT

British Library Cataloguing in Publication Data

A C.I.P. for this book is available from the British Library

ISBN 978 1 78220 056 7

Edited, designed and produced by The Studio Publishing Services Ltd
www.publishingservicesuk.co.uk
e-mail: studio@publishingservicesuk.co.uk

Printed in Great Britain

www.karnacbooks.com

CONTENTS

PSYCHOANALYTIC IDEAS AND APPLICATIONS SERIES

IPA Publications Committee

The Publications Committee of the International Psychoanalytical Association continues, with this volume, the series "Psychoanalytic Ideas and Applications".

The aim of this series is to focus on the scientific production of significant authors whose works are outstanding contributions to the development of the psychoanalytic field and to set out relevant ideas and themes, generated during the history of psychoanalysis, that deserve to be known and discussed by present psychoanalysts.

The relationship between psychoanalytic ideas and their applications has to be put forward from the perspective of theory, clinical practice, technique, and research so as to maintain their validity for contemporary psychoanalysis.

The Publication Committee's objective is to share these ideas with the psychoanalytic community, and with professionals in other related disciplines, in order to expand their knowledge and generate a productive interchange between the text and the reader.

This series is now enriched with a new important title: *Theory of Psychoanalytic Practice. A Relational Process Approach* authored by Juan Tubert-Oklander, to whom we offer our gratitude and appreciation. It is a comprehensive handbook, which deals with the psychoanalytic technique as a whole and with the analytic practice considered from a relational point of view, thus providing our readers with a general view upon a specific subject from a specific theoretical frame. But with the recent and constant internationalisation of our discipline the need for scholarship and analytic culture is growing accordingly. This text is didactically useful to everyone who wants to learn and master the core concepts of the relational approach, one which is nowadays always referred to. I am therefore sure this volume will encounter the favour of psychoanalysts and of many other students of related disciplines.

Gennaro Saragnano
Series Editor
Chair, IPA Publications Committee

ACKNOWLEDGEMENTS

For permission to reproduce material already in print, the author acknowledges with thanks the following:

To the Editor and the Analytic Press/Taylor and Francis, publisher of *Psychoanalytic Dialogues: The International Journal of Relational Perspectives*, for "The whole and the parts: Working in the analytic field", previously published in *Psychoanalytic Dialogues, 17*: 115–132, which is the basis for Chapter Six.

For Reyna,
who should share the billing

ABOUT THE AUTHOR

Juan Tubert-Oklander, MD, PhD, was born, studied medicine, and trained as a group therapist in Buenos Aires, Argentina. Since 1976, he has lived and worked in private practice in Mexico City, where he trained as a psychoanalyst, being now a Mexican citizen. He is the author of numerous papers and book chapters, published in Spanish, English, Italian, French, Portuguese, and Czech. He is co-author, with Reyna Hernández-Tubert, of *Operative Groups: The Latin-American Approach to Group Analysis* (Jessica Kingsley, 2004), and author of *The One and the Many: Selected Papers on Relational Analysis and Group Analysis* (Karnac, 2013). He is a full member of the Mexican Psychoanalytic Association, the Argentine Psychoanalytic Association, and the Group-Analytic Society International. He is a training and supervising analyst at the Institute of the Mexican Psychoanalytic Association.

PROLOGUE

A prologue is the opportunity an author has to warn any actual or prospective reader about what to expect from the volume presently in her or his hands (or, as things go nowadays, perhaps an e-book reader). So, I shall be frank about it: *this is not a book on psychoanalytic technique*. Indeed, its whole purpose may be thought of as an utter negation of the very possibility of such technique.

The previous statement is so extreme as to demand an immediate qualification. *Of course*, a psychoanalyst uses all sorts of techniques in his or her daily practice. There are many ways of conducting an interview, establishing a contract, conducting a treatment on a daily basis, making an interpretation, dealing with acting out, and so on, and not all of them are equally valid, useful, acceptable, or adequate for particular cases. Some are better, others not so good, yet others might be poor or outright bad, and what works perfectly in one case might fail calamitously in another. There might also be more than one alternative techniques that are equally adequate in any given situation or case. But this book is not about these detailed purposive operations, which really belong to a treatise and can only be truly learnt in clinical seminars conducted by experienced clinicians.

The statement that there is no such thing as a psychoanalytic technique refers to *the* technique, understood as a standard method to be applied in each and every case, some sort of protocol or algorithm that guarantees success to anyone who is able and willing to follow a preordained sequence of operations. This idea of the Method, which started with Descartes and Francis Bacon, is so much a part of our contemporary scientific–technologic conception of the world that it is scarcely thinkable that things might be otherwise. It has been argued that this claim was born with the ascent of the commercial bourgeoisie during Renaissance (Sabato, 1941). At a point in Western history in which money and commerce made social mobility possible, for the first time, for people who were not of noble birth, it became fashionable to disassociate prowess in knowledge and practical affairs from any claim to inborn talents. Hence this democratic ideal, synthesized in the well-known proverb that "the lame man who keeps the right road outstrips the runner who takes a wrong one", led to a mistrust of exceptional endowments in gifted individuals. It was Descartes (1637) who summarised this ideology, which still predominates, in the following terms:

> The power of judging well and of distinguishing the true from the false, which is properly what is called good sense or reason, is naturally equal in all men, and thus . . . the diversity of our opinions arises not because some are more reasonable than others, but only because we conduct our thoughts by different ways, and do not consider the same things. *For it is not enough to have a good mind, but the principal thing is to apply well.* (p. 16, my italics)

In the field of psychoanalysis, there are two polar positions: those who emphasise the personal contribution and idiosyncratic characteristics of the individual analyst to the therapeutic process and those who only acknowledge the intervention of theory, technique, and method in the therapeutic intervention. The former conceive the analytic treatment as a bipersonal relationship and, hence, find a need for an adequate match between the individual personalities of analyst and patient (the "analytic couple"); they also highlight the unique and creative aspects of each treatment, thus defining our profession as an art. The latter, on the other hand, consider psychoanalysis as a science and the psychoanalytic treatment as a technology, such as medicine, thus excluding any personal factor. For them, there is no such thing as an analytic couple and the best analyst for any given pati[...] precisely, the best analyst—that is, he or she who has a better know[...] ledge of theory and a greater command of technique (see Etchegoyen, 1986, pp. 35–40 for a statement of this position).

The first time I became fully aware of these contrasting perspectives, which are not merely of academic interest, since they bring about major consequences for our practice, was during the 34th International Psychoanalytical Congress, held in Hamburg in 1985. There I attended a Plenary Panel on "Identification and its vicissitudes in childhood". The two speakers were Selma Kramer, a Mahlerian analyst from Philadelphia, and Edna O'Shaughnessy, a committed Kleinian from London. The papers included clinical narratives of child analyses; the cases were quite similar, since both children had a borderline pathology, but there ended any possible resemblance. Simon, Kramer's (1986) patient, was a six-year-old adopted white child caught in midst of a fierce competition between his two primary care-givers—his white mother and a black nursemaid—for the possession of him, "each demanding loyalty to herself and to herself alone, [so] that his identity and identifications were confused, in fact duplicated" (p. 171). She managed the treatment with great patience and understanding, and very few interpretations, striving to establish a reliable relationship with the child. O'Shaughnessy (1986), on the other hand, had bestowed numerous subtle and intelligent interpretations, all of them framed in the Kleinian clinical language, on Timmy, her three-and-a-half-year-old patient. She also kept a strict analytic attitude of neutrality and abstinence, rejecting, for instance, a gift brought to her by the child, telling him "I do not accept any gifts from patients"—an action that many of us deemed to be unempathic. However, both children were clearly helped by their treatments.

The open discussion of their papers was begun by Professor Serge Lebovici, from Paris, who said, "Dr O'Schaughnessy's paper brings to us the problem of content interpretations. Frankly, I doubt that a three-and-a-half-year-old child may have understood such interpretations. I believe that it was the therapist's wonderful personality which really allowed the child to improve during the treatment." Half of the audience applauded heartily.

Edna O'Shaughnessy, totally impervious to this display of French gallantry, replied, "I would like to clarify for Professor Lebovici, in the first place, that I am not, and have never been, a "doctor". Second, I do

.lity—wonderful or otherwise—has anything
it I cure as a result of what I say, not of what I am."
.udience applauded, even more enthusiastically.
., I went to have a beer with three European
which had studied with me in the Mexican Institute
.s. For me and my former classmate, both identified
.pmental and object-relations perspective, Kramer's
clin. . was excellent, sensitive, and empathic, while O'Shaughnessy's ι. .s completely out of touch with the child. For our two
friends, the latter was a brilliant example of psychoanalytic work and
the former was only a mediocre supportive therapy. As you see, our
small group, just like the audience, was divided in halves.

This fifty-fifty division is something I have regularly witnessed in
the discussion of Plenary Panels in psychoanalytical congresses. (This
obviously does not occur in workshops and individual paper presen-
tations, since, there, people usually get together on the basis of a
common theoretical and ideological perspective.) Clearly, there are
major divergences in our conception of the psychoanalytic treatment
and of human life in general.

My own position on the matter leans towards the personological
conception of psychoanalysis, and away from that of scientific and
technological positivism. This precludes any attempt to describe the
treatment in terms of a predetermined sequence of stages, such as
Meltzer (1967) suggests in his book *The Psychoanalytical Process*. It also
avoids clear-cut definitions of terms, norms, and procedures. Hence,
what I intend to do in this book is pretty much what I do in my classes
at the Institute: to use the concepts, theories, and experiences as food
for a never-ending questioning and critical thought, by initiating an
open dialogue with my interlocutors: students, colleagues, and now
readers. They usually come out of it with a great many questions and
very few answers, but having exercised their capacity for critical
thinking. Some of them like it, while others hate the whole experience
(and myself).

Now comes the second point: *is this a textbook? The answer is yes and
no.* I have certainly made no effort to give a balanced account of all the
major trends in the understanding of the psychoanalytic clinical practice and experience, but, rather, developed a particular point of view,
that of relational psychoanalysis, as I understand and practise it. This
makes this book surely controversial, at best.

On the other hand, I have written it bearing always in mind the need of students undergoing psychoanalytical training. The chapters cover all the main points I usually teach in a second course in psychoanalytic technique, assuming that the students have already studied Freud's technical papers.

The whole book may be studied during a five-month term, while a more in-depth study, with additional material taken from the references, would take two such terms. I have already discussed successive versions of this text with several groups of students, during the years it took me to write the book, and they have found them useful, although quite a few of them did not agree with this way of conceiving the practice of psychoanalysis. I am also presently conducting a virtual study group of experienced colleagues who live in various locations, in which we are studying it.

Finally, there is still one point that should be specified: *my whole approach to the subject belongs to the Freudian tradition.* By this term, I do not mean that kind of thinking that strives to find the truth in the study of the minutiae of Freud's writings—this I would call "Freudism". I am, rather, referring to a way of approaching the problems of our clinical practice and experience, by taking Freud's first discoveries and thinking about these issues *as a starting point* for our critical and reflective dialogue, even if it leads us to some very different conclusions from his. Therefore, it should not surprise the reader to find that Freud is the most quoted author in this text. I fully understand and accept that other analysts and therapists, reared in different psychotherapeutic traditions, might take diverse authors as their starting point, but this should not interfere with our capacity to engage in a mutually respectful and productive dialogue with colleagues from other traditions.

My own preferred references draw from the work of Freud, Ferenczi, the Independent British tradition of object relations theory, the Latin-American tradition initiated by Enrique Pichon-Rivière, and the present-day intersubjective and relational trend in psychoanalysis. Being, as I am, both a psychoanalyst and a group analyst who finds these two theories and practices to be largely overlapping in their similarities and fully complementary in their differences, I have also made ample use of the group-analytic literature, in both the British tradition that stems from the work and teachings of S. H. Foulkes and the Latin-American tradition of Pichon-Rivière, a true pioneer of psychoanalysis and group analysis in Argentina. I particularly find Foulkes' concept of the group matrix to be enlightening for the understanding and further development of the contemporary concept of a "relational matrix". The fact that most present-day relational analysts have focused on bipersonal ("individual") therapy and lack a group-analytic training and experience has made it difficult for them to recognise that many of their relational concepts have been previously introduced and developed by group analysts. It has been the latter who have explored the area of confluence between group analysis and relational psychoanalysis, even before this name became fashionable—first with the Independent tradition and, more recently, with self psychology and relational analysis (Tubert-Oklander, 2013b).

The rest is to be found in the body of the book. It only remains for me the most pleasurable obligation of acknowledging the contribution of those who have aided me in my intellectual, professional, and personal journey that has made this book possible.

First and foremost, there is my wife, colleague, companion, and co-writer, Reyna Hernández-Tubert. Not only have many of the ideas that I put forward been developed in our endless conversation, thinking, working, and writing together, but she has also been my greatest critic and helped me to make a better text out of my initial efforts. Her more personal contribution to my existence, which has made me widely happier and much more creative, is perhaps more of a private matter that may not concern the reader, but I must mention the fact that she has given me the support and impetus I needed in order to traverse those moments of painful doubt and paralysis that haunt writers in general. This book would not exist without her. Writing is an act of love and, although love is what we really are, it remains forever incomplete unless one finds the right partner in this momentous journey. Thank God I found mine, and I hope my readers will also benefit from some of the side effects of my luck.

I have had several analysts in my life, and I would like to mention the two of them that have had the greatest influence on who I am now as a psychoanalyst and a human being. Betty Garma, my first analyst, treated me in Buenos Aires more than half a century ago, when I was still a child. She was then a young, warm, sensitive, intelligent, and beautiful woman, who not only understood my plight, but also took care of me and helped in the healing of the emotional wounds I was suffering at the time. My experience with her gave me a first imprint of what psychoanalysis can and should be. As decades went by and I became a psychoanalyst and grew as one, I gradually discovered that all my present conception of psychoanalysis is derived from this first analytic experience. She died in 2003, at the age of eighty-five, still vital and young at heart.

My last analyst and friend, Luis Moreno-Corzo, recently deceased at the age of ninety-four, helped me through a difficult period of mourning of my father's death, a few years ago. He also aided me in the consolidation of my identity as a senior analyst and author. I miss him as much as I am grateful to him.

Ricardo Horacio Etchegoyen, my first supervisor and teacher of technique, in Buenos Aires in the early 1970s, taught me the craft of our métier, and I can well say that I became a practising psychoanalyst under his guidance. However, he was such a good teacher that he helped me to identify my own thinking, in as much as it differed from his. I have always enjoyed reading his writings, whose clarity and lucidity allow me to specify, by contrast, my own views, which are very different from those he strongly believes in. His treatise, *The Fundamentals of Psychoanalytic Technique* (Etchegoyen, 1986), is a landmark in the evolution of the teaching of our discipline. He is still alive, although no longer active, at the age of ninety-four.

Then there are my two London great friends and colleagues, Malcolm Pines and Earl Hopper—both psychoanalysts and group analysts—with whom I have enjoyed a close friendship and a fruitful interchange of ideas during the last decade. They have also had a major influence on my present thought.

In the past few years, I have enjoyed sharing an ongoing discussion and interchange with my philosopher friend, Mauricio Beuchot, about his theoretical proposal of analogical hermeneutics. Together, we wrote the book *Hybrid Science: Psychoanalysis and Analogical Hermeneutics* (Tubert-Oklander & Beuchot Puente, 2008), in which we developed some of the philosophical ideas that underlie this conception of psychoanalysis.

I also wish to thank the members of the virtual group that is presently studying and discussing the manuscript of this book. They are all very experienced psychotherapists and psychoanalysts, and they have helped me to revise and correct quite a few flaws, both formal and substantial, that remained in the text. They are: Adriana Cuenca, Berta Loret de Mola, Jorge Luyando, Ignacio Mendoza,

Patricia Minjares, Marco Antonio Pérez-Mora, and María Luisa Saldaña.

The Institute of the Mexican Psychoanalytic Association is my intellectual home. There I completed my psychoanalytic education and still teach nowadays. My peculiar approach to psychoanalytic theory and practice has been largely determined by the fact that, during my training, I had the opportunity of studying with teachers who represented the various psychoanalytic schools, and helped me to know and understand writers as dissimilar as Freud, Abraham, Ferenczi, Reich, Fenichel, Fairbairn, Klein, Bion, Winnicott, Hartmann, Rapaport, Mahler, Greenson, Erikson, Pasche, Nacht, Lacan, Green, Kohut, and Kernberg, among others. From this variegated humus grew my present identity and views as an analyst.

Now it is my turn to convey what this perspective is, and this is what I shall do in the rest of the book.

Mexico City, 2013

CHAPTER ONE

Introduction

This text is an attempt to develop an integrative view of the theory of psychoanalytic practice. It is not, however, a theory of *classical* technique, but of a particular approach to clinical practice: that of *relational psychoanalysis*. Such view of our discipline is at odds with the traditional Freudian conception and with many of the prevailing schools in contemporary psychoanalysis. Nevertheless, it corresponds with the feelings and practice of many analysts, who have been trained in the various psychoanalytic traditions, but who have gradually found that their clinical experiences have led them to depart from some of the most cherished and adamantly sustained beliefs of their colleagues and friends. This new understanding of the nature and means of our work had been steadily unfolding in various areas of the psychoanalytic world, but until very recently it lacked a name that helped us to identify what the many clinical and theoretical contributions had in common. So, the various writers or groups developed their own terminology and concepts in order to account for their experience and practice. This tended to obscure the fact that they were unwittingly a part of an evolving collective movement.

Most of these developments tended to coalesce around the concept of *object relations*. Unlike traditional Freudian theory, which revolved around the theory of instinctual drives, for which the object was the most replaceable part of the instinct, a mere catalyst for the attainment of a discharge of organic tension, the object of object relations theory is always personal and non-replaceable, an object of love and hate, not only of pleasure and displeasure. This approach to the psychoanalytic understanding of the human being is also derived, of course, from Freud's original contributions—particularly in the second part of "Instincts and their vicissitudes" (1915c), in "Mourning and melancholia" (1917e), *Group Psychology and the Analysis of the Ego* (1921c), and *The Ego and the Id* (1923b). It was Ferenczi (1955, 1985), however, who initiated the systematic study of object relations.

Even though many object relations theorists have emphasised that this theory always refers to *internal* objects and the ego's fantasised relations with them, and not to interpersonal relations, presumably to avoid a conflict with the hallowed belief in the absolute priority of the intrapsychic, the fact remains that most of them—with the exception of Melanie Klein and her followers (Klein, Heimann, Isaacs, & Riviere, 1952)—consider that that psychic structure, what we may call the functional organisation of the mind, is derived from the internalisation of the child's relation with real persons in its entourage. A logical consequence of such belief is to acknowledge that the real person of the analyst—and not only his or her technical intervention—is involved in the analytic process and in the attainment of the cure.

Another characteristic of object relations theory is an emphasis on what came to be called a "two-person psychology", contrasted with the classic psychoanalytic theory, considered as a "one-person psychology" (Balint, 1968). Where Freudian metapsychology conceived the human mind as an almost closed system, which acted in a quasi-mechanical way, a conception that found an expression in terms such as "psychic apparatus", "mental mechanisms", "energy", "structure", "charge", and "discharge", object relations theory understood it as an open system, permeated by the individual's many relations with other significant people and with their environment, both social and non-human—physical and ecological, as Searles (1960) clearly described. When this point of view is applied to the analytic situation, it becomes a conviction that the observational data that pave the way for the analytic enquiry should be derived from the inner experience and the behaviour of both parties, and not only from one of them—the patient—as the objectivistic epistemology of classical theory demands.

Such a view is either explicitly stated, or implied and thinly disguised, in the work of writers such as Fairbairn, Balint, Winnicott, Searles, Rycroft, Milner, Khan, Little, Bollas, Pines, and Hopper, all of them members (with the exception of Searles) of the Independent Group of the British Psychoanalytic Society, and all of them heirs to the rich legacy of Ferenczi (Aron & Harris, 1993).

In the USA, Freudian psychoanalysis was dominated by one of the versions of psychoanalytic theory—that of ego psychology, nowadays referred to as the structural theory—which emphasised a metapsychological description of the functional structures of the mind, and minimisied the consideration of the sort of actual personal relations described by object relations theory. The other quite distinct psychoanalytic tradition in that country—that of Harry Stack Sullivan's interpersonal psychoanalysis, represented by the William Alanson White Institute for Psychoanalysis—was completely isolated from the former. Both traditions had been utterly split from each other, and both had developed their own conceptual language, theory, technique, clinical practice, training procedures, institutions, and patient following. Hence, for many years, there was no dialogue between them, although the Washington Psychoanalytic Institute retained the influence of Fromm-Reichmann's interpersonal approach to psychoses, thus allowing a more diversified theoretical base. One of the graduates of its Institute, Harold Searles, who worked with Fromm-Reichmann in Chestnut Lodge, became a pioneer in the psychoanalytic treatment of psychotic patients in the USA and a radical explorer of the field of countertransference, whose writings strongly resembled Ferenczi's (1985) yet-unpublished *Clinical Diary*.

Such neat separation began to crack during the 1970s, when a growing interest in British object relations theory and the appearance of Kohut's (1971, 1977, 1984) self psychology reopened the question of the alleged opposition between one-person and two-person psychologies. These theories were shocking and unacceptable for the more conservative members of both psychoanalytic groups. The Freudians found them non-psychoanalytic, or even anti-psychoanalytic, since they rejected or minimised the importance of instinctual drives, questioned the absolute primacy of intrapsychic processes, emphasised the importance of real external objects, both during infancy and childhood and in later years, suggested that analysts offered their patients much more than interpretations, and demanded a serious consideration of the participation of the analyst's subjectivity in the analytic process. The interpersonalists, on the other hand, felt that these theories were too Freudian, since they did not espouse a wholesale rejection of drive theory, placed too much emphasis on childhood experiences and their consequences for the organisation of the patient's personality and relational patterns, and insisted that the analyst should give expression to his or her subjective experiences only seldom and cautiously. But many other analysts in both groups read and were interested in these new ideas, and this set in motion a collective process that finally became a new trend in psychoanalysis.

In 1983, Greenberg and Mitchell, two analysts who came from the interpersonal field, wrote a book called *Object Relations and Psychoanalytic Theory*, in which they reviewed the Freudian and interpersonal points of view, and then contrasted them with that of British object relations theory. Thus, they identified and specified two widely diverging approaches to psychoanalysis: the *drive-structure model* and the *relational-structure model*, usually referred to simply as the "relational model".

Aron, from whose 1996 book, *A Meeting of Minds*, I have extensively drawn in order to present this historical evolution, recounts how some of the teachers at the New York University Postdoctoral Program in Psychotherapy and Psychoanalysis, in which he was trained, met in order to choose a name for their particular orientation. Such a decision was necessary because of the programme's peculiar organisation. Having been planned as a university programme committed to diverse viewpoints and academic freedom, its faculty represented the variegated panorama of psychoanalysis in the USA. This soon turned, however, into a two-track system, which allowed the students to decide what sort of training they were willing to follow: Freudian or Interpersonal. But when a number of faculty members began to feel that they were joined by a common point of view that was not represented by either track, they decided that they should start a new track, and then a name for it became an urgent need.

The group considered several alternatives, such as "interpersonal", "intersubjective", "object relations", or "self-selfobject relations", but discarded them all, on account of their sectarian implications. They finally compromised, though rather reluctantly, on the term "relational", borrowed from Greenberg and Mitchell (1983), as Aron (1996) describes in his book:

At first no one was happy with the term because it seemed to minimize both the role of the self and the biologically given components of the personality. It had the advantage, however, of seeming to borrow from the object relations tradition, the interpersonal relations tradition, and the self-selfobject relations [Kohutian] tradition; and it clearly seemed to distinguish itself from the drive theory perspective. (p. 13)

After that, the name rapidly helped the consolidation of a group, which gave birth to a new magazine called *Psychoanalytic Dialogues: A Journal of Relational Perspectives*, founded in 1991, which opened its doors to writers from all fields, such as object relations, interpersonal psychoanalysis, self psychology, Jungian analytical psychology, and intersubjective psychoanalysis, who were willing to enter an open debate on the implications of the relational view. Years later, in 2000, the group was to become institutionalised as the International Association for Relational Psychotherapy and Psychoanalysis.

But what, exactly, is relational psychoanalysis? It is not a new dogma or a systematic theory, but, rather, a new way of looking at things that have been known to clinicians since the beginning of psychoanalysis. Such a position was clearly stated by Ghent (2002), a distinguished interpersonal psychoanalyst and musician, one of the founding members of the Association, in his Introduction to the First IARPP Conference, in the following terms:

> There is no such thing as a relational theory, but there is such a thing as a relational point of view, a relational way of thinking, a relational sensibility, and we believe that it is this broad outlook that underpins the sea change that many of us recognize as breathing fresh life into our field. . . . [Among us], there are those who identify as Freudian, or Jungian, or intersubjectivists, or so called "relational analysts". (p. 7, my italics)

So, relational analysis is really a way of looking at the psychoanalytic experience, which is shared by numerous analysts formed by disparate traditions, and its community is a far cry from being uniform: a motley assembly of philosophers, artists, doctors, and freedom fighters of the mind, all sharing the same heart—as psychoanalysis was in its beginnings—rather than a battalion of well-trained soldiers, all marching to the same step. If relational analysis is a school, it is certainly not in the sense that Marxism is, a group unified by its adherence to its founder's point of view, to a set of established principles, or to a foundational text, but rather as Impressionism was—a collection of artists who share a similar interest and concern, that every one of them feels free to explore in his or her own particular way.

And what is this same heart, this shared interest? It is mainly a concern about relationships, with an emphasis on the emotional bond between human beings. This leads them to regard human affairs in the following terms.

1. A rejection of drive-orientated theories, in as much as these imply an impersonal causal explanation of human experience and behaviour, rather than a personal account of people's intentions and motives; therefore

2. A preference for those theories that conceive people as whole persons, with feelings, thoughts, perceptions, wishes, and fears, who relate to other whole persons who share this subjectivity, over those that postulate impersonal structures, mechanisms, and energies acting inside individuals—in Brierley's (1945) terms, *personology* rather than *metapsychology*;

3. An emphasis on the recognition, description, and understanding of subjective experience—both conscious and unconscious—of the two parties of the psychoanalytic encounter;

4. A conviction that a full understanding of what transpires during the analytic sessions should include a consideration of those relational events and processes that take place between analyst and patient—a *two-person psychology*—rather than solely relying on the study of the patient's internal processes (a *one-person psychology*); hence,

5. A special interest in the study of the mutual influences—both conscious and unconscious—that each of both parties of an analysis exert on the other, and on the process of negotiation— also conscious and unconscious—that lies under every event that occurs in it;

6. A constructivist epistemology, that understands psychoanalytic knowledge as the result of an interaction between two subjects who build together a new set of ideas, based on their shared experience and their mutual relationship that opens for them a new understanding of these;

7. A belief that all knowledge and ideas—including those of psychoanalysis—are determined by historical, linguistic, political, and contextual factors, and that they are based on emotional experiences derived from relationships;

8. A profound consideration of the effect of actual relations with other people—both past and present—on the conformation of the individual's experience and psychic structure and functioning; consequently,

9. A theory of the therapeutic process that attributes at least part of its results to the internalisation by both parties of the experience of their mutual relationship, and, finally,

10. A strongly held belief that, whenever a psychoanalytic treatment succeeds, it must necessarily have an effect on both parties, even though this is not equivalent for both of them.

Of course, this is my own construction of what I consider to be the basic principles of the relational approach to psychoanalysis, which would not be necessarily shared by many colleagues who consider themselves "relational analysts". On the other hand, many psychoanalysts who would not call themselves "relational" would share at least some of the propositions included in the previous list. This shows that the relational trend in psychoanalysis does not depend on the politics or the organisational aspects of our profession, but is, rather, an emerging tendency in the psychoanalytic community.

It might well be argued that this perspective has been a significant aspect of psychoanalysis from its very beginning, but the fact remains that psychoanalytic theory and practice acquire a very different feeling, organisation, and appearance when one takes personal relations as their basic concept, from when everything revolves around impersonal concepts such as "energy", "structure", "representation", or "drive". This is what Brierley (1945) was pointing out when she borrowed the term "personology" from General Smuts, to distinguish the science of personality from metapsychology. Smuts's (1926) argument is as follows:

> The procedure of psychology is largely and necessarily analytical and cannot therefore do justice to Personality in its unique wholeness. For this a new discipline is required, which we have called Personology, and whose task it would be to study Personality as a whole and to

trace the laws and phases of its development in the individual life.
... *Personology would study the Personality not as an abstraction or bundle of psychological abstractions, but rather as a vital organism, as the organic psychic whole which* par excellence *it is.* (Smuts, quoted by Brierley, 1945, p. 89, my italics)

So much for the use of the term "relational". And what about "process", which is also featured in the subtitle of this book? My choice of this word to characterise my approach to psychoanalytic technique might seem odd, especially in conjunction with the former, since the idea of a process approach is frequently opposed to that of a personal relations one (Guntrip, 1961, 1971). In such a line of thought, "process" implies a theory of impersonal events, articulated by causal relations, in the context of an allegedly scientific discourse—what Brierley (1944) calls an "objective theory". This is in sharp contrast with that other way of conceiving psychoanalysis—the "subjective theory" of personology—that understands it in terms relations of whole persons with other whole persons. From this perspective, Brierley (1944, 1945), however, considered that psychoanalysis needs *both* the subjective approach of personology *and* the objective view of metapsychology, which is a process theory. This is a consequence of the fact that each of these two kinds of knowledge is derived from a different type of relationship: one of them in terms of emotional contact and experience (subjective theory), and the other which deals with the same data from the standpoint of a temporarily detached observer.

There may be only one event, the psychological event, but there are very definitely two distinct methods of approaching and describing it. The results of both approaches have to be correlated, and can be used to correct each other. (Brierley, 1943, p. 120)

Another use of the term "process approach" to describe psychoanalytic treatment refers to Meltzer's (1967) contention that there is a "natural history" of the analytic process, with predetermined stages organised around the maternal transference and experiences of separation. What both conceptions have in common is to see the process as determined by something else than the wishes, aspirations, and feelings of the concrete persons that take part in the analytic encounter.

My own use of this term refers to the observation that, even though both parties enter the analysis with all their beliefs, values, motives, and thoughts, something else is set in motion when they start to meet in a closed room, in order to "do psychoanalysis", and this something has its own life and evolution, independent from their personal wishes and mental processes, determines them and is determined by them, and appears almost as a separate entity. A similar perception led Ogden (1994a) to postulate the existence of an "analytic third", which is created by the patient–analyst interaction, generating "analytic objects", which are the very stuff of the psychoanalytic enquiry.

The recognition that something is going on, which is independent from the individuals involved and somehow determines them, is a part of them, and is even taken by them as an object of relation, has been a regular observation in working with groups (Hernández de Tubert, 2006b; Tubert-Oklander, 2013b; Tubert-Oklander & Hernández de Tubert, 2004), and this led Foulkes (1964, 1975, 1990), the creator of group analysis, to formulate his concept of the *group matrix*. This is

> the hypothetical web of communication and relationship in a given group. It is the common shared ground which ultimately determines the meaning and significance of all events and upon which all communications and interpretations, verbal and non-verbal, rest. (p. 292)

From this point of view, a group—and this includes any ensemble of individuals-in-relation, starting with the analytic dyad—should be conceived as a network of multifarious relations, and the individuals would be the nodal points of such network (Foulkes, 1975). Now, this gossamer tissue of communications, in which individual human beings are embedded, is not only extended in space, up to the largest possible human system (Hernández de Tubert & Tubert-Oklander, 2005), but it also evolves in time, following a course with a consistent direction. This is the *process*, and in this sense we may speak of the psychoanalytic process.

The attempt to describe individual, dyadic, and collective events as a process with a direction and a course precludes thinking in terms of intrapsychic entities, such as those described by Freud in his topographic and structural models of the mind, or of the analyst and the patient as two isolated and almost closed "psychic apparatuses". Instead of thinking of separate structures, it conceives them in terms of *dynamic relations and their evolution*. Such relations and evolution are, of course, mainly unconscious, and need an interpretative activity in order to be unveiled. But, since the analyst is also a part of the process, there is no way in which he or she may be fully objective about it. This is why the analytic enquiry must be a co-operative exploration, shared between patient and analyst alike, since none of them could possibly see the whole picture.

The fact that the analytic relation is an intersubjective interaction—that is, that each of the parties has a personal perception, conception, feeling, and understanding of the other—makes its evolution unpredictable and ever-surprising. This is the rationale behind Bion's (1967) puzzling and certainly unorthodox statement that

> What is 'known' about the patient is of no further consequence: it is either false or irrelevant. If it is 'known' by patient and analyst, it is obsolete. . . . The one point of importance in any session is the unknown. Nothing must be allowed to distract from intuiting that. (p. 272)

In other words, the object of our enquiry is the unpredictable and uncontrollable spontaneous evolution of the analytic relationship.

When the process perspective is defined in these terms, it becomes fully compatible with the relational approach to psychoanalysis. This is why I have chosen the expression "a relational process approach" to describe my own view of psychoanalysis.

Now, if we accept this characterisation of the analytic process, it follows by necessity that we must reject not only any conception, like Meltzer's (1967), of a "natural history" of it, but also any attempt to establish a "standard technique", understood as a method, protocol, or algorithm that warrants the desired results, if followed as prescribed. Such an attempt to develop a "correct technique" stems from what I call "the dogma of the intrapsychic", the assumption that the essential determinants of an individual's behaviour and experience are "internal" and largely independent from "merely external" factors. This was stated by Balint (1968) in his classic book, *The Basic Fault*. There, he suggested that Freud was able to ignore external events and actual relations because he was working with obsessional and melancholic patients who had retired from objects and become interested only in their internal world. Hence,

> . . . all important events with these patients, both the pathological and the therapeutic, can be taken as happening almost exclusively

internally. It was this condition that enabled Freud to describe the therapeutic changes in a simpler form. *If external events and objects are only weakly cathected, the influence of their variation from one analyst to another, provided the analysts use a "sensible" analytic technique, will be still smaller, indeed practically negligible.* Forgetting that this is true only for this limit case and only as a first approximation, some analysts have arrived at the idea of "the correct technique", i.e. one that is correct for all patients and all analysts, irrespective of their individuality. *If my train of thought proves valid, "the correct technique" is a nightmarish chimera, a fantastic compilation from incompatible bits of reality.* (pp. 8–9, my italics)

This means that, if the patient's pathology is such that he or she acts as if the analyst did not really exist, the latter may safely cancel out his or her own personal contribution to the process in its interpretation. These conditions will subsist as long as no effort is made in order to analyse this defensive distortion in the patient's perception of the analytic relationship, and will be necessarily dispelled if and when he or she gets better, to the point of discovering that there is actually another person in the room. Then, the self-centred attitude derived from internalising relations gives way to the development of an intersubjective relationship, and the monotonous repetitiveness of pathology turns into the unpredictability of an open dialogue and a mutual interchange.

The impersonal view of the analytic interaction is a consequence of the fact that the psychoanalytic enquiry originally focused on psychopathology, and that only recently has greater attention been paid to the study of health. It is small wonder, then, that many of the recent developments in the study of personal relationships have been nurtured by the study of normal early development.

But, if we assume that the human being is intrinsically relational, then the analyst's whole personality, and not just her professional knowledge and skills, become a major factor in the therapeutic process. None the less, technique is still necessary, as a prop that keeps us going when we do not know what to do. When we are groping in the dark, it is certainly a great help to be able to adhere to the procedures generally accepted by our professional community, but we must not make too much of it. If an analyst knows what to do, he should do it, but if not, there are two ways to go: to follow the book or to accept and sustain uncertainty, and wait and see what happens.

In this, we should strike a delicate balance between the comfort of doing something one knows is bound to help, at least partially, and the anxiety of maintaining an uncertain situation, until a new development emerges or one of the parties concocts a creative response that paves the way for something new and unexpected.

These issues will, I hope, be clarified in the following chapters. I do not intend to write a guide for concrete action in the clinic, but, rather, open a reflective dialogue on the experiences gained from our practice, their implications, and the various concepts we use in order to think and talk about them. Such an attempt to theorise about the analytic experience represents for me the backbone of the psycho-analytic enterprise.

CHAPTER TWO

The psychoanalytic situation

The early evolution of technique

The early evolution of psychoanalytic technique is well known. At first, Freud used *suppressive hypnosis* for the treatment of neurotic symptoms. This implied giving the patient repeated commands that the symptom should disappear. In his 1893 paper "A case of successful treatment by hypnotism" (1892–1893), however, he introduced an interesting technical modification. He was then treating a young woman who had an obvious aversion to suckling her baby, rejected nourishment, and repeatedly vomited when forced to eat. After his initial injunctions met with a partial success, which was readily downplayed by the patient's family, Freud decided to try another strategy. Thus, he suggested to her that, five minutes after he left, she should face her family, rather violently, and demand of them why they were not giving her anything for supper, whether they were set on starving her, how on earth did they expect her to nurse her baby, and so on. From that moment on, her symptoms magically disappeared, although her husband was distressed by the fact that his wife had unwontedly expressed bitter reproaches against her mother. Obviously, the therapist had somehow sensed the existence of a family conflict and induced the patient to display it openly, instead of disguising it as a symptom. Not surprisingly, the family was not at all pleased with the treatment, in spite of the good therapeutic results! As could be expected, the relief was only temporary and Freud had to be called again after one year, when the birth of a new baby rekindled the problem.

Then came the *cathartic method*, which Freud had learnt from Breuer, who had himself acquired it from Anna O, his famous patient (Freud (with Breuer), 1895d). Unlike repressive hypnosis, this method implied an enquiry about the genesis of the symptoms, and this was particularly attractive for a staunch scientific researcher like Freud. He started this investigation by questioning the patients while in a trance, but soon he abandoned this practice, as he was not very good as a hypnotist, and replaced it by interrogating them in their waking state. In this, he relied on a further use of suggestion, when he placed his hand on the patient's brow and asked her to say the first thing that came into her mind at that time, which would be the sought-for representation. In the case of Catherine, however, he had only an ordinary dialogue with the patient, held in an informal setting, in which he managed to find out, in a single interview, the hidden meaning of her symptoms. But it was another patient, Fraulein Elizabeth von R, who prompted him to finally abandon his active questioning and his use of suggestion in order to extract associations from the patient, when she asked him to stop questioning her, because he did not let her follow the flow of her thoughts. Fortunately, Freud listened to her, and decided to keep silent and let her go on with her discourse, and this was the beginning of free association. About this, Jones (1953) points out that, just as Anna O was the inventor of the cathartic method, Elizabeth should be credited for the discovery of free association.

Later, in *The Interpretation of Dreams*, Freud discusses the free association method as a form of *self-observation*, which he contrasts with *reflection*, in as much as the latter implies applying the critical faculty, whereas the former is based precisely on the suppression of all criticism (Freud, 1900a, pp. 101–102). Then, in his 1904 paper on "Freud's psycho-analytic procedure", written in the third person, Freud (1904a) offers a description of the psychoanalytic situation that fits quite nicely with our present standard practice:

> The cathartic method had already renounced suggestion; Freud went a step further and gave up hypnosis as well. At the present time he

treats his patients as follows. *Without exerting any other kind of influence,* he invites them to lie down in a comfortable attitude on a sofa, while he himself sits on a chair behind them outside their field of vision. He does not even ask them to close their eyes, and avoids touching them in any way, as well as any other procedure which might be reminiscent of hypnosis. The session thus proceeds as *a conversation between two people equally awake,* but one of whom is spared every muscular exertion and every distracting sensory impression which might divert his attention from his own mental activity. (p. 250, my italics)

I have emphasised two expressions, because they might be open to criticism, as we shall see in the next section, but the fact remains that this is still an orthodox description of the outer setting of the psychoanalytic situation.

The psychoanalytic device

Free association

Apart from its usual physical setting (the patient lying on the couch, suspending temporarily all bodily action, and the analyst sitting behind, listening to his or her discourse), the analytic situation is classically defined by its rules and the roles that are assigned to both parties. The patient is required to comply with the *psychoanalytic rule*, usually referred to as the "fundamental rule" or the "basic rule", which demands that she adopts a passive attitude towards her own mental processes, observe them without trying to control or interfere with their course, and report them verbally to the analyst, without leaving out anything on any account. This means that she should not omit to report any of her internal experiences during the sessions, even though they might seem irrelevant, nonsensical, shameful, or offensive. In other words, it is mainly *a rule of non-omission.*

Freud (1900a) describes this method in the following terms:

My patients were pledged to communicate to me *every idea or thought that occurred to them* in connection with some particular subject; amongst other things they told me their dreams and so taught me that a dream can be inserted into the psychical chain that has to be traced backwards in the memory from a pathological idea. It was then only a short step to treating the dream itself as a symptom and to applying to dreams the method of interpretation that had been worked out for symptoms.

> This involves some psychological preparation of the patient. We must aim at bringing about two changes in him: an increase in the attention he pays to his own psychical perceptions and the elimination of the criticism by which he normally sifts the thoughts that occur to him. . . . It is necessary to insist explicitly on his renouncing all criticism of the thoughts that he perceives. We therefore tell him that the success of the psychoanalysis depends on his noticing and reporting whatever comes into his head and not being misled, for instance, into suppressing an idea because it strikes him as unimportant or irrelevant or because it seems to him meaningless. He must adopt a completely impartial attitude to what occurs to him, since it is precisely his critical attitude which is responsible for his being unable, in the ordinary course of things, to achieve the desired unravelling of his dream or obsessional idea or whatever it may be. (pp. 100–101, my italics)

I have emphasised Freud's reference to "every idea or thought that occurred to them" for two reasons. In the first place, to highlight an aspect of his conception that has been obscured by an inadequate translation of his expression *"freier Einfall"* (Rycroft, 1968, pp. 59–60, see entry "Free association"). The now standard expression "free association" does not convey the meaning of *Einfall*, which means "irruption", "sudden idea", or "occurrence", or even "incursion" or "invasion" (in the military sense), but not "association". Apparently, what Freud had in mind was not the idea of a network of associative connections, which was, none the less, present in his theorising, but the sudden irruption of an unexpected, uninvited, and extraneous thought. In other words, the relaxation of the conscious censorship of the patient's discourse paved the way for the emergence of the repressed. Such a concept underscores the importance of surprise as a signal of the advent of the unconscious.

In the second place, I want to pinpoint a bias in Freud's thinking. He was clearly isolating ideas and thoughts from all other mental processes that might be experienced by the patient during the sessions. This is a consequence of his emphasis on *verbal* thought and expression. Words are the only part of the analytic interaction that lends itself easily to objectification, and this was bound to appeal to his scientific aspirations. But this leaves out many experiences that are surely significant to our understanding of the analytic process, such

as emotions, impulses, yearnings, bodily feelings, sensory perceptions, mental images, or vague and ineffable sensations. I am not
saying that Freud would not have taken them into account, had they
emerged during a session, but that his inclination was heavily bent
towards verbal material, and that this he conveyed to the patient in
his wording of the basic rule.

I believe that there was a contradiction in Freud's thinking
between his strict adherence to a physicalist conception of science, and
the unavoidable hermeneutic nature of his discovery, and that this has
pervaded psychoanalytic theorising ever since, determining a significant gap between the linearity of metapsychological explanations and
the depth and complexity of the practice and discoveries of psychoanalysis (Tubert-Oklander, 2013b).

One thing was clear, however. Free association never meant just
"say everything that occurs to you", and not even "say everything,
without any omission". What Freud demanded of his patients was
that they adopt a self-observing stance. What he required was an
essentially passive contemplation of the unfolding of one's mental
processes, as that of a traveller who beholds the ever-fading images of
the scenery through a train window. Thus, he wrote, in "On beginning
the treatment" (Freud, 1913c), the following prescription,

> So say whatever goes through your mind. Act as though, for instance,
> you were a traveller sitting next to the window of a railway carriage
> and describing to someone inside the carriage the changing views
> which you see outside. (p. 135)

Now, the state of mind induced by the fulfilment of the psychoanalytic rule is not only a cognitive accomplishment, but also an alternative state of consciousness. This led Freud (1900a) to compare it
with the hypnagogic and the hypnotic states:

> What is in question, evidently, is the establishment of a psychical state
> which, in its distribution of psychical energy (that is, of mobile atten-
> tion), bears some analogy to the state before falling asleep – and no
> doubt also to hypnosis. As we fall asleep, "involuntary ideas" emerge,
> owing to the relaxation of a certain deliberate (and no doubt also crit-
> ical) activity which we allow to influence the course of our ideas while
> we are awake. (We usually attribute this relaxation to "fatigue".) As
> the involuntary ideas emerge they change into visual and acoustic
> images. (p. 102)

In such altered state of mind, the involuntary ideas that emerge are surely not restricted to verbal representations, and they certainly might involve "visual and acoustic images", as well as—even though Freud does not mention them—bodily sensations and emotional states. This regressive state—in the three aspects he described (1900a, pp. 533–549) as the *topographic, formal,* and *temporal regressions*—is what Kris (1936) called "regression in the service of the ego", considering it an essential requisite for both the psychoanalytic treatment and artistic creativity.

Freud (1920b) himself mentioned, in a brief paper called "A note on the prehistory of the technique of analysis", three likely precedents of his technique of spontaneous association, which linked it to artistic creation. One is Dr J. J. Garth Wilkinson's technique for enquiry and discovery, which consisted in choosing a theme and then noting down

> the first impression upon the mind which succeeds the act of writing the title [which] is the beginning of the evolution of that theme, no matter how strange or alien the word or phrase may seem [for] the first mental movement, the first word that comes is the response to the mind's desire for the unfolding of the subject. (Wilkinson, quoted by Ellis, quoted by Freud (1920b), p. 263)

A second precedent, which was pointed out by Otto Rank and quoted by Freud in a 1909 addition to Chapter 2 of *The Interpretation of Dreams*, comes from a letter from Schiller to Körner, in which he replies to his friend's complaint of insufficient productivity:

> The ground for your complaint seems to me to lie in the constraint imposed by your reason upon your imagination. I will make my idea more concrete by a simile. It seems a bad thing and detrimental to the creative work of the mind if Reason makes too close an examination of the ideas as they come pouring in – at the very gateway, as it were. Looked at in isolation, a thought may seem very trivial or very fantastic; but it may be made important by another thought that comes after it, and, in conjunction with other thoughts that may seem equally absurd, it may turn out to form a most effective link. Reason cannot form any opinion upon all this unless it retains the thought long enough to look at it in connection with the others. On the other hand, where there is a creative mind, Reason – so it seems to me – relaxes its watch upon the gates, and the ideas rush in pell-mell, and only then does it look them through and examine them in a mass. *You critics, or*

whatever else you may call yourselves, are ashamed or frightened of the momentary and transient extravagances which are to be found in all truly creative minds and whose longer or shorter duration distinguishes the thinking artist from the dreamer. You complain of your unfruitfulness because you reject too soon and discriminate too severely. (Schiller, letter of December 1, 1788, quoted by Freud, 1900a, p. 103, my italics)

I have highlighted the last two sentences because I believe they strictly apply to one of the obstacles to the analytic process, in both patient and analyst: the fear of a disorganisation of one's mental processes that invokes Reason as a watchdog, meant to keep away any unexpected and unknown alien visitors.

These two texts were not known to Freud when he devised his technique, so that they may be seen as precedents of, but not influences on, his thought. The next one, however, was certainly read by him during his adolescence, although he held no conscious recollection of the particular essay that foreshadowed his own contributions. This was Ludwig Börne's "The art of becoming an original writer in three days", and its influence on Freud was taken by him as an example of "the fragment of cryptoamnesia which in so many cases may be suspected to lie behind apparent originality" (Freud, 1920b, p. 265). There, the author says,

And here follows the practical application that was promised. Take a few sheets of paper and for three days on end write down, without fabrication or hypocrisy, everything that comes into your head. Write down what you think of yourself, of your wife, of the Turkish War, or Goethe, of Fonk's trial, of the Last Judgement, of your superiors – and when three days have passed you will be quite out of your senses with astonishment at the new and unheard-of thoughts you have had. This is the art of becoming an original writer in three days. (Börne, quoted by Freud, 1920b, p. 265)

Now, this "relaxation of the watch upon the gates of Reason" (Freud, 1900a, p. 103) is surely much more than a mere technique for generating new information, as it implies a very different frame of mind than that of the normal waking state. In this, it seems to be related to several psychological techniques, such as meditation, that have been applied by mystics and other esoteric teachers throughout history, which purport to teach, establish, and develop alternative states of mind in their pupils, claiming that these open the way for a direct perception of "True Reality". This was neatly phrased by the English poet, engraver, and mystic, William Blake, in his famous aphorism, "If the doors of perception were cleansed every thing would appear to man as it is, infinite. For man has closed himself up, till he sees all things thro' narrow chinks of his cavern" (Keynes, 1972, p. 154).

If this interpretation of the functional meaning of free association were valid, we should consider the hypothesis that this artificially induced state of mind might be a therapeutic factor in itself. The practice of free association would then be an exercise aimed at developing a particular function of the personality: that of engaging in partial regressive states, in order to transcend the limits imposed by the chains of Reason and open the way for a deeper understanding of our true selves. But, of course, Freud never suggested such an idea, and it would have been incompatible with his conception of the analytic method.

Evenly-suspended attention

Freud also posed a special task for the analyst, which is equivalent to that imposed on the patient by the basic rule: the analyst should strive to be, during the sessions, in a state of *evenly suspended attention*. This meant "not directing one's notice to anything in particular and in maintaining the same 'evenly-suspended attention' (as I have called it) in the face of all that one hears" (Freud, 1912e, pp. 111–112). Such a rule had more than one aim. In the first place, it was a way of avoiding note-taking and other efforts to remember what the patient said, replacing it by the spontaneous emergence of any preconsciously stored information that happened to be relevant for that particular moment.

It was also a way of avoiding a bias in the analyst's listening. Just as free association was a way to invoke the unexpected emergence of mental contents that were extraneous to the patient's consciousness, this deliberate suspension of the analyst's judgement allowed him to surprise himself with previously unthought ideas. His first mention of this technique was in the case history of "Little Hans" (Freud, 1909b), in which he used it as an aid in reading the notes sent to him by the boy's father. This was his rationale:

We will not follow Hans's father either in his easily comprehensible anxieties or in his first attempts at finding an explanation; we will begin by examining the material before us. It is not in the least our business to "understand" a case at once: this is only possible at a later stage, when we have received enough impressions of it. *For the present we will suspend our judgement and give our impartial attention to everything that there is to observe.* (pp. 22–23, my italics)

A few years later, in his "Recommendations to physicians practising psycho-analysis" (Freud, 1912e), he further developed this notion, in the following terms:

It will be seen that the rule of giving equal notice to everything is the necessary counterpart to the demand made on the patient that he should communicate everything that occurs to him without criticism or selection. If the doctor behaves otherwise, he is throwing away most of the advantage which results from the patient's obeying the "fundamental rule of psychoanalysis". The rule for the doctor may be expressed: "He should withhold all conscious influences from his capacity to attend, and give himself over completely to his 'unconscious memory'". Or, to put it purely in terms of technique: "He should simply listen, and not bother about whether he is keeping anything in mind". (p. 112)

So, the need for the analyst to keep an evenly suspended attention is something more than a mere technical trick. Quite on the contrary, it is the other side of the coin of a unit that it forms in an inextricable blend with the patient's free association. Just as the latter implies an alternative state of consciousness, so does the former. The patient and the analyst are, therefore, coupled by their partaking in a similar mental state, in which communication may become a communion of minds. The set of technical norms and measures that foster this most peculiar encounter—the articulation of free association and evenly suspended attention—is we may call the *psychoanalytic device*.

The relational perspective

Up to this point, I have discussed the establishment of the psychoanalytic situation as if the analyst and the patient were two primarily isolated mental systems that are secondarily articulated by their communication—that is, in terms of a one-person psychology. In this, I followed Freud's argumentation, even as I drew a few conclusions that he would have taken exception to. I shall now try to reformulate these concepts in relational terms—that is, of a two-person psychology.

Free association is certainly much more than "relaxing the watch upon the gates of Reason", since the latter may be done in isolation, while the former is always carried out under someone else's gaze. For the patient, complying with the fundamental rule is always a personal relationship with the analyst, in which he or she exhibits his or her most intimate experiences and thoughts to the analyst's consideration—in its twofold meaning of "continuous and careful thought" and "thoughtful and sympathetic regard". The ability to free associate in the presence of the analyst is, therefore, contingent on the quality of the analytic relationship.

This assertion may be compared to Winnicott's (1958b) concept of "being alone in the presence of another person", a feature of what he calls "ego relatedness", that is, a form of intersubjective relation that is neither characterised nor driven by instinctual tension, which he deems to be "the stuff of which friendship is made" and perhaps also "the *matrix of transference*". When the analytic relation is characterised by closeness, intimacy, and trust, free association comes out easily; on the other hand, when distrust and suspicion prevail, the flow of communication becomes blocked by resistance. Therefore, the mere fact of requiring the patient to free associate throws her relational capabilities and conflicts into a bold relief. It is, at one and the same time, a diagnostic tool that might be compared to an electrocardiogram under stress, which reveals deficiencies that might have remained dormant under less exacting conditions, and an exercise in relating, which might pave the way for the development of new relational and perceptual patterns (Horney, 1987).

But a relation is never one-way only; trust and suspicion are always mutual, and they need to be solved by means of a shared understanding—that is, insight. So, when free association finally ensues, it is a sign and a consequence of the evolution of the analytic relationship. Showing one's intimacy is always a sign of confidence, in the same way that sleeping in the presence of someone else necessarily implies a full trust in that person. This is why a patient who falls asleep during his session is not always acting a resistance; quite the contrary, this might be an expression of his deepest trust in the analyst. But, in the very same way, the analyst can only let go in the flow of her own stream of consciousness when the obstacles to the development of an intimate and mutually trusting relationship have been removed by interpretation, insight, and mutual testing.

All this implies a mutual regulation of both parties' mental processes, which takes the form of an unconscious bilateral communication. Freud (1912e) was the first to describe the "communication from unconscious to unconscious" that takes place during the psychoanalytic treatment, in the following terms:

> It is easy to see upon which aim the different rules which I have brought forward converge. They are all intended to create for the doctor a counterpart to the "fundamental rule of psycho-analysis" which is laid down for the patient. Just as the patient must relate everything that his self-observation can detect, and keep back all the logical and affective objections that seek to induce him to make a selection from among them, so the doctor must put himself in a position to make use of everything he is told for the purposes of interpretation and of recognizing the concealed unconscious material without substituting a censorship of his own for the selection that the patient has forgone. To put it in a formula: he must turn his own unconscious like a receptive organ towards the transmitting unconscious of the patient. He must adjust himself to the patient as a telephone receiver is adjusted to the transmitting microphone. Just as the receiver converts back into sound-waves the electric oscillations in the telephone line which were set up by sound waves, so the doctor's unconscious is able, from the derivatives of the unconscious which are communicated to him, to reconstruct that unconscious, which has determined the patient's free associations. (pp. 115–116)

Such a formulation seems to imply, by sheer omission, that unconscious communication acts in only one direction, from the patient to the analyst. This simply does not fit with what we know about the workings of the unconscious: there is no way in which the patient's unconscious might not react to the analyst's unconscious, and this is bound to be expressed in her behaviour and utterances. Of course, it might be argued that the analyst is trained, by studies and personal analytic experience, to recognise and understand the productions of his own unconscious, and to translate the impact of the patient's unconscious communications into interpretations that she may use to her benefit, and that of the treatment. In Freud's terms, "he should have undergone a psycho-analytic purification and have become aware of those complexes of his own which would be apt to interfere with his grasp of what the patient tells him" (p. 116). But this argument really poses a question. Perhaps the patient is not trained to identify and understand the impact that the analyst's unconscious has on her own unconscious, and therefore cannot put it into words; she might even misinterpret in terms of the transference what is actually happening, but this does not mean that she is not receiving—and suffering—its consequences. In such a situation, the analyst should help the patient, by means of interpretations, questions, or other communications, to make conscious the unconscious—in this case, her unconscious perception of the analyst's unconscious—and this implies a much greater personal commitment by the analyst than what is usually considered desirable in terms of the established version of the psychoanalytic treatment.

The very fact that the analyst is offering the patient an opportunity to put into words and understand the hidden aspects of their mutual relationship offers the latter an experience that she might have lacked during her formative years. How often do parents acknowledge the accuracy of their children's perceptions of them, especially when these perceptions go beyond what they are inclined to reveal, or even beyond what they are willing to admit to themselves? The same is true for almost any other relationship that involves authority, such as that of a teacher with a student, or a physician with a patient. The fact that analysts endeavour to uphold truthfulness over the preservation of a narcissistically retouched image of themselves is one of the features that sets psychoanalysis apart from almost every other relationship, and this must be part of its momentous effect on patients and analysts alike.

Hence, we may take exception at Freud's allegations that (a) he treats his patients without exerting any other kind of influence, apart from giving them interpretations of their "material", and (b) an analysis is a conversation between two people who are "equally awake"— that is, in a normal state of consciousness. Quite on the contrary, we have seen that both parties are placed by the psychoanalytic rule in a position that fosters in them a non-ordinary state of consciousness, and that they exert a mutual influence on their respective mental states, which then become a shared state of mind, which may well be called a "communion".

Even though the considerations put forward in the last two paragraphs are not compatible with Freud's understanding of the method that he had created, they are consistent with the experience of many present-day analysts in the practice of such method. Of course, this is still a moot question, but it should not obscure the fact that the psychoanalytic device created by Freud is not only a technical resource for gathering information, but an opportunity for an entirely new form of relationship, one that allows a process of cognitive and emotional development to ensue. And this brings us to the question of the personal contribution of the analyst to the psychoanalytic process, which might be summarised as the *analytic attitude*, as we shall see in the next chapter.

CHAPTER THREE

The analytic attitude

The analyst's contribution to the analytic situation

In the previous chapter, I have made a case in favour of considering the analytic situation as an instance of interaction—both conscious and unconscious—between analyst and patient. Now, "interaction" means "mutual or reciprocal action or influence". This represents a serious questioning of the usual allegation that "there is no room for action in psychoanalysis". It also implies that the analyst's participation in the analytic situation goes far beyond his or her conscious and purposeful technical interventions.

Such contentions are inevitably disquieting for analysts and patients alike, since they suggest that the former might not be in full control of the situation while conducting an analysis. But, if there is any chance that this might be true, we should confront it, try to understand it, and benefit from the ensuing knowledge.

From this point of view, the analyst contributes to the analytic situation in three different but interrelated ways. In the first place, there is the *mutual interaction*, which is mainly unconscious, that is set in motion whenever two people meet in any given situation. In this, psychoanalysis is no different from any other relationship.

In the second place, the analyst participates by means of *conscious and purposeful interventions*, which might either be technical and orientated by formal theory, or more spontaneous and guided by intuition and common sense. These actions are of a peculiar nature, which is characteristic of psychoanalysis, and this turns them into a subject matter for any account of psychoanalytic technique (Heimann, 1978).

Finally, there is a special kind of participation, which lies halfway between the other two, since it is neither a discrete act, under fully conscious control, nor an unconscious automatic expression or reaction, but, rather, a consciously undertaken disposition, which fosters the emergence of spontaneous reactions that are, nevertheless, consistent in their being orientated by such tendency. In other words, it is an *attitude*. Such a term condenses a series of implied meanings, such as: (a) the arrangement of the parts of a body of a person, an animal, or an inanimate object—that is, a posture; (b) a position or bearing as indicating action, feeling, or mood, and also the feeling or mood itself; (c) a mental position with regard to a fact or state; (d) an organismic state of readiness to respond in a characteristic way to a stimulus (as an object, concept, or situation); (e) any posture held momentarily in dancing (Merriam-Webster, 2002, see entry "Attitude"). The special attitude that analysts strive to maintain during the sessions has, therefore, been named the "analytic attitude", and this shall be the subject matter of this chapter.

The dimensions of the analytic attitude

The analytic attitude may be studied along several axes or dimensions. These are: (i) *impartiality*, (ii) *circumspection*, (iii) *passivity*, (iv) *tolerance*, (v) *neutrality*, (vi) *abstinence*, (vii) *rationality*, and (viii) *anonymity*. The framing of these names as if they were abstract qualities suggests that they are absolute values. I believe that this is not a useful way of thinking about the analytic attitude. I would rather discuss these dimensions as axes that describe the dialectic relation between opposites; thus, it would be much better to think in terms of: *impartiality–partiality, circumspection–reactivity, passivity–activity, tolerance–severity, neutrality–commitment, abstinence–indulgence, rationality–irrationality*, and *anonymity–disclosure*.

The explicit recognition that all these values are really dialectic pairs would also help us to avoid one very common pitfall in our customary thinking: that of attributing one value—usually a positive one—to the analyst, while leaving the opposite value, or anti-value, to the patient. Thus, it is not unusual in psychoanalytic literature to consider the analyst as cautious and the patient as impulsive, the analyst as impartial and the patient as biased, the analyst as anonymous and the patient as almost transparent, and so on. A truly dialectic view of such opposites would allow a multi-axial analysis of the dynamics of the psychoanalytic process, which would help us to identify and describe the various features that make up the analytic attitude.

Impartiality–partiality

The very concept of evenly-suspended attention implies an effort to keep an impartial attitude towards anything and everything that may transpire in the psychoanalytic situation. The idea, clearly stated by Freud (1912e) in his paper on "Recommendations to physicians practising psycho-analysis", is that the analyst should keep an unbiased attitude towards the patient's expressions, in order to be open to that new way of understanding things that is the token of the emergence of the unconscious. This is usually accompanied by a feeling of surprise. For some analysts, such as Bion (1967, 1970), this is the gist of psychoanalysis: the discovery of the unknown. This was clearly stated by this author in the following—rather extreme—terms:

> What is 'known' about the patient is of no further consequence: it is either false or irrelevant. If it is 'known' by patient and analyst, it is obsolete . . . The only point of importance in any session is the unknown. Nothing must be allowed to distract from intuiting that" (Bion, 1967, p. 272)

Of course, such a view is in sharp contrast with the conventional way of understanding psychoanalysis, which sees it as a therapeutic intervention, orientated by previously established knowledge. From this perspective, the psychoanalytic treatment is a clinical application of psychoanalytic theory, and not a part of the process of the construction of such theory.

Both points of view are to be found in Freud's writing. On the one hand, he emphasised the essential incompleteness of any analysis and the investigative nature of the analytic enquiry. For instance, in *The Interpretation of Dreams*, he asserts that "There is at least one spot in every dream at which it is umplumbable-a navel, as it were, that is its point of contact with the unknown" (Freud, 1900a, p. 111n.). Later, in Chapter 7 of the same book, he elaborates on the same idea, in the following terms:

> There is often a passage in even the most thoroughly interpreted dream which has to be left obscure; this is because we become aware during the work of interpretation that at that point there is a tangle of dream-thoughts which cannot be unravelled and which moreover adds nothing to our knowledge of the content of the dream. This is the dream's navel, the spot where it reaches down into the unknown ... The dream-thoughts to which we are led by interpretation cannot, from the nature of things, have any definite endings; they are bound to branch out in every direction into the intricate network of our world of thought. It is at some point where this meshwork is particularly close that the dream-wish grows up, like a mushroom out of its mycelium. (p. 525)

Such awareness of the boundlessness of the unconscious led Freud (1912e) to postulate that "one of the claims of psycho-analysis to distinction is, no doubt, that in its execution research and treatment coincide" (p. 114). The corresponding frames of mind for both endeavours were, however, quite different, so he suggested a non-systematic approach to psychoanalytic research, on account of the difference of the analytic attitude of passive reception and the scientific attitude of active questioning of hypotheses:

> *The most successful cases are those in which one proceeds, as it were, without any purpose in view, allows oneself to be taken by surprise by any new turn in them, and always meets them with an open mind, free from any presuppositions.* The correct behaviour for an analyst lies in swinging over according to need from the one mental attitude to the other [i.e., the analytic and the investigative attitudes], in avoiding speculation or brooding over cases while they are in analysis, and in submitting the material obtained to a synthetic process of thought only after the analysis is concluded. *The distinction between the two attitudes would be meaningless if we already possessed all the knowledge (or at least the*

essential knowledge) about the psychology of the unconscious and about the structure of the neuroses that we can obtain from psycho-analytic work. At present we are still far from that goal and we ought not to cut ourselves off from the possibility of testing what we have already learnt and of extending our knowledge further. (pp. 114–115, my italics)

I have emphasised two fragments of this quotation, because they clearly depict Freud's contradictions. The first one underscores the need to avoid bias by means of an "aimless wondering"—what Racker (1960) would have called "sending your not-search" to look for new findings (p. 17). This is akin to Bion's (1967, 1970, 1980) "suspension of memory and desire" in order to allow the analyst's intuition to grasp the unknown. But we are then astonished to find, in the second fragment, that the author seemed to believe that some day we shall posses "all the knowledge . . . about the psychology of the unconscious and about the structure of the neuroses that we can still obtain from psycho-analytic work". Whatever happened to the "dream's navel", that "spot where it reaches down into the unknown"? Did Freud really believe that we would one day be able to exhaust the deep well of the unconscious?

Obviously, the founder of psychoanalysis experienced mixed feelings towards the most unusual characteristics of the therapeutic and research method he had invented. He was keenly aware of the uniqueness of psychoanalysis as a never-ending enquiry, but he also wished it to be accepted as a science, according to the standards of nineteenth-century epistemology, and to defend its effectiveness as a form of treatment. Therefore, he oscillated between what could be called a *process view* and an *objectivistic view* of psychoanalysis.

Nevertheless, he clearly valued those treatments which implied an open enquiry over those that were restricted to the application of pre-existent knowledge:

Analyses which lead to a favourable conclusion in a short time are of value in ministering to the therapeutist's self-esteem and substantiate the medical importance of psycho-analysis; but they remain for the most part insignificant as regards the advancement of scientific knowledge. Nothing new is learnt from them. In fact they only succeed so quickly because everything that was necessary for their accomplishment was already known. *Something new can only be gained from analyses that present special difficulties, and to the overcoming of these a great deal of time has to be devoted.* Only in such cases do we succeed in descending into the deepest and most primitive strata of mental development and in gaining from there solutions for the problems of the later formations. *And we feel afterwards that, strictly speaking, only an analysis which has penetrated so far deserves the name.* (Freud, 1918b, p. 10, my italics)

On this basis, I have put forward the idea that the essential difference between psychoanalysis and psychoanalytic psychotherapy is that the latter applies pre-existent psychoanalytic knowledge to the conduction of a treatment aimed at attaining therapeutic goals, while the former is boldly exploring the unknown and trying to think through, conjointly with the patient, the enigmatic experiences that emerge whenever two people meet in a closed room with the intention of "doing psychoanalysis" (Tubert-Oklander, 2000). This implies a fundamental revision of the epistemological assumptions that underlie psychoanalytic thinking, since the analyst, unlike the psychotherapist, cannot take his or her own theory as granted, but is bound to also take it as an object of the analytic enquiry.

If this is so, psychoanalysis has undermined, by its very existence, the traditional concept of "objectivity" in science and epistemology. The analyst is no longer an uncommitted observer who is studying a patient lying at the bottom of a well. He is, rather, an audacious explorer who does not mind going down the well and trying to find a way out in co-operation with the patient. He is not only trying to understand the analysand, but also trying to understand his or her self, experiences, beliefs, and theories. The end result of such a process is a wider and deeper understanding of what it means to be a human being that relates to other human beings, trying to think through the experience at the same time.

These ideas do not imply a form of discrimination based on status: psychoanalysis is not "something that psychoanalysts do" and neither is psychotherapy "something done by psychotherapists". Neither is the difference between these two approaches to treatment clear-cut and established for the duration of the process. Quite the contrary, every psychoanalytic treatment starts by being psychotherapy, in as much as it must necessarily apply pre-existent knowledge, if the analyst is to find his or her way through the initial stages. It is only occasionally that a new and unexpected opening happens, and both parties find themselves saying things that are entirely new for them. It is as if they had been possessed by an alien spirit, even though they feel pretty much themselves, perhaps more than ever before. Such moments of meeting and discovery, perhaps of creation, are what we may call "analytic moments" (something akin to what Stern and colleagues, 1998, call "now moments"). No treatment can be made up only of such moments, but, on the other hand, there are many treatments in which this never happens. Attempting to do true psychoanalysis implies trying to create the conditions for the occurrence of such moments, and having the patience to wait for them.

In any case, the analyst's contribution to the analytic process implies trying to keep a dynamic balance between the partiality of pre-established knowledge and the impartiality of an unrestricted openness to the unknown.

Circumspection–reactivity

Analysts have traditionally endeavoured to observe a cautious attitude during the sessions. Knowing how easy it is to act out a state of emotional tension without being aware of it, as the act is usually rationalised by all sorts of conscious justifications, they strive to keep a measured behaviour and to weigh all circumstances and possible consequences before taking any decision. Such overtly prudent conduct is usually contrasted with the patient's tendency to effect a "motor discharge" and acting out.

This is an instance of how a clinically useful practice might be invalidated by its one-sided application and its ideological distortion. Prudence is certainly an asset in the face of emotional turmoil, but it could become a liability when the patient is timid and afraid of action. In such a clinical situation, it might be therapeutically useful if the analyst were to spontaneously express his or her reactions, in order to avoid an unconscious collusion—what Baranger and Baranger (2008), called a "bastion"—in the form of an overtly cautious, and ultimately sterile, behaviour by both parties. And if such bilateral resistance were to occur, it should also certainly have to become a subject for the analytic dialogue (Little, 1957).

Therefore, a valid technical recommendation ("look before you leap") becomes an ideological statement in two different, but complementary ways. In the first place, a measure that is useful in some clinical situations is generalised as an absolute value in every conceivable circumstance, thus depriving it of its usefulness. In the second, not only has one of the polar qualities of this axis been taken as "good" and the other as "bad", but there is also an *a priori* attribution of the "good" trait to the analyst and the "bad" one to the patient.

In this case, it is also a question of the analyst endeavouring to maintain a dynamic balance between the two polar qualities: that of a discreet and judicious attitude, and that of a disposition to spontaneous reaction.

Passivity–activity

Pretty much the same is to be said about our next axis, and it may even be argued that there is no essential difference between this and the previous one. Analysts usually strive to attain and keep an attitude of passive receptiveness, avoiding any active interventions, with the exception of interpretations of the latent meaning of the patient's material and of some other technical manoeuvres—such as questions or confrontations—that aim to set the ground for interpretation. Such a norm certainly has its virtues, as many patients are in sore need of experiencing being-with-themselves in a non-intrusive environment. For such patients, who have been the object of multiple impingements during their formative years, the analyst's silence and passivity give them an opportunity to "be alone in the presence of another person", as Winnicott (1958b) aptly phrased it, and this experience of ego-relatedness is truly curative in itself. But what is sauce for the goose might not be sauce for the gander, as there are other patients who have been deprived, from infancy onwards, of the experience of being well cared for. These patients experience the analyst's passivity as aloofness, carelessness, and rejection. This compounds the original traumatic experience of loneliness, abandonment, and helplessness, originating an iatrogenic effect. This issue has been treated by Kohut and Wolf (1978) when describing the different needs and therapeutic handling of patients with an *under-stimulated* or an *over-stimulated self*.

On the other hand, even at the beginnings of psychoanalysis, it became obvious that some treatments soon reached a deadlock, when the analyst adhered strictly to the principle of passivity. Thus, several active measures were suggested in order to overcome such therapeutic impasses. Ferenczi (1919) was the first to describe such technique in his paper "Technical difficulties in the analysis of a case of hysteria". There, he described a female patient who, in the midst of a phase of transference love, kept her legs crossed during the whole session. Ferenczi, following an oral suggestion of Freud, readily interpreted this as a masturbation equivalent and forbade the patient to adopt this position. This opened the way for the analysis of the erotic fantasies that had been previously concealed behind this drive-satisfying activity.

Freud (1919a) immediately took over these experiences and discussed, in "Lines of advance in psycho-analytic therapy", their theoretical implications. In this paper, he strongly favoured a moderate use of active interventions, intended to help the patient overcome his or her resistances. Such activity on the part of the analyst he considered to be "unobjectionable and entirely justified" (p. 162).

From this, he goes to a discussion on abstinence, in which he reminds us that "it was a *frustration* that made the patient ill, and that his symptoms serve him as substitutive satisfactions" (p. 162), but since it is the suffering generated by the illness that impels him towards the cure, it is essential that there should be no premature amelioration of his condition. Therefore, the analyst should see to it that the suffering be kept alive, by means of an administered frustration he called "abstinence", to avoid an untimely interruption of the treatment. This is the first kind of active intervention that Freud mentions.

The second one is the now classic observation about the phobic neurosis, in which he recommends compelling agoraphobic patients "to go into the street and to struggle with their anxiety while they make the attempt" (p. 166), so that the hitherto concealed memories and associations come to the fore and may be finally analysed.

Both Freud and Ferenczi, therefore, considered active interventions as a means to neutralise the homeostatic function of neurotic symptoms and symptomatic actions, thus mobilising anxiety and aiding in the analysis of their unconscious meanings. In the next few years, Ferenczi (1921, 1925) continued his experimentation with the active technique, which finally led him to a severe criticism of its drawbacks. One of them was the fact that the analyst became stereotyped in an authoritarian role, thus increasing the patient's resistance and even compounding his or her childhood traumatic experiences. He had, in the meantime, written with Otto Rank the book *The Development of*

Psychoanalysis (Ferenczi & Rank, 1924), in which they stressed the unique importance of emotional experience as the only basis for conviction about the findings of an analysis. Therefore, he started to explore another vein, by means of the "elasticity of psychoanalytic technique" (1928b) and the "principle of relaxation" (1930), which I shall explore in the following subsections.

Of course, the analyst's activity does not necessarily imply formulating prescriptions or proscriptions for the patient. An interpretation is also, after all, an action that interferes with the patients spontaneous psychic activity and turns the thought in a given direction. This Ferenczi (1921) called a "midwifery of thought".

Consequently, the discussion the analyst's activity and passivity soon turned towards the question of when, how much, and how frequently we should interpret. In the 1950s and 1960s, this took the form of a controversy between "classical technique" (usually more passive) and "Kleinian technique" (usually more active in its interpretations). Racker (1960), who did a comparative study of both techniques, argued poignantly in favour of the analyst's total participation in the analytic process, in the following terms:

> "Evenly-suspended attention", for instance, is but one aspect (though fundamental) of the complex process of understanding the unconscious. . . . We tend to identify, and identification is, partially, an active mental process, besides implying the reproduction of the object's pathological activity. . . . Thus as in the sexual act the woman is, in one aspect, receptive and therefore "passive", nevertheless fully active within this passive role—if she is healthy and loves the man—so also is the analyst towards his patient. An exaggerated passivity on the part of the analyst has a certain similarity to the behaviour of the frigid woman, who does not respond, who does not really unite. . . . [T]his analytic-synthetic understanding can only be achieved if the passive position is joined to an active striving to understand, to a good measure of active identification, and to sufficient energy for struggle against the resistances, not only those of the patient, but also one's own. (pp. 29–30)

In other words, the analyst must *relate* to the patient with his whole personality, actively *identify* with her, *fight* against their shared resistances, *work* towards understanding whatever emerges during the sessions, and also, of course, *communicate* his understanding, ideas, and findings to the patient. This is what Little (1957) called "the analyst's total response to his patient's needs". In all of this, as Freud remarked, we are active enough.

The psychoanalytic attitude, therefore, starts as a state of passive receptivity towards the patient's multiple expressions, but must soon evolve into a dynamic interplay between activity and passivity, in patient and analyst alike, which should be always geared to the patient's therapeutic needs.

Tolerance–severity

The traditional analytic stance implies an attitude of tolerance and unconditional acceptance of the patient. The analyst is especially careful to avoid any moral judgements about the patient's fantasies and actions. The very fact that the analyst is willing to accept the patient's experiences as intrinsically valid, and to strive to understand them without passing judgement on them, builds up the patient's confidence and contributes to the overcoming of resistances. Freud (1913c) commented on this in his paper "On beginning the treatment", saying that, if the analyst exhibits a serious interest in the patient, clears the resistances, and maintains an empathetic attitude, abstaining from any moralising, the patient "will of himself form such an attachment [an "effective transference"] and link the doctor up with one of the imagos of the people by whom he was accustomed to be treated with affection" (pp. 139–140).

But the analyst should not only abstain from adopting a judgemental attitude towards the patient, but she must also avoid it in relation to the patient's objects of love and hate, such as his spouse, parents, siblings, or friends. As Fairbairn (1952) pointed out, a patient's objects might be "bad", but they are certainly his, and he clings to them unrelentingly, for being deprived of one's objects is far more terrifying than being harassed by "bad" objects that are, none the less, present, and neither is he willing to change any of his "bad" objects for a "better" one.

For this author, the child internalises the "bad" aspects of the parents in order to preserve an idealisation of them as external objects. Therefore, the "bad" objects are truly a part of her self. That is why patients feel attacked and offended whenever the analyst criticises them. These objects may be "bad"—i.e., hostile and rejecting—but the patient needs them and loves them, and if the analyst reproves and rejects them, she feels that it is her need and love that are being condemned.

All this supports the clinical value of tolerance. There are quite a few instances, however, in which the patient's behaviour should not be condoned or accepted. This is particularly so in the case of destructive acting out, either during the sessions or out of them, which demands that the analyst impose some limits on the patient's actions. This is generally accepted in the case of suicidal, delinquent, or criminal behaviour, as well as in that of clearly aggressive acts towards the analyst or his environment, but it becomes a moot question in some other instances. Should the analyst, for example, actively intervene when a patient indulges in promiscuous acts, exposes herself to contagion of sexually transmitted diseases, or engages in a series of abortions? Many analysts would definitely take exception to such interventions, since they look too much like a moral judgements, and they feel strongly that the analyst should never accept the role of the superego. The question is, however, rather complex, since the superego does not only have moral and repressive functions, but it is also a protective agency, as a result of the internalisation of the "good"— i.e., loving, caring, and protecting—parents (Freud, 1927d). And the patient might well have lacked the experience of having someone care enough for her as to admonish her about such perilous behaviour. In this, just as in the case of the circumspection–reactivity axis, the analyst's attitude *vis-à-vis* the patient should be geared to the latter's personal history and therapeutic needs.

So, once again, we are faced with a need to keep a balance between both poles, and to exhibit tolerance without condoning unacceptable acts, and severity and limits without rejection or moral condemnation.

Neutrality–commitment

The question of the analyst's neutrality has been a matter of debate. Sometimes, it is framed as if the analyst could and should operate in an axiological vacuum, be purely "objective", and offer interpretations that were completely devoid of values. This is, of course, nonsense. No human expression could ever be neutral, in this sense. Values are implicit in thought, since they offer the very categories that make up the framework of our thinking processes. They are not "things" that may be observed, described, or quantified, but abstract entities, which derive from our interaction with objects and pervade all our behaviour and our experience of ourselves, others, the world, and life in general. They are immanent in all our cognitive and affective processes, and in our concrete actions, as a "style" that gives them substance (Tubert-Oklander, 2011a, 2013b; Tubert-Oklander & Hernández de Tubert, 2004). The eight axes that I am using as a tool for the analysis of the concept of the analytic attitude are, for instance, values.

Therefore, the analyst comes to the analytic encounter provided with a complex and mainly unconscious set of values, and so does the patient. And the friction created by their mismatch is probably a part of that tension that gives the transference–countertransference field its structure. When this becomes the subject matter of the analysis, the analyst's values and their articulation with the patient's become one more element to be accounted for (see Chapter Nine).

So, neutrality does not mean, and can never mean, that the analyst does not participate in the generation of analytic objects and events. We shall, therefore, have to seek another, more restricted, technical meaning. The very concept of "neutrality" implies non-alignment in regard to two or more conflicting groups—for example, two countries at war. Therefore, the analyst's attempt to remain neutral implies an avoidance of taking sides with one of the parties in conflict, in the experiential world of the analysand. This may be an *internal* conflict, as in the case of a clash between two instinctual or emotional needs, an *external* one, for example, a conflict with one's parents or spouse, or an *internalised* one, such as a conflict between one's actual behaviour and the demands (moral, aesthetical, or otherwise) of the internalised parents (Freud, A., 1936). In any case, the analyst strives to remain equidistant from the conflicting factions, to identify temporarily with every one of them in order to understand them empathetically, and return to her neutral position, from which she will attain a better understanding of the whole situation. This was defined by Anna Freud, in terms of Freud's (1923b) structural model of the mind, as follows: "when he [the analyst] sets about the work of enlightenment, he takes his stand at a point equidistant from the id, the ego, and the superego" (Freud, A., 1936, p. 28). In a similar vein, albeit in a more humanistic language, Racker (1960), tells us that interpreting the repressed instinctual wish without including the libidinal aspect of the ego's defences, which tend to preserve the object and the relation with it, is tantamount to adopting a moralistic stance, and that interpretation should always include and be based on an empathy with both sides of the conflict. And he adds that, "the absence of this aspect from the interpretation is felt, with reason, as lack of affection and often has negative consequences" (p. 33).

Everyone would agree that this is an ideal model, and that a real analyst seldom complies with its demands, but that he should never-theless endeavour to do so. However, is it really always desirable that the analyst be "neutral", in this restricted sense? Many patients feel such an attitude—which fits nicely with the ideal of a circumspect, impartial, passive, and always rational analyst, who is beyond the maelstrom of human passions—to be a display of indifference, or even hypocrisy. Thus, Ferenczi (1933) wrote about "professional hypocrisy" to refer to the analyst's polite and uncommitted stance, which, more often than not, conceals intense negative feelings in the countertransference. His technical answer to the problems derived from this situation was to disclose his true feelings to the patient and analyse them with her. This is certainly not accepted by most analysts.

What such patients expect and demand is a greater commitment by the analyst. This is a response that they often find in the latter's spontaneous, and unavoidable, emotional reactions. One woman patient, for example, told me, "I felt that my analyst was utterly insen-sitive. How else would he be able to sit quietly and continue his polite and considerate questioning, while I was emotionally bleeding to death? But one day, at the end of the session, I noticed tears in his eyes, and I knew that he had been really with me."

But perhaps we should not wait for our unintentional reactions to give the patient a hint that we are also made of flesh, blood, and heart, and that we are partaking of his suffering. Some patients need more than that, since they are not yet able to detect and understand such hints, and they truly need to know that the analyst is fully there with them. In such cases, the analyst should have clear expressions of his emotional commitment towards the patient, such as an empathic ges-ture or utterance when the latter is speaking of a situation in which he has been abused or victimised. For, if there is no such response on the part of the analyst, the patient might doubt whether his suffering was truly justified; perhaps he was exaggerating after all, or even, maybe, the event did not happen at all! Such doubts are a part of his defences vis-à-vis the traumatic experience, and also perhaps an identification with parents who denied that anything had happened. Such a situation might be impossible to solve by analytic means, unless the analyst is willing to identify with the patient and share his unbearable suffering, and this implies getting in touch with the analyst's own experiences of suffering, which resemble those of the patient. No wonder that analysts and patients so frequently engage in unconscious pacts in the service of resistance, aimed at avoiding such suffering for both of them, thus forming what the Barangers (2008) have called "bastions" of resistance. Such bastions can only be dismantled by means of further and deeper analysis of what is actually happening in the analytic situation.

The analytic attitude, therefore, requires both neutrality and commitment, and only a careful perusal of the total situation may reveal which of them is germane to that particular moment. But such analysis can usually be done only after the fact, and not during the session, so that, when things are actually happening, the analyst can only rely on her intuition, experience, and emotional contact with the analysand, in order to respond.

Abstinence–indulgence

The concept of "abstinence" was introduced by Freud (1919a) in his paper "Lines of advance in psycho-analytic therapy", in the context of his discussion of the "active technique". There, he stated that the "analytic treatment should be carried through, as far as possible, under privation – in a state of abstinence" (p. 162). This is in order to prevent, as we have already discussed, an early alleviation of symptoms. In other words, the patient should be kept in a state of *frustration*, so that the analysis may continue. This argument is based on the classical theory of instinctual drives, which maintains that all human experience and behaviour is ultimately motivated by a need to relieve organic tension, by means of concrete acts that bring about satisfaction. Mental processes, in general, and thinking processes, in particular, appear only when there is a frustration of instinctual (i.e., sexual or aggressive) wishes. If it were true that there is an intrinsic opposition between thinking and action, on the one hand, and thinking and satisfaction, on the other, it would certainly follow that psychoanalysis requires a suspension of action and the maintenance of frustration for the patient.

But, is this theory a fair account of mental life? Many psycho-analysts have questioned the assumption that the release of organic tension is the only source of human motivation. Fairbairn (1952) formulated a radical criticism of drive theory when he suggested that "libido is primarily object-seeking (rather than pleasure-seeking, as in the classic theory), and that it is to disturbances in the object-relation-ships of the developing ego that we must look for the ultimate origin of all psychopathological conditions" (p. 82). In a less radical vein, Winnicott tried to reconcile his object-relations view with that of clas-sical theory when he differentiated the "ego needs" ("the meeting of infant's needs") from "id needs" ("the satisfaction of instincts") (Winnicott, 1960, p. 141). In his previous classical paper on regression (Winnicott, 1955), he had contrasted "wishes" with "needs" as follows:

> It is proper to speak of the patient's *wishes*, the wish (for instance) to be quiet. With the regressed patient the word wish is incorrect; instead we use the word *need*. If a regressed patient *needs* quiet, then without it nothing can be done at all. If the need is not met the result is not anger, only a reproduction of the environmental failure situation which stopped the processes of self growth. The individual's capacity to "wish" has become interfered with, and we witness the reappear-ance of the original cause of a sense of futility. (p. 288)

Guntrip (1961), who was analysed by both Fairbairn and Winni-cott, formulated a cogent argument against drive theory, which he considered to be a major theoretical mistake. This rather extreme posi-tion was, of course, the subject of much controversy.

All these criticisms and revisions came from the Independent group of the British Psychoanalytic Society, at that time called the "Middle Group", but quite similar questionings sprang from the inter-personal and culturalist traditions in the USA. Authors such as Sullivan (1940, 1953), Horney (1939), and Fromm (1941, 1979) criti-cised the theories of libido and instinctual drives, described—in argu-ments that resembled Winnicott's—various ego needs as the major motivation of human experience and behaviour, and interpreted the significance of erogenous zones as channels for relationship, as Fairbairn did. These two independent trends of psychoanalytic thought finally met in the inception of relational psychoanalysis, as described in Chapter One.

Coming from the field of Freudian psychoanalysis in the USA, Kohut developed his theory of self psychology, as a radical criticism of drive theory and the structural point of view that prevailed in his country. For him, the sexual and aggressive drives originally described by Freud are really the result of a psychopathological fragmentation of the self as a result of a non-empathic response from its selfobjects (Kohut, 1982). He also emphasised that the individual definitely needs an empathic response from objects, whenever they are not experienced as separate, but as an extension of the self (selfobjects) (Kohut, 1984). This self–selfobject relationship lasts for, and evolves during, the whole life span. In other words, autonomy is always relative, and we never cease to depend on the empathic responses from our near and dear. This concept is strikingly similar to Fairbairn's (1952) contention that "the development of object-relationships is essentially *a process whereby infantile dependence upon the object gradually gives place to mature dependence upon the object*" (p. 34).

Such revision of the motivational theory of psychoanalysis implies a different view of the analytic relationship, since not all the patient's yearnings are to be considered an expression of instinctual wishes, to be kept in abstinence. On the contrary, there are other needs—relational needs, what Winnicott (1960) called "ego needs"—that have to be responded to, such as the need to feel that the analyst truly sees, understands, and cares for the patient.

Therefore, from the particular point of view that I am putting forward in this book, the analyst should keep a balance between frustrating the patient's instinctualised wishes—which are usually a manifestation of his or her resistance towards closeness, intimacy, and dependence—and adequately responding to his or her relational needs. More about this shall be said when we discuss the analytic relationship and the therapeutic aspects of regression, particularly in Chapter Twelve, on "The healing process".

There is, however, another, quite different meaning that has been assigned to "abstinence", and this is the principle that the analyst should not use the patient for the satisfaction of his or her own wishes or needs. In other words, the analyst is at the service of the patient's (therapeutic) needs, and not the other way round. This clearcut injunction will be partly revised when we discuss mutuality in the analytic relationship—mainly in Chapters Eight and Nine—but even if we accept that the analyst may personally benefit from his participation in the analytic process, it is still the case that such gain is a by-product of the experience, and that the treatment should always be aimed at responding to the patient's needs.

There are various grounds on which the analyst might exploit the patient: (a) instinctual exploitation (sexual or aggressive), (b) economic exploitation, (c) political exploitation, and (d) narcissistic exploitation. The first three are easy to detect, and an ethical and adequately trained analyst usually manages to avoid them. The real problem is narcissistic exploitation, since it is usually unconscious, and it refers to areas of the analyst's personality that have not been touched in his or her personal analysis. If this were the case, how could we identify such a situation? The patients frequently give signals that this is happening and, if the analyst were willing to listen to them, he might get a hint. This is more likely to happen when the analyst is partially aware of his narcissistic trends from analytic experience, even though he might not be conscious of the fact that this particular character trait is active in the analysis at the time. However, this is much more difficult when there is an unconscious narcissistic collusion between both parties, as we shall see when we discuss the bastion (see Chapter Ten).

Obviously, this meaning of "abstinence" is absolutely justified, and a basic ethical precept for the analyst. Although Freud never used the term in this sense, there are indications that he was aware of these dangers. In his paper on "Recommendations to physicians practising psycho-analysis" (1912e), he warns the beginning analyst against several "ambitions" or "temptations"; all of them refer to the analyst following her or his wishes, instead of acting in the best interests of his patient.

The first ambition is the *desire to do research*. As we have already seen, Freud recommends that any research work be postponed until the completion of the treatment. The second one is the *therapeutic ambition*—that is, the narcissistic desire to cure, in order to augment the therapist's prestige and self-esteem. In this, he suggests that the analyst must model himself "on the surgeon, who puts aside all his feelings, even his human sympathy, and concentrates his mental forces on the single aim of performing the operation as skilfully as possible" (p. 115). One of the readings of this recommendation, which understands it as an injunction towards unemotionality, has been rebutted in the previous subsections, and we shall see more of this when discussing the anonymity–disclosure axis. But there is still another meaning to it, and this is that analysts do not "cure", but only aid a natural healing process. This is implied in Freud's suggestion that they should imitate the French surgeon, Ambroise Paré, whose motto was "*Je le pansai, Dieu le guérit*" ("I dressed his wounds, God cured him"). The third temptation is that of *exhibiting one's individuality*. This we shall discuss when dealing with anonymity. The fourth is that of *educating the patient* and turning him or her into a better person— according to the analyst's values, of course. This he found unfeasible and ethically unacceptable.

Even though I do not share Freud's assumption that the analyst's values and beliefs can be left aside during the treatment, as we have seen before, I certainly endorse his admonition against the narcissistic exploitation implied in "forming the patient in our own image".

In sum, the principle of abstinence is aimed at blocking the satisfaction of pathological or unethical desires, both in the patient and in the analyst, but it does not imply a relegation of valid needs in any of the parties. Even the fulfilment of the analyst's needs becomes acceptable when this helps him to be in a position to better comply with the requirements of the treatment, as long as it is always subordinate to the patient's therapeutic needs. This last statement is, of course, a moot question, which requires further discussion.

Rationality–irrationality

One of the values that have been inherent in psychoanalytical theory and practice is that of rationality. Even though Freud exposed the non-rational source of all mental life, he nevertheless remained a staunch supporter of the primacy of rational thought over all other mental processes. This made him distrustful of any approach based on intuition, emotional experience, or "mere" relationship. No doubt this played an important role in his rejection of Jung's mysticism, his dislike of Ferenczi and Rank's (1924) emphasis on analytic experience as the ultimate basis for conviction about the findings of an analysis, and his final repudiation of Ferenczi's technical and clinical experiments.

Nevertheless, if we were to seriously consider his discovery that the major part of the mind is unconscious, and therefore subject to a peculiar logic (the *primary process*), which is quite different from that of conscious rational thought (the *secondary process*), we might expect that a substantial portion of what goes on in the analytic process should occur in terms other than those of the conscious. The analyst would then participate in the analytic process with her total personality, and not only with her rational thinking (Little, 1957).

There certainly is much worth in the fact that the analyst strives systematically to use his capacity for rational thought in order to understand the patient's expressions, his or her own internal experiences, and whatever happens during the sessions, as long as this does not imply a suppression of other functions of his mind that would allow him or her to display a fuller response. What sometimes interferes with a deeper understanding of the analytic process is not the use of rational thought, but its ideological enthronement as the only valid access to knowledge.

Therefore, the analyst strives to be sensitive and reasonable at the same time, keeping a dynamic balance between both frames of mind. It is easier, of course, to purport to be sensible than to be sensitive, since reason is naturally dependent on will, and the heart is not, but the analyst's disposition, personal development, and training, all help him to listen with both a clear mind and an open heart.

Anonymity–disclosure

Freud (1912e) warned analysts, as we have previously seen, against "bring[ing] their own individuality freely into the discussion, in order to carry the patient along with them and lift him over the barriers of his own narrow personality" (p. 117). He felt that this practice would yield no useful results, and that it would interfere with the resolution of transference. Therefore, he recommended that "the doctor should be opaque to his patients and, like a mirror, should show them nothing but what is shown to him" (p. 118).

Apparently, the author was warning against a certain exhibitionistic tendency in the analyst, and also a naïve belief that showing oneself as similar to the patient might help to gain his or her confidence and attain a greater intimacy. I would certainly agree that offering oneself as a model is not a good idea, especially since we analysts are not necessarily the paradigm of mental health and maturity. But Freud's injunction has been understood as a plea for an absolutely impersonal attitude on part of the analyst. This is simply not possible since, no matter what we do or do not do, we shall be expressing our personality. If an analyst manages to keep his face practically devoid of expression, he would only be revealing a social phobia—unless, of course, he happened to suffer from Parkinson's disease! Besides, many analysts believe that this is not even desirable. Racker (1960), for instance, argued poignantly against the orthodox interpretation of this recommendation, in the following terms:

> "Be a mirror" . . . meant "speak to the patient only of himself". It did not mean "stop being of flesh and blood and transform yourself into glass covered with silver nitrate". The positive intention of not showing more that the indispensable of one's person does not have to be carried as far as to deny (or even inhibit) in front of the patient, the analyst's interest and affection towards him. For only Eros can originate Eros. . . . Just as the positive transference is of fundamental importance for analytic work, so also is the positive countertransference and its full unfolding through the hard work the analyst must do to understand and inter- pret. (p. 31, my italics)

This is, of course, an attempt to reintroduce the analyst as a person, from within the Freudian tradition. Analysts who have been trained in the interpersonal school would perhaps find this text rather timid, and limited in its recognition of the intersubjective nature of the analytic situation, just as those trained in the classical Freudian tradi- tion would find it soft, and perhaps anti-analytic. But Racker's description of the essential unity of transference and countertransfer- ence, of the patient's and the analyst's emotions in the relation, is simi- lar to the ideas of some contemporary authors who believe that the analytic relationship is constantly being damaged and repaired, as a part of the analytic process (Aron, 1996, pp. 148–150).

So, even though Freud's advice that the analyst should not unduly expose her personality—especially when it is clearly in the service of her narcissistic–exhibitionist traits—is still valid, this should not obscure the fact that psychoanalysis is always a two-person situation and that our patients know much more about us than we are willing to acknowledge. Therefore, the participation of the analyst's person- ality and reactions in the process should be systematically analysed, lest our discretion be turned into an outright denial of a most signifi- cant part of the analytic situation. This would probably require an explicit disclosure of some of the analyst's experiences and mental processes. As this is a controversial issue, we shall discuss it extensively later. For the time being, let it be said that the analytic attitude implies attaining a dynamic balance between a discreet, self-effacing attitude on the part of the analyst and a cautious self disclosure, whenever she deems it necessary and adequate for the good evolution of the treatment.

In summary

I have presented a rather lengthy discussion on the various dimensions of the analytic attitude. Indeed, it turned out to be much longer than I had expected. I had intended to offer a brief description of the classical conception of this attitude, adding some comments on the contemporary challenges against it, but I found out that this was a major element in my own approach to psychoanalytic technique. It now seems obvious to me that any relational view of psychoanalysis must place the analytic attitude at the centre of its thinking, since the analyst's automatic participation in the process becomes much more important than any technical measure that he may purposely apply. And the only part of such automatic participation that is under our control is precisely the analytic attitude. We cannot control our unconscious contribution to the interaction; we can only try to identify and analyse it. But the analytic attitude may well be learnt and practised until it becomes for us a second nature. An inner attitude, just like a bodily posture, helps us to react automatically in the desired direction, without having to think about it beforehand. In analysis, just as in ballet, the very first step is to acquire the correct and necessary attitude or posture. And such an attitude is not just a position; it requires a certain tension, which will provide the energy needed in order to react. In our case, the tension is generated by the dialectic interplay of the opposite poles of each pair of values that I have described as "axes".

Nevertheless, I feel that a young analyst who is starting his practice would do well to adhere to the more cautious and self-effacing traditional analytic attitude, until he becomes acquainted with the nuances of the analytic treatment and experience. I also feel that such an attitude is more useful at the beginning of a treatment, when one does not yet know the patient very well. But this might be only a reflection of my own Freudian upbringing, and probably an analyst who came from some other analytic school would exhibit a quite different bias.

Aron (2003a) relates how, during his training in the New York University Postdoctoral Program in Psychotherapy and Psychoanalysis, he had two supervisors: one of them was Freudian and the other one was Interpersonal. Whenever he told his Freudian supervisor that he had said something to the patient, the former would ask him, "Why did you say this?" On the other hand, the Interpersonal supervisor would invariably ask, "Why didn't you say it?" when he told him about his thoughts, feelings, and perceptions during the sessions. Obviously, both supervisors reasoned from two quite different sets of assumptions: the Freudian assumed that an analyst should never actively intervene, thus giving the patient an opportunity to be-with-himself in the presence of another person, unless there were a good reason for it; the Interpersonal supervisor assumed that the analyst should always engage in a fluid interchange with the patient, thus fostering a mutual generation of analytic data, unless there were a good reason against it. It is not a question of saying who is right and who is wrong—they are probably both right in certain respects and wrong in others—but to clearly identify an analyst's assumptions in order to understand what he or she does and says.

The relational psychoanalysis movement was born precisely from the need to create a common ground in which analysts from various origins who are united by a similar set of questions about the analytic experience may develop a fruitful interchange of ideas and clinical experiences. In my own particular case, I moved from a Freudian training, with an object relations bias, towards an increasing study of the impact of interpersonal and transpersonal processes on the analytic situation and process. In this, I was aided by the fact that my first training had been in group-analytic psychotherapy, that I then evolved towards group analysis, and that I have also had a long-term practice in marriage and family therapy, which sensitised me to relational and contextual processes. I had some trouble in finding an adequate term to refer to my approach to psychoanalysis—I played with "object relations", "interpersonal", and "intersubjective", none of which fully satisfied me—until I met the term "relational", and finally added the idea of a "process", which I had been using for some time in my clinical teaching. The result of this evolution is this book.

CHAPTER FOUR

The context of analysis

What is a context?

The concept of "context" is not a part of psychoanalytic theory. None the less, we are constantly unwittingly referring to the context of the patient's expressions, since no human communication can be understood without it.

A *context* is that set of subsidiary information about a *text* that helps the reader to determine the meaning or meanings that may be found in it. Such information may be of various kinds. For instance, the passages that precede or follow a certain portion of the text might shed light on the meaning intended by the author. The reader may also use some external information about the circumstances in which the piece was written—such as the author's personality and biography, the intended audience, and the social and political environment at the time. But the reader–interpreter might go even further, and attempt to discover meanings that had never been conscious for the author, but that may be plausibly inferred from the juxtaposition of the text and its context.

Now, "text" does not only mean "the original written or printed words and form of a literary work", but also "the form and substance of something written or spoken" (Merriam-Webster, 2002, see entry "Text"), "something (as a story or movie) considered as an object to be examined, explicated, or deconstructed" and "something likened to a text"—as, for instance, when the occurrences of everyday life are described as "texts" to be interpreted. The word also originally meant "tissue"—that is, a woven product:

> Just as the effect of a thread in a fabric must needs depend on its location within a larger whole, the effect of interwoven words always depends on the complex interrelation within the whole word-tissue in which they are embedded. But the effect of context goes even further: a piece of tapestry can only be appreciated in its relation with the wall on which it hangs, the room and the house where it is, and the culture and sensitivity of those who behold it, and a book also derives an additional meaning from the circumstances in which it is being read. A conversation [or a session] is a tissue made of words, phrases, intentions, emotions, and relationships, but it does not have a real boundary, since its edges are woven into a wider context, set up by language, culture, other groups, institutions, history, and society-at-large. Interpretation thus acquires a kaleidoscopic dimension, which never finds an end. . . .

> What one deems to be an adequate behaviour depends on the context. A certain conduct that would be perfectly acceptable in a wedding would not be so in a wake or burial, and the expectations in both cases vary from one culture to another. During a psychoanalytic session, both parties are allowed—and even required—to say things that would be frankly shocking in an ordinary social environment. Clearly, psychoanalysis creates its own particular context, which starts to operate when the door of the analyst's office closes, leaving two people alone in a room, engaged in the business of "analysing". (Tubert-Oklander & Hernández de Tubert, 2004, pp. 83, 84)

In everyday life, we use contextual information in order to determine how a particular message should be understood. A person's demeanour while speaking helps us to decide what kind of message we are receiving. Is it an aggression or a joke? Is it a suggestion, an admonition, or a reprimand? Is it praise or sarcasm? Is it courtesy or seduction? Such *metacommunication*—that is, a message that is parallel to, and comments on, the manifest verbal expression—represents a proposal for the listener to engage in a certain type of relation with the speaker. Therefore, every time that one person speaks to another, he or she is simultaneously sending a non-verbal message, which could be framed in words such as: "I want you to be my (boss, subordinate, parent, sexual partner, persecutor, conscience, nurturing breast, toilet, castrator, victim, etc.)". This is what communications theorists such as Bateson (1972) convey with their distinction between the *report* and the *command* that are implicit in every communicative act. Thus, speaking to another person has a *referential function* (a report about something) and a *relational function* (a command—order, suggestion, demand, invitation, or plea—to engage in certain type of relation).

In other words, relationship is one of the contexts that determine how any particular act of communication is to be understood, and if two or more people are to reach a satisfactory understanding, they should create a common context for their mutual communication. Such context building occurs in any human interaction, and certainly must happen also in the analytic relationship. One could even say that the analytic process *is* the constitution and evolution of a particular context: the analytic context, and it behoves the analyst that he or she should do whatever is necessary for bringing about such context.

The creation of the analytic context

The analytic context is created by both parties, even though the greater responsibility for this falls on the analyst. Leaving aside, for the moment, the unconscious relational proposals by the two of them that constitute that aspect of the analytic relation that we call the transference–countertransference, the patient's main contribution to the creation of this new context is her request for help and willingness to engage in the treatment. The analyst contributes in several ways. First, there is that consistent position and way of doing things that we have named the *analytic attitude*, which has been the subject of the previous chapter. Then, there are many specific instances of his *technical interventions*, aimed at: (a) setting the minimum and adequate conditions for the establishment and development of the analytic relationship and process, (b) establishing and nurturing the analytic relationship, and (c) modulating the evolution of the analytic process. The rest is, of course, his *personal contribution*, derived from his personality, personal history and experience, sensibility, knowledge, capabilities, beliefs, values, and even oddities.

I have already discussed the analytic attitude, and shall deal with the analyst's personal contribution and the technical interventions aimed at the analytic relationship and process in the next chapters. Now, I intend to focus on those "minimum and adequate conditions" required by the analytic treatment. These are what we usually call the analytic "set-up", "setting", "frame", or "contract".

These names usually refer to the fact that the analyst has to clearly define for the patient, at the beginning of the analysis, the conditions in which such enterprise is to be carried out and the rules that will govern their interaction. This problem was dealt with by Freud (1913c) in his paper "On beginning the treatment". The traditional psychoanalytic set-up is based on the norm that he introduced at the time. This contribution to the creation of the analytic context, however, goes further than the mere utterance of what has been called the "analytic contract", as we shall presently see.

The functions of the analytic setting

In the following discussion, I shall use the term "setting" in order to refer to that set of regularities that encompass and contain the analytic process, which is the dynamic aspect of the psychoanalytic situation, hence defining its context. These certainly include, but are not restricted to the set of explicit rules that are known as the "analytic contract".

Since the various writers that have dealt with the functions of the setting have explored and emphasised some of them, while leaving aside others, there will be some discrepancy among my various references. I trust, however, that I shall be able to demonstrate that they blend together to form a harmonious polysemic concept, which might help us to attain a better understanding of the analytic process.

The setting as a stable frame for perception

One way to approach the study of the setting is in terms of the psychology of perception. We know very well that perception is based on comparison. This is the reason why any constant stimulus—such as, for instance, the background noise in a factory—soon ceases to be perceived. In order to perceive movement, we need to compare whatever is moving with something that remains static or, at least, moves considerably slower.

Such a course was taken by the Argentine psychoanalyst, José Bleger (1967a), in his now classic paper "Psychoanalysis of the psychoanalytic frame". His approach was methodological, in as much as he was trying to describe the analytic situation in terms of constants and variables. Thus, he defined the analytic situation in the following terms:

> I suggest . . . that we should apply the term "psycho-analytic situation" to the totality of phenomena included in the therapeutic relationship between the analyst and the patient. This situation comprises phenomena which constitute a process that is studied, analysed, and interpreted; but it also includes a frame, that is to say, a "non-process", in the sense that it is made up of constants within whose bounds the process takes place. (p. 511)

According to this author, something that moves or evolves—that is, the process—may only be studied when the same set of variables is kept steady—that is, the frame or setting. That is why we include in the psychoanalytic setting the analyst's role, the definition of space and time parameters, and the rules of the treatment (schedule, fees, absences, holidays, and so on). But Bleger goes beyond this methodological definition when he describes the function of the setting as the depository of the patient's "psychotic part of the personality", as we shall see in the subsection on "the setting as continent object relation".

Another Argentine psychoanalyst, Joel Zac (1968), built on Bleger's concepts in order to further conceptualise the setting and its functions. He defined the analytic situation as "the whole set of facts and relationships that take place during the session or in the course of a treatment, between the analyst and the patient, in the analytic environment space" (Zac, 1968, p. 29, my translation). Such situation may only be understood as a "field", that is, as a "transversal" description of a "moment" of the evolution of the treatment. This concept of "the analytic situation as a dynamic field" was introduced by the Barangers (2008), as we shall see in Chapter Six.

This implies a few consequences: (a) that the analytic field is a dynamic whole; (b) that the analyst and the patient form a functional unit, not as *parts* of static situation, but as *members* of an evolutionary relationship; (c) that the events that we observe are not pre-existent to the analytic situation, but are generated in it, and (d) that the analyst–patient functional unit and the facts which are thus generated are expressed in the analytic relationship, in terms of transference–countertransference.

The analytic situation is dynamic. This means that it is continuously evolving, but one can distinguish two aspects in it, according to the speed of their evolution: the *process* and the *setting*. The process is the moving part of the situation—the variables—which is in sharp contrast with the more stable part of it—the constants, that is, the setting. The latter includes five kinds of constants: *theoretical, functional, temporal, spatial*, and those derived from *the analyst as a real person*. These are the following.

1. Theoretical constants. They include the analyst's theories about: (a) the personality (theory of psychoanalysis); (b) the interpretive technique; (c) the setting; (d) the group and society.
2. Functional constants. They include: (a) the aims of the treatment; (b) the patient's role; (c) the analyst's role; (d) fees.
3. Temporal constants. They include: (a) the duration of sessions; (b) their frequency; (c) their rhythm: (i) *continuous or "analytic week"*—sequential sessions (e.g., Monday through Thursday or Friday) and *a single interval or "analytic weekend"*; (ii) *discontinuous*—four or five sessions with one or more intervals; (d) periods of separation: from session to session, weekends, vacations, holidays, and other previously agreed and announced breaks.
4. Spatial constants. They include: (a) the place of the sessions (preferably an office); (b) the quality and quantity of objects that are to be found there; (c) their distribution.
5. Constants derived from the analyst as a real person. They include: (a) his personality; (b) his internal and external attitudes, behaviour, demeanour, and external appearance; (c) his ideology and ethics; (d) the social and scientific institutions he belongs to. (Zac, 1968, p. 33, my translation)

In a previous paper, called "The analytic situation as a dynamic field" and quoted by both Bleger and Zac, the Barangers (2008 [1961–1962]) use the concept of "field", taken from Gestalt psychology and the work of Merleau-Ponty (1942, 1945), in order to describe the analytic situation as a situation between two persons who remain unavoidably connected and complementary as long as the situation obtains, and involved in a single dynamic process. *In this situation, neither member of the couple can be understood without the other.* (2008, p. 796, my italics)

These ideas represent an attempt to fully include the analyst as a whole person in the psychoanalytic situation. These authors clearly understand the unavoidable mutual regulation between the two parties of the psychoanalytic situation. All of them have been clearly influenced by the work of Enrique Pichon-Rivière, one of the founders of the Argentine Psychoanalytic Association, who was their teacher and mentor, and who is also an ever-present influence in this text. None the less, as Pichon-Rivière was never much of a writer, and developed his teaching mainly through the spoken word, his ideas have been kept and publicised mainly though the work of his disciples, and in a few books made up from his papers and the notes taken by his students during his classes (Pichon-Rivière, 1971, 1979; Tubert-Oklander, 2011b; Tubert-Oklander & Hernández de Tubert, 2004). Pichon-Rivière always emphasised the importance of what he called the "bond", understood as the relation between the analyst and the patient as two real persons, each with his or her own personal history and social context, as an essential part of the analytic situation. (The original Spanish term, *vínculo*, is better translated as "bond", on account of its contractual, moral, and chemical connotations, than as "link", which suggests a more mechanical tie.)

Nevertheless, Bleger's description of the analytic situation as composed of an evolutionary element—the process—and a stable one—the setting—is still somehow imbued by the scientific tradition of "objective" observation. The truth is that the whole situation is a process, since the setting also evolves, even though at a slower pace than the dialogue and the relationship, and every now and then it must become a subject for the analytic enquiry. The whole situation is, therefore, dynamic, and the necessary distinction between that part of it that evolves rapidly and that which evolves slowly and imperceptibly, although adequate and necessary for the comparative process of perception, can be readily reversed when the setting becomes the focus of the analytic dialogue. This is a classical figure–ground phenomenon, in which the picture and the frame reverse their respective positions, when our attention is directed towards the latter.

The setting as a frame that defines the meaning of its contents

We have already seen that the context is a frame that defines how the expressions that are included in it are to be understood. Whatever happens on a theatrical stage, for instance, acquires a very different meaning from what it would have had in everyday life. (No sane person runs to call the police when there is a murder on stage.) The same happens in the Catholic rite of confession: as this is considered a sacrament, the believer is not really confessing to that other poor sinner, who happens to be a priest, but to God, since the minister has now become the channel for communicating with the Deity. In the same vein, anything that is said or happens in the psychoanalytic situation is imbued with a most unusual meaning after the door of the analyst's office is closed and the session starts. The analyst also becomes a quite different character, when invested with his analytic function, and this is surely an essential part of transference.

This function has been extensively studied by Milner (1952a,b), who, when comparing her experiences as a painter and as a psychoanalyst, says,

> I told how I saw the frame as something that marked off what's inside it from what's outside it, and to think of other human activities where the frame is essential, a frame in time as well as in space; for instance the acted play, ceremonies, rituals, processions, even poems framed in silence when spoken and the space of the paper when written. Also the psychoanalytic session framed in both space and time. I said I thought that *all these frames show that what is inside has to be perceived, interpreted in a different way from what is outside*; they mark off an area within which what we perceive has to be taken as symbol, as metaphor, not literally. (Milner, 1952a, pp. 80–81, my italics)

> The frame marks off the different kind of reality that is within it from that which is outside it; but a temporal spatial frame also marks off the special kind of reality of a psychoanalytic session. And *in psychoanalysis it is the existence of this frame that makes possible the full development of that creative illusion that analysts call the transference*. Also the central idea underlying psychoanalytic technique is that it is by means of this illusion that a better adaptation to the world outside is ultimately developed. (Milner, 1952b, p. 87, my italics)

Liberman (1976a), another of Pichon-Rivière's disciples, once suggested an imaginary experiment. Suppose that a person somehow manages to unexpectedly listen to a psychoanalytic session, from some nearby apartment, and does not know who these people are and what they are doing. What would this witness think about the conversation? Perhaps the listener would surmise that they were a parent and a child talking, but would then suddenly have the strange feeling that they were two lovers discussing their relationship, or a person who is confiding a personal secret to an intimate friend, and all this would then be blurred by their formal tone, which might suggest a teacher–student or a doctor–patient relationship. In Liberman's example, the imaginary listener finally despairs of his attempt to understand the conversation and decides that "these two people are mad".

Now, what sort of information might give the listener a signal that he is witnessing a psychoanalytic session? Of course, he would need to have some information about the existence of a peculiar kind of relationship called "psychoanalysis", and also have a hunch that this applied to what he was hearing. In Liberman's experiment, the listener had to have another analyst, with a certain knowledge of that particular treatment, explain to him the meaning of such extraordinary conversation.

Liberman suggests that an essential requirement for a speaker and a listener to understand each other (and for an external listener to understand their conversation) is that their mutual relation be clearly defined, recognised, and accepted by both of them (and by the "occasional listener"). They also need to share a common code, which is germane for that particular context.

This function of the analytic setting is generated by the analyst's analytic attitude. But such an attitude is based on a series of theoretical, practical, ontological, axiological, and relational assumptions that are not necessarily shared or known by the patient, and that might even be unthinkable for her. For instance, the fact that the analyst is not willing to offer much information about herself might be experienced by the unsophisticated patient as a violent rejection or a boorish attitude. It behoves the analyst to give some information about this unusual behaviour, as a contribution to the development of a common context for both parties.

But the analytic context is also inserted in two much wider contexts: the *institutional* and the *social* contexts. Therefore, the meanings assigned to the symbolic interchanges that take place during an analysis also depend on their insertion in such contexts. For instance, a male patient's behaviour towards a female analyst will surely be influenced by his socially acquired beliefs about what sort of conduct is acceptable or mandatory towards a woman, his expectations of her behaviour towards him, and the sanctioned forms of man–woman interaction. But the analyst is also bound to come to the analytic encounter with such beliefs, habits, and expectations. These cultural factors, which become obvious whenever the patient and the analyst come from different backgrounds, but tend to go unnoticed when they do not, should always be exposed and analysed (Hernández de Tubert, 2006a).

On the other hand, sometimes psychoanalytic procedures run contrary to the usual social habits and expectations. One example of this is the analytic norm of paying for unattended sessions. Such unusual behaviour and demands by the analyst should not only be openly explained and discussed with the patient, as Etchegoyen (1986) explains in his textbook of psychoanalytic technique, but also analysed in terms of their consequences and unconscious implications for both parties and their mutual relationship.

All this is a question of mores, but the institutional context also includes the laws of society. If a patient asks for a receipt on the fees that he is paying, this is only exercising a right bestowed upon him by law. In Mexico, and in many other countries, such a receipt marks the difference between being able to deduct this expense from taxes, or not (and, for the analyst, between paying taxes on it, or not). In such a situation, if the analyst were to interpret—as some do—that "the patient is trying to control the analyst's economy", as a justification for not giving the receipt, it would be tantamount to fraud.

In sum, the analytic situation creates a most peculiar context, but this cannot, and must not, be divorced from the social and institutional contexts in which the treatment takes place.

The setting as a containing object relation

The setting creates a peculiar environment that the patient relates to. The regularity of the sessions and of the analyst's behaviour makes it reliable and predictable—on the whole, much more than that provided by other relationships. In this, the analytic setting is akin to the type of environment that, in our culture, a family builds for a newborn baby. As babies are fragile, sensitive, and dependent, we create a simplified environment that responds to their needs, and protects them from extreme stimuli, such as hunger, physical pain, heat and cold, noise, rough touch, and loneliness. The fact that the analytic setting closely resembles, in its isolation and simplification, that of the baby's room, acts as an invitation to regress for those patients who have a need for it.

This point of view, which is characteristic of object relations theory, is in sharp contrast with that of ego psychology, which emphasises that the patient regresses in response to the frustration and lack of stimuli in the analytic setting. Macalpine (1950) and Menninger (1958), for instance, maintain that the patient regresses because the analytic environment infantilises him or her. The recumbent position and the analyst's silence generate a sensory deprivation that forces regression upon the patient. From this perspective, analytic regression would be equivalent to that which is induced by solitary confinement in jail. Such a comparison is certainly not a happy one, since it relates our practice to a maltreatment of our patients. And, of course, there is still the unanswered question raised by Macalpine of why the permissiveness of the analytic situation does not prevent regression, instead of inducing it.

Of course, such an argument is based on drive theory and assumes that it is frustration that leads to regression. Object relations theorists, such as Ferenczi and Winnicott believe regression to be a natural response to a mild and protective environment, although the former only arrived at this conclusion after abandoning his "active technique", based on drive theory, which imposed on the patient an additional frustration in order that his wishes and conflicts be forced into consciousness (Ferenczi, 1919, 1921, 1925). In his later work, however, he asserts, in "The unwelcome child and his death instinct" (1929), that some patients who exhibit a set of self-destructive traits that have been encompassed under the term of the "death drive" have been "unwelcome guests" in their family. In other words, their parents did not wish to have these children, and their expressions of rejection of towards them barely hid an unconscious wish that they should never have been born, or even that they should die. In the treatment of such patients, Ferenczi applied his concept of a certain "elasticity" in the analytic technique (1928b)—that is, a greater permissiveness and an attempt to adapt the analytic situation to the patient's needs, just as he maintained that the family should adapt itself to the child, and not

the other way round (1928a). This is how he describes the technique
that he developed for the treatment of this type of patient:

> In these cases of diminished desire for life, a situation became appar-
> ent which could only be described as one in which the patient had to
> be allowed for a time to have his way like a child. . . . Through this
> indulgence the patient is permitted, properly speaking for the first
> time, to enjoy the irresponsibility of childhood, which is equivalent to
> the introduction of *positive* life-impulses and motives for his subse-
> quent existence. (Ferenczi, 1929, p. 128–129)

Winnicott follows the same path in his classical paper "Metapsychological and clinical aspects of regression within the psychoanalytical set-up" (1955). Just like Ferenczi, he believes that some
patients have suffered an anomalous situation during their infancy,
and that this is what creates in them "an organization which enables
regression to occur" (p. 18). For him, the sequence is as follows:

a. A failure of adaptation on the part of the environment that results
    in the development of a false self.
b. A belief in the possibility of a correction of the original failure
    represented by a latent capacity for regression which implies a
    complex ego organization.
c. Specialized environmental provision [the analytic setting],
    followed by actual regression.
d. New forward emotional development, with complications. (p. 18)

This last assumption is clearly equivalent to Balint's (1932, 1952)
suggestion that such patients undergo what he called a "new beginning" in the later stages of an analysis.

It is obvious that this point of view does not consider regression as
a defence mechanism, or as an adaptation to an abnormal environment, but as a path towards healing. When the patient regresses, she
or he is expressing trust in the analyst and a deep-rooted hope that
there might still be a second opportunity for him or her to live
through the structuring experience of being *truly* dependant on a reliable caring object (Hernández de Tubert, 1999).

And what is Freud's clinical setting, according to Winnicott (1955)?
On this, he argues that, on account of his or her regular, predictable,
reasonable, committed, and ethical behaviour,

In the analytic situation the analyst is much more reliable than people are in ordinary life . . . [and] the whole thing adds up to the fact that the analyst *behaves* himself or herself, and behaves without too much cost simply because of being a relatively mature person. (p. 21)

Winnicott believed that, if Freud had not been up to such an ethical standard of behaviour, he would not have been able to develop either the psychoanalytic technique or the theory that he derived from the clinical experiences that he had when applying such technique, no matter how clever he might have been. In this, he was clearly stating that intelligence is never enough, unless it is coupled with sensitivity and ethics. And every single detail of this setting was shown to be of extreme importance at a specific phase in the analysis of patients who had a need for regression.

Of course, we could ask whether all patients might need an experience of regression at certain stages of their treatment. If our answer happened to be positive, then these observations would be valid for every treatment. I shall come back later to this issue.

Another approach to the question of the setting as a particular kind of object relation comes from Bleger (1967a). As we have already seen, this author believed that the setting was the depository for what he called the patient's "psychotic part of the personality"—that is, the most primitive and severely traumatised one. This part of the personality is mute as long as the treatment proceeds as usual, but it suddenly emerges when there is some disturbance in the setting. And this emergence of disorganisation and pathological traits should be analysed accordingly.

The analyst is, therefore, obliged to preserve the setting and defend it from any attacks on it, whether from the patient or from himself, but he should also pay special attention to whatever emerges when the setting is broken, since this might give a clue to some phenomena that had remained invisible up to that moment. And, even though Bleger, from his traditional psychoanalytic outlook, does not consider this possibility, the disturbance that ensues when there is a fracture in the setting becomes manifest in both the patient and the analyst. This is related to the Barangers' (2008) concept of the "bastion", and to the contemporary conception of *enactment* as an unavoidable element in the psychoanalytic process. This we shall discuss in Chapter Ten, on "The evolution of the analytic process".

These ideas suggest that the analytic situation is built on the basis of the setting, the analytic attitude, and the analytic relationship, but that all these are disrupted every now and then, and that both parties have to work together in order to heal it. This process of integrity–rupture–healing–new integrity is what allows the development of an evolutionary process.

The setting as a co-creation and part of the analytic relationship

In our customary thinking, the setting is seen as the structural aspect of the analytic situations, while the process would be its dynamic facet. However, the concepts "structure" and "process" are relative to the circumstances, the time span, and even the speed of their progress. A tree is definitely a structure when you crash your car into it, but it is a process if you watch it patiently over the years. In the same vein, water is fluid when you are swimming in it, but it appears to be as solid as a wall when you collide with its surface when falling from a height. So, the setting or frame is that part of the analytic process that changes at a much slower pace than the other parts. Thus, the former not only allows us to observe them by comparison, but it also acts as a container for their variability and push (Tubert-Oklander, 2008).

In any case, the setting certainly does evolve during the course of the treatment, and this evolution is a part of the development of the analytic relationship. Such changes should, therefore, be thoroughly analysed in terms of their unconscious meaning and impact on the analytic relation. Moreover, not only the changes, but also their very inception, are the result of a complex negotiation, which is largely unconscious, between the analyst and the analysand, as we shall see when we discuss the analytic process. Also, the way in which this process of negotiation is transacted is as important as the specific agreements that are thus reached. Hence, the form and spirit of the conscious and unconscious negotiation between the parties is an essential part of the construction of the analytic relationship and process.

The setting as a legal commitment for both parties

The psychoanalytic treatment requires that both analyst and patient are able and willing to comply with a formal commitment to the rules of the treatment. Whenever the patient is not capable—on account of age, pathology, or vital situation, as in the case of children, adolescents, or psychotic adults—of keeping such a commitment, someone else—usually the family—has to do it, in order for the treatment to be possible.

This commitment clearly refers to what is known as the "analytic contract" (that is, the explicit agreements reached by both parties about the conditions of the treatment), but also to a series of implicit agreements about what might be termed the "spirit of the treatment"—for example, there is no formal rule forbidding a patient from bringing in a portable media player and spending the session listening to her favourite tunes, but this is clearly a transgression of the very purpose of an analysis. This we shall discuss in the next section, when dealing with the explicit and the implicit settings.

The idea of viewing the analytic situation in terms of a two-party contract was developed by Menninger (1958). Some analysts, such as Roustang (1976), have taken exception to this view, upon the argument that the unconscious knows nothing of contracts, so that this concept would really be alien to psychoanalysis. It is true that the unconscious, like small children, does not have the concept of "rules" or "laws", and is, therefore, unable either to comply with them or break them. But the analysis cannot deal only with the unconscious, but must consider the whole of the patient's personality. There must be some functional conscious ego to allow the analysis to begin, in order that the patient can get to his sessions on time, leave when they are over, pay for them, and understand, albeit on a superficial level, the formal rules of psychoanalysis.

But, even though the unconscious does not conceive or understand rules as such, it is bound to perceive somehow that the analyst is obeying some higher instance, and this is experienced as the presence of a third party, both uncanny and enormously powerful. This vivid experience of the Law has a structuring impact on the patient, just as it has on small children during early development. All this must be duly analysed.

So, the contract is a legal situation that regulates the relationship. The Law has a life and a power of its own, independently from the wishes and feelings of both parties, who also have an object relationship with the Law as the Third, which is binding for both of them. The Law is either imposed by the analyst or co-created by both parties as an explicit contract or as tacit agreements, but there is also a higher and more abstract moral law: the Law of Analysis, which is borne, but not created, by the analyst. This is part of what Lacan (1981) conveys with his metaphor of the Phallus as a symbol: the Father (and the analyst) bears the Phallus, but they *are not* the Phallus. This means that they impose the Law, but they are not the Law, since they are also subject to its power, just as a judge who imposes the law has to obey it as much as those whom he is judging.

The analyst conveys this legality of her or his behaviour not only by obedience to the rules of the explicit contract, but also by his submission to the norms of the profession, in keeping the analytic attitude and its ethical standards. In this, he is not acting alone, but as a member of a community, which is therefore invisibly present in the session. This is an absolute requirement for the practice of psychoanalysis, and if it is lacking, the analyst will be "merely clever"—in Winnicott's (1971) terms—but will never be able to develop a true psychoanalytic practice.

The setting as a secluded space that defines a subgroup

It was Bion (1961) who pointed out that the fact that analyst and analysand have to meet in a closed space in order to conduct psychoanalysis implies that they become an isolated subgroup that segregates itself from the community. In the unconscious life of groups, this is invariably conceived as if it were a sexual meeting, thus defining a fantasised mating group, from which an idealised product would be born. This he considers to be a universal collective fantasy, one of the three basic assumptions unconsciously held by groups about their *raison d'être*. The members of a group either believe that they are there in order to find an idealised leader to depend on (the *basic assumption dependency*), or one who would lead them to fight against an enemy or escape from it (*basic assumption fight/flight*), or a pair that would lead them through mating and giving birth to an idealised product that would by itself solve all their problems (*basic assumption pairing*). This sort of magical thinking obviously operates in terms of the primary process, and groups oscillate between this sort of functioning—the *basic assumption group*—and another way of thinking in terms of the secondary process, which is able to tackle the group's problems in a rational and, therefore, scientific way—the *work group*. (It should be noted that, for Bion, the basic assumption group and the work group are not two different groups, but two kinds of mental activity that take place, alternately, in any given group.)

In the psychoanalytic situation, the frame defines the limits—spatial, temporal, relational, and legal—that isolate a subgroup, a pair, from the larger community, thus making it the depository of certain collective fantasies that involve mating, conceiving, and giving birth to a product (a Messiah) in terms of Bion's conception of the basic assumption of pairing. Small wonder that such a technical device should have been imbued with sexual fantasies, as Freud soon discovered.

The implicit and explicit settings

One thing that becomes obvious when we examine Zac's (1968) list of the constants of the analytic setting is that most of them are not a part of the explicit contract that is established between the patient and the analyst. The functional and the temporal constants are certainly discussed and agreed at the very beginning of the treatment; the spatial constants are usually taken for granted, but the theoretical constants and those derived from the analyst as a real person are usually not mentioned at the contract stage. All the elements of the setting might, however, become involved in the analytic process, and then they should be duly enquired into and analysed.

We are, therefore, dealing with two aspects of the setting: the explicit *contract* and the implicit *tacit setting*. Both of them are relatively stable, acting as a context for the analytic process, and both might suddenly become the subject of the analytic dialogue; in this case, the process becomes the context for the analytic understanding of the setting and its implications. One possible result of this reversion of the figure–ground organisation of the analytic situation is that there might be a change in either the contract or the tacit setting.

The contract

After one or more interviews—which should not be too many—with a prospective patient, and if the analyst has arrived at the conclusion that psychoanalysis may be the treatment of choice for that particular individual and situation, he or she will propose such a therapeutic approach to the patient. This implies letting the patient know what an analysis is all about by clarifying the following points: (a) the aims of the treatment, (b) the patient's role, (c) the analyst's role, and (d) how they are going to understand each other. In other words, the patient has to know what to expect from the treatment and the analyst, and what is expected from him.

This approach assumes that we should strive to enlist the patient's conscious co-operation in a common endeavour. Some analysts feel this to be pointless, since reasonable explanations have no effect on unconscious anxieties and defence mechanisms, so that the only way to get an analysis going would be to interpret unconscious conflicts and transference phenomena as they arise, and to form a relationship with the patient on the basis of the relief given by such interpretations. This was, for example, Klein's (1932) stance on the question.

Others, including myself, feel that one needs to muster the patient's conscious co-operation, and that this requires offering him some sensible explanations that he may understand. This was perhaps one of the major differences between Melanie Klein and Anna Freud on the subject of technique, which surfaced when discussing the technique of child analysis, but is truly applicable to all kinds of analytic treatment. Klein (1932) relied mainly on immediate interpretations of the unconscious conflicts and the transference, hoping that the relationship would develop spontaneously on the solid ground offered by the feeling of relief that ensues after a successful interpretation. In other words, she was looking for the patient's *unconscious co-operation*. Anna Freud (1927), on the other hand, tried to gradually build a relationship with the child at a conscious level, and then proceed with the analysis with the *conscious co-operation* of the patient.

Winnicott (1958c) tried to strike a balance between these two positions, in which each of them would be partly right. He also emphasised the need to take into account the patient's intelligence:

> It is necessary for us to deal with the situation as we find it in each case that we treat. With very intelligent [patients] we need to be able to talk to their intelligence, to feed their intelligence. It is sometimes a complication when we are doing work with a [patient] and the [patient] feels that something is going on, and yet has no intellectual understanding of what it is all about. In any case it would seem to be

a pity to waste the intellectual understanding of the [patient], which can be a very powerful ally, although of course in certain cases the intellectual processes may be used in defence, making the analysis more difficult. (pp. 119–120)

I fully agree with Winnicott on these considerations, and I have published a paper on the analysis of an adolescent boy in which I emphasised the need to rely on the conscious co-operation of the patient's intelligence for the analysis to go on (Tubert-Oklander, 1988). I would also call attention to the fact that, even though Freud (1913c) discouraged "lengthy preliminary discussions before the beginning of the analytic treatment" (p. 125), he was apparently referring to a theoretical discussion, aimed at convincing the patient of the validity of the psychoanalytic treatment. Of course, if the patient has persistent doubts, they are probably derived from her ambivalence towards treatment, and they will not be solved by explanations, but would probably require a tentative interpretation, even during the interview stage. But Freud always made every effort to explain to the patient what analysis was and what her contribution should be to this shared endeavour. So, we should always try to count on both the conscious and the unconscious co-operation of the patient; the former depends on the conscious non-defensive contribution of the patient's intellect, while the latter is a result of effective interpretations that alleviate unconscious anxiety, this being a valid argument for the use of early interpretations, even during the interviews.

Another necessary part of the contract corresponds to the arrangements about fees, form of payment, policy about unattended or cancelled sessions, the duration, frequency, and rhythm of the sessions, as well as routine and foreseeable interruptions. In the management of such practical matters, as well as in every other aspect of the contract, there are several ways of establishing it. Etchegoyen (1986) describes three kinds of contract: the *authoritarian, demagogic,* and *democratic* contracts. The first one is unilaterally imposed by the analyst, and the patient can only choose to accept it as it is or reject it wholesale by not entering treatment. The second one implies a magnanimous indiscriminate accommodation of the patient's wishes, in an attempt to establish the analyst as a "good" object. The democratic contract requires an open discussion of both parties' positions, possibilities, and interests, in order to attain an even-handed agreement. This is obviously my own way of approaching the contract, but not only on account of such ethical values as the consideration and respect for the analysand's rights, but also on analytic grounds. The establishment of the contract is the first significant interaction between the analyst and the analysand, and it sets the key for the whole analytic relationship that is to develop between them. Taking into account the patient's opinions, possibilities, and needs, as well as the analyst's, defines the relation as non-abusive for either party. It puts forward an ideal model of rationality and negotiation, and this implies considering the point of view of the other. All of this sets the tone for all future analytic interactions.

But the establishment of the contract offers yet another opportunity for the creation of the analytic situation. The analyst might choose to reflect with the patient on the implications that each of the alternatives under consideration might have for their future relation. This brings home the message that everything that happens in the analytic sessions will be subject to scrutiny, as a part of the analysis. Such procedure may be called a *reflective contract*.

The tacit setting

Several of the constants of the setting are usually not included in the contract, but they are rather taken for granted. These are: (i) spatial constants, (ii) constants derived from the analyst as a real person, (iii) theoretical constants, (iv) institutional and social constants, and (v) constants related to the "spirit of the analysis".

(i) *Spatial constants*: these are usually taken for granted; the rationale for this is probably that, as the place of the sessions, the quantity and quality of the objects to be found there, and their distribution are usually kept constant, they may be safely cancelled out as part of a formless ground, which passes unnoticed behind the more striking and apparent process. This argument leaves out the fact that patients keenly observe, interpret, and are obviously affected by every detail of the analyst's entourage. It is clearly not the same if the analyst works at her home or in an office, if she works alone or sharing the premises with other therapists, if the office is in a residential area or in a hospital setting, if there is a waiting room or not, a secretary or an answering machine. The furniture and other objects in the analyst's office, and the part of the city where it is located, tell the patient a great deal about who the analyst is and what her values and aspirations are. The geographical disposition of the office is also revealing of the analyst's personality. For instance, if the analyst's chair is removed from the couch, or if there some other piece of furniture in between them, this might be an indication of a phobic rejection of intimacy. If the office is extremely impersonal, this gives the patient as much information about the analyst as if he had his family's portraits on his desk. The impact of all these details should be, but almost never is, thoroughly analysed in terms of the transference–countertransference.

Besides, the objects and their distribution also vary during a treatment. It is unrealistic to expect that a space where people live and work will not change over a period of years, and every change sends a set of messages to the patient. New objects appear and others vanish, the office must perforce be cleaned, the walls painted, the curtains repaired or changed; if there is a vase of flowers, they have to be replaced periodically, and so on. And all these changes frequently reveal the presence of some other person who is taking care of things. For instance, when a male analyst marries, it is not unusual for his wife to have some influence on the arrangement of his office; this is readily perceived by the patients, and should be duly analysed.

There is, however, one of the spatial constants that is not taken for granted, and this is *the couch*. Of course, this might be included in the functional constants, as a part of the patient's role, if one considers that the recumbent position as a *condition sine qua non* for psychoanalysis. But, if the use of the couch is taken as facultative, it becomes certainly one of the spatial constants. The requirement that the patient should lie on the couch during the analytic sessions while the analyst sits out of sight behind him was introduced by Freud (1913c) as "the remnant of the hypnotic method out of which psychoanalysis was evolved" (p. 133). Nevertheless, he considered that it deserved to be maintained for two different, although mutually related, reasons. First, because he felt that he could not "put up with being stared at by other people for eight hours a day (or more)" (p. 134). Second, because he wanted "to prevent the transference from mingling with the patient's associations imperceptibly, to isolate the transference and to allow it to come forward in due course sharply defined as a resistance" (p. 134).

What these two reasons have in common is the assumption that the patient's transference might develop without any interference from the analyst's personal characteristics. The attempt to study the patient's mental processes without any contamination from the analyst's personality led Freud to control his spontaneous expressions when the patient was looking at him, and this was part of the effort that he wanted to avoid by means of the couch. Now, I have been arguing extensively that such objectivity is, in fact, impossible, and that the analyst inevitably participates in the analytic process. If this were true, Freud's two reasons would no longer be valid, except as an expression of his own personality traits. Why, then, do I still consider the couch to be a useful tool?

Although I usually introduce the couch as an option for the patient, and not as a rule, I frequently suggest that patients should lie on the couch, if they have not done so by themselves. This I do because I think that there are some periods in the analysis in which the patient is truly aided by lying down and cutting out the visual interaction with the analyst. This is particularly so during a period of regression, since, if the patient is to surrender herself to the experience, she might not be able to keep erect, or the effort of so doing might act as a deterrent to further engagement in the process. But I also sometimes ask a patient who has been lying on the couch to sit down and enter into a face-to-face contact with me, if I feel that he has been using the couch as a resistance against emotional contact, or as an autistic retreat.

(ii) Constants derived from the analyst as a real person: as I have already discussed in previous sections and chapters, the analyst is very much a real presence for the patient, and her personal characteristics have a permanent impact of the development of the process. They include: (a) her personality and history, (b) her internal and external attitudes, demeanour, and appearance (c) her ideology and ethics, and (d) the social and scientific groups and institutions she belongs to. All these factors remain in the background, until some disturbance of the analytic relationship or transference development compels them to come to the fore and become a subject matter for analysis. Of course, several of these personal factors might change over the years, and this also requires further analytic enquiry, whenever there is some indication that the patient has noticed or reacted towards them. It is also frequently necessary that the analyst should actively explore what the patient has actually perceived, imagined, interpreted, or thought about him. (See Chapter Eight for a further discussion of the matter.)

(iii) *Theoretical constants*: these are a part of the constants derived from the person of the analyst, since they are an expression of his conception of the world, values, beliefs, personal experiences, studies, and the groups and institutions to which he belongs. They include the analyst's theories about: (a) the personality (theory of psychoanalysis); (b) the analytic technique; (c) the setting; (d) the group and society. This even has a bearing on the very diagnosis of the patient, whose psychopathology, as observed and conceived by the analyst, is really an artificial dissection of a much wider and more complex network (Baranger, W., 1992; Hernández de Tubert, 2005), which includes both parties' family, personal, professional, and social relations, the institutions in which they participate, and the wider social context, as well as the theories and prejudices held by all of them about mental health, illness, and healing.

Such participation of the analyst's theories in the analytic process should also be analysed whenever its impact on the analytic relationship makes it impossible for both parties to understand what is actually happening between them, with an explicit reference to the analyst's assumptions. Besides, these theories might also change over time, sometimes even dramatically. For instance, Kohut (1979) describes, in his paper on "The two analyses of Mr. Z", how a patient who had finished his first analysis with him found out, when he came back for further treatment, that he was now a radically different analyst, as a result of being in the process of developing his new ideas on the analysis of the self.

In other cases, the change in the analyst's theories is the result of his being under the influence of some other author, teacher, or supervisor. For example, José Remus Araico, a senior Mexican psychoanalyst who trained in Buenos Aires during the 1950s, used to speak of one episode of his training analysis with Heinrich Racker. He humorously recounted that the analysis was proceeding quite satisfactorily along the Freudian path, until his analyst returned from London, after supervising with Melanie Klein, and he found him to be "a completely different analyst".

Such incidents in the evolution of an analytic treatment have not frequently been the subject of theoretical or clinical discussions, but they ceertainly demand to be taken into account by the analytic enquiry.

(iv) *Institutional and social constants*: these were not included in Zac's analysis of the setting, but they are very important, and also usually taken for granted, since they are assumed to be constant and shared by both parties. This assumption is not necessarily true. In the first place, the patient and the analyst might come from, and live in, two quite different social environments, and this might result in many a misunderstanding between them. This is not very frequent, since generally they both belong to the same social class and have been reared in similar environments, and may, therefore, safely ignore the social dimension. However, whenever an analyst takes a patient who comes from another country or social class, or belongs to a minority group or religion, the social and institutional factors come to the fore. More or less the same happens when there is a significant divergence between them, in terms of their respective conceptions of the world; this is quite obvious when there are differences in their political, ideological, religious, or moral values.

Freud (1919a) considered that these subjects ought to be left aside, in order to avoid turning the analysis into indoctrination, as we have seen in Chapter Three, when discussing abstinence. He rejected any active intervention aimed at educating the patient, and believed that a correct analytical stance would allow him to help people who differed from him in these matters, as we can see in the following quotation:

> I have learnt by experience, too, that such a far-reaching activity towards patients [of educating them into superior values] is not in the least necessary for therapeutic purposes. For I have been able to help people with whom I had nothing in common – neither race, education, social position nor outlook upon life in general – without affecting their individuality. (pp. 164–165)

The underlying assumption was that psychopathological processes were related to the universal human conflicts—that is, to what all human beings have in common, and not to what differentiates them. This does not mean that Freud did not take into account the impact of social factors on individual dynamics. On the contrary, he used them as valuable elements for interpretation, as can be readily seen in his analyses of his own dreams in *The Interpretation of Dreams* (1900a). He took into account, therefore, the social and cultural origins of his patients, and analysed them accordingly. What he did not do was to enquire into the impact that his own upbringing had on the patients, and neither did he analyse what he and the patients had in common, which, therefore, remained unnoticed.

Such invisible aspects of the social and institutional context are also suddenly revealed when there is a sudden change in such context, as in the case of wars, political and economic crises, elections, or the death of public figures. Such commotions unveil what had been concealed behind the regularities of everyday life and the analytic routine. This is a case of what Bleger (1967a) described as a mobilisation of the "psychotic part of the personality" that had been previously contained by the setting. However, far from being a shock that affects only the patient, these situations deeply disturb both parties of the analytic relationship, since such changes are a part of the wider world that they share. We shall discuss this further when addressing the phenomenon of the "overlapping worlds" (Puget & Wender, 1982).

(v) Constants related to the "spirit of the analysis": there is a tacit norm in psychoanalysis, apart from the explicit agreed-on rules, that must be preserved in order that the treatment may proceed. This is what I call the "spirit of the analysis". It is impossible to enumerate in the contract all the conceivable transgressions of this norm, since patients are extremely ingenious in creating new and unexpected ways of violating it, in the service of resistance. For instance, there is no provision in the contract, as we have already discussed, forbidding the patient to bring in a portable media player and spend the session listening to his favourite music, as some adolescents try to do, but this is clearly at odds with the very aim of the analysis, so the analyst will probably have to interpret this as an attack on the treatment, and sometimes even forbid it, if interpretation has not been enough to solve this situation, unless there is some relational reason in favour of accepting this behaviour for the time being. Of course, if a patient keeps inventing new ways of distorting the analytic situation, and forcing the analyst to become a repressive authority or a passive ineffectual one, this is a severe disturbance of the analytic relationship that will have to be dealt with, as we shall see in Chapter Ten, on "The evolution of the analytic process".

Transgressions to the provisions of the contract or to this tacit norm might be due to an unconscious intention to violate, weaken, distort, or sterilise the analysis, or to a misunderstanding by the patient of their true meaning. For instance, a young university student had been proceeding uneventfully with his analysis. At the end of each month, he duly paid for all the sessions, even if he had not attended, but once he paid one session less. I pointed this out to him, and he told me that it was because he had missed a session when he had an exam. I pointed out that, in the past, he had paid for the unattended session, even if he had informed me in advance that he was not going to come. "Yes", he said, "but that was because I had personal things to do, and on this occasion it was not my fault." Finally, I discovered that for him the rule of having to pay for the unattended sessions was a punishment for his absence, and that he felt that it would be unfair for him to be punished for something that was not for him to decide—the time of his exam. I had to explain to him that the rule was not intended to punish him for not coming, but to respond to an economic necessity, derived from the standard organisation of the professional practice of psychotherapy. I then suggested that we try to understand his outlook on life in terms of obligations and punishments. Finally, at the end of the session, we agreed that, if he were to tell me in advance about any such absence, we would strive to find a way to replace the session.

The other alternative—a destructive attack on the setting and the very existence of analysis—we shall discuss in Chapter Ten when dealing with the evolution of the process and the obstacles to it.

The dynamic evolution of the setting

As we have already seen, the setting should be actively constructed by the analyst, through an open dialogue with the patient, and it must be kept constant, even when the former fully knows, and the latter will soon discover, that it is a fragile structure, which is constantly being fractured by the impact of external and internal reality and the evolution of the analytic process. So, the analyst and the patient must work arduously in order to restore it, over and over again. Such a job is truly shared, but the analyst's responsibility in this is always greater than the patient's.

Meltzer (1967) emphasises the importance of the creation of the setting at the beginning of the treatment for the maintenance of the analytic process as a modulator of the patient's anxieties. He also feels that the analyst must constantly rediscover the setting with every patient, until it is clearly defined in such a way that these anxieties are contained in it.

Therefore, the setting is not something that can be created once at the beginning of the treatment, and then kept static. On the contrary, it is a living structure, which not only contains the process, but evolves with it and periodically becomes a subject for the analytic enquiry, and needs to be recreated by the conjoint efforts of analyst and patient.

There are also changes in the setting that have to do with the evolution of the institutional, social, cultural, and political context that acts as a frame for the whole psychoanalytic treatment. For instance, the profound changes that have taken place in our society—changes that include values, mores, economical and living conditions, as well as the prevailing forms of psychopathology—have determined that the analytic community must revise the minimum requirements for the conduction of an analysis. Even though most analysts within the Freudian tradition would agree that the technical model of regular and frequent sessions, introduced by Freud, is still the ideal form of conducting a psychoanalytic treatment, they also acknowledge that it has become increasingly difficult, and even impossible, to follow it in many cases. This has led to the introduction of various new clinical arrangements, in order to respond to the demands of our present situation, such as extended sessions, condensed analysis, shuttle analysis, discontinuous analysis, analysis on demand, and distant analysis, both by telephone and through the Internet (Hernández-Tubert, 2008a). Whether such major modifications should still be considered "psychoanalysis" or not is a moot question. Other types of psychoanalytic approach to therapy, such as group psychotherapy, brief therapy, and family and marriage therapy, are usually considered to be different from psychoanalysis, although few doubt their analytic inspiration or their clinical value. There has been, however, a growing acceptance and mutual tolerance of the various psychoanalytic traditions on the matter of frequency. While most analytic groups consider a four-times-a-week frequency to be standard, British analysts still adhere to the five-session week, while the French have settled for a frequency of three sessions a week. These different standards are surely in part a matter of tradition, but they might also be related to the diverse theoretical conceptions of the analytic process, as we shall see in the following chapters.

CHAPTER FIVE

The substratum of analysis

The analytic relationship and experience

The analytic situation may be viewed in terms of several components: (a) the *context of analysis*, provided by the setting and the
contract; (b) the *analytic process*, represented both by the verbal,
non-verbal, and emotional interchanges that take place between both
parties; (c) the *substratum of analysis*, on which the process is founded.
The latter is the analytic relationship.

Everything that happens in an analysis is rooted on the analytic
relationship and without it there is no analysis. Interpretation, for
instance, is not only information that the patient receives about
herself—or, rather, about what the analyst thinks about her—but also,
and foremost, a particular form of relationship with another human
being.

Freud (1913c) clearly realised the importance of this relational
basis for interpretation and insight. In his paper "On beginning the
treatment", he posed the question about which is the right moment to
begin the analyst's communications to the patient, and his answer was
definite:

Not until an effective transference has been established in the patient, a proper *rapport* with him. *It remains the first aim of the treatment to attach him to it and to the person of the doctor* [my italics]. To ensure this, nothing need be done but to give him time. If one exhibits a serious interest in him, carefully clears away the resistances that crop up at the beginning and avoids making certain mistakes, he will of himself form such an attachment and link the doctor up with one of the imagos of the people by whom he was accustomed to be treated with affection. It is certainly possible to forfeit this first success if from the start one takes up any standpoint other than one of sympathetic understanding [*Einfühlung*, i.e., empathy], such as a moralizing one, or if one behaves like a representative or advocate of some contending party – of the other member of a married couple, for instance. (pp. 139–140)

Interestingly enough, in the first edition of this paper, the latter part of this quotation read: ". . . if one behaves like a representative or advocate of some contending party *with whom the patient is engaged in a conflict – of his parents*, for instance, *or the other member of a married couple*" (p. 140, n1, my italics). Apparently, this original version gave too much credit to present external conflicts for Freud's taste, so he suppressed it. It also underscored the existence of an actual—that is, not just internal—conflict with the parents, a subject that had become anathema for the psychoanalytic movement. This deletion is similar to his omission of only one line from his published report of his first interview with Dr Lorenz (the "Rat Man", Freud, 1909d), which is readily found in his original notes on the case (1955a): after Freud had explained to him the nature and conditions of a psychoanalytic treatment, the patient said that he had to consult with his mother about this, and only the next day, when he came back, did he accept. This is hardly surprising, if we consider that his mother had full control over his monies, but it emphasised his unusual dependence on her (as he was almost thirty), an aspect that Freud totally omitted in his case history; so, this observation had to be deleted (Zetzel, 1966).

Going back to the analytic relationship as the substratum of the analytic process, it would seem that Freud's recommendation to wait until "an effective transference has been established" before starting to interpret was intended to avoid raising the patient's resistances to such a level that he might abandon the treatment. In other words, the patient had to be "hooked" by his emotional bond with the analyst, before being able to tolerate listening to some unsavoury truths. This is the idea that he puts forward in "On beginning the treatment" (Freud, 1913c), but in his *Introductory Lectures on Psycho-Analysis* (Freud, 1916–1917), he suggests a different explanation:

> If the patient is to fight his way through the normal conflict with the resistances which we have uncovered for him in the analysis, he is in need of a powerful stimulus which will influence the decision in the sense which we desire, leading to recovery . . . [W]hat turns the scale in his struggle is not his intellectual insight – which is neither strong enough nor free enough for such an achievement – but simply and solely his relation to the doctor. In so far as his transference bears a "plus" sign, it clothes the doctor with authority and is transformed into belief in his communications and explanations. In the absence of such a transference, or if it is a negative one, the patient would never even give a hearing to the doctor and his arguments. In this his belief is repeating the story of its own development; it is a derivative of love and, to start with, needed no arguments. Only later did he allow them enough room to submit them to examination, *provided they were brought forward by someone he loved. Without such supports arguments carried no weight, and in most people's lives they never do.* Thus in general a man is only accessible from the intellectual side too, in so far as he is capable of a libidinal cathexis of objects. (pp. 445–446, my italics)

Now, this raises the phantom of an objection that Freud always feared: that the results of his analyses were nothing more than a reflection of his own bias, imposed on the patients by suggestion. This he rejects, by showing that it is by no means easy to induce the patient to accept such prejudiced interpretations when they do not fit with his personal experience. It is, however, quite possible for the patient to turn into a staunch supporter of the analyst's particular theory, but this collapses, sooner or later, if the transference is duly analysed. It is the fact that analysts regularly strive to denounce and dismount the transference that deprives suggestion of its power.

This is, of course, related to the issue of neutrality, already discussed in Chapter Three. Menninger (1958) gave a most interesting example of the problem of the analyst's influence on the patient's persuasions:

It is odd that so excellent a clinician as Otto Fenichel could write: "If we do not break off the analysis too soon and if we consistently show the patient his intrapsychic reality, he will recognize that clinging to inappropriate ideals and moralities [i.e., those disavowed by the analyst [Menninger's addition]] has a resistance function. . . . It has been said that religious people in analysis remain uninfluenced in their religious philosophies since analysis itself is supposed to be philosophically neutral. . . . Repeatedly, I have seen that with analysis of the sexual anxieties and with the maturing of the personality, the attachment to religion has ended". *Of course*, Fenichel saw it (as a temporary phenomenon, at least). His personal preoccupation with and devotion to psychoanalysis were well known. And his patients strove to please. I have seen the *reverse* of Fenichel's observation, for *my* patients strive to please, too. In the long-run the ex-patient finds his own attachments and commitments. (p. 94n)

It must be remembered that Fenichel was an atheist—as was Freud—while Menninger was a devout Christian. His observation, therefore, meant that, when the patient has a positive transference with his analyst, he guesses or infers the latter's values and beliefs, and tries to please him by offering a reasonable imitation of them. Menninger thought that this was an inevitable but transitory phenomenon, without any relevance for the patient's future. He does not seem to have considered, however, the option of investigating what the patient rightly perceived and thought about the analyst's beliefs, thus analysing their mutual influence. Such an approach—which could only be clearly formulated after the development of relational psychoanalysis, for instance, in Hoffman's (1983) now classical paper on "The patient as interpreter of the analyst's experience"—may comply with Freud's injunction that the positive transference should also be analysed, in order to dispel these suggestive phenomena.

Freud's observation that, for most people, logical arguments only carry weight when they come from someone they love implies that the patient's ego might well function as an executive officer who is only willing to interview candidates for a post who come with recommendations from his friends, but who anyway scrutinises them thoroughly, and only accepts one who fits the requirements of the job. In this version, the use of the positive emotional bond is only tactical, in so far as it gives the patient an opportunity to consider the analyst's arguments. But there is an even more radical way to understand it, if we think that psychoanalysis has shown that cognitive mental processes, such as reasoning and judgement, cannot be isolated from their emotional foundation. If this were true, it would imply a revolutionary subversion of that well-established Western epistemology that began with the Classical Greeks (Popper, 1958).

Ever since the pre-Socratics, classical Greek philosophers endorsed a pluralistic theory of knowledge that fostered the discussion among the various schools of thought, and even within a same school. This assumption certainly still stands as a landmark in the development of Western thought. They also underscored that such discussion should be an exclusively *rational* interchange of ideas; this implied leaving aside all personal and emotional considerations. But now Freud was suggesting that, in the field of psychoanalysis, recognition of truth did not depend only on the rational validity of an argument, but also on the emotional relationship between whoever poses it and he who is on the receiving end of such communication. This is a veritable epistemological scandal, but perhaps psychoanalysis is bound to raise such commotions in everything it touches.

As we have already seen in previous chapters, Ferenczi and Rank (1924) presented, in their book *The Development of Psychoanalysis*, a revolutionary point of view, which placed emotional experience at the very centre of the psychoanalytic enquiry. For them, the analytic experience is not only a welcome confirmation of our theories, but its very source, and the only thing that can make any sense out of our theoretical constructs. Consequently, "just psycho-analysis could for the first time clearly show that there are . . . two kinds of knowledge, one intellectual, the other based on a deeper 'conviction'" (p. 45). These considerations clearly strive to keep a balance between subjective experience and objective analysis, between feeling and talking, between psychology and natural science.

This should be enough to dispel the usual criticism of Ferenczi's position as being "merely subjective". Fenichel (1941), for instance, suggested that, in the narrow passage between the Scylla of too much talking and intellectualisation and the Charybdis of too much feeling and acting out, Ferenczi and Rank's book represented a reaction against the former, but they "went too far to the other extreme" and "in their emphasis of experiencing they became admirers of abreaction, of acting out, and thus working through was the loser" (p. 100).

This was certainly not the case, as we shall see later when we discuss therapeutic regression and working though.

More recently, Maroda (2002) deals with this problem in the light of recent experimental research on emotion and cognition. Here, she takes exception to the classical analyst's efforts to suppress or disguise his or her emotional reactions. She deems such behaviour—which follows Freud's (1913c) rationale for the use of the couch ("I do not wish my expressions of face to give the patient material for interpretations or to influence him in what he tells me", p. 134)—to be clearly anti-therapeutic, since analysts "often have strong feelings in response to their patients". She believes that "these moments of strong feeling offer great opportunities for therapeutic change" (p. 115).

Her answer to the question of "how to accomplish this in the patient's best interest" is to allow the analyst's non-verbal expression of his or her emotional reactions, and leave it to the patient to decide whether or not to comment about his perception of the analyst's feelings. From a rather different quarter, that of the Independent Tradition of British Psychoanalysis, Heimann (1978) emphasised the need for the analyst to be "natural" with her patients—that is, to openly express a true emotional response to them. This necessity she feels to be "genetically founded" on the fact that "the experience of psychoanalysis represents a developmental process, [which] links the natural element with the creative and lends analysis its artistic, creative character" (p. 322). None the less, she emphatically rejects any suggestion that the analyst should communicate "his feelings to the patient and [give] him an insight into the analyst's private life, because this burdens the patient and distracts him from his own problems" (p. 319). What Heimann is pointing out is the need for the analyst not to deny or hide her emotions, but not to discuss them with the patient. Other authors, such as Little (1981) disagree with her on this point.

However, regardless of the technical stance one might take regarding these matters, it seems to be clearly established that the analytic experience and knowledge rest on a peculiar combination of cognition and feeling, whose epistemological consequences we shall further discuss when dealing with interpretation.

So, from my own point of view, the analytic relation is the *substratum* of the analytic experience, the analytic process, and the discoveries of an analysis. This is a complex metaphor, based on the various meanings of the term, which are the following: (1) something that is laid or spread under or that underlies and supports or forms a base for something else; (2) an underlying structure, layer, or part that serves as a basis or foundation; (3) in agriculture, a layer of rock or earth beneath the surface soil, specifically the subsoil; (4) in biology, the base or material on which an organism lives; (5) in philosophy, substance, considered as that which supports accidents or attributes; (6) in photography, a layer of material placed directly on a film or plate as a foundation for the sensitive emulsion (Merriam-Webster, 2002, see entries "Substratum" and "Substrate").

The analytic relation underlies the analytic process (1), and serves as its basis or foundation (2); it nurtures the process (4), and offers a sound support for its creative and sensitive aspects (3, 6), that is, the analytic experience; finally, it is the very stuff of analysis, the substantial support of its more evanescent manifestations (5). If we accept this perspective, once the initial context is established, everything that happens in an analysis will hinge on the evolution of the analytic relationship, which should, therefore, be the object of our closest attention.

Enquiring into the analytic relationship

When Freud began the analytic enquiry, he took the doctor–patient relationship for granted. When a patient asked him for his professional services, he took this at face value, as a rational demand from an adult to another adult, and therefore answered in those very same terms. Such view held fast for some time, during the first stages of a treatment, but this initial peace was soon ruptured by the emergence of passionate outbursts from the patient, which had the analyst as its object. Such violent feelings took either the form of a hostile expression of fear, anger, and mistrust, which Freud found to be more frequent in male patients, or of a passionate declaration of love, which might fall into erotomania—this being the case in the analysis of women, in Freud's (male) experience (Freud, 1915a).

When such situations developed, the analytic process seemed to stagnate, since the patients no longer cared for continuing the joint effort with their analyst, but, rather, insisted in their amorous demands, in the case of the "positive" (erotic) transference, or in their persistent quarrelling with him in the case of the "negative" (hostile) transference. Freud, therefore, interpreted this as a resistance; it was obvious to him that everything that hindered the progress of analysis was a resistance (Freud, 1900a, p. 517), so that the patient ought to be creating a "false connection" (Freud, 1895d, p. 302) with the person of the analyst in order to avoid remembering the repressed painful memories. Therefore, "the patient repeats instead of remembering, and repeats under the conditions of resistance" (Freud, 1914g, p. 151). He or she is *acting out* the repressed contents, instead of taking cognisance of them.

This phenomenon was called the "transference", since Freud assumed that it was the result of transferring affects and unconscious wishes from their original objects in the past to the analyst as a present object. The term had already been used by him in *The Interpretation of Dreams* (Freud, 1900a); there, it referred to the expression of an unconscious wish, by means of transferring its intensity to a preconscious thought, and getting itself covered by it.

The underlying metaphor is that of a transference of funds from one account to another. In the case of the analytic relationship, he believed that a repressed idea—a painful memory—could only become conscious by being syncretised with a preconscious representation, in this case, the image of the analyst. Of course, all these considerations were framed in the language of the topographical model of the mind, which is part of a one-person psychology, but we shall see later how they may be reformulated in terms of a two-person psychology.

The emphasis on the repetitious nature of the transference presented it as a direct expression of the past, with no real relation to the present situation. It was, therefore, considered to be a confusion of time, space, and person: the patient mistook the here-and-now situation with the analyst for a there-and-then situation with someone else—the parents or any other significant childhood figures.

Such emphasis on the past stemmed not only from Freud's attempt to develop a causal theory and therapy of neurosis, which would require identifying the past origins of present events, but might also have had an emotional meaning. Anyone who has ever treated a patient with psychoanalysis is fully aware of the awesome impact of the passions unleashed in the transference, and this can only be tolerated and accepted when one has already worked through these issues in his own analysis. But Freud never had the benefit of a psychoanalytic treatment; his self-analysis was mainly a cognitive enterprise, and lacked the experience of transference. And even then, he had to look for a sympathetic listener in Wilhem Fliess, but this listener was not capable of interpreting Freud's passion towards him, so that this experience of transference was missed as an opportunity for knowledge and development, and finally turned into bitterness and resentment. Therefore, Freud was quite unprepared to deal with his patient's transferences. In his "Observations on transference love" (Freud, 1915a), we find him struggling in an attempt to demonstrate that this "transference love" was merely a pathological phenomenon, an expression of the patient's neurosis, which should be approached with the same objectivity as any other symptom. Of course, he failed in this endeavour, since "being in love in ordinary life, outside analysis, is also more similar to abnormal than to normal mental phenomena", so that he had to conclude, uneasily, that "we have no right to dispute that the state of being in love which makes its appearance in the course of analytic treatment has the character of a 'genuine' love" (p. 168).

The anxiety generated in him by his patient's transferences must have been even more intense when he found himself and his family woven into the fabric of his patients' erotic and sadistic fantasies. Dr Lorenz (the Rat Man (Freud, 1909d)), for example, had perverse conscious fantasies and dreams featuring Freud's daughter; in the session of 26 November 1907, for instance, he told of a dream in which he lay on his back on her, and penetrated her with the faeces that came out from his anus (Freud, 1955a). One can only wonder about this father's feelings at listening to such expressions; he must have felt enraged, insulted, and fearful for his daughter, just as he must have been threatened by his female patients' passionate demands for romantic and sexual love, so that he probably defended by reminding himself, over and over again, that "this has nothing to do with me or my family, it is only a remnant from the past".

Such efforts to find protection from the full impact of unconscious passions, which every analyst must have relied upon sometimes, when things became unbearable in an analysis, had the benefit of helping him to hold fast and continue with the treatments, but it also had the disadvantage of eschewing cognisance of those present factors, stemming from the actual patient–analyst interaction, that acted as stimulus to such transference developments.

This, of course, was in line with his programmatic rejection of all present causes in the genesis of neurotic symptoms. One most significant omission in Freud's (1918b) case history of the Wolf Man, pointed out by Calvo (2008), is that the patient inflicted on him vicious anti-Semitic attacks, combined with sadistic homosexual fantasies in the transference, as Freud told Ferenczi in a letter dated 13 February 1910 (Falzeder & Brabant, 2000, pp. 136–139). Such apparently sexual fantasies were really an acting-out of traditional vernacular anti-Semitic insults. But Freud completely omitted any reference in his case history to the fact that his patient was anti-Semitic and that he himself was a Jew, which nowadays we would consider essential for the understanding of the transference–countertransference.

Ferenczi (1933), in contrast, became painfully aware that his patients' accusations that he had somehow mistreated or abused them by being insensitive, cold, or even hard and cruel towards them, selfish, heartless, or conceited, had a basis in their observation and sufferance of some less than amiable aspects of his personality and behaviour, which he had not been aware of. He also identified his own resistance to listening to them and his tendency to explain their reproaches away by attributing them to their neuroses. Therefore, he encouraged them to openly express any criticism of him, and even tried to interpret any veiled expressions of such criticism, since patients frequently are afraid of expressing, or even consciously acknowledging, the existence of such feelings, perceptions, and thoughts. In this, he paved the way for an entirely new way of approaching the practice of psychoanalysis. In his own words: "That means that we must discern, not only the painful events of their past from their associations, but also— and much more often than hitherto supposed—their repressed or suppressed criticism of us" (Ferenczi, 1933, p. 226).

Such recognition of the objective basis of the patients' complaints, which ran parallel to his revaluation of Freud's original traumatic theory of neuroses, was violently rejected by the latter, as well as by the whole analytic group (Masson, 1984; Tubert-Oklander, 1999). His suggestion that the analyst should, after engaging in an analytic self-criticism, recognise and discuss with the patient such unsavoury reactions on his part was even more shocking to the analytic community. Freud (1937d) went as far as discussing, in "Constructions in analysis", written six years after Ferenczi's untimely death, what was obviously an answer to his disciple and friend when he suggested that, if a construction of the patient's past proved false after having been communicated to him, the analyst should find a suitable moment to recognise his previous failure "without diminishing his authority" when he had a new construction to offer in its stead.

The divergence is clear now: Freud was worried about protecting his authority over the patient; Ferenczi (1933), on the other hand, was concerned about gaining his or her confidence. In this, he had to face and disengage from the analytic tradition of what he called "professional hypocrisy"—that is, the maintenance of the illusion that the analyst is always calm, in full control of himself, well-disposed, and only interested in the patient's welfare. Surprisingly enough, when this was actively dispelled, the result was a strengthening of the analytic relationship and a deepening of the analysis:

> A great part of the repressed criticism felt by our patients is directed towards what might be called *professional hypocrisy* [my italics]. We greet the patient with politeness when he enters our room, ask him to start with his associations and promise him faithfully that we will listen attentively to him, give our undivided interest to his well-being and to the work needed for it. In reality, however, it may happen that we can only with difficulty tolerate certain external or internal features of the patient, or perhaps we feel unpleasantly disturbed in some professional or personal affair by the analytic session. Here, too, *I cannot see any other way out than to make the source of the disturbance in us fully conscious and to discuss it with the patient, admitting it perhaps not only as a possibility, but as a fact.* [my italics]
>
> It is remarkable that such renunciation of the 'professional hypocrisy'—a hypocrisy hitherto regarded as unavoidable—instead of hurting the patient, led to a marked easing off in his condition. The traumatic–hysterical attack, even if it recurred, became considerably milder, tragic events of the past could be reproduced *in thoughts* without creating again a loss of mental balance; in fact the level of the patient's personality seemed to have been considerably raised. (Ferenczi, 1933, p. 226)

Here, for the first time, Ferenczi took the phenomenon of the analyst's transference towards the patient, called *countertransference*— first mentioned by Freud in "The future prospects of psycho-analytic therapy" (1910d) as an obstacle induced in the analyst by the influence of the patient on his or her own unconscious, and which had to be duly recognised and overcome—as an essential part of the analytic enquiry. This was many years before authors such as Winnicott (1949a), Heimann (1950), Little (1951), and Racker (1953) rediscovered the countertransference as a source of most valuable information for analytic understanding. Symptomatically, none of them quoted Ferenczi in their papers, with the exception of Heimann, who explicitly declared her disagreement with him.

It is interesting to note that Racker's contribution was read to the Argentine Psychoanalytic Association in 1948—that is, one year after Winnicott's, which was presented to the British Society in 1947 and published in 1949—but it was much criticised by his colleagues, who argued that "if Racker has countertransferences, he should go back to analysis, and not theorise about it", and he was not allowed to publish it in an international journal until five years later, since they felt that "it was dangerous to let the public know that analysts had countertransferences". This was pretty much the same argument that led Freud and Jones, in an exchange of letters dated 29 May 1933 and 3 June 1933, respectively (Paskauskas, 1993, pp. 721, 722–723), to consider that the publication in English of Ferenczi's last paper could only be deleterious to the reputation of both psychoanalysis and its author.

It seems that the impact of the conflict between Freud and Ferenczi became a trauma for the psychoanalytic community, so that "the first reaction of the analytic movement to it was denial and silence" (Balint, 1968, p. 149). The trauma and the defences against it were then transgenerationally transmitted to each new generation of analysts. Balint wrote, in 1968, of the resistances that he found whenever he tried to salvage Ferenczi's contributions to psychoanalysis, asking for "a critical reappraisal—not an uncritical acceptance—of what was valuable in the ideas developed in Budapest under Ferenczi's leadership . . . [t]here was no response" (p. 133). He believed, however, that things might have changed at the time, so he was willing to try again.

Balint was wrong. It took some fifteen years more—fifty after Ferenczi's death—for a part of the psychoanalytic community to reopen that line of analytic enquiry that had been summarily closed after his demise, as we shall see in the following chapters. This type of collective censorship in the references to dissident individual authors or groups is by no means unusual in our profession, as Aron (1996) has pointed out in the case of the blatant omission of the work of interpersonal analysts, in the work of those Freudians who have recently leaned towards an intersubjective or relational critique of the classical theory of psychoanalytic technique. (I would also add that of the group-analytic tradition by the sage group of thinkers.) But there is still one more general aspect of the analytic relationship that should be dealt with now, and that is the various *dimensions* of such relationship.

The dimensions of the bond

At first, there was no attention paid, in the analytic literature, to the more conscious and rational aspects of the analytic relationship, since they appeared to be absolutely commonplace and uninteresting. Transference was the real riddle to be solved, as it was a definite outgrowth of the unconscious, in its awesome and tragic repetition; the other aspects had really nothing to teach us, being just a plain, ordinary, common-or-garden-variety doctor–patient relationship.

It soon became apparent, however, that such everyday doctor–patient interactions in clinical medicine included some very intense transference phenomena, which usually went unnoticed by the physician, and which baffled and horrified him when he was no longer able to disregard, on account of their intensity. This, according to Jones (1953) is what happened to Josef Breuer, in his relationship to his famous patient, Anna O (pp. 246–247).

Doctors were clearly (and still are) at a loss when dealing with the emergence of human passions in their consulting rooms. Psychoanalysts, on the other hand, soon learnt to expect, recognise, and analyse such disruptions of the initially placid analytic dialogue. But then they discovered that some severely disturbed patients were not able, from the very beginning of the treatment, to establish a sufficiently reasonable relationship that would act as a base for the development of the analytic process. Such cases demanded a reconsideration of the rational and conscious aspects of the relationship.

As early as 1934, Sterba had suggested that, in order that the analytic treatment might function, a part of the personality of the patient should identify with the analyst and view his or her own behaviour and experiences from the latter's perspective. Such objective understanding by the patient of his own plight and motivations—"objective" in as much as it represents the point of view of the object—would be an essential part of psychoanalytic insight. These ideas were further developed by Bibring (1937), who speaks of an "observing and criticizing ego" that attains a "progressive objectivation" (p. 180).

In 1955, Zetzel (1956), a Boston analyst who had trained in and practised psychiatry and psychoanalysis in the UK between 1938 and 1949, developed an ego-psychological critique of Klein's technique of transference analysis, in which the reproduction of early object relations in the patient's relation to the analyst is interpreted from the very first session. She then stated that

> A differentiation is made between transference as therapeutic alliance and the transference neurosis, which, on the whole, is considered a manifestation of resistance. Effective analysis depends on a sound therapeutic alliance, a prerequisite for which is the existence, before analysis, of a degree of mature ego functions, the absence of which in certain severely disturbed patients and in young children may preclude traditional psychoanalytic procedure. (p. 370)

The idea that these analysts put forward is that the constitution of the analytic relationship requires a differentiation and opposition between two discrete aspects of this relation: the *transference* and the *therapeutic alliance*. The former is defined as a clearly pathological phenomenon, a manifestation of the patient's neurosis; it is a wholesale repetition of the past, with no consideration for actual reality, which is either ignored or distorted. The transference is, therefore, always inappropriate to what is actually happening in the analysis (Greenson, 1967; Greenson & Wexler, 1969).

The therapeutic alliance, on the other hand, is reality orientated, and an expression of the healthy and mature part of the patient's personality. This includes both his capacity to keep in mind the reason for being in analysis and the formal definition of this treatment, as well as his adequate perception of the real characteristics of the analyst's personality and behaviour, and of the actual interchanges that take place between the two parties.

Stone (1954) had already used—in his paper "The widening scope of indications for psychoanalysis", the term "real personal relationship" to refer to this aspect of the analytic bond, to be contrasted with "true transference reactions". Anna Freud (1954), in her own contribution to the same panel, added,

We see the patient enter into analysis with a reality attitude to the analyst; then the transference gains [full] momentum until it reaches its peak in the full-blown transference neurosis which has to be worked off analytically until the figure of the analyst emerges again, reduced to its true status. But—and this seems important to me—so far as the patient has a healthy part of his personality, his real relationship to the analyst is never wholly submerged. With due respect for the necessary strictest handling and interpretation of the transference, I feel still that we should leave room somewhere for the realization that *analyst and patient are also two real people, of equally adult status, in a real personal relationship to each other. I wonder whether our-at times complete-neglect of this side of the matter is not responsible for some of the hostile reactions which we get from our patients and which we are apt to ascribe to "true transference" only.* But these are technically subversive thoughts and ought to be "handled with care". (pp. 618–619, my italics)

This last comment seems to be a reaction against the too frequent practice of interpreting every expression of the patient's relation with the analyst as if it were nothing but a pathological symptom, thus ignoring the possibility that the patient might be accurately perceiving his analyst, or rightly evaluating some aspect of their mutual relationship. Interestingly enough, Anna Freud reaches the same conclusion as Ferenczi, more than two decades before, but she not only fails to quote him, but also appears reluctant to assume the full consequences of this observation, clearly out of fear of the possible reactions of the analytic community.

Later, Greenson (1967) made a further distinction within the therapeutic alliance. He suggested that we distinguish between two parts of it: the *working alliance* and the *"real" relationship*. The former is considered to be transference-free, while the latter is described as a non-transference relation. The working alliance represents the contribution of the patient's intelligence and conscious co-operation to the constitution of the analytic situation. It includes her ability to understand a formal working proposal and to play the conventional patient role that it requires from her, in spite of the vagaries of emotional reactions. This clearly implies at least a theoretical assumption which is characteristic of ego psychology: the existence of a *conflict-free ego sphere*, which allows the development of rational thought, understanding, and behaviour, in spite of the existence of conscious and unconscious conflicts.

When this particular mental position is achieved, the patient might be able to formulate such a complex utterance as: "I am feeling utterly rejected and despised by you. I know, of course, that you have done nothing that supports this perception of mine; quite on the contrary, you have been kind, patient, and understanding, but the fact is that I still feel this way, and this hurts and angers me". Whenever a patient thus clearly discerns his realistic perceptions from passionate transference reactions, things become quite easy for the analyst, who only has to interpret what she believes to be the unconscious source of these emotions. But patients only rarely humour us to such extent; on the contrary, they are usually passionately certain that their present perception of the analyst is both realistic and wholly justified. This requires that the analyst do *something* in order to help the patient attain, or recover, an operative split between his conscious rational understanding of, and identification with, what the analyst is trying to do, and his intense emotional experiences, which have been necessarily aroused by the treatment. Whether this "something" should be restricted to interpretation only, or should be expanded to include other kinds of interaction, is, of course, a moot point, and it is one of the landmarks that distinguish the various technical schools in psychoanalysis.

The "real" relationship refers to the perceptual and emotional interchanges that take place between analyst and patient, which show no sign of being either repetitive and non-realistic, or rational and conventional working agreements. Thus, a patient might be justifiably angry if the analyst has actually done something that hurt him, as Ferenczi (1933) clearly showed in his last paper and Anna Freud suggested in 1954. He might also be understandably grateful for the help that he has received from the analyst. As Freud (1937c) pointed out, in "Analysis terminable and interminable", "not every good relation between an analyst and his subject during and after analysis was to be regarded as a transference; there were also friendly relations which were based on reality and which proved to be viable" (p. 222).

Just as the working alliance implies the conflict-free ego sphere, the real relationship pre-supposes the establishment of *object* and *self constancy*, which allow a person to preserve an emotional relationship with an object, in spite of its absence or of the conflictual disturbances of their bond. Both features are clearly lacking in very small children and in borderline and psychotic patients, so that, from the point of view of ego psychology, such patients are clearly non-analysable, unless the analyst engages in some sort of preparatory therapy, in order to establish them before starting the analysis (Freud, A., 1927; Zetzel, 1956).

Many analysts who do not share the theoretical assumptions of ego psychology have taken exception to this dissection of the analytic relationship. The Kleinians, for instance, do not recognise a structural, functional organisation of the mental apparatus, but, rather, think in terms of a two-tier disposition of subjective experience: a conscious and pre-conscious experience of one's self, objects, and world, which is rational and realistic, and an unconscious phantasmic experience of the very same elements, which is neither rational nor realistic, but is, rather, framed according to instinctual and affective motions. This perspective has been tersely summarised by Meltzer (1981), as follows:

> Mrs. Klein . . . made a discovery that created a revolutionary addition to the model of the mind, namely that *we do not live in one world, but in two*—that we live in an internal world which is as real a place to live in as the outside world. (p. 178, my italics)

These are clearly experiential "worlds", one of them conscious and the other unconscious.

This is the rationale for the Kleinians' early and constant interpretation of the transference. For them, transference is not defined by being repetitive, but only by being unconscious, and this implies, of course, being ruled by the primary process and not by conscious rational thought—the secondary process. From this perspective, the transference is just the unconscious correlate of the conscious patient–analyst relationship. The differences between the ego-psychological and Kleinian concepts and their handling of the transference have been discussed by Greenson (1974, 1975) and Rosenfeld (1974).

Without engaging in a theoretical discussion about the various models of the mind, it is still worthwhile to point out that the sort of clear separation between cognitive and affective mental processes, although perhaps conceptually useful, does not seem to comply with the reality of concrete psychological functioning. Human beings are not apparatuses, made up of separate parts or components, but, rather, organic wholes, which react as a totality. Every cognitive function or process is, therefore, accompanied by and founded on an emotional and relational substrate. For instance, the accurate perception that the analyst has been truly generous and helpful is based on the experience and feeling of being well-cared for, protected, and ultimately loved by a present and attentive object, but it is also a repetition of previous experiences of love and care; as Freud (1913c) put it, if one treats the patient with kindness and serious interest, he will develop an attachment to the analyst and the analysis.

Another line of questioning of this dissection of the analytic relationship is derived from our current understanding of it in terms of a two-person psychology. Relations always include more than one person, and every party is included in, contributes to, and is determined by such a complex field. Although some descriptions of the components of the analytic relationship seem to imply that they belong only to the patient, this bipersonal perspective has not been overlooked by analytic theoreticians. Greenson (1967), for instance, is clearly aware that the working alliance must be constructed by analyst and patient alike, and he describes the contributions of the patient, the analyst, and the analytic situation—meaning the frame or setting—to its development. The real relation is also, of course, dyadic by definition. In addition, the transference, which had originally been conceived in terms of a one-person psychology, has become a bipersonal phenomenon, ever since the deepening of the analysis of the countertransference led us to acknowledge the essential unity of transference and countertransference (Racker, 1960).

It seems that those psychoanalysts like myself, who have been trained in, and are identified with, the classical Freudian tradition, have been awkwardly attempting to develop an understanding of the inherently interpersonal and relational nature of the psychoanalytic situation and process without forsaking the one-person language and theory that we inherited from Freud. This is, of course, a no-win endeavour, since the need to affirm our heritage unduly encumbers the development of our thinking and clinical practice. On the other hand, interpersonal theoreticians have always emphasised the importance of the unconscious interactions that ensue between patient and analyst, as an essential determinant of the analytic process. The problem is that there has been very little dialogue between these two schools of psychoanalytic thought.

This question is, of course, more political than theoretical. Each school has defined its identity, not only in terms of what it includes and affirms, but also of what it leaves out or utterly rejects. Thus, interpersonal psychoanalysts have tended to emphasise the here-and-now factors and reduce the importance of those childhood experiences that Freudians consider most important. Hence, the interpersonalist version of the subject appears more amenable to being shaped by environmental and contextual influences, both present and past, than that of the orthodox Freudians. On the other hand, the latter systematically reject any suggestion that such influences play a significant part in pathogenesis or in the therapeutic process, underscoring instead the importance of the repetition compulsion and the steady structure of the personality, derived from childhood experiences.

Such social organisation of our profession hinders the efforts of those who infringe the traditional boundaries between the theoretical grounds of the various schools. This sometimes leads them to camouflage their movements, concealing the true import of their statements, not only from others, but also, and perhaps even more importantly, from themselves. For instance, Hoffman (1983) has shown that the conservative critics of the blank screen concept, within the Freudian field, have tended to restrict their observations to specific sectors of the analytic relationship, thus avoiding a full recognition of the ongoing participation of the analyst's personality in the process. In a similar vein, Aron (1996) suggested that the use of terms such as "actualisation", "enactment", and "projective identification" has helped some contemporary Freudian theoreticians to build a bridge between the individual personalities of the patient and the analyst, while at the same time refraining—on the basis of their being allegedly discrete events in the course of a treatment—from taking full cognisance of the pervasive and ever-present unconscious interaction and communication between them. In other words, it is a theoretical strategy that delays the acknowledgement of what he has called "the interpersonalization of psychoanalysis". Such strategy is also found in the writings of the Barangers (2008, 2009), who, even though they had proposed, in their original paper on "The analytic situation as a dynamic field" (published in Spanish in 1961–1962 and in English translation in 2008), the universal validity of field phenomena in the psychoanalytic treatment, later (Baranger, Baranger, & Mom, 1983) retreated to treating the field as a regressive—that is, psychopathological—phenomenon that appeared whenever the analytic asymmetry was lost (Tubert-Oklander, 2007, 2013a). (See Chapter Six.)

Perhaps we are in sore need of a new language for psychoanalysis, a language that might take into account the multiple dimensions of human existence and experience. When speaking about the analytic relationship, we were traditionally bound to choose between two opposite terms, which became, at one and the same time, both useful, on account of what they described, and restrictive, as a result of what they left out. A new way of thinking about such matters would require a dialectical approach to these opposites.

One such approach was that of the Argentine psychoanalyst and social psychologist, Enrique Pichon-Rivière (1971, 1979), who suggested that, in order to develop a comprehensive psychoanalytical theory of mental disease and healing, we need to keep up a constant enquiry of the individual within his or her context. This implied, for him, taking into account *three dimensions*: the *individual*, the *group*, and *society* with its institutions. These three fields of enquiry are not clearly separated, but they are successively integrated, and the point where they intersect is what he called the *bond*. This he defined in the following terms:

> [Such considerations] have led us to take, as the material for our work and permanent observation, the particular way in which an individual connects or relates with the other or others, thus creating a structure, which is specific to each case and to each moment, which we call the bond. (Pichon-Rivière, 1979, p. 22, translated for this edition)

But why introduce the term "bond"? Is it not enough to speak of "object relations"? For Pichon-Rivière, the bond is a more comprehensive and concrete concept than that of object relations. The latter refers to the internal structure of the bond, and is, therefore, restricted to the intrapsychic reflection of a much wider structure; it is "the heir to atomistic psychology" (p. 35). The bond includes the subject, the object (which is really another subject), their mutual behaviour, and the group, institutional, and social contexts in which their relation takes place. Such interaction he compared to a sports match which has to be simultaneously played in two fields: the outer field and the inner field. This I have previously described in the following terms:

> In this, Pichon-Rivière is following George Herbert Mead's (1934) suggestion that self-consciousness stems from the identification with and internalization of the other people's roles in their interaction with

the subject. When one has internalized the others' roles, attitudes, and behaviour, one becomes proficient in interacting with them. Pichon-Rivière, ever a sportsman, was delighted to find Mead's description of group interaction in a football team, which is organized and integrated by the internalization of the "generalized other". This term is used to refer to the organized community or social group—in our present case, the team—that gives the individual a sense of unity—i.e., of self—by being a part of this whole. For example, in the case of football [which to Pichon-Rivière could only mean soccer] "in each player there is a representation of the eleven adversaries, of his ten companions, and also of himself participating in the action" (Pichon-Rivière & Quiroga, 1985, p. 186). (Tubert-Oklander & Hernández de Tubert, 2004, pp. 53–54)

Now, Mead, as a representative of American pragmatism, as well as James (1907), surely had a great influence on Sullivan's (1953) conception of interpersonal relations. Thus, both interpersonal psychoanalysis and Pichon-Rivière's innovative approach to psychoanalysis and group analysis stemmed from a similar philosophical root, which is quite different from Freud's philosophical background.

The analytic bond, therefore includes, according to Pichon-Rivière, both the analyst and the patient, their internal and external objects and relations, the groups and institutions to which they belong, and the institutional and social context in which the treatment takes place. This is a most complex dynamic structure that cannot be fully viewed at any given time, but which may be enquired into and analysed by means of the psychoanalytic method. If we accept such a perspective, we shall no longer be able to dissect the analytic relationship into alleged "components". The apparently discrete elements that we have described in it—the transference–countertransference, the working alliance, and the real relationship—are only the various dimensions of this complex interaction system. Just as we cannot understand any of the parties involved without considering the other and the total organisation of the relationship, neither can we conceive any of these dimensions without the others. The bond is a living organic whole, which cannot be divided into parts.

What are we referring to, then, when we speak of these various aspects of the therapeutic relationship? It is a conceptual dissection and a perceptual reorganisation, akin to the reversion of the figure–ground relation, which allows us to highlight one of the dimensions of the bond, which becomes the figure, while the others recess into the ground. This manoeuvre might be compared to that of listening to and understanding music. A piece of music is also a unity, but we might well describe, and selectively perceive, several aspects of it, such as the melody, the rhythm, the tempo, and the harmonic sequence; however, it is plain nonsense to speak about them as if they were separate entities, instead of the various aspects of a complex whole.

The above-mentioned dimensions of the analytic bond are, therefore, those aspects that come to the fore when we look at it with various conceptual "lenses". The working alliance is just what we see when we consider the relationship in terms of a formal arrangement for co-operative work between two informed and consenting adults; it highlights the participation of conscious wishes and intentions, as well as those sophisticated abilities that allow people to work with others. The "real" relationship is what comes into focus when we approach it with a question about what these two people actually are, what they are doing and giving to each other, and what are the effects on them of their mutual encounter. Finally, the transference–countertransference is that view of their interaction that emerges when we concentrate on both parties' automatic and unconscious participation, in which we discern a repetitive pattern that connects their present experience with some of their previous and emotionally significant ones.

In order to illustrate these concepts, I shall present a brief clinical vignette.

A very disturbed patient, who had already recovered somewhat, expressed an intense anxiety *vis-à-vis* my vacations. Such a reaction had been common for several years, but it had significantly diminished with time and the evolution of her analysis. This break, however, was to be longer than usual, and this had generated a great anger in the patient, which was clearly related to some childhood traumatic experiences of abandonment and loss that she had lived through in her relation with her parents. The analysis of these well-known factors, however, was not enough to dispel her anxiety. In the last session before I was due to leave, she suddenly asked me, "But, are you *really* coming back?" I feel bewildered by her question. I would like to assure her that I am certainly coming back and that I shall be here to receive her at the appointed time, but I also remember that I am travelling by air, and I think that some accident might prevent me from fulfilling my promise. All of this leads me to reflect upon the fragility of human life. I finally answered as follows: "My intention is to come back and be here to receive you at the date and time that we have agreed. If it is up me, I shall be here." The patient stayed silent for a while, and then said, "What you have just said is really soothing to me. If you had told me that you would certainly be here, I would not have believed you. Now, you are telling me instead that, although not everything depends on you, you do want to come back, and you shall do all that is necessary to achieve it. I think that this is what my parents could never tell me." Before putting an end to the session, I informed her that I would be travelling abroad, and that, although I had planned to be back before the date of her next session, there might be some unexpected inconvenience with the flights, so I asked her to phone me before her session, to confirm the appointment.

In this episode, we have a *transference expression* of the patient, which resonates with my corresponding *countertransference reaction*. She is afraid that I might die or disappear, according to the pattern of her childhood experiences, and I fear my own death, both as a reaction to her anxiety and also on account of some personal emotional situations, including the universality and inevitability of death. It is also possible that she might have unconsciously perceived my uneasiness about these vacations, and that this might have nurtured her own fears. It is pointless to ask who has "really" initiated this interaction, since all interactions are always circular; what matters here is that both of us recognise that our relationship is, for the moment, shadowed by fear of fatality and tragedy, and to do something that might conceivably modify this emotional situation.

My first reaction is the impulse to deny any danger, just as her parents apparently used to do. But once I manage to assume the existential and personal character of my anxiety, I decide to respond with the truth, and say, "I intend to come back, but I cannot assure you that I will." The patient thanks me for my answer, and describes the meaning that it has had for her. This part of the interaction is better understood in terms of the *real relationship*, and brings about a *corrective emotional experience* (Alexander & French, 1946) for both of us. Finally, once that the transference–countertransference anxiety has been dispelled, I am now ready to discuss with the patient the practical aspects of our next meeting, to inform her of a certain element of uncertainty about my trip, and to suggest some measures to protect her if such a situation were to happen. This last interchange may be understood in terms of the *working alliance*, although it is certainly also germane to consider it in terms of the real relationship (I am concerned about the patient) and of the transference (I, as the analyst, am not like her parents, since I am able and willing to speak clearly about real problems). It is also, of course, a countertransference expression, since I am attempting to repair any damage that I might have been felt to have caused her by acknowledging that I am neither invulnerable nor fully in control of events at the same time that I manage to overcome my own personal anxiety by turning into a concerned parent who is taking care of a frightened child.

I believe that the analysis of this episode might clearly illustrate the way in which I use the terms that I have introduced in this section, as well as my understanding of the dynamics of the therapeutic relationship. More about this will be said in the following chapters.

CHAPTER SIX

The analytic field

The concept of "field"

In the early 1960s, the Barangers published a paper in Spanish titled "The analytic situation as a dynamic field" (Baranger, & Baranger, 1961–1962), which was published in English only in 2008. There, they claimed that the analytic situation should always be understood as a two-person setup, in which neither party may be conceived without the other, since they are inescapably bound and complementary. This they called a "dynamic field".

The concept of "field" was first used in science by physicists, who used it to refer to a region of space in which a given effect (such as magnetism or gravity) exists. But it also implied a certain organisation of such a region, in which any change at a given point had effects on every other point of the field. Field theories implied an epistemological revolution in science, since they replaced linear causality, as an explanatory principle, by complex interdependence. They also had the characteristic of being atemporal, since they explained the phenomena that took place in the field in terms of its organisation and dynamics, without any reference to its previous history.

Such concepts were imported by Gestalt psychologists, who were particularly interested in the study of "wholes", as opposed to that of "parts". From such a perspective, *the whole was considered to more than, prior to, and more elementary than the sum of its parts*. This meant that, in the complex organisations that characterise living phenomena—such as organisms, their structure and functions, and their interactions with other organisms and their environment—this complexity is a primary phenomenon, and its so-called "parts" are artificially created by our analytic activity, whether intellectual or physical. The functional apparatuses described by physiology, for instance, do not exist in nature as such, as they are always integrated in the functioning of a whole organism and placed within a physical, biological, psychological, and social context. It is the physiologist who creates them, by means of several techniques—either anatomical or functional—that isolate a group of mutually related organs from the rest of the organism. And this isolation is akin to, as Goldstein (1940) pointed out, that which develops in pathological conditions.

Therefore, the "parts" that we create by means of our analytical—that is, severing—techniques are necessarily studied in an abnormal situation that resembles pathology, and the results of such studies can only be used for the understanding of the activity of the normal organism if we identify the ways in which this isolation modifies normal function, and take the necessary measures to compensate for such distortion. This implies reintegrating this information into the functioning of the organism-as-a-whole, and restoring the organism to its normal context, from which it had been segregated when it was placed in the laboratory. The same applies to any study or conception of the individual in isolation. The human being always acts as a whole and is always inserted in a relational and social context.

These concepts were introduced in the field of social psychology by Lewin (1951), who had studied chemistry and philosophy before turning to psychology. He conceived the human being as existing in a "vital space", defined as a field in which many different forces interacted, thus shaping his behaviour and experience. Surprisingly enough, these forces correspond to a variegated assortment of disparate elements, such as childhood experiences, wishes and aspirations, membership of groups, organic characteristics and transformations, physical and social climates, geographic environment, language, cultural values, institutional and social environment, political events, and accidental happenings. Although this would seem akin to "multi-plying apples by pears", it becomes quite possible when we consider the nature of the psychological field. All the factors that take part in such a field are psychological events. Thus, any physical event that has an impact on the field becomes a "quasi-physical" factor—that is, the psychological representation of such event. In the same way, biological and social events become "quasi-biological" and "quasi-social". Thus, any somatic change, such as the metamorphosis of puberty, menopause, hunger, sexual deprivation, mutilation, or surgical interventions, enter the field only in terms of their impact on psychological functioning. The same happens with social and environmental events, which become relevant in terms of their psychological counterparts. Even non-existent entities, such as ghosts and vampires, take part in the field, if the individual believes in them.

The same applies to interpersonal and group situations, which, according to Lewin, also constitute a psychological field. In such a field, the whole—the group—is more than, prior to, and more elementary than the sum of its parts—the individual members. It is, therefore, possible to understand the latter's behaviour and experiences in terms of the organisation and the dynamics of the group field.

The field approach to human affairs implies taking into account *contemporary factors* only. Everything is viewed in terms of the present, and the past and the future have a purely psychological existence, as remembrances of what has happened and expectations of what is to come. In this, once again, it is belief, rather than actual occurrence, which determines the psychological relevance of an event.

Another representative of this kind of thinking is the French philosopher, Merleau-Ponty, who, in his books, *The Structure of Behaviour* (1942) and *Phenomenology of Perception* (1945), critically discussed the Gestalt point of view. Where the classical Gestalt psychologists had emphasised the study of perception and Lewin that of motivation, Merleau-Ponty adopted the phenomenological–existential point of view, thus focusing on the study of *personal experience*. This brought him into contact with one possible way of understanding psycho-analysis: as a methodology for the study of unconscious experience.

The Barangers explicitly derived their conception of the analytic field from the writings of Merleau-Ponty. This is consistent with their whole approach to psychoanalysis, which is mainly philosophical and humanistic, in sharp contrast with Lewin's quasi-physical perspective. However, they had certainly been influenced by their teacher and mentor, Enrique Pichon-Rivière, an avid reader of Lewin.

Pichon-Rivière (1971) conceived human existence in terms of *three areas of behaviour and experience*: the *body*, the *mind*, and the *external world*. Therefore, the individual would place a certain emotion, thought, or impulse in one of the three areas, experience and interpret it as belonging to that realm, and act accordingly. Thus, for instance, if a person deposits an anxiety in the body, it will be expressed, perceived, and interpreted in hypochondriacal or psychosomatic terms, and he will take actions believed to be appropriate to cure a disease. Of course, in this context, "action" does not only refer to purposeful and consciously engaged acts, but also to that sort of automatic unconscious bodily expressions that are the very stuff of emotions and psychosomatic disturbances. On the other hand, if a person places it in the external world, it will be seen as a reaction to an objective danger, which demands taking measures intended for defence or for the destruction of enemies. When the anxiety is manifested in the mind area, it might turn into doubt, an active search for meaning, or complex theorising, which might even become a delusion. But the mind, the body, and the external world are not only depositories for emotional experiences, but also the source of psychic movements. Pichon-Rivière, therefore, found it easy, just as Lewin did, to interpret the psychological field in terms of mental, bodily, and external events.

The analytic field is, therefore, a psychological field, in Lewin's terms, or an experiential field, as defined by Merleau-Ponty, Pichon-Rivière, and the Barangers, which is generated whenever two people meet in a closed room, in order to "do psychoanalysis". This implies a certain conventional and social definition of the situation—the setting—as well as the physical, institutional, and social environment in which all of this takes place, which are usually kept tacit, unless some psychological event in the field makes them relevant and worthy of mention. Such complex psychological space is essentially dynamic; this means that every element within the field interacts with all the others, that its configuration evolves with time, and that its limits are also variable, expanding and contracting according to the fluctuations of feeling, thought, and meaning within the field.

Field concepts in psychoanalysis

That the analytic situation is always bipersonal would appear to be a truism: nobody has ever denied that there are physically two persons present in every analysis. But the crux of the question is whether both of them actually determine the analytic process, or whether it is driven only by the patient's mental processes. Although Freud created the psychoanalytic device as the meeting of two people, each with his own particular task, his whole scientific perspective demanded that his descriptions should be framed in objective terms— that is, that they should describe the object of study as if the observer were not there at all. This resulted in a one-person theory, which described and explained the events that took place in the analytic situation solely as a manifestation of the patient's personality—his "mental apparatus"—thus assuming that the analyst was nothing but a neutral observer, who had no influence on the "material" under scrutiny.

The relational approach to psychoanalysis was really inaugurated by Ferenczi, who conceived the psychoanalytic treatment as a veritable meeting of two minds. This implied an interweaving and mutual determination of transference and countertransference. He also emphasised the crucial role played by emotional experience, as the true basis of psychoanalytic discoveries. Nowadays, researchers tend to think of affects as a primitive form of communication among individuals, one that appears from the very beginning of life, long before the acquisition of language. It is certainly the only way in which a baby can influence and generate reactions in its mother that are appropriate to its needs (Bion, 1962). Emotion is, therefore, not only a private experience, but an event shared with other human beings— what we might call a *communion*. But, since the gist of this process appears to be unconscious, it can only be truly comprehended as an inference from the inner conscious experiences and outer behaviour of the parties involved.

This was obviously Ferenczi's view. In his clinical writings—especially in his *Clinical Diary* of 1932 (1985), a private document that was not intended for publication—the analyst's and the patient's mental processes freely intermingle, and their simultaneous unravelling enriches and deepens both parties' understanding, thus generating a true emotional insight:

> It is as though two halves had combined to form a whole soul. The emotions of the analyst combine with the ideas of the analysand, and the ideas of the analyst (representational images), with the emotions of the analysand; in this way the otherwise lifeless images become events, and the empty emotional tumult acquires an intellectual content. (p. 14)

Such a point of view demanded a *mutual generation of data* (Aron, 1996), in order to attain a fuller understanding of what was actually happening at the unconscious level of the encounter, and Ferenczi found it in his technique of "mutual analysis". This was suggested to him by Elizabeth Severn, who features in his *Diary* as "R. N.". Severn was a very ill person, what we would call nowadays a "borderline patient". She had been sexually abused in childhood, exhibited a severe personality disorder, and was incapacitated by her symptoms. She was also a rather mystical psychotherapist. She seems to have developed what Balint (1968) calls a "malignant regression", in which she stormed Ferenczi with her reproaches and demands. At some point of her analysis, she demanded that he accept being analysed by her, in order to solve what she believed to be his negative counter-transference, which she claimed to be the cause of the stalling of her analysis. Ferenczi resisted this suggestion for a year, but he finally accepted it, since he was painfully aware that she was right about his countertransference. Therefore, they embarked on a bold experiment, in which they alternated the sessions of her and his analyses (Aron, 1996; Fortune, 1993; Ragen & Aron, 1993; Smith, 1998, 1999; Tubert-Oklander, 2004a,b, 2013b). Ferenczi was quite surprised when he found out that his confession of his antipathy towards her gave place, after an initial stormy reaction on her part, to a new calm and a progress in the analysis.

In the entry of Ferenczi's (1985) *Diary* corresponding to 19 January, he records how he analysed with her one of his own traumatic childhood memories that was in resonance with the patient's dream. The result was that

> The analyst is able, for the first time, to link *emotions* with the above primal event and thus endow that event with the feeling of a real experience. Simultaneously the patient succeeds in gaining insight, far more penetrating than before, more strongly than ever before, into the reality of these events that have been repeated so often on an intellectual level. (pp. 13–14)

This experiment in mutual analysis was interrupted by Ferenczi's illness—a severe pernicious anaemia—which led eventually to his death. It was truly fruitful in its clinical discoveries, although it is certainly not a technique to be recommended. Apparently, the development of a highly pathological transference–countertransference stalemated the analysis, in spite of Ferenczi's courageous and extremely creative efforts. From a therapeutic point of view, it was certainly successful: according to Fortune, who has done the deepest historical research on Severn's life, her daughter told him, many years later, that she had no doubt that the analysis with Ferenczi had saved her mother's life (Fortune, 1994). Perhaps this treatment should be classed with Freud's self-analysis as two unique paradigmatic psychoanalytic experiments.

After Ferenczi's death, there seemed to be a collective ban in the psychoanalytic community on the subject of countertransference. It was only in the late 1940s, as we have already seen, that a series of papers on the subject started to emerge (Winnicott, 1949; Heimann, 1950; Little, 1951, Racker, 1953). Of these, Little's contribution was, perhaps, the nearest to Ferenczi's original stance.

But it was Racker who, in 1948, introduced the microscopic analysis of countertransference reactions. Since the paper was considered too subversive to be published at the time, it appeared in English only in 1953. Therefore, Heimann's (1950) "Countertransference", a more superficial paper, is still considered to be the precursor of the literature on the subject in the English-speaking world. As already stated, Heimann was overtly critical of Ferenczi, but she did mention him, even though only to express her disagreement with his views about countertransference disclosure, while Winnicott, Racker, and Little did not.

During the 1950s, Racker continued his systematic investigation of the countertransference and its interweaving with the transference, which is summarised in his book *Transference and Countertransference*, originally published in Spanish as *Studies on Psychoanalytic Technique* (Racker, 1960). There, he introduced the revolutionary concept that resistance is always coupled with a counter-resistance (a term introduced by Little) in the analyst. This was turned by the Barangers into their concept of the "bastion"—an unconscious collusion between analyst and patient on not to analyse, or even mention, a particular subject.

During the past two decades, a group of writers, such as Jacobs (1993a), Ogden (1994a), Ponsi (1997), Renik (1998), and Schwaber (1998), among others, have developed a new way of presenting clinical papers, in which they register the minutiae of their own mental processes and emotional experiences during a session, and show how they intertwine with the patient's. This mutually generated material is the basis for interpretation during the session of the transference–countertransference configurations that emerge in the analytic field. All this is clearly much in the spirit of Ferenczi's (1985) *Clinical Diary*, but they do not refer to his pioneering studies in this endeavour.

On the other hand, relational psychoanalysts, such as Aron (1996), have found in Ferenczi a forefather of their own concerns and explorations. All this developed since the publication, in 1988, of the English translation of the *Clinical Diary*, which fostered a burgeoning interest in Ferenczi's work.

Other writers have taken exception to this approach to clinical practice. Green (1993), for instance, severely criticised Jacob's (1993a) interactional description of a session, presented during the Amsterdam International Psychoanalytic Congress. This led to a controversial discussion, mitigated by Wender's (1993) sympathetic and understanding approach to the same paper. This is certainly an issue in the psychoanalytic world, which seems to be based on contrasting epistemologies and world views (Hernández de Tubert, 2004; Tubert-Oklander, 1999, 2011a, 2013b).

Now, all of this evolution occurred in the Freudian field. In the interpersonal domain, field concepts had been current from the very beginning. Sullivan (1953) was clearly sympathetic to Lewin's field concepts, although he specified that "however, Kurt Lewin's conceptions are by no means identical with those that I am about to unwind" (p. 35n). He then developed his own view of human existence in terms of the individual's participation in an interpersonal field, considering that "the study of interpersonal relations . . . in the end calls for the use of the kind of conceptual framework that we now call *field theory* (p. 368).

Nevertheless, he never went as far as to include the analyst's subjectivity in his clinical data. Ever faithful to his particular brand of rationalism, which led him to value the precision of language above everything else (Mitchell, 2000, pp. 6–7), he saw himself as a detached observer of the patient's interpersonal field. As Aron (1996) points out,

"Sullivan's interpersonal theory, while interpersonal in its examination of the patient's life, was asocial in its neglect of the subjectivity of the therapist as inevitably participating in the analytic interaction" (p. 58).

But in spite of his objectivistic restrictions, Sullivan had already opened the door, and it was not long before other interpersonal analysts took the enquiry one step further. Erich Fromm, Frieda Fromm-Reichmann, and Clara Thompson developed, under the influence of both Ferenczi and Sullivan, the interpersonal analytic technique towards an ever greater participation of the analyst as subject and object of the enquiry (Aron, 1996, pp. 134–135). This new perspective went as far as suggesting that patients may also be helpful to their analysts, in their own personal development, that the latter could—and sometimes should—be explicitly grateful to them for this help, and that the enquiry of their mutual relationship is the very stuff of analysis (Levenson, 1993; Searles, 1979; Singer, 1971). As Levenson clearly put it, "Ultimately, the patient does not learn from us how to deal with the world. *The patient learns to deal with us in order to deal with the world*" (p. 396, my italics).

Relational analysts in general have adhered, explicitly or implicitly, to some conception of the analytic field, since this is the only theoretical construct that seems to be able to accommodate the dialectics of the analyst's and the patient's subjectivity that is the very basis of the relational approach to psychoanalysis (Aron, 1996; Hoffman, 1983). Stolorow and Atwood (1992) have explicitly defined their "intersubjective theory" as a field theory, in the following terms:

> Intersubjectivity theory is a field theory or systems theory in that it seeks to comprehend psychological phenomena not as products of isolated intrapsychic mechanisms, but as forming at the interface of reciprocally interacting subjectivities. (p. 1)

(For these authors "intersubjectivity" is defined as a mutual influence among minds, regardless of whether there is also a mutual recognition of the other as a like subject, while others, such as Benjamin (1990, 1998) restrict its use to refer to the more sophisticated capacity for mutual recognition.)

So, we truly need to develop a better understanding of the concept of "field", in order to account for the complex unconscious interactions that evolve during the psychoanalytic treatment.

The dynamic properties of the analytic field

I shall start by presenting the main concepts introduced by the Barangers, and then discuss my own understanding of it. These authors enumerate, in their paper "Insight in the analytic situation" (Baranger & Baranger, 2009, pp. 1–15), the following characteristics of the psychoanalytic situation.

1. *The analytic situation is a bipersonal field*, in which both parties determine each other and whose experience and behaviour in this context cannot be fully understood without due reference to the other. However, following Pichon-Rivière, they specify the paradox that it always is a two-body but three-person situation, since there is always a third present–absent party that completes the Oedipal triangle, which is the basis of all other relational structures, from the bipersonal to the multi-personal.

2. *The analytic situation is essentially ambiguous.* This ambiguity is indispensable, in order to create and maintain a special context in which any given event is amenable to various interpretations.

3. *The bipersonal field of the analytic situation is structured along three lines,* derived from three basic configurations: (a) the *structure derived from the analytic contract,* which not only defines the spatial, temporal, and functional constants, but also the indispensable asymmetry between the parties; (b) the *structure of the manifest material* (the analytic dialogue); (c) the *unconscious fantasy* that underlies all manifest expressions (the latent or unconscious content). This fantasy does not belong only to the patient; it is, rather, a co-creation by both parties, a dyadic fantasy.

4. *The point of urgency for interpretation is defined by the meaningful convergence of these three configurations.* Since the unconscious fantasy of the session is created from the confluence of the unconscious contributions of both parties, this does not depend only on the patient, but on their mutual interaction. Of course, the authors do not use the terms "mutual" and "interaction", which would have been incompatible with their analytic conception and tradition, but the meaning is clear in their writing, for instance, when they say, "The point of urgency is an unconscious fantasy of the couple (which is *created* within the couple as such). This fantasy

can be defined as 'the dynamic structure (of the couple) that at any moment confers meaning to the bipersonal field'" (p. 3).

5. *The analytic situation must be indefinite and mobile,* so that it may become "a couple situation in which all the other imaginable situations of the couple (and others) are experienced, but none is acted upon" (p. 3). This actualisation is based on mutual projective identifications by the patient and the analyst, even though their respective positions *vis-à-vis* these unconscious processes are not equivalent.

6. *The unconscious dynamics of the analytic situation depends on two factors: the primary field that integrates and subsumes the common factors of both parties' unconscious experiences, and the analyst's interpretations.* The latter depend not only on the patient's verbal and non-verbal expressions, but also on the analyst's personality, technique, theoretical persuasion, experience, and ideology. From this interchange, each patient–analyst couple develops its own particular dialect, a common language, which is used for understanding. It is worthwhile noting that the authors, in accordance with their originally Kleinian orientation, conceive the goal of analysis as "making conscious the unconscious, by means of the analyst's interpretations". This defines a unilateral conception of the analytic process, which is precisely what they are trying to transcend. (In Chapters Eight and Nine, I shall introduce the concept of the "interpretative process", in order to highlight the fact that mutuality in psychoanalysis is not restricted to the pathological aspects of the analytic relationship—conceived as "transference" and "countertransference"—but is also an essential part of the reflective thinking that sustains the analytic enquiry.)

7. *The transference neurosis (or psychosis) is really a transference–countertransference micro-neurosis (or psychosis), a pathology of the bipersonal field.* The analysand necessarily tends to recreate his own pathology and personal history in the analytic situation. The analyst must let herself be absorbed in this pathology of the field— an event that is, however, inevitable, as a result of the analytic relation—but also analyse this experience, so that she may rescue herself, and the analysand, from this shared pathology.

8. *Such a double rescue is achieved by means of successful interpretation,* which mediates the passage from a symmetrical configuration of

the field, in which both members of the analytic couple are equivalent and act on each other by means of projective identification, to another kind of asymmetric communality, in which the repetition compulsion has been overcome by reflective thinking and understanding.

9. *Psychopathological diagnoses of the patient have no operational value in themselves, but only in relation to a particular analyst and context.* In a later paper, Willy Baranger (1992) further develops the idea that all diagnoses are relative, since they are constructed by the analyst, on the basis of a series of assumptions about the patient's suffering, held by the analyst, the patient, his or her relatives, and society. "The 'private' individual neurosis, in its concept, comes from an artificial dissection made by the psychopathologist" (p. 89, translated for this edition).

10. *Insight is also a field phenomenon, which may be defined as a restructuring of the field, a gradual development of both parties' understanding of their shared unconscious situation.* This conception is clearly shown in the following quotations.

> Any development in theory should be based on the changes in the field induced by interpretation. Insight, conceived as a restructuring of the field that follows an interpretation, is our essential tool for the validation of our interpretations and, less directly, of our theories (Baranger, & Baranger, 1969, p. 89, translated for this edition)

> The process of elaboration of the field consists in the analyst's interpretation and the patient's "understanding". If we delve deeper into this we realize there are not two processes, but only one. An interpretation that does not reach the patient is useless and can be dispensed with. The patient's single understanding has no bearing on the analytic process. The specific analytic insight is the process of joint understanding by analyst and patient of the unconscious aspect of the field, which permits it its pathological present content to be overcome and the respective involved parts to be rescued (Baranger & Baranger, 2009, p. 5)

This description makes it clear that, for the authors, the concept of the analytic situation as a dynamic field had a general application—that is, it referred to everything that happens in an analysis, and not to a part of it. It was a perspective, a new way of looking at things. This is particularly clear in their treatment of the concept of the "unconscious fantasy", which they also consider to be bipersonal, a "fantasy of the couple", and they add "in analytic group psychotherapy, the appropriate expression is 'group phantasy'" (Baranger & Baranger, 2008, pp. 805–806).

This shows the radicalness of their revision of the traditional understanding of the psychoanalytic treatment. In a later paper, written with Jorge Mom (Baranger, Baranger, & Mom, 1978), they further examined the perverse configurations of the analytic field, showing how the analyst's theories participate in the constitution of bastions of resistance, as we shall see in Chapter Ten, on "The evolution of the analytic process".

In later publications, however, the Barangers and Mom were more cautious. In a paper titled "Process and non-process in analytic work" (Baranger, Baranger, & Mom, 1983), they seemed worried about the risk implied by taking the field concept as an affirmation of a total symmetry of the positions of the analyst and the patient. Therefore, they appeared to restrict the use of the term "field" to those configurations of the analytic relation in which the necessary asymmetry instituted by the contract or pact has been lost and substituted by a pathological symmetrical organisation.

Since field phenomena appear to be based on Melanie Klein's concept of "projective identification", they discuss her tendency to overextend its use, to the point of conceiving transference as a continually active process of projective identification, and understanding the evolution of the analytic session as a succession of projective and introjective identifications. From their point of view, such excesses tend to obscure the unavoidable differences that are necessary to define the psychoanalytic situation, as they clearly affirm in the following extract:

> It was a great temptation to try to arrive at a unified theory of transference, countertransference and projective identification. It would suffice to allow that the field created by the analytic situation consists of a transferential–countertransferential field formed on the basis of crossed-over and reciprocal projective identifications between analyst and analysand. Thus, the asymmetrical function of this field would constantly aim to undo the symbiotic structurings originating in the projective identifications by means of interpretation. *In fact, we realized that such a definition could only apply, and without great precision, to extremely pathological states of the field: a field characterized either by an*

invincible symbiosis between the two participants, or by the annihilating parasiting of the analyst by the analysand [my italics]. The simplification and unification of the theory led, not to greater coherence but to flattening. Today, we consider differentiation of the phenomena indispensable, *since their correct technical management depends on this differentiation.* (p. 3)

Of course, I can only agree with their contention that the analytic process oscillates between moments of symmetry and asymmetry, and that insight is the key to the recovery of the functional asymmetry of analyst and analysand, whenever it has been lost. Nevertheless, I cannot accept the idea that symmetry is necessarily pathological, and neither do I believe that the concept of "field" should be reserved for the obstructions to the wished-for evolution of the analytic process. Their concern that the field concept might be misused—as indeed it has been—to sustain a wholly symmetrical conception of the analytic relation is well based, but it seems to me that they are throwing away the baby with the bath water. The analytic field has a paradoxical organisation: it is, at one and the same time, both symmetrical and asymmetrical, thus allowing space for both mutuality and autonomy of the parties (Aron, 1996), a paradox that creates the dialectic tension that fuels the analytic process. From this perspective, I consider that it is more useful for our thinking to use the term "field" to refer to all configurations, both symmetrical and asymmetrical, and "process" for any kind of movement of the field, instead of limiting the latter to its desired evolution. Thus, what they prefer to call a "non-process" would be better described as a "stagnated process".

From my point of view, the analytic field is created from the interaction between the analyst and the analysand, and this involves their whole personalities, incorporating both their differentiated parts and the more primitive and indiscriminate levels. This generates a threefold field, as we shall see in the following chapters, in which *the parties are two, but also one, and they strive to become three, among many.*

The phenomenology of the field

Up to this point, we have discussed the field from the objectivistic perspective of an external observer. I shall now endeavour to achieve a phenomenological description. By this, I mean a description of the experience of both parties' being-in-the-field (Merleau-Ponty, 1945). In a similar vein, Atwood and Stolorow (1984; Stolorow & Atwood, 1984) originally named their explorations "psychoanalytic phenomenology", but later changed it to "intersubjectivity theory".

The analytic field is, definitely, an experiential field, and a highly complex one, since it is made up of the articulation and dialectic tension of various kinds of experience. There is one level of experience that is organised by our everyday socially shared conception of the world. In this realm, the analytic hour is forty-five or fifty minutes long, the space of the session is an office, to be measured in feet, yards, or metres, the analyst is a professional healer, the analysand is a patient, and their relationship is ruled by a service contract. This is, of course, the area of the "working alliance"—that is, of conventional reality, geared towards purposeful action.

There is another level of experience, which is organised by emotions. Here, time stretches and contracts according to the vagaries of feeling, and a session might be almost instantaneous or never-ending. The distance between the patient's couch or chair and the analyst's seat might stretch to an astronomic void, or collapse into nothingness. The relationship between analyst and analysand might change into something else, and become mother–child, torturer–victim, hunter–prey, baby–womb, student–teacher, brother–sister, mouth–nipple, eye–landscape, guinea pig–scientist, or seducer–seduced relations, among many others, and all of them reversible, following the symmetrical logic of the primary process (Matte-Blanco, 1975, 1988). The limits of the field may be extended in time, space, and fantasy, to encompass a distant past or a foreseen future, faraway lands and characters, or mythological beings, such as vampires or fairies. Sometimes, both parties feel alone; at other times, they are in such an intimate contact that nothing else exists; on occasions, other people, or the social, political, and physical environment, are keenly present in the session. And these experiences, derived from the structural and dynamic characteristics of the field, are the very stuff of our psychoanalytic enquiry. I shall now present a brief clinical vignette that illustrates these field phenomena.

Catherine was a middle-aged married woman, who started her treatment with me soon after I came to Mexico. She had an overpowering presence and a tendency to flout social conventions, which made her fearsome for many of her acquaintances. From the very start of her analysis, she defined her relation with me in terms of being concerned about my welfare. I was younger than she, and she knew that I had recently arrived from Argentina, so she assumed that I had serious economic difficulties (which was not so far from the truth). She therefore started fantasising about buying me a car. When Christmas came, she asked me how old my children were, so that she might buy some presents for them, since I "was surely not in a position to do so". Even though her proposal to adopt me was somewhat tempting, I interpreted that she needed to see me as totally helpless, in order to deny her own need for care and help.

For a long time, she sat on the chair and acted as the very intelligent and cultured woman that she was. She politely disagreed with any interpretation about her emotional relation with me, especially if it referred to any feelings of need; if I insisted, her response was a cool and ruthless anger, which made me feel impotent and stupid.

Once, she left for a trip abroad, after rejecting any interpretation that might allude to the possible emotional meanings of this separation. When she came back, she could not find the way to my office, which she knew well. When, after having missed two appointments, she finally managed to come to her session, she was very disturbed, and said, "It is as if I were losing all my mental faculties, one by one." I suggested that perhaps she had come to need my presence, after all.

Soon afterwards, she decided to lie down on the couch, without any suggestion from me that she should do so. Then, everything changed: she suddenly started to express some very childish and tender feelings, speaking in a soft and drowsy voice, which was very different from her usual speech. At those moments, I felt that we were very near to each other, as if she were snuggling against my chest. This feeling of mine was fully shared by her, as was evident when she expressed the fantasy of becoming very little and hiding underneath my beard. But at the end of the sessions, when she sat up, she experienced a lacerating pain in her neck, as well as a feeling of dizziness, as if she were falling. I interpreted that we had been as one during the session, and that lifting her head off the cushion, which represented her union with me, was felt by her as tearing apart from our fusion and falling into a bottomless void.

Outside of her sessions, she began to feel insecure and anxious in her everyday activities. On one occasion, when her anxiety became unbearable, she decided to take a bath in warm water, and then urinated in the water, stirred it with her finger, and felt that this calmed her down.

This state of affairs became so intolerable to her that she had to turn to action. She then demanded a reduction in the frequency of her sessions. At the time, she was coming three times a week. Her argument for reducing her weekly sessions to two was that she lived on the other end of town, that sometimes it took her more than an hour to get to my office, the traffic was insufferable, and so on . . . I knew that all of this was true, but I believed she should keep the frequency. None the less, she insisted fiercely, and I decided to give her some slack, in order to avoid an escalating conflict. In retrospective, I now feel that this was a mistake, since she immediately went back to her usual domineering self, acting towards me as a stern teacher, who reprimanded me over and over, making me feel clumsy and stupid. My interpretations that she had deposited her helpless self in the third session, so as to recover her usual position of strength, and my pleas to return to the previous frequency were all to no avail, and soon afterwards she left treatment. I have since, however, learnt from third parties that she is faring well and that people who know her have noticed an important change in her behaviour since she had been in therapy.

This clinical example is, of course, open to discussion on many levels, but I have presented it in order to illustrate the sudden, and sometimes startling, changes in the organisation of the field. Catherine acted, both in her everyday life and in her sessions, as a veritable juggernaut. In her analysis, she turned into being a fairy godmother to a helpless child—namely, myself—but only as far as she felt that I went along with it; whenever I showed any potency or, indeed, any independent existence, she turned again into a bulldozer that promptly cleared me out of the way.

My own emotional stance towards her oscillated with these movements; I alternately felt helpless, stupid, ashamed, angry, and sometimes compassionate towards her, so that our very identities and relationship changed from moment to moment. Then, she became a needy child, even a baby, and I turned into a nursing mother. This brought about a total collapse of the distance between us; the world around us had disappeared, and we were glued to one another in such an intimate connection that one could say I was the space for her existence, and she was for mine, at least for the duration of the session. Then again, when this symbiotic bond was interrupted by the end of the hour, she felt a physical laceration at being severed from such fusion. So, she effected a move in order to recover her previous autonomy, which she felt to be threatened by this regression; I could not stop it, and suddenly the field had metamorphosed again into an adult "teaching" situation, which was well known and non-threatening to her.

I contend that such phenomena cannot be understood only in terms of the patient's personal history and organisation of her personality, or of the impact of her communications on my own psychic functioning. A better understanding may be attained when we include the concept of the analytic situation as a dynamic field, co-created by the analyst and the analysand, drawn from their own personalities, feelings, experiences, and beliefs. In this case, my own personal situation as an immigrant, my youth, and a certain feeling of awe towards such a towering woman must have helped to construct this configuration of the field. And, even during her regression, was she the only one to feel the loss of her usual self? Although I believed this development to be positive and necessary for her healing, was there, perhaps, a part of me that missed her imposing, but also overtly attractive, demeanour, now being replaced by a needy, helpless child? Was this a case of what the Barangers call a "bastion", defined as an unconscious collusion between the analysand and the analyst, aimed at preserving a certain emotional situation (in this case, the myth of Catherine's alleged strength and invulnerability)? I was not able to formulate these questions at the time, as I lacked the experience and the theory that would have allowed me to do so. I believe that nowadays I would have at least tried to question my own position *vis-à-vis* my patient. I do not know whether such an effort would have changed the final outcome, but it surely would have meant a difference in our mutual experience.

The metapsychology of the analytic field

The title of this section might seem rather strange, if one considers the radical criticism of metapsychological theory that I put forward in Chapter One. That criticism was basically aimed at two characteristics of this theory: (a) the formulation of impersonal causal explanations of human experience and behaviour, rather than a personal account of people's intentions and motives, and (b) the use of quasi-physical models to describe and explain mental functioning. I believe such criticisms to be fully valid. However, I still feel that there is room in our discipline for metapsychological discussions, provided that we define metapsychology as "the set of general assumptions about mental functioning that the analyst uses in order to frame her or his clinical thinking". Such assumptions are inevitable, even though they frequently remain implicit in clinical theory. Metapsychological discussions are an attempt to make explicit these implicit assumptions, so that analysts can become aware of what sort of theory they are really using. This might be described as an epistemological critique of clinical theory.

What metapsychology is not, and should not be, from my point of view, is a higher order and more abstract causal theory, which would allow us to derive, by deduction, the whole of the clinical theory. The term "clinical theory" refers to a theory of psychoanalysis framed in terms of the experiences, wishes, feelings, fears, and defensive manoeuvres of concrete human beings. Such theory is psychological and experience-near, and it aims at an interpretative and empathic understanding of individuals. This is in sharp contrast to metapsychology, which is abstract and naturalistic, in as much as it seeks to find causal explanations of human events that are quite similar to those posed by the natural sciences. These distinctions were formulated by George Klein (1973, 1976), who sharply criticised metapsychology as reductionistic and claimed that, far from being a sound theoretical basis for clinical theory, it was truly incompatible with the latter. In a similar vein, Guntrip (1961) emphasised the need for psychoanalysis to become "a truly personal psychology", quite distinct from, and opposed to, the impersonal explanations of natural science. Such points of view generated, of course, many bitter confrontations.

The fact is that, if one strives to strip Freud's metapsychology of its mechanical and physical models, there still remains a series of assumptions about mental functioning, which can be proved to underlie most of psychoanalytic theory and practice, even in the case of those analysts who would be happy to reject metapsychology wholesale. I believe that it is worthwhile to identify and explicitly formulate these assumptions, if only to be able to question them, and perhaps discard or replace those that do not stand up to serious criticism.

Besides, much is to be gained if we manage to articulate the relational and personal theory of the psychoanalytic treatment with the
impersonal and abstract theory of mental processes proposed by
metapsychology, especially in those parts of it that can be recognised
as strictly psychological. This is the case, for instance, for Freud's
conception of the primary and the secondary processes as the two
modes of mental functioning. Also, such concepts might help us to
clarify our conception of the analytic field.

Freud's great discovery was that human behaviour and experience
are intentional and meaningful, but that such intentions and meanings
are largely unknown and inaccessible to the subject who lives these
experiences and carries out these actions. Such inaccessibility derives
largely from the fact that the subject makes a continuous effort—
which is also unknown to him or her—in order to avoid becoming
aware of them. This is what Freud (1900a, 1915d, 1915e) called
"repression". Consequently, if we intend to explore this unconscious
dimension of human experience, we shall have to apply a certain
method and make an effort in order to neutralise repression and allow
the emergence of what has been previously kept at bay. This is the
work of psychoanalysis.

Of course, such early formulation of the nature and status of the
unconscious has been revised and amplified by later research and
theorising. Sullivan (1940, p. 91) suggested that one only really has
information about one's experience after turning it into communicative speech, either by telling it to some other person, or by thinking
about it in communicative terms (what Pichon-Rivière (1971) described as "a dialogue with the internal objects that constitute the inner
group"); therefore, much of what is unconscious is not repressed, but
unformulated. Donnel Stern (1983, 1997) has built upon this observation in order to explore the realm of unformulated experience,
which he considers not in terms of specific repressed contents, but
of inchoate domains of feeling, sensation, and thought, which need
to be reframed by language, in order that the subject may become
aware of them. This reformulation of the theory of the unconscious
radically changes our understanding of it, since its scope is enlarged
to include much more than those mental contents that the subject
is defending against. The idea that the unconscious includes many
valuable mental processes and capabilities, and not only those parts
of the personality that are incompatible with civilised life, leads us to

a conception of the human being that significantly differs from Freud's.

None the less, the acceptance of Freud's discovery of the unconscious and the determination to explore it does not imply that we necessarily have to adhere to many of his ideas about the nature of the unconscious that were formulated simultaneously with his discovery, and have since been linked by tradition with the latter (Mitchell & Aron, 1999, pp. 77–79). The unconscious, thus, appears as a particular dimension of human experience, defined by being unknown to the individuals who undergo it, and by presenting a resistance to any effort to reveal it. But nothing in this concept compels us to restrict its use to the sphere of the individual. Quite the contrary, there is an unconscious dimension for every human event, regardless of the number of people involved. This allowed Freud (1921c) to develop a psychoanalytic study of collective phenomena, in *Group Psychology and the Analysis of the Ego*.

If we follow this trend of thought and apply it to the psychoanalytic situation, we cannot fail to consider the analytic treatment as a collective phenomenon—what Ferenczi and Rank (1924) called "a mass of two"—and that its unconscious dimension needs to include both members of such a small group. The analytic encounter must then set in motion a complex unconscious interchange between both parties, which follows an unpredictable and uncontrollable path, ruled by the logic of unconscious mental processes.

One of the few things about the unconscious on which there is a general agreement among psychoanalysts is that unconscious thinking does not abide by the laws and categories that rule conscious rational thought—what Freud (1900a) called the "secondary process". Unconscious thinking follows its own course, called the "primary process", distinguished by the absence of the ordinary categories of space, time, causality, and contradiction as well as by the effect of two particular rules of combination of ideas—condensation and displacement. It also formulates abstract considerations in terms of their plastic representation, thus suggesting that its basic units are iconic signs—that is, images derived from sensory perceptions—rather than the verbal signs characteristic of the secondary process. The result is a peculiar kind of thought, which corresponds to the world of dreams, poetry, and myths, that Fromm (1951) called "the forgotten language".

Matte-Blanco (1975, 1988) developed an in-depth enquiry into the logic of the unconscious. He concluded that what characterises the primary process is that it follows a *symmetric logic*, which allows the reversibility of all relations. In traditional Aristotelian logic, most relations are not reversible: if John is Peter's father, Peter is not John's father. This is an *asymmetric logic*. In unconscious thinking, on the contrary, all propositions are reversible: John and Peter have a father–son relationship, in which they may alternately occupy either of the poles.

But with this reversibility of relations, all the categories of the secondary process vanish. Causal relations, for instance, are necessarily irreversible: a lighted match causes a fire, but the fire does not cause the match; the same happens with the concept of time, which requires an irreversible succession of moments, and that of space, since, if any given place may be replaced by any other, spatial relations lose their meaning.

Another feature of unconscious thought is the reversibility of the relation between a class and any of its members. A certain lady is a woman and a mother; this means that she is a member of the class of women and of the subclass of mothers. In the irreversible logic of the secondary process, such relation is immutable: the class of all women is not a woman, and any given woman is not the class. But in the reversible and symmetrical logic of the primary process, this is not so, and any given mother—let us call her "Mrs Jones"—becomes interchangeable with the class of mothers as a whole. We may then say that Mrs Jones is, at one and the same time, part of the set of all mothers, and that this set is part of Mrs Jones. The relations between whole and part, class and member of the same have collapsed, and we are left with an imposing concept of Maternity, in which Mrs Jones becomes the bearer of the archetype of the Great Mother, and the latter is incarnated in the face, the body, and the voice of this particular woman. But, since every one of the members of the class of mothers partakes of this reversibility, any of them is equivalent to any other, and all mothers are one. This is the basis of those two mental motions that we name "condensation" and "displacement".

If we now apply these general propositions about the workings of the mind to the analytic situation, we shall find that, at the unconscious level, there is no differentiation between subject and object, and that both are equivalent and may be interchanged with the utmost ease. The analyst and the analysand are identical and interchangeable, and neither of them can possibly avoid it.

Of course, human beings are not just the unconscious and primary process; consciousness and secondary process also exist, so that thinking always follows a double track. This is what Matte-Blanco (1988) calls "bi-logic", that is, the confluence and alternation of both kinds of logic: symmetric logic and asymmetric logic. This he states in no uncertain terms:

> Bi-logical structures are most abundant. They are seen in the various ways of conceiving and living all aspects of human life, religion, art, politics, and even science, in the differences between psychoanalysts, and in every other aspect of life. Once one gets used to seeing them, *one cannot avoid the surprising conclusion that we live the world as though it were a unique indivisible unit, with no distinction between persons and/or things. On the other hand, we usually think of it in terms of bi-logic and, some few times, in terms of classical logic.* (p. 46)

This is not only concordant with the Freudian discovery, but also with the Kleinian conception of a realm of unconscious fantasy, which determines a particular kind of experience that underlies, and is in sharp contrast with, everyday conscious experience. Meltzer (1981), who developed the theoretical consequences of this concept, affirms that "*we do not live in one world, but in two . . .* we live in an internal world which is as real a place to live in as the outside world" (p. 178, my italics). These are experiential "worlds", one of them conscious and the other unconscious. Consequently, there is a conscious level, in which the analyst is the analyst, the patient is the patient, and both are doing psychoanalysis, but this coexists with another level, in which things are quite different; thus, the patient might feel that interpretations become venom that poisons her, or the analyst might unconsciously experience himself as a good mother who nurses a hungry baby.

But these unconscious fantasies do not pertain only to the individual; as a result of the automatic unconscious communication between the analyst and the analysand, a new sort of fantasy is created from the confluence of the contributions of both parties. This corresponds to the Barangers' (2008) "dynamic field" and to Ogden's (1994a) "analytic third". This symmetrical experience of the fusion of the patient and the analyst coexists in dialectical tension with a differentiated, asymmetrical, experience of both of them as separate subjects. This is the reason why the analyst does not get lost in the fascination of merging, nor does she lose the track of ordinary time, or forget that she is an analyst, with a personal and professional responsibility towards the patient. Such duality is clearly depicted in the following vignette.

A woman analyst, who was supervising with me the case of a deeply disturbed child with a psychotic mental structure, brought a session in which she had found herself unable to think cogently and experienced all sorts of paranoid ideation. For instance, even though she knew that the child's father had left and would only come back at the end of the hour, she felt certain that he was on the other side of the door, listening and ready to burst in and confront her with her ineptitude. I suggested that she had fully identified with the child's inner world, and that she was feeling like a mother who deems herself incapable of dealing with a baby and fears her husband's reproofs. She answered that this was precisely the conflictive interaction between the parents, in as much as she had been able to ascertain in her interviews with them. I added that this kind of identification, albeit being quite painful to her, was a sorely needed requirement for the child's healing. She then said that what surprised her was that, even though she was completely at a loss during the session, she never lost track of time and ended it punctually. I suggested that her immersion in the experience of merging with the patient had not been total, that she had somehow managed to keep a part of her anchored to adult experience, as a differentiated member of other, larger groups in which she participates, such as her professional community. She suddenly remembered that, when feeling utterly lost during the session, she had striven to evoke my image, and that that helped her to go on with her work. I took this as a confirmation of my previous suggestion and added that she had taken me as a complex symbol of her participation in the analytic community, which included her analyst, teachers, fellow students, and authors, thus keeping an alternative organisation of her experience simultaneous and in dynamic contrast with her immersion in her patient's and his family's psychotic world.

Fromm (1979) once questioned, in a discussion about Freud's concept of transference, whether it was really desirable for the patient to regress, in the analytic situation, to a state of childhood, so that he may express those experiences that he learnt to suppress as a child in order to be accepted by the adults. His answer was affirmative, but with an important qualification:

> If the analysand during the analytic hour becomes a child altogether, he might as well be dreaming. He would lack the judgement and independence which he needs in order to understand the meaning of what he is saying. *The analysand during the analytic session constantly oscillates between the infantile and the adult existence; on this very process rests the efficacy of the analytic procedure.* (p. 42, my italics)

But what is sauce for the goose is also sauce for the gander: the analyst must also oscillate, during the sessions, between an adult discriminate and rational position and an infantile indiscriminate and magical one. It is the dialectic tension and the dialogue between them that generates insight in both parties. The infantile type of experience is not, as we shall later see, a primitive stage to be overcome in the course of a successful development; quite the contrary, it subsists during the whole of our life, coexisting with, and enriching, our adult experience. And this internal dialogue among the various parts of the personality, which resonates with the external analytic dialogue, is the source of a new kind of knowledge, what we might call, following Ogden (1994b) the "subject of analysis", a concept that I shall elaborate later, when discussing the interpretative process.

CHAPTER SEVEN

The analytic process

The concept of process

Both the concept of *field* and that of *process* constitute attempts to describe and conceptualise the non-personal (and, hence, non-interpersonal) aspects of the analytic interaction. This is what we might call the *transpersonal* dimension of the analytic treatment. If we look at a psychoanalytic session with the eyes of ordinary consciousness and common sense, it is obvious that there are two people in the room, that the latter is a consulting room, and that they are there to engage in a sophisticated interchange, framed in terms of a service contract aimed at restoring what is considered to be one party's "mental health". Such is the manifest content of the experience, but what about its underlying unconscious dimension? Bion (1980) approached this problem in the following terms:

> Every psychoanalyst has to have the temerity, and the fortitude which goes with it, to insist on the right to be himself and to have his own opinion about this strange experience which he has when he is aware that there is another person in the room. Pressure against it is considerable: your senses tell you that it is your office; you are used to the windows here, the furniture there; there is every pressure to make you

feel you are at home. It is difficult to resist that. I have suggested this: Discard your memory; discard the future tense of your desire; forget them both, both what you knew and what you want, to leave space for a new idea. *A thought, an idea unclaimed, may be floating around the room searching for a home.* Amongst these may be one of your own which seems to turn up from your insides, or one from outside yourself, namely, from the patient. (p. 11, my italics)

This is a compelling perspective: something is happening in the analytic office, which transcends the testimony of our senses and the categories of ordinary thought, and this is independent from both persons involved. For instance, new and unknown ideas might be there in the room, without either analyst or analysand having thought them; they are, rather, "thoughts in search of a thinker", following Pirandello's (1921) suggestive metaphor of the "characters in search of an author". Nevertheless, Bion seems still to be caught in one of the traps of ordinary consciousness when he suggests that such thoughts must necessarily spring either from the analyst's insides, or "from outside . . . namely, from the patient". From the point of view that I have been advancing, it is more likely that these ideas—that is, mental configurations—spring from an interactive process that does not have a subject and, hence, requires a subject in order to think them through.

In other words, mind is not coextensive with what we recognise as the person (Foulkes would say that "intra-psychic does *not* convey . . . 'intradermic'" (Foulkes & Anthony, 1965, p. 21)); it occupies the space between individuals and goes through them, extending in all directions, both spatially and temporally, fading away beyond the dim horizon of our personal perception. It is also dynamic and dialectical, in as much as it involves an evolution, which follows its own logic. *Such an extension is what we call the field, and the corresponding evolution is the process.* Field and process are but two perspectives of one and the same complex reality, the former being constructed, experienced, and thought in terms of a spatial model, and the latter in those of a temporal model.

We have already discussed in detail the concept of field; now, I intend to do the same with that of process. To begin with, a process is a sequence of changes over time, though not just any such sequence, but an organised one—that is, an evolution with a direction and a course. This implies that the sequence is not random, but subject to the action of self-regulating mechanisms, aimed at some end state, although probably the latter is not a definite point of arrival, but some sort of dynamic equilibrium that is a new kind of process. This is the case of the therapeutic process, which necessarily implies change, and change which is orientated towards a certain accomplishment that one deems to be desirable; therefore, the therapist must necessarily intervene periodically, in order to ensure that the evolution follows the preferred course (Klimovsky, 2004, pp. 160–168).

This analysis seems to assume that the process really belongs to the patient, and that the analyst, complying with the scientific tradition of objectivity, merely observes its course "from the outside" and sometimes intervenes rationally, in order to steer and modulate the process and to further investigate its characteristics. This corresponds to Sullivan's (1953) "participant observation", assuming that the therapist (psychiatrist or psychoanalyst) intervenes with

> actions or operations . . . which are scientifically important [because they] are accompanied by conceptual schematizations or intelligent formulations which are communicable. These, in turn, are those actions or operations which are relatively precise and explicit—with nothing significant left equivocal or ambiguous. (pp. 13–14)

What this overtly rational approach to the problem of clinical knowledge and corrective intervention leaves aside is the non-rational substrate of all cognitive processes, purposive interventions, and interpersonal relations. This is the very same problem we found when studying the analytic field: it would seem that a large part of what is usually referred to as "mainstream psychoanalysis" does not take seriously the implications of the discovery of the unconscious, since it stubbornly keeps describing the analyst's participation in the analytic situation in strictly rational terms, even though it has been thoroughly demonstrated that the major part of mental activities does not conform with rational thought. Evidently, a therapist cannot be exempt from a form of functioning that is common to all human beings.

The other impediment derived from this attempt to describe the evolution of an analysis solely in the terms provided by secondary process thinking is that the analytic process appears to be something that pertains only to the patient, with the analyst standing aside, acting as a participant observer. Of course, Sullivan (1953) has warned us against ivory tower fantasies, but the participation that he allows for the therapist is that of a curious enquirer and an interventionist who co-creates and modifies the phenomenon that he is studying. The observer, who uses his personality as the data-collection instrument is "an only imperfectly understood tool, some of the results of the use of which may be quite misleading" (p. 368), since his own anxiety might well distort observation and understanding. Nevertheless, he is still mainly a tool, rather than a human being in full contact and participation with another human being.

From yet another quarter, that of contemporary Kleinian analysis, Meltzer (1967) conceives the analytic process as something that takes place in the patient's unconscious, from which its "natural history" derives. The evolution of the process mirrors the very structure of mind, which imposes an unavoidable series of stages that lead to its natural ending in an inescapable, painful weaning. The analyst's contribution is restricted to the establishment and preservation of the analytic setting, and the creation of the interpretative process by means of verbal interventions. Once again, such description takes for granted the very subject–object differentiation that psychoanalysis has shown to be only a rather superficial stratum of our experience.

Of course, Meltzer recognises that during his work the analyst must become "immersed" in the analytic process, rather like a musician does with her instrument, trusting the virtuosity of her mind while in the depths. Afterwards, she must "emerge" from this absorption, when talking with colleagues and writing. This description is much nearer to the living experience of the practice of psychoanalysis, but it still seems to imply an analyst in full control of herself, and hardly participating with her own subjectivity, with the exception of the sensitivity that stems from the exploratory use of normal projective identification as a means to gain access to another person's feelings (Klein, 1955). This is akin to Kohut's (1959, 1982) assertion that the analyst's systematic use of "prolonged empathic immersion" in the patient's subjective experience bestows upon him a quasi-objective knowledge of such subjectivity.

The concept of process that I am putting forward is rather different. I contend that, whenever two or more people enter into some kind of relationship, there is an immediate interweaving of their unconscious mental processes and other such interpersonal and transpersonal events in which one, the other, or both partake. The result is the development of a highly complex mental process, which encompasses their individual subjectivities within a larger collective matrix. This process is definitely mental, but it does not have a subject, and it evolves on its own, quite independently from the intentions and will of the parties involved. It is like a wave or wind that carries them along and penetrates them through their very insides. Paradoxically, this current both springs from the most intimate and unknown aspects of their personalities, and possesses them as an alien force.

The very idea of such a power is thoroughly uncanny and begets rejection. Sullivan (1953) referred to *uncanny emotions*, when trying to convey the feel of the earliest and severest anxieties undergone by infants; these are *awe, dread, horror,* and *loathing.* It seems that all of us feel this way when faced with something so much larger and overwhelmingly powerful that recreates the earliest experience of utter dependence. Such negative feelings are a reflection of the emotional disturbance that ensues whenever there is a disruption of the mothering relationship, and the baby is faced with a premature awareness of its mother's presence. There is another side to it, of course, which corresponds to those moments of harmonious resonance and fusion, in which there is no perception of the other's separate existence, but only the experience of a holding, nurturing, warm, caring, and mirroring environment, which is indistinguishable from its very being.

Strikingly enough, even those positive feelings frequently evoke anxious forebodings, whenever early traumatic experiences have left their mark, inducing the pervasive expectation that any kind of letting go, of submitting to superior forces, will surely bring about catastrophic disillusion and unbearable suffering. Then, the initially pleasant feelings of intimacy, tenderness, and fusion are experienced as a bait that lures the heedless to their doom.

Such intimations of disaster cannot but set in motion all sorts of defensive manoeuvres—Sullivan's (1953) "dynamisms", aimed at "minimizing or avoiding anxiety in living" (p. 11). This is true not only of the patient, but also of the analyst, and this is an essential factor in the construction of that bipersonal obstacle to the evolution of analysis that we call "resistance" (see Chapter Ten).

The patient feels endangered by the perception of an all-powerful force that emerges there in the room and carries both parties along;

therefore, he would rather believe that it is the analyst, as a person, who bears this power, or even *is* this power, and this generates a paranoid negative transference, frequently masked by seduction and idealisation. Such transformation of the analyst into an omnipotent narcissistic object has been discussed, in terms of knowledge turned into omniscience, by Lacan (1973), in his concept of the *sujet supposé savoir* (the "supposed subject of knowledge" or "subject supposed to know"). The analyst also feels threatened by the loss of control implied in giving in to this underlying current, and would rather identify himself with the omnipotent object that has been defensively created by the analytic couple in order to contain and deny the real magnitude of the power that has been unleashed. This is probably the reason why Bion (1974–1975) once said that whenever there are two people in a room, doing psychoanalysis, both of them should be terrified.

Meltzer's (1967) and Kohut's (1959, 1982) image of an "immersion" in the patient's mental processes is apparently more friendly than that of being possessed and carried away by an alien impersonal force. Nevertheless, the real prowess of the analyst emerges when she is able and willing to be swept by this current and, like a surfer who manages to ride an enormous wave, suddenly finds herself capable of unexpected accomplishments that transcend her personal capacities. In actual practice, this frequently takes the form of the analyst suddenly uttering words that convey an understanding that she had never known before. The experience is rather like that of the artist who feels that he is not creating the emerging work—a text, a painting, a musical score, or an acting, dancing, or musical performance—but that the opus is using him as a means in order to create—or recreate—itself. From our psychological perspective, this is necessarily conceived as a manifestation of the unconscious at work, although this need not be restricted to the personal unconscious.

Creativity implies a particular way of "letting-go", of renouncing rational conscious control and being possessed by the "not-me", in order to let its impact fructify in our insides, and give birth to a new mental development—experience, knowledge, action, or production. This was lucidly described and analysed by Ghent (1990) as "surrender", in his paper "Masochism, submission, surrender: masochism as a perversion of surrender", where he notes several features of this phenomenon:

1. [Surrender] does not necessarily require another person's presence, except possibly as a guide. One may surrender "in the presence of another", not "to another" as in the case of submission.
2. Surrender is not a voluntary activity. One cannot choose to surrender, though one can choose to submit. One can provide facilitative conditions for surrender but cannot make it happen.
3. It may be accompanied by a feeling of dread and death, or of clarity, relief, even ecstasy.
5. It is an experience of "being in the moment", totally in the present, where past and future, the two tenses that require "mind" in the sense of secondary processes, have receded from consciousness.
6. Its ultimate direction is the discovery of one's identity, one's sense of self, one's sense of wholeness, even one's sense of unity with other living beings. This is quite unlike submission in which the reverse happens: one feels one's self as a puppet in the power of another; one's sense of identity atrophies.
7. In surrender there is an absence of domination and control; the reverse is true in the case of submission. (pp. 110–111)

Ghent's description of surrender seems near to Bion's (1967) abdication of memory and desire, or to Marion Milner's indefatigable search—related to mystical experience and artistic creativity—for an inner "answering activity" (Parsons, 1990). She was a British psychoanalyst, a member of the Independent Group, who published a series of books of self-exploration, initially under the pseudonym of "Joanna Field", in which she chartered her life-long investigation of her inner self. In her first book, titled *A Life of One's Own* (Field, 1934), she included the following description of this deep change in the attitude towards experience:

> It was then that the idea occurred to me that until you have, once at least, faced everything you know – the whole universe – with utter giving in, and let all that is "not you" flow over and engulf you, there can be no lasting sense of security.
>
> Only by being prepared to accept annihilation can one escape from that spiritual "abiding alone" which is in fact the truly death-like state. (Field, 1934, p. 152)

Perhaps one of the most compelling descriptions of this passive surrender to the unknown currents of the soul is to be found in D. H.

Lawrence's (1994) poem "Song of a Man Who Has Come Through", from which I have extracted the following fragment:

> Not I, not I, but the wind that blows through me!
> A fine wind is blowing the new direction of Time.
> If only I let it bear me, carry me, if only it carry me!
> If only I am sensitive, subtle, oh, delicate, a winged gift!
> If only, most lovely of all, I yield myself and am borrowed
> By the fine, fine wind that takes its course through the chaos
>   of the world
> Like a fine, an exquisite chisel, a wedge-blade inserted;
> If only I am keen and hard like the sheer tip of a wedge
> Driven by invisible blows,
> The rock will split, we shall come at the wonder, we shall find
>   the Hesperides.

(p. 195)

Such surrender, letting go, giving in, is what psychoanalysis is looking for, what is truly demanded by the articulation of free association and free-floating attention. In this endeavour, both parties have to surrender to a not-me evolution that utterly subverts their conventional identity, and paves the way for a new knowledge of what it really means to be human.

But what is it that one has to "let go" in order to access this new and different experience? Apparently, it is the hard-earned benefits of the secondary process, in as much as they have acquired a defensive function—that is, a *false self* (Winnicott, 1949b, 1960); it is not surprising, then, that there should always be a resistance against this process. The aim is to recover the capacity for having the kind of candid view of the world that children have, that Balint (1968) referred to with the German term *arglos* (innocent, guileless, unsuspecting). As Ghent (1990) points out, "Here, regression and surrender are close relatives" (p. 109).

This discussion clearly shows that the psychoanalytic process might be somehow related to the earliest experiences in an individual's life, and this demands from us that we study this phenomenon from a developmental perspective.

The developmental basis of the analytic process

The first question that we should answer when tackling this problem is whether psychoanalysis actually needs a theory of development. This is far from being a merely academic dispute, since a number of psychoanalysts have taken exception to the developmental point of view. Their argument is as follows: developmental theories deal with causal explanations; psychoanalysis, being a part of the humanities, deals with relations of meaning, not of causality; therefore, genetic theories of development are alien to, and incompatible with, the psychoanalytic view of the human being. This position can be found in the writings of many French psychoanalysts, as illustrated by André Green's controversy with Daniel Stern (Sandler & Sandler, 2000).

Such a line of reasoning is based on a radical dichotomy between causal–naturalistic and semantic–humanistic knowledge. This opposition is most probably biased and unfair, as dichotomies usually are. It is true that the humanities tend to organise their problematic in terms of semiotic systems, which can be studied quite apart from their genesis, but this is mostly a question of methodology. The Swiss linguist, Ferdinand de Saussure (1916), suggested that there are two ways of studying cultural phenomena. One of them, called *diachronic*, deals with these as they occur or change during a period of time—as, for example, in the study of etymology, the origins of words. The other, called *synchronic*, is concerned with events that coexist in a limited lapse, ignoring their historical background—as in the case of the study of language as a complex system of terms, their meaning, and the syntactic rules for their combination. These two approaches are complementary, and they can be found in any enquiry into human affairs.

In the case of psychoanalysis, this binocular vision can be found in the synchronic study of the field and the diachronic study of the process. But there is a similar double view in the area of motivation. Pichon-Rivière (1971), who always thought of psychoanalysis in terms of a dialectic between individual and group, underscored the fact that meaningful behaviour is always both an expression of the individual's personal history and of his present situation as a member of a group or groups. In family therapy, for example, the identified patient is, at one and the same time, a spokesman for herself (that is, for her inner reality, derived from her unique history and conflicts) and for the family group (as the talebearer of its unspoken conflicts and secrets). The therapist must, therefore, interpret in both directions: first in a *vertical* direction, pointing at the individual's inner problems, and then in a *horizontal* direction, showing how her behaviour is an expression of a present conflict that is active in the group, but which is unperceived by its members. In an individual psychoanalytic treatment, this implies interpreting any analytic event both as an expression and continuation of the patient's previous problems, and of the present configuration of the bipersonal analytic relationship and its larger interpersonal and transpersonal contexts, as we shall see later.

The main difference between psychoanalytic theory and other approaches, such as general systems theory, which eschew historical references in order to focus on the present dynamics of the field, is that the former always takes into account the previous process that led to the present state of affairs. But this does not imply adhering to a simplistic view of causality that views the present as "nothing but" the necessary consequence of the past. Science has come a long way from the nineteenth-century's conception of the universe as a perfectly oiled machine, in which nothing unforeseen could ever happen. Contemporary scientific thinking has incorporated uncertainty, ambiguity, and the emergence of new and unexpected configurations and experiences. Therefore, understanding the developmental processes that led to any present situation enriches our comprehension of the latter, without falling prey to any sort of reductionism.

In this sense, Meltzer (1967) is right in his contention that the analytic process is determined by the structure of mind, even though I cannot subscribe his idea of a "natural history" of such process. But the structure implied in this is that of *any* mind, including the patient's and the analyst's; therefore, both parties engage in a process that is at the same time bipersonal and contextual in terms of the unavoidable organisation of their mental functioning.

What are the characteristics of the human mind that have a bearing on the nature and course of the analytic process? Some of these we have already discussed in the previous chapter, when considering the dialectics of the primary and secondary process; now, I shall focus on the various forms in which experience is organised.

One of the basic disagreements about early development refers to whether there is a subject–object discrimination at the beginning of life, or not. Many accounts of the developmental processes of the infant, such as Spitz's (1965), Mahler's (1968; Mahler, Pine, & Bergman, 1975), and Winnicott's (1958a, 1965), suggest that its first experiences correspond to an indiscriminate blend of the baby and the mother, a primeval fusion from which the former must emerge, through a complex and protracted process of maturation and learning from the interaction with the care-giver. This idea was first posed by Freud (1930a), in *Civilization and its Discontents*, when he suggested that

> originally the ego includes everything, later it separates off an external world from itself. Our present ego-feeling is, therefore, only a shrunken residue of a much more inclusive – indeed, an all-embracing – feeling which corresponded to a more intimate bond between the ego and the world about it. (p. 68)

Another, quite different, point of view postulates the existence of a capacity for discrimination from the very beginning, which sustains the development of object relations at that early stage. Klein (1975) and her followers have described highly complex relational fantasies, based on a clear distinction between subject and object, from the dawn of life. Etchegoyen (1985), for example, summarises this position when he writes that "I am inclined to believe that the idea of space comes to us with the genome and so the introjective and projective mechanisms are active from life's beginning, because ego and object are present from the start" (p. 13).

Daniel Stern (1985), working from the vantage point of infant observation, dismisses such claims, on the basis of the immaturity of the infant's cognitive functions, and suggests that the elaborate fantasies described by Klein actually correspond to a later period. Nevertheless, he finds in his observational studies many behavioural signs of the existence of highly complex interchanges between the infant and its mother, from the first week of life, which make him reject Mahler's concept of a symbiotic phase. Winnicott (1962a) characteristically sidesteps the issue when he argues, "Is there an ego from the start? The answer is that the start is when the ego starts" (p. 56). But the question of the subject–object differentiation cannot be omitted, since it has numerous clinical consequences.

However, this dichotomy might well be an artifice of our either/or reasoning, and several authors, such as Benjamin (1990, 1995) have suggested that both theories are partly right, that the baby has, from the very beginning of life, a dual relation with its mother of both fusion and differentiation, and that this generates a paradoxical bonding with her, who is simultaneously an object and a part of the subject. Rycroft (1962) has suggested that the baby shows from the beginning an emerging reality principle, which operates simultaneously with the pleasure principle; if this were not the case, the baby would not be able to identify the breast and relate with it, or respond to the mother in any way. Therefore, "one is forced to conclude that the infant engages in realistic and adaptive behaviour, that the secondary processes operate coevally with the primary, and that ego-functions cannot initially be differentiated from instinctual discharges" (p. 388). This is quite similar to Ogden's (1991b) reply to Mitchell, when questioned in an interview about the paranoid–schizoid position: "I do not think of the depressive position as following the paranoid schizoid position, but as existing from the beginning as an element of experience" (p. 372). In a similar vein, Grotstein (1981) has posed the "dual-track theorem", which states that the baby has both a clearly differentiated relation with the breast, which sets the basis for projective identification, and a fusion with the mother that is only gradually solved. These two quite different experiences are there from the beginning, coexist, and contribute to the complexity of the mind. It is, therefore, doubtful that there may be a "solving" of the fusional aspect of the relationship with the others and the world, as we shall presently see.

The most primitive experiences, characterised by a lack of discrimination, are very difficult to access and describe, since they are quite alien to those of our ordinary consciousness. Their peculiarity lies in the impossibility of differentiating between good and bad, subject and object, inner and outer, material and mental, light and shadows, here and there, now and then; in other words, they are organised according to the logic of the primary process, as we have seen in the previous chapter. Bleger (1967b, 1974) suggested the term *syncretism* for this coexistence and confluence of all opposites, and that of *ambiguity* for the particular kind of object relation that corresponds to this level of organisation. Having been trained in the Kleinian tradition, he found it necessary to postulate a third position, earlier and more primitive than the paranoid–schizoid and the depressive positions described by Klein (1975). With this he tried to solve some of the difficulties posed by the concept of the paranoid–schizoid position, which seemed to telescope phenomena corresponding to different moments of early development, thus ascribing later and more complex experiences to an earlier and more primitive stage.

The earliest position proposed by Bleger was what he called the *glishcro-karyc position*, a less than euphonic term, derived from the Greek, which referred to an "agglutinated nucleus". This was defined, just as in the case of the two Kleinian positions, by a particular kind of anxiety—confusional anxiety—and a specific set of defences—cleavage, immobilisation, and fragmentation. *Confusional anxiety* is the fear of indiscrimination and fusion. *Cleavage* differs from splitting, in as much as it does not tear apart a unitary structure, but, rather, dissects it along a natural plane, which marks the boundary between the various levels of organisation of the mind; in this case, what is massively excluded from conscious experience is the whole of the primitive and indiscriminate level. The implied metaphor is that of the tendency of some rocks or crystals to split in a preferred plane or direction, as well as that of the cell division, especially of the fertilised egg. *Immobilisation* implies "freezing" the particular object that corresponds to this position—the agglutinated nucleus, which includes both subject and object in their primeval fusion. This might well be related to Laing's (1959) concept of "petrification" and Tustin's (1986, 1990) "encapsulation". Finally, *fragmentation* implies a comminution of psychic structure, quite different from the neat divisions of splitting and from the dissections of cleavage.

From Bleger's point of view, the three positions—*glishcro-karyc*, paranoid–schizoid, and depressive—were not conceived only as developmental stages, but also as three coexistent forms of experience, which lasted for the whole life span. Consequently, at any given moment, the subject would have three simultaneous and alternative versions of reality. Where Meltzer (1981) suggested that Klein discovered that "we do not live in one world, but in two" (p. 178), Bleger propounded that we actually live simultaneously in three worlds.

Such a theoretical proposal is strikingly similar to Ogden's (1989, 1991a, 1994b) introduction of an "autistic–contiguous position", which is in a dialectical interplay with the paranoid–schizoid and depressive positions. These "three modes of creating and organizing psychological meaning . . . [constitute] three fundamental psychological organizations. . . . None of the three modes exist in isolation from the others: each creates, preserves, and negates the others dialectically" (1991a,

p. 594). Even though a detailed comparison between Bleger's and Ogden's conceptions would be too extensive to expound here, we may safely assume that both authors are referring to one and the same phenomenon, viewed from different perspectives, since both emphasise the primitiveness and lack of discrimination of the corresponding experiences, the ambiguity of relationships (indeed, Bleger considers that ambiguity *is* the particular form of object relations that corresponds to the *glishcro-karyc* position), the use of superficial imitation as a defence, and the catastrophic nature of anxiety at this level of experience. Ogden, however, does not remain committed to a mainly psychopathological view of the matter, as Bleger did, but, rather, moves towards a comprehensive conception of normal mental functioning (Civitarese, 2008).

It is also interesting to point out the remarkable similarity of Bleger's view of a primitive but continuously active indiscriminate level of experience with Loewald's (1951, 1980) contention that the primeval fusion of the subject, the object, and the whole environment subsists side by side with the more differentiated view of the world that clearly distinguishes between ego and outer reality. This he derives from the same passage from *Civilization and its Discontents* that I quoted above, which he reframes in the following terms:

> We know from considering the development of the ego, as a development away from primary narcissism, that to start with, reality is not outside, but is contained in the pre-ego of primary narcissism, becomes, as Freud says, detached from the ego. So that *reality, understood genetically, is not primarily outside and hostile, alien to the ego, but intimately connected with, originally not even distinguished from it.* (Loewald, 1951, p. 12, my italics)

As a consequence, mental health appears to him, much as in Bleger's and Ogden's work, as the capacity to keep a dialectical balance between the experiences of fusion and discrimination, this being one of the main functions of the ego:

> Freud has raised the problem of psychological survival of earlier ego-stages side by side with later stages of ego development, a problem which he says has as yet hardly been investigated. If we look closely at people we can see that it is not merely a question of survival of former stages of ego-reality integration, but that people shift considerably,

from day to day, at different periods in their lives, in different moods and situations, from one such level to other levels. In fact, *it would seem that people are more alive (though not necessarily more "stable"), the broader their range of ego-reality levels is. Perhaps the so-called fully developed, the* [sic] *mature ego* is not one that has become fixated at the presumably highest or latest stage of development, having left the others behind it, but *is an ego that integrates its reality in such a way that the earlier and deeper levels of ego-reality integration remain alive as dynamic sources of higher integration.* (p. 18, my italics)

The most primitive experiences of fusion between the self, the object, and environmental reality become more apparent in regressive states and in the treatment of severe personality disorders. It is, therefore, understandable that they were initially described by analysts involved in the treatment of psychotic states, such as Ferenczi, Winnicott, Mahler, Searles, Bleger, and Tustin, among others. Nevertheless, such experiences are readily found in ordinary, common-or-garden-variety analyses, when one looks for them.

One important difference between Bleger's contribution and that of the other authors mentioned above is that the former used these concepts as a bridge between the understanding of the individual and that of groups, institutions, and society (with the exception of Ferenczi, who, although he never worked clinically with groups, was from the beginning of his career interested in the social and political implications of psychoanalysis). Ever interested in politics and social issues, like his teacher and mentor Pichon-Rivière, Bleger strove to find a psychoanalytic basis for the study of collective phenomena. This he found in the concept of syncretism. Therefore, he described in every human group—starting with the dyad—two levels of social relations: the well-known *interactional sociability*, which consists in interchanges between differentiated individuals, and a *syncretic sociability*, in which there is a fusional continuity of subject, object, and environment. The latter he describes in the following terms:

In every group [there is] a type of relation which is, paradoxically, a non-relation, in the sense that it is a non-individuation imposed as a matrix or a basic structure of the whole group, and which persists during its whole life span. (Bleger, 1971, p. 89, translated for this edition)

In order to describe this "non-relation", represented by primeval unity, he used the biological metaphor of a syncytium. This is a continuous mass of protoplasm with many nuclei, which is not differentiated in discrete cells. He postulated, therefore, the existence of a deep "syncytial structure" of the personality: just as in a syncytium we find numerous nuclei that share a common cytoplasm, human groups represent a single continuous mass that acts like a matrix, in which are embedded the nuclei of individual identifications and personal experiences that correspond to the egos of its members.

Bleger believed that the non-discriminated structure that he called the "agglutinated nucleus" is regularly cleaved away, in order to avoid confusional anxiety, and deposited in the invariant aspects of the environment, which, therefore, become the containers for such primitive parts of the personality. This is the case with the regularities and rituals of maternal care for the baby, but also that of the psychoanalytic setting for patient and analyst alike, and of social institutions, norms, traditions, and laws, in the individual's and the group's relationship with the wider social context. When such stable containing structures change or break down, as in the case of climatic or telluric catastrophes, social crises, and the rupture of the psychoanalytic setting or of the child-rearing environment, the result is an abrupt emergence of unexpectedly disorganised or violent mental phenomena or behaviour. This led the author to the rather unfortunate formulation that institutions—including the psychoanalytic setting—are the containers for the "psychotic part of the personality", and I consider this unfortunate because it falls back on the traditional psychoanalytic vice of confusing the primitive with the psychopathological. On the other hand, he clearly conceived this syncretic level of experience and mental functioning as simultaneous with the differentiated construction of reality, and indispensable for the very existence of human relations.

Montevechio (1999, 2002), one of Bleger's students and continuators of his work, further developed this point of view. Being an ardent student of Latin-American mythology, she naturally sought further clarification of this obscure dimension of human experience in ancient myths, and found it in the myth of Dionysus. From her point of view, the three basic myths of psychoanalysis are those of Dionysus, Narcissus, and Oedipus. The former was unlike the other gods in the Greek pantheon: he was the only one to have been born of a mortal woman, did not reside on Olympus, and was a god who suffered, in sharp contrast with the imperviousness of the other deities. But his main characteristic was that he was a god of contradictions: he came from fire and rain, and his cult represented liveliness and creativity, on the one hand, and ruthless destructiveness, on the other (Hamilton, 1942). This is precisely the way in which the most primitive stratum of the mind works, since it contains the most lively part of the human being, both in its loving and caring aspect and in its more sombre one, which brings about violence and destruction.

It is also responsible for the individual's deep connection with his community, as well as with the whole non-human environment (Searles, 1960). In this level of existence, there is a true continuity of the individual with everything that surrounds him. Such stratum is referred to by Bion (1963) as "the primitive mind and the primitive social capacity of the individual as a political or group animal" (p. 16).

Dionysus, with his inner ambiguities and contradictions, as well as his deep connection with nature, enjoyment, and suffering, is a most fitting image for the syncretic level of human existence, with its fleshly continuity and essential identity with all that is. In this, Montevechio followed Nietzsche's (1983) argument in *The Birth of the Tragedy*. In this book, the philosopher dialectically opposed two types of existence, which the Greeks personalised in the characters of Apollo and Dionysus. Apollo, the Sun-God, was the deity of light and appearance, of prophecy and dream; he was, therefore, the master of the plastic arts— based, as they are, on visual imagery—and of poetry. Dionysus, on the other hand, was the god of drunkenness, of passion and frenzy, both destructive and creative; he was also the master of the non-figurative arts—music and dancing. Greek tragedy, according to Nietzsche, is born of the conjugation of the Apollonian and the Dionysian.

Dionysus represents, in his essential ambiguity, the deep currents of Life, of formless fusional existence, and the essential unity of Man and Nature. Apollo represents the *principium individuationis* that estranges human beings from each other and from Nature, figurative forces, and the calm and measure derived from detachment. Nevertheless, he is not free from ambiguity, since he stands both for appearance and illusion, on the one hand, and light, reason, and truth, on the other. This apparent contradiction might be solved by Freud's (1914c) introduction of another mythological figure: Narcissus.

In Greek mythology, the latter was a beautiful young man who disdained love from both men and women, until the gods decided to punish him by making him fall in love with his own image, reflected on the surface of a pond. Echo, the nymph, who was in love with him, had been condemned to never to speak again independently, but only to repeat what others said. Therefore, although she always followed the youth, she could not talk to him. But this contributed to Narcissus's belief that the image he saw in the waters was truly another young man, since his illusion was compounded by the fact that Echo repeated the words of love he said to the youth in the pond. But he could never touch or kiss his beloved, since, whenever he touched the water, the image was distorted by the ripples that were thus induced. So, he finally became depressed, withered, and died. Echo's pain at her loss was beyond consolation, and she sought refuge in a cave, losing all her flesh and bones, until only her voice remained, reflecting the words of anyone who entered her domains (Hamilton, 1942). This is, therefore, a story of images and reflections, both visual and acoustic.

The first phase of mental development (and here I prefer the term "phase" to that of "stage", since the latter suggests the idea of a step in an evolutionary process, as in classical developmental theory, while the former may be understood as "a particular appearance or state in a regularly recurring cycle of changes with respect to quantity of illumination or form of illuminated disk (as of a planet, the moon)", that is, a cyclic change of emphasis or appearance (Merriam-Webster, 2002, see entry "Phase"), with its passionate bodily and sensuous yearnings, impulsive actions, ambiguous relations, and a primal unity of subject, object, and environment, might well be symbolised by Dionysus. This would seem to correspond to Bleger's *glishcro-karyc* position and Ogden's autistic–contiguous position.

The second phase, which centres on figurative experience and imaginary thinking, creates a world of images, always complementary and reversible, which lack substance and depth, like the young man in the pond that Narcissus loved. This type of thinking seems to correspond to the Kleinian description of unconscious fantasy (Isaacs, 1948), and we may well relate it to Klein's concept of the paranoid–schizoid position. Such organisation of experience may be represented by the myth of Narcissus and Echo.

The third phase, ruled by the individuation principle and language, sets the stage for interpersonal relations and the conflicts derived from the need to distribute love and hate among the few members of the child's family. This was originally described by Freud in terms of the myth of Oedipus. Perhaps Nietzsche's description of the Apollonian might be conceived as a condensation of the Narcissistic and Oedipal experiences. The latter is the realm of discrimination, and revolves around two basic differentiations: subject and object, on the one hand, and male and female, on the other.

Traditional psychoanalytic descriptions of development tend to end here. Nevertheless, recent psychoanalytic developments, focused on the problem of intersubjectivity (Benjamin, 1995, 1998), have pointed out that the Oedipal child's gender differentiation is based on a rigid exclusion of everything defined by culture as "belonging to the other sex". Symbolisation at this level is, therefore, still of an excluding nature, framed, as Aristotelian formal logic, on the "either/or" principle of the excluded middle. The over-inclusive identifications of the pre-Oedipal narcissistic phase, which allowed the child to alternatively fantasise himself as male and female, in a bisexual conception, are replaced by an exclusive heterosexual complementarity that will only be transcended with the emergence, during adolescence, of a post-Oedipal organisation. This implies the recovery of the pre-Oedipal over-inclusive identifications, to be kept in a state of dialectical tension with the exclusive heterosexual identification of the Oedipal organisation, thus attaining a new type of including symbolisation, in terms of "both–and", which corresponds to a principle of inclusion (Hernández de Tubert, 2000).

This sequence of phases of development is, of course, an artifice of theoretical description. We have already seen that all these organisations are present from the very beginning, albeit in an embryonic form, so that the successive phases do not imply a substitution of previous organisations, but a prevalence of one of them. In later life, the Dionysian, the Narcissistic, and the Oedipal organisations are kept in a dialectic tension and mutual relation, which constitutes the post-Oedipal organisation. I have not found any Greek myth that might represent this more complex form of experience, but perhaps we can find a suitable image in the Catholic concept of the Trinitarian Godhead (Tubert-Oklander, 2011a, 2013b).

Therefore, in every human encounter there is an instantaneous connection between the parties involved, which encompasses these three dimensions of relationality in a dialectical interchange. An interpersonal relationship does not only evolve as a meeting of clearly differentiated individuals, who communicate and act upon each other by means of all sorts of messages, signals, gestures, and actions. It is also a vivid interchange of images, mutual reflections, and fantasies, and also an essentially carnal continuity and identity of the parties, and their successive contexts, which fade into the dim horizon of their experience.

Bleger (1971) used the image of the syncytium for this paradoxical structure, which is simultaneously individuated and fusional. Tubert-Oklander and Hernández de Tubert (2004, pp. 66–69) used the time-honoured metaphor of an island, which is only apparently separated from the continent on the surface level, but is continuous with it in the deeps, as shown in one of the most famous quotations in the English language, taken from John Donne's well-known Meditation XVII, written in 1624:

> No man is an island, entire of itself; every man is a piece of the conti-
> nent, m part of the main. If a clod be washed away by the sea, Europe
> is the less, as well as if a promontory were, as well as if a manor of thy
> friend's or of thine own were: any man's death diminishes me, for I
> am involved in mankind, and therefore never send to know for whom
> the bell tolls; it tolls for thee. (pp. 108–109)

Donne's idea is quite clear: the individual is an illusion, since he or she is really an integral part of the community, just as every island is really connected to the mainland at the bottom of the sea, and is only hidden by the deep waters. Pichon-Rivière was also fond of this quotation, which to him represented the essential unity of the individual and the group. The same idea was expressed by Foulkes (1948), who conceived that "each individual [is] itself an artificial, though plausible, abstraction" (p. 10). So, of course, is the group (Tubert-Oklander, 2011b).

The same is valid for any personal relationship, and this certainly includes the analytic relation. The analytic process, set in motion by the initial contact between two people who intend to do psycho-analysis together, navigates through all the phases of human experi-ence and relationship, over and over again, and this process has a momentum, an evolution, and a steerage of its own, quite apart from the thoughts and intentions of the individual parties.

This phenomenon might be, and often is, interpreted as the mani-festation of a regressive process. Thus, Bion (1961), for instance, suggested that group phenomena are essentially a by-product of the regression of its members, as shown in the following quotation:

> The belief that a group exists, as distinct from an aggregate of individuals, is an essential part of [the members'] regression, as are also the characteristics with which the supposed group is endowed by the individual. Substance is given to the fantasy that the group exists by the fact that *the regression involves the individual in a loss of his "individual distinctiveness"* (Freud, 1921c), *indistinguishable from depersonalization, and therefore obscures observation that the aggregation is of individuals.* It follows that *if the observer judges a group to be in existence, the individuals composing it must have experienced this regression.* . . . [The word] "group" . . . [means] an aggregation of individuals all in the same state of regression. (p. 142, my italics)

Nevertheless, the very same author had discussed, in his original writings on "Experiences in groups", published in 1948–1951, the dual nature of social life, which encompasses both a primitive fusional dimension—the "basic assumption group"—and a well differentiated and rational one—the "work group". Consequently, there is more in the group than that which we know as the individual, and the group is more than the sum of its members.

> My experience in groups, indeed, indicates that man is hopelessly committed to both states of affairs. . . . In the group the individual becomes aware of capacities that are only potential so long as he is in comparative isolation. *The group, therefore, is more than the aggregate of individuals, because an individual in a group is more than an individual in isolation.* (Bion, 1961, p. 90, my italics)

These two statements are, apparently, contradictory. The possible reasons for this have been discussed in a previous book, called *Operative Groups: The Latin-American Approach to Group Analysis* (Tubert-Oklander & Hernández de Tubert, 2004, pp. 62–65). But each might have a portion of truth: the group, including the case of that particular two-member group that we call "psychoanalysis", is certainly different from, prior to, and more than an aggregate of individuals, as shown by the Gestalt theorists, such as Goldstein (1940) and Merleau-Ponty (1942, 1945), but some group phenomena become evident only when there is a diffusion of the boundaries of the individual ego.

The question here is how adequate it is to use the concept of "regression" to account for the fact that analyst and patient regularly merge in one of the dimensions of their relationship. Such a merger would be considered a "regression" if, and only if, we accepted the claim that, in the course of normal development, individuals *must* leave behind such merger relationships, and that their appearance necessarily implies going back on the steps of development. But if we adhere to the point of view that I have put forward in the preceding pages, that there is a coexistence of the various organisations of experience, such loss of subject–object boundaries can only be thought of as a normal dimension of human relations, which usually goes unheeded, until the psychoanalytic device reveals its existence.

Some clinical consequences

Looking at the experience of an analysis in terms of the analytic process brings about some consequences for our participation in it. For instance, it de-centres the question of content. When one is viewing the analysis as a process, it is no longer germane to ask what the patient is really saying with this or that expression. Instead, we shall be concerned about where the analysis is going, what sort of evolution is developing in the dialogue and the relation. Are we now more capable of meaningfully conversing about emotional experiences, whether they take place in the sessions or in the patient's life? Have we managed to expand the emotional scope of our relation? Is our verbal communication subtler and richer than it used to be? Have we developed together an ability to conjointly repair the unavoidable fractures in the relationship? If the answer to these questions is affirmative, then we are on the right track, no matter what happens in individual sessions, or in certain stages of the analysis.

I have often found, when supervising child analysts and therapists, that there are moments when they feel they are frauds. This is usually expressed as follows: "I feel that I am deceiving the child's parents: the truth is that I am not really doing anything, I am only playing with the child." My first response to this is to ask the therapist if there is any other adult in the child's life who takes him seriously, who listens to him, who honours every appointment previously agreed and does not cancel it because something more important has come about, who is willing to play with him and considers play to be an important matter, who does what she has promised and does not promise what she cannot do. The answer is regularly that there is no one else. But, of course, these considerations refer to the non-specific factors of the treatment, which we psychoanalysts tend to take for granted: "This is all very nice, but what about interpretation, insight, making conscious the unconscious?"

So, my second response is to invite the supervisee to consider the changes that have occurred, in both patient and therapist, since the beginning of the treatment. If there has been a relief of symptoms and changes in the child's behaviour, in and out of the sessions, if patient and therapist are more comfortable and fluid in play and dialogue, if the child is ever more capable of expressing his needs and emotional experiences, and the analyst is more comfortable and fluid in her responses, whether interpretative or otherwise, if both parties are succeeding in the task of sharing, communicating, and reflecting about significant emotional experiences, then everything is evolving as it should.

By then, the supervisee most probably will be re-evaluating her previous criticism of the labour implied in child analysis and therapy. Perhaps she has been sharing society's and the parents' deprecation of emotional life and personal relations. This might well be a part of the self-mutilating process of growing up in the social context.

We all have in us, to a certain extent, a compulsion for figures and facts. This is why we insist on finding objective indicators of analytic work, and, ever loyal to the Biblical mandate, stubbornly adhere to the unwarranted belief that achievement must come as the offspring of hard labour. The idea of psychoanalysis as play seems to upset one of our most cherished beliefs.

The same is true in the case of the treatment of adults, in which the equivalent of play is a free-floating conversation. Even I frequently feel that a session has been wasted if I have failed to provide an interpretation, until I manage to reorganise my perception in process terms. Then the feeling that "I have not been doing anything really; we have only been chatting, and the patient does not need an analyst for that" dissolves into a growing wonder at the vitality and the beauty of the psychoanalytic process. When the matter is viewed from the perspective of the evolution of the process, what seemed to be rather pointless conversations, sometimes focused on seemingly external general events such the news, politics, or a film, acquire new meanings in terms of the unfolding of the analysis. Nowadays, I feel free to enter into a lively conversation with my patients, while at the same time monitoring the course followed by our shared experience and dialogue.

A similar approach has been advocated by Ferro (1996), who frequently restricts his interventions to comments at the level of the manifest content of the patient's communication, postponing interpretation, when he feels that the latter would not be open to a discussion of the relational implications of what is going on between them. This might be misunderstood as implying that the analyst already knows everything about the patient's fantasies, and that the postponement is made in consideration of her inability to incorporate a premature revelation. This is certainly not Ferro's idea; quite the contrary, he cautions us about the danger of merely translating the patient's expressions into the analyst's theoretical jargon. Such interventions are logically unobjectionable, and even possibly true, but they betray the analyst's lack of openness and sensitivity *vis-à-vis* the patient. They also saturate thinking prematurely, thus foreclosing the opportunity for the emergence of new thoughts.

For instance, Ferro tells us of the case of Cosimo, a thirteen-year-old schoolboy who seemed to be out of touch with life (pp. 28–32). During their first interview, the child told the analyst his elaborate fantasies about UFOs and extraterrestrials, and then recounted a dream in which he went through a gate and entered a terrifying and dangerous territory, but fortunately there were guardians looking after the region, who might perhaps protect him from falling into a terrible chasm.

The transference implications of these expressions are obvious. Yet, Ferro decided against interpreting the terrifying quality of the present meeting, and said only that it seemed to him that Cosimo was entering a mysterious world, in which he might get lost, but only to a certain point, because the guardians were there to protect him from falling into the void, with the result that, just as he was captured by this world, he emerged from it again and found himself in his ordinary, familiar reality. In this interpretation, he was opening the way for the possibility that both Cosimo and himself might dwell together in this other bizarre dimension, while remaining clearly rooted in quotidian reality. Nevertheless, it also avoided any explicit reference to either unconscious content or the patient–analyst relationship. Ferro's comments about this vignette are as follows.

> Unforeseeable developments may be facilitated by a welcoming and containing listening attitude that takes into account the narremes [elements of the narrative] and is able to encourage their activation (without premature interpretative caesuras), and in which a relative degree of unsaturation of the field is tolerated. . . . Precisely this quality, seen in negative terms as *non-persecution, non-intrusion and non-decoding*, will allow the climate of terror and nightmare to be transformed into the familiar domestic climate that the patient will be keen to investigate and explore. . . .

> It would have been possible from the very first session to interpret the terror of the meeting, the uncertainty of what he might have found "in this house and inside himself", and so on. That is how I used to work, and different stories and perhaps silences would have been activated. I now consider it closer-to-life, more creative and useful to the patient to follow him in his account, encouraging and taking a keen interest in it—while remaining *conscious* that there is also another level to the story and that a long road must be travelled over a prolonged period to bring the two levels together and construct a new, original language common to both, without emotional or linguistic colonization of either. (pp. 31–32)

This is a view of psychoanalysis as something quite different from a decoding procedure, but rather as a living and creative process, which unfolds along unforeseen paths, building a bridge between the familiar and the unknown. Such evolution develops simultaneously in three dimensions: the emotional relationship, the clarifying dialogue, and the mutual interaction. In the following chapter, I shall explore each one of them under the titles of the *relational process*, the *interpretative process*, and the *interactional process*. This discrimination should not be understood as if I were referring to three discrete processes, but, rather, to three inseparable dimensions of one and the same process.

The process point of view implies, as Meltzer (1967) pointed out, relieving the analyst from the responsibility of setting any definite goals for therapy, but, rather, to "preside" over the process, thus warranting that it evolves in the right direction, even though neither he nor the patient knows anything about a point of arrival. It is an

open journey of relation, growth, and discovery, in which the
analyst's seamanship fosters the survival of both members of the crew
while still retaining an ample space for wonder at, and discovery of,
the new. This has been fittingly described by Meltzer (1984), in the
following terms:

> I suggested the usefulness of viewing psychoanalytical treatment from
> a process point of view, that is of a continuum of transference–coun-
> tertransference [i.e., relational] events which the analyst monitored,
> contained in his setting, and tried to assist with interpretation. In this
> view the content of the process was seen to emerge from the uncon-
> scious of the patient as an externalization of his internal object rela-
> tions and narcissistic organization, while the analyst was described as
> "presiding" over its evolution. (p. 170)

This is undoubtedly true, but it is not the whole story. The analytic
process certainly emerges "from the unconscious of the patient", but
also from that of the analyst, of their mutual relation, and of the
community to which both of them belong. As Ferro (1996) puts it, "the
field that is activated and transformed depends on the mental functioning of the couple, on the freedom of the analyst and on his *negative capability* [understood, in Bion's (1970) terms, as the capacity to
tolerate uncertainty]" (p. 32). The new entity that is created by the
analytic interaction is built from both parties' minds—in their functioning and contents—and their interactions, as well as from the
impersonal mental processes that emanate from the various groups
and institutions they belong to, society, and culture.

In the following chapters, we shall see how this way of looking at
the psychoanalytic experience determines a fresh understanding of
such well-known concepts as transference, countertransference, material, interpretation, insight, resistance, acting-out, negative therapeutic reaction, enactment, and impasse.

CHAPTER EIGHT

The dimensions of the process

The golden braid

The very idea of the psychoanalytic process, framed in these terms, implies a goal-directed evolution that is set in motion by the encounter of these two human beings, which has a development of its own, quite apart from the conscious intentions and will of the two parties. Of course, any relationship between human beings initiates an unconscious process, so what is it that defines a bipersonal process as "psychoanalytic"? There is the initial intention and agreement about a shared goal and the way in which they are going to try to attain it, and a general setting—both explicit and implicit—which creates a new context for their dialogue and mutual relationship. There is also the analyst's conscious participation in the interaction that ensues, which is based on his or her knowledge of theory and technique, previous experience (both personal and professional), and best judgement. And there is the patient's own conscious contribution and judgement. All of this fuels the manifest dialogue and interaction, but the major part of what is happening between these two people is still unconscious, and can only be partially known as a result of an ongoing effort to examine, interpret, and understand their shared experience. This effort is originally introduced by the analyst, but it is expected that, sooner or later, it might turn into a shared endeavour to find out "what is happening to us, and what does it mean".

The fact that this whole effort is goal-orientated—albeit this might be a very abstract and indefinable goal—determines that not everything that happens in an analytic treatment corresponds to a process that may be called "psychoanalytic". There are stagnated processes, in which what Pichon-Rivière (1971) called the "dialectic spiral" has turned into a vicious circle, and also deteriorating processes, which go from bad to worse. This is what the Barangers and Mom (Baranger, Baranger, & Mom, 1983) meant when they wrote about "Process and non-process in analytic work". But perhaps these accidents in the analytic process should be considered as an inherent part of it. Such was the stance taken by Giovacchini and Boyer (1975), who suggested that the psychoanalytic impasse is an inevitable phase of the analytic process, albeit

> while the development of threatened or actual impasses appears to be inevitable in all analyses . . . they are more frequent and often more severe in the treatment of those patients whose personality structures lie nearer the psychotic end of the continuum of psychopathological conditions. (Boyer, 1978, p. 63)

(More about impasse in Chapter Ten, on "Evolution of the analytic process".)

Now, in order to better describe the psychoanalytic process, I have found it useful to consider it in terms of three dimensions: the *relational*, the *interpretative*, and the *interactional* processes. Just as in the case of the various aspects of the psychoanalytic relation (transference–countertransference, working alliance, and "real" relation), we are not speaking of three different things, but of three aspects of one and the same process, which are conceptually distinguished in order to attain greater clarity in understanding them. This corresponds to the "golden braid" of emotional experience, cognition, and action, whose "seamless unfolding" comprises much of mental life, according to Clark (2009). In the case of the analytic process, the evolution of the treatment follows the braid formed by its emotional, interpretative, and interactional dimensions.

The relational process

The three aspects of the process that I have identified correspond to the three dimensions of mind—emotion, cognition, and conation—that Rapaport (1951) included in his "conceptual model of psychoanalysis". Hence, I was in doubt about whether this first thread of the braid should be called "relational process" or "emotional process". I finally chose the former, in spite of the fact that it may be cogently argued that the analytic relation necessarily includes the three aspects, because in contemporary psychoanalysis we tend to use the adjective "relational" to refer to the emotional experience of being-with-the-other. Therefore, I shall use the term "bond", whenever I want to speak about the analytic relationship in its threefold quality of being an experience of feeling with, knowing, and doing to and being done by the other.

In the previous arguments, we have seen how the dual perspective offered by the concepts of *field* and *process* requires a redefinition of most, or perhaps all, the traditional concepts of psychoanalytic technique. Even though we may still use such classical concepts as transference, resistance, insight, or working-through, they necessarily acquire a new meaning when placed in the context of a new theoretical understanding of the analytic process, based on a different epistemology and conception of the human being (Hernández de Tubert, 2000, 2004; Tubert-Oklander, 2011a, 2013b).

Perhaps the greatest discrepancy between the point of view that I am putting forward in this book and traditional psychoanalytic theory is the rejection of the common-sense assumption that the analytic situation is based on the encounter of two discrete personalities, which can know each other only on the basis of their utterances and gestures. In such a view, both parties are fully individuated and rational adults, whose inner experiences are necessarily a mystery for the other, and can only be surmised from a careful perusal and a logical analysis of the other's verbal and non-verbal behaviour.

If this were the case, the essential asymmetry of the analytic situation would determine a true impossibility for the patient to know who the analyst really is and what is going on "inside" him. The fact that the latter sits out of the former's view, does not speak about her or his own experiences, either in or out of the sessions, and endeavours to keep a formal professional attitude during their encounters, would automatically turn any perception by the patient of the analyst's mental processes into a projection of his own unconscious fantasies—that is, a transference.

This is what theory says, but it is not what we have found out in the actual practice of psychoanalysis. Many analysts have observed that patients frequently seem to know much more about their therapists' personal characteristics, history, silent thoughts, feelings, sufferings, and conflicts than the latter are willing to acknowledge. Nevertheless, patients frequently silence their observations, since the alleged anonymity of the analyst, as implied by the setting and his transference interpretations, are understood—perhaps quite rightly—as an expression of a ban on knowing anything about the analyst. The patient feels that it is wrong that she should have such knowledge—something like an analytic sin—and so tries to hide it and avoid discussing it in the sessions. Sometimes, she opts for repression, and forgets having ever known anything of the sort. In such cases, this suppressed knowledge can only be detected from its indirect expressions, or symptoms, which require that the analyst identify them and interpret their hidden meaning, that is, if he is willing to consider the possibility that the patient's new symptom might be an expression of a denied knowledge of the analyst's mental state and processes.

Such patient reactions might well be described as a "countertransference" *vis-à-vis* the analyst's state of mind. I shall now present one example of this kind of interaction, taken from the analysis of Alicia, a neurotic young woman who came to treatment during the mourning period for her father's death. This episode happened years ago, during her third year of analysis (Tubert-Oklander, 2004a,b, 2013b).

The old woman in the mirror

> One morning, I arrived at my office just in time for Alicia's session. It was a bad day for me, as I was feeling very sad. I decided, however, not to cancel her appointment. My patient came in and lay on the couch, as usual. I was glad that I did not have to face her. Alicia immediately started a humorous account of her dealings at her work. She was witty, and her stories were pleasant to hear. I did not say much, and the session was soon over, or so it seemed.

> The next day, she was quite distressed. "I must be crazy", she said. "Yesterday, when I left, I got into my car and, when I looked at myself in the mirror, I clearly saw an old woman's face."

I asked what she thought about this experience. She did not know what it meant, but she was frightened. All her hypotheses pointed to a self-destructive melancholic state. I did not know what to do. I was certain that this illusion was related to my state of mind during the last session, so I tried to explore whether she had perceived anything unusual the day before, but nothing came out of this. So, I decided to give her some information that might help us in understanding her symptom.

I told her then that I believed that this vision was related to the fact that yesterday's session had been different from others. She asked me why. I answered that I had been quite sad at that time. She immediately asked, in a worried tone of voice, "What's happening to you?" I assured her that nothing serious had happened, that I was only sad. We now had to analyse what this situation meant to her.

She said that her fantasy had been that my mother had died. I was surprised at the accuracy of her perception, since, even though my mother had died a few years ago, my gloomy mood stemmed from a belated working-through of the mourning for her death; but I said nothing about this. Alicia then said that, anyway, she knew nothing of this on the previous day.

I replied that I thought she had unconsciously perceived my mood at the time. She had given me forty-five minutes of agreeable conversation. It seemed to me that she had taken up the task of entertaining me and taking care of me, as she had always done with her father.

She suddenly remembered that when she had arrived for yesterday's session, she had noticed that my eyes were red, as if I had been crying, but she immediately put it out of her mind and forgot everything about it, until now.

I interpreted that she had somehow absorbed the venom of my sadness, in order to make me wholesome again. But this had poisoned her emotionally; this might have been the reason why she saw herself as an old woman in the mirror. She had also become my mother in her fantasy, to give me back what she believed I had lost. This taking care of me was a reproduction of the role she had had in her relation with her father, and she was recovering this relationship, when recreating it with me.

The rest of the session was devoted to analysing her relationship with her father, and its new edition in the analytic relation. When she left, at the end of the session, her farewell was: "I hope you get over your sadness soon."

Alicia's symptom is clearly an expression of her suppressed perception of the analyst's mental state. Here, it was my whole personality, in its present state, that acted as a stimulus for the patient's transference reaction, in which she related to my fragility in the same way that she had always done towards her father's. Standard analytic technique would require that her reaction be analysed without any "countertransference confession". But how can you analyse a reaction to a stimulus whose perception has been suppressed by the patient and is being silenced by the analyst? In such an instance, the disclosure of the analyst's circumstances that acted as the stimulus becomes mandatory, since any other behaviour would impede the analysis of the transference.

Of course, the whole episode could be seen as an enactment of the patient's attitude towards her father's and her own fragility, condensed with the corresponding attitudes in her father and her analyst. The truth is that my emotional state during the first of the two sessions had made me lose my analytic stance. I was there, physically present and maintaining our usual routines, but I could barely wait for the session to end, and I certainly thanked her in my heart for taking care of me, instead of analysing her attitude. Alicia's illusion shocked us both back into analysis; it was a brisk call to attention that made me recoup my analytic function.

The patient, who has long since finished her analysis, has read this report, and her comment was as follows.

> This account is very similar to what I remember, and I like the way you have told it. When reading it, I felt a longing for that time. I was then completely in love with you—not sexually, but romantically—and this love helped me through most difficult times. I no longer feel this way about you; this is growing up, but it is also a loss.

I also discussed with her, in this post-analytic meeting, the impact that our concurrent mourning processes had had on her analysis. When she came to me for treatment, soon after her father's death, I was also going through the initial stages of my own mourning for the loss of my mother. This circumstance certainly aided my understanding of her plight, but it also set in motion a series of resonances between us, in which our common resistances took the form of bastions to be analysed.

In this case, we could retrospectively identify the moment in which she perceived that something was amiss with me. On many other occasions, such perceptions are only inferred from their results. None the less, there are numerous instances of almost instantaneous perceptions, by either analyst or analysand, of the other's mental, emotional, or physical state, which take place at the very moment in which one opens the door and welcomes the patient. Of course, we know more about our own flashes of insight than about the patients', since the latter very frequently repress or silence their intuitions about the analyst. But the fact is that very intense and clear countertransference responses frequently occur on the spur of the moment, sometimes taking no more than a second, and there is no reason to suppose that the same might not be true for patients, especially since we have quite a few instances of evidence that it is so. Let us consider one further example of such occurrences.

Arlette's fear of disgust

Arlette is a mature woman in her second analysis. She is quite melancholic and prone to intense emotional outbursts, both in the transference and in her everyday relations. One day, as I open the door, I feel a sudden dislike for her. Why on earth did she come today? She frequently misses sessions, and could just as well have had the courtesy of sparing me the burden of her presence. I am flabbergasted at the intensity and quality of these feelings, which stand in sharp contrast with my usual friendly and sympathetic stance towards her. Once in the consulting room, she starts with perfunctory information about her everyday life and her conflicts with her husband, and then, in an abrupt and passionate spurt, utters that I must be absolutely fed up with her for repeating the same things over and over again. After some exploration of her feelings and thoughts about it, I interpret that it is she who has a feeling of disgust towards her suffering, which she considers unworthy of a mature and intelligent woman. To find herself at the end of her tether and to need help is something that humiliates her. I also decide to tell her about my unexpected emotional experience at the beginning of the session. She feels hurt, but hardly surprised, since we have had numerous experiences of such sudden inductions: sometimes it is I who has these flashes of something that is happening to her, other times it is she who instantaneously reacts to an emotional state that she senses in me, just as she enters my office. We then manage to relate this event to her present domestic conflicts, in which she clearly projects her anxieties into her husband, provoking impulsive reactions in him, and with the peculiar quality of interpersonal relations in her family of origin, in which ever since her childhood she seemed to be at the receiving end of her parents' projections.

These vignettes illustrate the fact that, whenever two or more human beings get in touch with each other, there is an instantaneous flow and admixture of their mental contents and processes that breeds the development of a new mental organisation, which does not belong to any of them. Ogden (1994a) has coined the name "the analytic third" in order to refer to this phenomenon, since he takes it as the appearance of a third, bodiless subject, which is there in the room, generating emergent fantasies and thoughts, which are quite alien to patient and analyst alike. This proposal, which is quite similar to Bion's (1980) idea of "thoughts in search of a thinker" and to the Barangers' (Baranger & Baranger, 2008) conception of a "couple fantasy", emphasises that the third is actually a subject, in as much as it is a source of experience, fantasies, and ideas. I fully agree with this description, which corresponds to what I prefer to call the "analytic process". None the less, I would take exception to the suggestion of considering it a subject, but, rather, regard it as an impersonal mental development that does not have a subject. Why? Of course, I do not believe that Ogden is referring to a sort of invisible imp that appears in the room, side by side with analyst and patient, although the third might well take such shape in the imaginary language of the unconscious. This is part of the trouble generated by the fact that the impact of primary experience—always of a sensuous and bodily nature—is processed in two distinct ways: the reveries of unconscious fantasy and the conceptual precisions of discourse. So, the third may be conceptualised as a process, that is, in impersonal terms, or it may be experienced in highly personal terms, by applying the mechanism described by Klein (1929) in her paper "Personification in the play of children". This is also true of any other process that might be perceived by the human mind: Cronus devouring his children, for instance, is an embodiment of the subject's inkling of the inescapable passage of time.

But which of these two languages is the more suitable for the job of theory building? And to which of these two realms does each conceptual term belong? When speaking of the person, "I" would seem to correspond to the primary experience of being and acting, "me" to the individual's imaginary representation in the theatre of the mind, and "subject" would be an abstract term that refers to his or her experience of "I-ness". So, granting that the third is a locus for the generation of meaning, does it carry a feeling of I-ness? We know that it might be perceived as a character in the personification game of fantasy and play, and that it also might—and should, by grace of the analytic process—be incorporated into the subject's definition of who he is, but is the third an "I" in itself? I prefer to think that it is not, and this is because I am keenly interested in social processes and their impact on personal relations and the organisation of the personality. Social and cultural phenomena are clearly mental processes, but they do not include a feeling of I-ness. Of course, there always is the first person plural, but "we" is better suited to describe the experience of commonality in action, as in the case of a football team that is playing a game on the field, while "us" is always an object, like "me". This is why I chose the name "I, thou, and us" for one of my papers (Tubert-Oklander, 2006a), thus underscoring the objective nature of our common production.

Is this the right answer to this riddle? I would say that it is a workable answer, and that the choice of one or the other point of view would depend on the nature of one's queries. Such instantaneous fusion, which corresponds to the Dionysian-syncretic—level of the relationship, seems to occur spontaneously, without any effort by the parties' discrete personalities. This implies a difference from the Klein–Bion model of projective identification, which postulates that the most primitive interpersonal relationship consists of an interchange of projected fragments of non-symbolised emotional experience, which are, thus, deposited in the other person, who acts as a container for them (Bion, 1962; Ferro, 1996, 1999, 2002). From this perspective, projective identification serves both defensive and communicative functions, but it is always spurred by painful emotions and fuelled by instinctual drives. I believe that such a view condenses two quite different processes: one is the natural flow of mental contents between individuals, at the level of syncretism, that Bleger (1971, 1974) called the "syncytial structure"; this would not be an active process, but, rather, a direct consequence of primeval fusion. The second is an active expulsion, which fulfils a defensive function, of painful experiences into a human container. This is, of course, an active and rather violent process that invades the privacy of the other person. Both processes are vectors for communication, but they lead to different results. While the second one is experienced as an intrusion and automatically breeds new defensive manoeuvres as a response, the first one is felt as an expression of one's own mental processes, in the form of countertransference occurrences and reveries. Much of Ogden's (1994a,b) work on the vagaries of his thoughts during sessions is better understood in this light.

On the other hand, Bion also suggested, in his early work on groups (1961), that human beings initially relate to each other in terms of what he calls "valency". This is "the capacity of the individual for instantaneous combination with other individuals in an established pattern of behaviour", which he called a "basic assumption" (p. 175). And he added,

> Although I use this word to describe phenomena that are visible as, or deductible from, psychological events, yet I wish also to use it to indicate *a readiness to combine on levels than can hardly be called mental at all but are characterized by behaviour in the human being that is more analogous to tropism in plants than to purposive behaviour* such as is implicit in a word like "assumption". (pp. 116–117, my italics)

This hardly psychological primitive level, in which mind and body, individual, group, and environment are indistinguishable, clearly corresponds to what I have been calling the Dionysian aspect of human existence. Bion calls it the "proto-mental system", defined as "one in which physical and psychological or mental are undifferentiated" (p. 102). It should be remembered that the author was writing at the time about small therapeutic groups; therefore, he constantly refers to group phenomena *vis-à-vis* the individual. None the less, his ideas on the subject are germane for our consideration of the analytic process, provided that we consider the analytic couple, as Ferenczi and Rank (1924) did, as a small group, or, perhaps, as Bion himself pointed out, as a subgroup that has isolated itself from the larger group, but which is still subject to the aegis of group phenomena.

Of course, there are differences in the kind of unconscious mental processes that are studied best in a bipersonal or in a multi-personal field (Tubert-Oklander & Hernández de Tubert, 2004; Hernández de Tubert & Tubert-Oklander, 2005), but the fact remains that what Bion (1948–1951) wrote then about groups seems to be perfectly applicable to the bipersonal psychoanalytic situation. Individual and group—that is, relational—phenomena are just two sides of the same coin:

> The individual cannot help being a member of a group even if his membership of it consists in behaving in such a way as to give reality to the idea that he does not belong to a group at all. In this respect the psycho-analytical situation is not "individual psychology" but "pair". *The individual is a group animal at war, not simply with the group, but with himself for being a group animal, and with those aspects of his personality that constitute his "groupishness".* (p. 131, my italics)

This last observation is the reason why transference interpretations are so difficult for the patient to hear and for the analyst to utter. Both of us are always trying to reaffirm our existence as individuals, and, therefore, naturally reject the very idea that perhaps we are being acted on by unconscious collective fantasies, rather than being the agents of our own existence.

Such view represents a severe challenge to our ordinary conscious conception of the world. Freud (1917a) described the narcissistic offences implied by three scientific revolutions: Copernicus's demonstration that Earth is not the centre of the universe, Darwin's contention that the human being is just another animal, and his own discovery that "the ego is not the master in his own house". Perhaps we should add to them a fourth such offence. It is not just the case that the ego—that is, the conscious subject—is not the master in his own house, but also that what we had taken to be our house was not ours to begin with. Our most private and intimate mind, our *sancta sanctorum*, is traversed and determined by a gossamer web of multiple relations and contexts, which stem from everything we had declared to be alien to our personal selves. As Mitchell (1993) points out, the very notion of the self is built upon a series of inclusions and exclusions.

The very same resistance seems to act, with increasing strength, when we try to extend such understanding to the effect of collective phenomena, such as groups, institutions, culture, and society-at-large, on the individual's experience and behaviour. In my own practice, I look for this groupishness in the way my patient and myself enact cultural and mythical relational patterns, which stem from the society to which both of us belong. One relevant example is the appearance of stereotyped gender roles and relational patterns (Hernández de

Tubert, 2006a). Of course, all of this is unconscious and requires extensive and painstaking analysis. There is an intense resistance by both parties—and by the whole psychoanalytic community—to acknowledging that we are somehow the puppets of a narrative that has no subject, since it stems from the collective. But all this belongs to our next topic, that of the interpretative process.

In any case, most analysts would agree that this objective aspect of the unconscious analytic relation shows an evolution during the course of the analytic treatment in the direction of a greater amplitude, depth, intensity, fluidity, and meaningfulness. The relational process evolves, from its initial separateness and stereotypy, towards an ever more intimate, fluid, and emotionally significant relationship between the parties, in which the other is conceived as a true partner and fellow, and holder of an interior life and subjectivity that should always be respected and taken into account. Thus, the original psychoanalytic asymmetry, which appeared to be absolute, is mollified by the mutual discovery that the other is much more than a patient or an analyst, that he or she is a human being after all. This, of course, is not a novel discovery for the analyst, who has been there many times before, but who has to rediscover it anew in every treatment. It might, however, be an absolutely revolutionary experience for the patient, who still has to find this out in the case of his parents, siblings, friends, spouse, children, and fellow citizens.

This major change in the way the relation is experienced by both analyst and analysand is manifested as a greater intimacy, amplitude, depth, and mobility of mutual feelings. This is an essential part of the mirroring that many of us feel is a major factor in the healing process (Pines, 1982, 1985). There is more on this in Chapter Twelve, on "The healing process".

The interpretative process

Interpretation has been, from the very beginning of psychoanalysis, one of its most distinctive features, a veritable *shibboleth* that tells us apart, as psychoanalysts, from the practitioners of other kinds of psychotherapy. Freud (1904a) used it as a landmark in his definition of the discipline he had created when he described it as "an art of interpretation which takes on the task of, as it were, extracting the pure metal of the repressed thoughts from the ore of the unintentional ideas" (p. 252).

This quotation shows what kind of theory of interpretation the author had in mind: for him, the text represented by the patient's discourse and behaviour had a *latent content* that lay hidden behind their apparent meaning, called its *manifest content*. The former was the valuable aspect of communication, the "pure metal" to be extracted from the coarse ore of the patient's actual expressions, which had been distorted and contaminated by his resistances. One possible consequence of this approach is that psychoanalytic technique be turned into something akin to cryptography—breaking a code—or police investigation—discovering the truth behind a pack of lies. (I actually remember one of my early teachers saying, "The patient is always dishonest."!)

However, this is not the only possible way of conceiving the nature of interpretation. Since the question of how to interpret a text has been with us ever since the beginnings of Greek philosophy, we might as well look for help in the various answers given by the science of hermeneutics.

Hermeneutics is the discipline that studies the theory and practice of the interpretation of texts. But the concept of "text", in its hermeneutical technical sense, is far from obvious, since it is not restricted to written documents, but has instead been extended to include discourse, dialogue (with Gadamer, 1960), intentional action (with Ricoeur, 1965), and every other form of expression, such as music, dancing, ritual, manners, customs, the plastic arts, and culture in general. Thus, we arrive at the contemporary definition of hermeneutics as "the theory of the rules that preside over an exegesis—that is, over the interpretation of a particular text, or of a group of signs that may be viewed as a text" (Ricoeur, 1965, p. 8).

Traditionally, there have been three forms of hermeneutics: *univocality*, *equivocality*, and *analogy* (Beuchot, 1997; Tubert-Oklander, 2009, 2013b). *Univocality*—from "univocal", which means "only one voice"—asserts that, for any given text, there is one, and only one, correct interpretation, which is considered to be "true", while all others are "false". Such a position, which in our time has been characteristic of the modern thought that determined the intellectual climate in which Freud became a scientist, gives us clarity and certainty, while paying the price of rigidity and dogmatism.

Equivocality—from "equivocal", meaning "equal voices"—holds that, for any given text, there are multiple, perhaps infinite, interpretations, and that all of them are equivalent, so that personal taste and convenience are the only possible criteria for choosing one among them. This position, which has become one of the tenets of postmodernism, is particularly sensitive to the effects of history, context, and perspective on any interpretative activity, thus allowing a more varied and nuanced understanding of the text, but it breeds ambiguity, relativity, and uncertainty, as well as an abandonment, in its extreme form, of any concept of truth.

The third form of interpretation is *analogy*, or *analogism*, which means an acceptance that there are more than one, albeit not infinite, possible interpretations for a text, but that they are not necessarily equivalent; some of them are better, others not so good, others still are poor, and some are outright bad. The criterion for choosing among them is to take into account not only the *meaning*, derived from the inner logic of the semiotic systems used by the author and the interpreter, but also the *references* of the text and its interpretations—that is, the non-textual reality that they are talking about. The result is a certain flexibility and recognition of the difference in points of view, but without relinquishing the search for truth, a relative, partial, and humble truth, it is true, but good enough to go on thinking and acting.

Analogical hermeneutics, as proposed by Mexican philosopher Mauricio Beuchot (1997; Tubert-Oklander, 2013b; Tubert-Oklander & Beuchot Puente, 2008), is a hermeneutical theory based on analogy; this makes it particularly useful for clarifying the nature, aims, and methods of psychoanalytical interpretation. In understanding and interpreting the patients' utterances and behaviour during the sessions and psychoanalytical theories and texts, we have the opportunity of considering the various perspectives and possible interpretations without either claiming that only one of them is right, which would be a univocal interpretation that disqualifies all other points of view that differ from one's own, or that all of them are equivalent, an equivocal interpretation, for which all points of view are equally valid, which makes any rational discussion meaningless. From the analogical point of view, there is a recognition of the existence of alternative interpretations and theories, but there would still be, however, the possibility of evaluating them in terms of their comparative ability to identify, clarify, and account for the problems and experiences that they are trying to understand and solve. The orthodox psychoanalytic view of interpretation has been that of a univocal conception of meaning, as suggested by the above-mentioned quotation from Freud.

Interpretation actually refers to two kinds of activity by the analyst: one of them is internal, a particular way of processing the information received from the patient, in order to establish its underlying meaning; the other one, external, corresponds to the means used in order to convey to the patient this new information about himself.

There might also be some translation issues when discussing interpretation in psychoanalysis. Laplanche and Pontalis (1967) point out that the German term *Deutung*, used by Freud, does not carry the same connotations as the English "interpretation". This is how they state it:

> A terminological point: "interpretation" does not correspond exactly to the German word *"Deutung"*. *The English term tends to bring to mind the subjective—perhaps even the forced or arbitrary—aspects of the attribution of a meaning to an event or statement.* "Deutung" *would seem to be closer to "explanation" or "clarification" and, in common usage, has fewer of the pejorative overtones that are at times carried by the English word.* . . . Freud writes that the *Deutung* of a dream consists in ascertaining its *Bedeutung* or meaning. (p. 228, my italics)

But does this mean that the contemporary views that stress the bipersonal and creative aspects of interpretation are nothing but a misunderstanding, based on a translation error? Certainly not. It is true that Freud emphasised, in his theoretical and epistemological discussions, the univocal and objective nature of *Deutung*. This was quite in line with the positivistic conception of science that he had received from his teachers, which represented a main feature of his ego ideal, but there was another side to it, which stemmed from his roots in German Romanticism, represented by Goethe and by the unavoidable ambiguity and equivocality of the psychoanalytic enquiry that he had created. This is an internal tension that can be found throughout Freud's lifetime work, between two seemingly contradictory ideals, which might have blinded him to some aspects of the full subversive impact of his creation and discoveries, which represented a major challenge to the theory of knowledge in which he had been reared. We have already discussed this dual attitude of Freud towards the discipline and method he had created, particularly in the section headed

"Impartiality–partiality" in Chapter Three. What is now relevant for our present discussion is that this dialectic tension between a univocal theory of interpretation, which emphasises its reference to a single state of affairs that constitutes its "true" meaning, and an equivocal one, which suggests a never-ending process of exploring the gossamer network of meaning that fades into an unfathomable horizon (Freud's "dream's navel"), can only lead us to an analogical conception of psychoanalytic interpretation.

But nowadays, many of us no longer conceive interpretation as an operation that the analyst carries out on the patient's "material" and later communicates to the latter as a piece of verbal information about his or her hidden mental processes. This revision goes much further than the mere admission that "both patient and analyst may contribute to it", since such formulation still assumes that interpretation is an objective account of the patient's mental processes, and that the latter's contribution to it would be restricted to a rational discussion of the adequacy of the analyst's "explanation" or "clarification". In our present intersubjective understanding of interpretation, this is conceived as a bipersonal process of creation of meaning, which can only emerge from a true dialogue, as Gadamer (1960) suggested in the case of hermeneutics (Orange, 2011).

The idea of "creating meaning" does not imply that this work is in any way arbitrary. On the contrary, the analyst's and the patient's creativity is fuelled by the momentum of the emotional experience that they are presently sharing, but it is restrained by the structure and potentialities of the language they use, the modes of imagination determined and allowed by the structure of mind, their own personal histories and experiences, the symbolic matrix of the culture they both belong to, the circumstantial context of the session, and the degree of adequacy of their communicative productions to the nature, intensity, tone, and feeling of the emotional experience they are both trying to articulate in terms of speech. This is akin to the poet's need, when trying to convey a certain emotional experience to other human beings, to submit to the requirements of language, the symbolic lore of culture, and literary form—for example, a sonnet—in order to construct her final product. But the result might or might not ring true to the reader. Poetic truth is not the same as common-sense truth or scientific truth. The latter are *truth by correspondence*, which is when a verbal expression matches a concrete state of affairs, while the former is an *expressive truth*, which is when a verbal communication fits, transmits, and is able to recreate a particular emotional experience. A poetic expression is true when it induces in the receiver a new emotional experience, which is analogous to the poet´s original one. The result is a refinement of their mutual perception and understanding, not only of the emotional experience they have shared, but also-one hopes—of some aspect of the universal experience of being human. This is the kind of truth that we seek in psychoanalysis.

When the patient speaks or uses some other means of expression, the aim is to make his emotional experience known to another human being—the analyst. The greatest obstacle to such communication is that our everyday language, that of the secondary process, is not meant as an instrument to speak about emotional experience, but only about concrete material events. It is most adequate for the purpose of saying such things as "Pass me the salt", "The cat is on the mat", "Jesus of Nazareth died at the age of thirty-three", "Mars has two small moons, Phobos and Deimos", "Every material body persists in its state of being at rest or in uniform rectilinear motion, unless it is compelled to change its state by a force acting on it", or "The patient was late for his Monday session". But it is pitifully inadequate to describe, convey, understand, or account for emotional experiences. In this, patients, analysts, and poets share a common predicament: that of finding a way to stretch the use of language to its very limits and beyond, in order that it may be able to speak the ineffable. This is what we call "poetic language" (Tubert-Oklander, 1994).

The main instrument for this expansion of the limits of language is the use of *metaphor*. This is the use of an analogy, which acts in terms of its *connotations*, or implications (what Bion (1962) called a "penumbra of associations"), rather than its *denotation*, which is its concrete reference to a non-linguistic fact (Tubert-Oklander, 2013a). The result is that metaphor does not convey information about a state of affairs, but induces in the receptor (reader or listener) an emotional state that is akin to the emotional experience that the emitter (speaker or writer) wanted to be shared and understood. For instance, in Hamlet's "To be or not to be" monologue, the complex use of metaphor gives us an intimate knowledge of the character's state of mind, which could never have been attained in terms of a conceptual description:

> To be, or not to be,—that is the question:—
> Whether 'tis nobler in the mind to suffer

The slings and arrows of outrageous fortune,
Or to take arms against a sea of troubles,
And by opposing end them?
(Shakespeare, *Hamlet*, Act III, Scene 1)

The patient is always facing, during the sessions, the same challenges that befuddle the poet, when trying to make the analyst know
something about his or her emotional experiences. Then, all of her
behaviour—verbal, paraverbal, or non-verbal—becomes a vast metaphor of the emotional experiences that she is trying to communicate.
This has an impact on the deepest layers of the analyst's being, thus
generating an emotional response. Now, the analyst is listening
intently, not only with his mind—understood as the split-off intellect
of the scientific attitude—but with his whole being, including
emotions and the body, and has developed the ability and the habit
of identifying such incarnate reactions, turning them into dream-
thoughts (fantasies), and finally verbalising them. He then makes
some behavioural response, which might be verbal (usually an interpretation), paraverbal (the rhythm and tone of his speech), or non-
verbal (a gesture, a movement, an action). This, in turn, induces an
emotional response in the patient and, if this new experience is somehow akin to the original emotional experience that the patient was trying to communicate, then he or she will know for sure that the analyst
has understood something. If that were not the case, the patient would
have to try again, until the analyst gets it, or until he loses all hope of
being understood. Fortunately, this does not happen very often.

The analyst is also painfully aware that her verbal formulations
when interpreting are only a very partial and inexact rendering of her
experience during the session and the intuition she has had of the
patient's inner experiences. So, only the latter's response to the interpretation might allow the analyst to evaluate its adequacy and expe-
diency (Freud, 1937d). In other words, the patient's immediate
response provides answers to two basic questions: (1) to what extent
has the analyst managed to make herself understood by the patient,
in what she was actually trying to say? and (2) if the patient has
reached a good enough understanding of the meaning of the interpretation, to what extent has he felt understood by his analyst? But the
patient does not only either understand or misunderstand what the
analyst had meant to say, but also frequently understands more than

the analyst had been consciously trying to say; in such cases, the patient's response acts as an interpretation for the analyst of a part of her own mental processes, of which she had not been conscious at the time of making the interpretation. This same process of mutual adjustment and increasing communication occurs in the case of the paraverbal and non-verbal aspects of the analytic dialogue.

The result of this pendular movement is the development of a new language or dialect, which is peculiar to this particular analytic couple. The whole process follows a spiral course, which expands and advances with each new turn of the dialogue. The use of the spiral as a metaphor of mental development has a long history, starting with Hegel. Pichon-Rivière (1971) and Baranger (1979) used it to depict the evolution of the analytic dialogue, which, just like a spiral, has a triple motion: (a) a *circular motion*, by going over and over again back to the same themes; (b) a *forward motion*, the equivalent of the lead of the thread in a screw, by which each turn determines an advancing linear movement, so that it never comes back to the same place as before, but always moves a little bit forward, and (c) a *widening motion*, so that each turn determines a wider circle, thus turning the spiral into a cone. Hence, Pichon-Rivière conceived analytic work—in both the bipersonal and the group settings—as an ever-widening spiral of free communication through dialogue. This is obviously a very powerful image that lends itself to describe the various processes implied in analytic work.

However, the point I wish to underscore here is that this spiral process, albeit being initiated and fostered by the analyst by means of the setting, the analytic attitude, and his interpretations, has an evolution and a momentum of its own, which is quite independent from the conscious intentions and contributions of both parties. The analyst should always keep a sense of direction, in order to evaluate whether the process is moving forward as intended, but the fact is that he cannot control its development, but only observe it and comment it with the patient, in order that they may gain some understanding of it together. The evolution of the interpretative process does not depend on what happens during a particular session or on any discrete act of interpretation, but, rather, on the analyst keeping an interpretative attitude towards everything that happens and inviting the patient to do the same, through their collaborative analytic dialogue.

When everything goes as it should, the interpretative process evolves from a purely referential language, which centres on conventional everyday reality, towards a growing and ever richer and plural verbalisation of the experience of internal and external reality, in which there are no excluded or forbidden themes, and which recognises and respects the similarities and differences between the two parties. This change in the use of language occurs in both the patient and the analyst, the former being now able to provide a more deeply moving and nuanced account of her emotional experiences, while the latter finds himself talking much more freely and communicating interpretations that ring alive and true, instead of the routine translations of the patient's utterances to the language of the analyst's theories, with which psychoanalytic treatments usually begin. So, both parties have become freer and deeper in their ability to speak to each other, and their dialogue has acquired a much more vital, creative, joyful, and veracious quality.

Therefore, it is not a question of the analyst having to reveal to the patient the true previously unknown content of his expressions, but of both developing together a mutual capacity for using their dialogue in order to speak about, share, and think through the kind of emotional experiences that they have to deal with. Whatever they find along the way is usually novel and surprising for both, which gives an inkling of the inexhaustible well of human experience and meaning—Freud's (1900a) "dream navel".

This conception of the interpretative process may be further clarified by comparison with the experience of group analysis. Foulkes (1948, 1964, 1990) conceived the group analytic dialogue as a free-floating conversation, the equivalent of free association in psychoanalysis, which determines a process of *translation*, in which verbal expressions of emotional experiences become ever more articulate, leaving behind the more primitive forms of expression, such as symptoms, acting-out, or psychosomatic disturbances. The analyst is in a liminal position, both within and without the group; within, because, being a member of the group, she is always a part of what is happening in the dynamic matrix of communication, and without, because she strives to keep an inquisitive stance *vis-à-vis* what is happening to all of them together, including herself in it. The analyst's role is not that of a leader, but of a *conductor*, just like the conductor of an orchestra, who does not play an instrument, but creates the conditions for the musicians to play theirs and to do it together, in a creative and truthful way. It not her job to know or say what has been left unsaid, but to help the group members to find it out by themselves through dialogue.

If this model is applied to the bipersonal psychoanalytic situation, we have a two-person group, whose dialogue is mainly unconsciously determined, but in which one of the members—the analyst—has the ability to observe himself, the patient, and their mutual relationship, just as it is occurring, and to invite the other to do the same. The basic feature of the analytic attitude is *curiosity*, not the scoptophilic curiosity of nosiness and gossip, but the sincere wish to know and understand of love, philosophy, and science. The analyst strives to keep his or her curiosity alive, instead of merely reacting to whatever is happening in the analytic situation, and interpretation is an invitation for the patient to do the same. The basic analytic question is, at least from a relational point of view, "What is happening to us right now?"

Hence, the interpretative process is a way of making conscious the unconscious background of the session—albeit in terms of a much wider conception of the unconscious that Freud's idea of "the repressed"—by means of an enquiring and reflective dialogue, and not of interpretations, conceived as a merely technical intervention by the analyst.

The interactive process

This is a particularly difficult subject, since the concept of "interaction" in the analytic process is a highly controversial one. Throughout the history of psychoanalysis, there has been an open conflict between the advocates of "active technique" and those who demanded an exclusively verbal communication in analysis. This was one of the main reasons for questioning whether child analysis was really a form of psychoanalysis, since, in the treatment of children, action is the name of the game. Nowadays, no one would deny that child analysis is a valid form of psychoanalysis, and some, like Meltzer (1967), would even suggest that it is its purest form, since in adult analysis we are always trying to deal with the child within the patient. There is still, however, a discussion about whether the analyst should actively participate in the child's play or remain as a passive observer, who intervenes only with interpretations.

Psychoanalytic technique has demanded, from its very beginning, that action must be suspended by both parties, in order to foster the symbolisation process and to prevent the acting out of instinctual impulses. In Freud's (1900a) topographic model, the obstruction of the motor pole of the psychic apparatus determined a topographic regression towards the perceptual pole; this was supposed to force the reconversion of verbal thoughts into their original imaginary form, thus originating regressive phenomena such as dreams and transference. The reclining position imposed on the patient would, thus, favour the emergence of fantasy, which would be then verbally interpreted by the analyst. The fact that the latter was subject to a behavioural restriction that demanded that he should intervene only with words compounded the analytic device.

However, there were clearly diverse clinical situations that required that the analyst take a more active stance *vis-à-vis* some behavioural resistance by the patient, the most obvious one being the need to restrict some forms of destructive acting out. But in 1918, as we have seen in Chapter Three, there were two papers, by Freud (1919a) and Ferenczi (1919), that introduced the possibility of using an "active technique" in order to neutralise certain unshakable resistances that took the form of concrete behaviours of the patient which implied a magical omnipotent control and/or a disguised instinctual gratification. The analyst's technical response would be to impose on the patient a proscription against continuing with this conduct. Ferenczi, who carried out a thorough research on the use of this technique, finally abandoned it, because he felt it to be authoritarian, perhaps as a remnant of the traditional medical emphasis on the physician's authority, and replaced his positive and negative injunctions, which had been intended to increase the inner tension in the patient, with a new flexibility (1928b) that initiated his later studies on the therapeutic regression. In these (1929, 1930, 1931, 1933) he posited the thesis, later endorsed by Balint (1932, 1952, 1968), Fairbairn (1958), and Winnicott (1955, 1956), that the structural imprints and consequences of early traumata are beyond the reach of any symbolic approach, in a quasi-organic state, and can only be contacted and modified by concrete behavioural responses, given during a regression to infantile dependence—what Winnicott called "management". This will be further discussed in Chapter Twelve, on the "The healing process".

Of course, these theoretical and technical proposals generated much controversy and opposition, and still do. One staunch opponent of this way of understanding the analytic process is Etchegoyen (1986) in his widely acclaimed textbook, *Fundamentals of Psychoanalytic Technique*, which attempts to synthesise an ecumenical integration of the various schools and technical approaches that are considered to be "mainstream psychoanalysis". Another enthusiastic critic of any active or interactive conception of psychoanalysis is André Green, as we shall see below. But the fact remains that a large number of analysts from various schools of analytic thinking and practice are sympathetic to such non-standard views.

The main objection to the theory and practice of psychoanalytic action is that "There is no place in an analytic session for acts, either by the analysand or by the analyst" (Green, 1993, p. 1135). But such an argument reflects a rather simplistic view of the analytic encounter. It is true that the patient is under the injunction (at least in the traditional conception of the setting) to remain in a recumbent position on the couch and abstain from any action, other than speech. It is also true that the analyst has learnt to restrict his automatic or impulsive reactions to the patient's expressions and maintain a professional demeanour that strives to avoid any spontaneous expression of emotion and keep a neutral attitude of non-committed interest. But we cannot ignore that the major part of the human mind is unconscious, and that this is as true for the analyst as for the patient. We know very well that, as the patient speaks and, hopefully, freely associates, he is also latently expressing all sorts of unconscious meanings, and that a large part of them go beyond mere information to include things that are being unconsciously done to the analyst. But the very same is true for the analyst; even when she is conveying a well-thought interpretation, there is no way to know beforehand what kind of unconscious contents are being expressed behind this professional intervention and what unconscious intentions are being acted on the patient. These are sometimes partially identified after the fact, mainly through the analysis of the patient's response to interpretations, which, more often than not, is a covert (and sometimes overt) criticism, commentary, amplification, or correction of them. In this, as Bion (1985) said in his *Italian Seminars*, the patient is our best colleague, teacher, and supervisor:

We could say that there is one collaborator we have in analysis on whom we can rely, because he behaves as if he really had a mind and because he thought that somebody not himself could help. In short, the most important assistance that a psychoanalyst is ever likely to get is not from his analyst, or supervisor, or teacher, or the books that he can read, but from his patient. The patient—and only the patient— knows what it feels like to be him or her. The patient is the only person who knows what it feels like to have ideas such as that particular man or woman has. *That is why it is so important that we should be able to hear, see, smell, even feel what information the patient is trying to convey.* He is the only one who knows the facts; therefore, those facts are going to be the main source of any interpretation, any observation, which we are likely to be able to make. . . . It appears to me that *the evidence which is available to my senses directly is worth incomparably more than the evidence which can be brought to me through "hearsay".* (pp. 3–4, my italics)

However, "available to [the analyst's] senses" includes everything that he or she is "able to hear, see, smell, even feel"; it includes the living feeling of being related to and acted upon by another human being who is there in the room, as well as that of perceiving, feeling, thinking, talking to, and acting upon that other person—in other words, the full experience of interaction, both conscious and unconscious.

In any relation between two or more human beings who are living, awake, and aware of each other's presence, there is a constant flow of mutual communication, at both the conscious and the unconscious levels. This is what Freud (1912e) described as an unconscious communication between the two parties. To his description, which emphasised the use of the analyst's unconscious as a receiver for the emissions of the patient's, we should add, with the benefit of the hindsight offered by one hundred years of additional psychoanalytic practice, two other features: (a) that the communication is necessarily bilateral—that is, that the patient's unconscious is also a receiver for the emissions of the analyst's—and (b) that this unconscious communication includes not only information about the emitter's ideas, fantasies, wishes, and beliefs, but also a set of actions aimed at influencing his or her partner.

This is basic: the major part of human communication is unconscious; therefore, by definition, it is unknown and uncontrollable by the subject and always includes an element of action. To communicate something, verbally or otherwise, always implies acting upon the receiver. As early as 1921, Ferenczi had remarked that every interpretation is a form of action and influence on the patient, but so are the patient's associations and comments on or replies to the analyst's interventions (or non-interventions). The Argentine psychoanalyst Álvarez de Toledo (1996) wrote in 1994 a landmark paper in which she enquired as to the unconscious meanings of speech and words during analysis, in the cases of associating and interpreting, which are always relational actions. Her lead was followed by several of her colleagues at the Argentine Psychoanalytic Association: Racker (1958a), who studied the transference implications of the analysand's relation with the analyst's interpretation; de Racker (1961), who described the effect of the *form* of the interpretation, quite apart from its *content*; Liberman (1976a,b), and showed how the effectiveness of a psychoanalytic interpretation depends on the stylistic complementarity between the patient's material—verbal or otherwise—and the analyst's interpretation, which should be formulated in terms of the elements of communication that are lacking in the patient's mental processes and the consequent semiotic disturbance. Obviously, there is much more to psychoanalytic communication than the mere content of verbal expressions, whether associations or interpretations.

Communication theorists (Bateson, 1972; Watzlawick, Jackson, & Beavin, 1967) have identified two basic axioms of human communication. First, that *it is impossible not to communicate*, because every behaviour communicates something; even such apparently passive behaviours as silence or lack of response send a message and have an effect on other human beings. Second, that *every communicative act has two discrete levels*: it is a *report* and a *command*, at one and the same time, as we have seen in Chapter Four. This is because language, both verbal and non-verbal, has a *cognitive or referential aspect*, which gives information about some state of affairs, and a *conative or pragmatic aspect*, as an action directed to the other, in order to determine some kind of relation that is being wished by the emitter. So, whenever we say that "So-and-so is the case", we are simultaneously enquiring "Will you be my . . . (parent, child, lover, teacher, student, rival, friend, enemy, breast, toilet, and so on)?" Of course, being psychoanalysts, we are always interested in the relational quality of the request: is it an authoritarian demand, a humble plea, a seduction, an allurement, an extortion, a threat, an enticement, an attempt to convince, or some other form of enticement? Besides, we would add a third dimension to the cognitive or referential and conative or pragmatic aspects: that of the *affective aspect* of communication, which invites an emotional resonance in the other human being, this being the basis of the relational process, as we have already seen.

Now, if we accept the proposition that analyst and patient are influencing each other all the time, by means of conscious and unconscious action, then it is mandatory that these interaction processes be duly taken into account and analysed in the analytic dialogue. This implies observing and enquiring about how the presence, demeanour, and behaviour of the other act as a constraint, both positive and negative, on both parties' feeling, thinking, and acting. But this process goes far beyond the mere interaction between two discrete agents, since it acquires a direction, a goal, a meaning, and a momentum of its own, just as we have seen in the cases of the emotional and cognitive bipersonal processes. It also goes beyond the boundaries of the pair and the time and circumstances of their concrete meetings, extending in space and time, including all sorts of group, institutional, social, political, and cultural factors, as well as the past history and future expectations of each of the parties and the groups, institutions, and communities to which they belong. Such transpersonal processes go through the individuals, determining them and leaving their mark in the deepest layer of the unconscious, but they are also reframed and worked through during their passage, and then turned into actions that contribute to ratify or redirect the process. And most of this goes on unconsciously.

Now, the unconscious part of the interactive process is, by definition, not directly accessible to observation, so that it has to be inferred, enquired into, and interpreted. Hence, we should start by studying the more conscious aspects of the analytic interaction, and then see if what we have learnt from them aids us to understand the hidden part of it.

The first thing that comes to our attention is that interaction becomes manifest in the negotiation of differences and conflicts between the parties. Whenever two or more people get together in a certain context, there are bound to be some agreements and disagreements about how they conceive the nature, aims, and procedures of their mutual relationship. There is also frequently a conflict of interests between them. Such differences have to be dealt with, by struggle, imposition, submission, indifference, or negotiation. Indeed, each psychoanalytic treatment starts with such transactions, during the interview and contract stage. Etchegoyen (1986, pp. 65–68) states that there are three kinds of contract: an *authoritarian* one, which only takes into account the analyst's needs and conveniences, a *demagogic* contract, which seeks to please and appease the patient by letting him or her determine all the conditions for the treatment, and a *democratic* contract, which is rational, task-orientated, and open to negotiation. Obviously, the author favours the third one. But this choice of one of these three forms is not only a question of rationality and fairness, but also an essential element of the analytic attitude and process, since it determines what sort of relationship is going to ensue and what model of argumentation and transaction will be offered for the patient to internalise.

But the need to negotiate conflicts and differences is not restricted to the norms of the explicit contract, but also to the values and procedures that constitute the implicit part of the setting. All these are usually the background for the analytic process, which becomes the figure in our enquiry, but they suddenly come to the fore when the agreements, whether implicit or explicit, are broken, or when an underlying difference that has previously gone unnoticed turns into an open disagreement. This breeds a need for a new negotiation of the disagreement, in order to heal the fracture in the working relationship. Such conflicts also occur, obviously, as a consequence of transference–countertransference motions, which are unconscious and, hence, have to be identified and interpreted, before they can be openly negotiated, as an essential part of their working through.

There are also unconscious negotiations of differences and conflicts, which generate more or less stable accommodations between the parties. These have to be sought, interpreted, and discussed, for two reasons. First, because the unconscious agreement that has been arrived at might have a defensive function, as an unconscious collusion between them, such as that which the Barangers (2008) call a "bastion". Second, because even healthy and progressive adaptations should be duly examined and talked through, in order to attain a conscious understanding of the ways in which we develop sound and mutually satisfying relationships, this being an essential part of the process of learning from experience.

Negotiation is not restricted to some specific moments, but can be conceived as an ongoing process that constitutes one of the essential elements of psychoanalytic treatment. Pizer (1992) deems that "the negotiation of paradox may be considered as an essential vehicle of the therapeutic action of psychoanalysis" (p. 215). In his use of the concept of "paradox", he follows Winnicott's (1971) approach. A paradox is something quite different from a contradiction or a conflict; in logic, it is a statement that is true if, and only if, it is false, or that is only true if its contrary is also true. Human relationships are always paradoxical, since every feeling implies and includes its contrary. This is a consequence of the non-unitary nature of mind, which is always divided, both vertically (i.e., operating in diverse levels at the same time) and horizontally (i.e., presenting simultaneously opposite feelings and relations). A logical contradiction may only be solved by establishing which of the opposite statements is true, the other necessarily being false; a conflict is solved by modifying the situation or its definition, so that the conflict no longer exists; paradox, on the contrary, is never solved, but transacted so that one finds a way to live with it. This is the dialectical operation that accepts the coexistence of opposites and the maintenance of the tension between them as the very basis of life.

Consequently, the analytic situation is necessarily paradoxical, as a result of the many-layered, multi-faceted, and hypercomplex nature of the relationship. This paradox needs to be accepted, faced, talked about, and negotiated, without ever trying to solve it by turning it into a straightforward affair. The opposites whose coexistence has to be accepted and maintained in a state of creative tension are many: inner–outer, subjective–objective, individual–group, withdrawal–relationship, selfishness–altruism, competitiveness–cooperation, ruthlessness–concern, independence–dependence, love–hate, knowledge–ignorance, instinct–environment, conscious–unconscious, present–past, repetition–novelty, among others. This overlapping coexistence and tension are the very stuff of which Winnicott's (1971) "third area" of transitional space is made. This is lucidly expressed by Pizer (1992), in the following terms:

> In analysis, the framework for the transitional area of illusion is maintained through a continuing intersubjective process of negotiation, by which analyst and patient seek to straddle the paradoxes of their

many-layered relationship. This ongoing process of negotiation carries both the potential for structure building and the delicate hope for a reworking of repetitions in the transference–countertransference construction. Exploration of these issues includes consideration of the analyst's and patient's coauthorship of metaphorical communications and a definition of the analyst's neutrality in terms of his responsibility to preserve the area of illusion for ongoing negotiation. (p. 215)

This negotiation occurs at the intrapersonal, interpersonal, and transpersonal levels. (I prefer not to use the term "intrapsychic" for the intrapersonal, because all these three levels are mental processes, which would deserve to be called "intrapsychic".) At the intrapersonal level, negotiation has been with us since the very beginning of psychoanalysis, as the transactions between unconscious instinctual wishes and moral censorship, in order to arrive at the end product of the dream work, is a clear instance of negotiation (Freud, 1900a). But this concept becomes central in the theory of psychoanalysis with the publication of *The Ego and the Id*, in which the main function of the ego is defined as the ability to negotiate between id wishes, superego values and injunctions, and reality (Freud, 1923b).

Negotiation becomes particularly visible when we come to the interpersonal level, in which conflicting interests, values, points of view, and procedures must be transacted, as described by Pizer (1992):

Negotiation is intrapsychic, interpersonal, and intersubjective, and it is vital to our biological existence. Negotiation is intrapsychic in the sense that we must each mediate within ourselves the containment and expression of drive and affect, as well as the tension in living between engagement in the fresh potentials of the present moment versus enmeshment in the conservative grip of repetition of our past experience; in this sense, negotiation is an ego function necessary for the internal management of paradoxical experience. Negotiation is interpersonal in the sense that we are always arranging with one another matters of desire, safety, anxiety, power, convenience, fairness, and so on. Negotiation is intersubjective in the sense that we constantly influence one another, consciously and unconsciously, from infancy onward in a myriad of ways, from minute adjustments to gross adaptations. (pp. 216–217)

Negotiation at the transpersonal level is less obvious in the bipersonal setting, since it corresponds to the inter-group, institutional, and social spaces, although it might be more readily enquired into in group analysis, especially in large groups (de Maré, Piper, & Thompson, 1991; Hopper, 2003a,b; Kreeger, 1975; Schneider & Weinberg, 2003). None the less, it may be explored interpretatively, if one looks for it, since we are all—including both analysand and analyst—traversed by these transpersonal processes, just as X-rays go through our physical bodies, and these processes organise and leave their marks on the unconscious, both personal and interpersonal. So, they are necessarily a part of the analytic field and process, and consequently must be analysed.

The experience of being a part of such an effort of enquiry and negotiation, unprecedented in the patient's life, brings about a true revolution in the organisation of his mental processes, relationships, and actions, and gives him a truly novel perspective of life in general. Alexander and French (1946) introduced the term *corrective emotional experience* to refer to the mutative effect of the analytic experience. But this concept, which is essentially a reframing of Ferenczi's (1929) idea of permitting the patient "properly speaking for the first time, to enjoy the irresponsibility of childhood, which is equivalent to the introduction of *positive* life impulses and motives for his subsequent existence" (p. 106), is only partial, in as much as it only takes into account the affective component of the process. The healing analytic experience comprises, as we shall see in Chapter Twelve, the three dimensions of affectivity, cognition, and conation. Hence, we have come back to the golden braid of emotion, thought, and action, with which we started this chapter, as a way to better understand the nature and dimensions of the analytic process.

CHAPTER NINE

Interpretation, insight, and working through

To interpret or not to interpret?

Psychoanalysis was defined by Freud (1904a), as we have already seen, as "an art of interpretation" (p. 252), since it was set on the task of "making the unconscious conscious" or, as Pichon-Rivière (1971) used to say, "making explicit the implicit". Of course, Freud's (1915d) original conception of the unconscious as identical with the repressed seemed to restrict its contents to the set of antisocial or immoral impulses and wishes, and to the most painful or unpleasant memories that had been mercifully forgotten. Any other mental contents of which the subject was not aware really belonged to the pre-conscious, and not to the dynamic unconscious (Freud, 1912g, 1915e). But with his later revision—in *The Ego and the Id* (Freud, 1923b)—of his theory of the structure of the mind, it became obvious that the unconscious was much wider than the repressed, and that it included not only mental *contents*, but also mental *structures, functions,* and *processes*. Hence, not only the id, conceived as a boiling cauldron of primitive impulses and wishes, but also large parts of the ego and the superego could now be regarded as belonging to the unconscious. So now all kinds of thoughts, beliefs, feelings, arguments, values,

decisions, strategies, and assumptions could be a part of the unconscious mental processes and contents, and, consequently, become a
valid object for interpretation.

For instance, every human being has what, in philosophic
parlance, is known as a *Weltanschauung*, which is usually translated as
"conception of the world". This is a set of assumptions, beliefs, values,
conviction, habits, and procedures that act as prejudices (in the sense
of prejudgements, i.e., judgements made without sufficient previous
information) in all our dealings with reality. Such a conception of the
world is a real psychological structure for the individual, which is
mainly unconscious and derived from a similar set of values that rules
social life, communication, perception, thought, and action, in the
community in which the subject has been born and reared. The fact
that this view of the world is incorporated through the very first identifications with the adult care-givers and the intimate family group
makes it almost impossible for it to become conscious as such, since
these convictions are not perceived as assumptions at all, but only as
"the way things are" (Hernández de Tubert, 2004; Tubert-Oklander &
Hernández de Tubert, 2004, pp. 77–82).

But this conception of the world is not only unconscious on account
of cognitive limitations (one cannot perceive something that is always
there and has always been there, because there is no possible point of
comparison without it), but also for dynamic reasons. A significant
part of the *Weltanschauung* is actually repressed, because society
needs to keep out of the awareness of its members some major contradictions between the principles and values that are openly declared,
and what is actually happening and being done to make it function.
This is usually referred to, in social and political science, as "ideology".
The same is valid for organised groups, such as institutions and
families, in which there are regularly flagrant incongruities between
what is being said and what is actually done, reinforced by a tacit
prohibition of acknowledging and even perceiving them. A child
readily incorporates these mandates and learns not to know what he
is not supposed to know and not to feel what he is not supposed to
feel (Bowlby, 1985). The result is that, as Freud discovered, the individual ends up by showing a similar split between his ideal self-image
and what he actually is and does; but not only that: there is a similar
blindness to many disappointing, distasteful, or even destructive
aspects of the care-givers, in the case of the child, or of institutions and

society, in that of adults. So, there is an intentional blindness towards quite a few aspects of the inner experience of oneself and the outer experience of others, society, and the world.

This means that repression does not only bar from awareness any knowledge of forbidden libidinal or aggressive wishes and impulses, or the memories of traumatic, shameful, or guilty experiences, but also the knowledge of some aspects of self, others, and collective entities that evoke unpleasant feelings or forebodings. For instance, a person might not want to know that he harbours racist, sexist, or class-based prejudices; that someone he loves and trusts is being dishonest; that some institution he relies on is marred by corruption or ineptitude, or that his welfare is based upon the exploitation of other human beings. These instances of actively ignoring a non-instinctual aspect of the self or a part of external reality are usually referred to as "denial" or "disavowal", rather than "repression", but the dynamic result is the same as in repression: a segment of personal experience is treated as non-existent and banished from perception, memory, and thought. It is the task of analysis to reinstate it as a part of the patient's world of experience, and this requires putting it into words so that it may be shared by the analytic pair.

Now, this brings to us an essential question: who is to utter these words? Is it the analyst's job to speak whatever she has surmised about what the patient has left unspoken—that is, to interpret it? Or would it be better to wait patiently until the patient is able to word it himself? The answers we give to these questions determine two radically different approaches to psychoanalytic practice. On the one hand, many analysts feel that a true analytic enquiry of the patient's mind demands an essentially passive attitude on the part of the analyst, in order to avoid contaminating the patient's material with the analyst's theories. Besides, it is argued that only when the new idea emerges freely and unexpectedly from the patient's insides will it carry real conviction for him. This point of view is usually held by those psychoanalysts that identify themselves as "truly Freudian".

Indeed, there is some basis for the belief that this was Freud's approach to the clinic. For instance, in "Analysis terminable and interminable" (Freud, 1937c), he calls into question the assumption "that we have the power, for purposes of prophylaxis, to stir up a pathogenic conflict . . . which is not betraying itself at the time by any indications, and that it is wise to do so" (p. 223). This stems from the previous discussion of a former analysand's—whom we now know to be Ferenczi—reproach that he had failed to interpret the negative transference. The account of this episode, phrased in the third person in order to preserve the anonymity of the patient (and perhaps also of the analyst) is as follows:

> Many years [after the end of the analysis] . . . the man who had been analysed became antagonistic to the analyst and reproached him for having failed to give him a complete analysis. The analyst, he said, ought to have known and to have taken into account the fact that a transference-relation can never be purely positive; he should have given his attention to the possibilities of a negative transference. *The analyst defended himself by saying that, at the time of the analysis, there was no sign of a negative transference. But even if he had failed to observe some very faint signs of it – which was not altogether ruled out, considering the limited horizon of analysis in those early days – it was still doubtful, he thought, whether he would have had the power to activate a topic (or, as we say, a "complex") by merely pointing it out, so long as it was not currently active in the patient himself at the time.* To activate it would certainly have required some unfriendly piece of behaviour in reality on the analyst's part. Furthermore, he added, not every good relation between an analyst and his subject during and after analysis was to be regarded as a transference; there were also friendly relations which were based on reality and which proved to be viable. (pp. 221–222, my italics)

It is obvious in this passage that Freud was reaffirming his previous recommendation of not interpreting prematurely, since

> Even in the later stages of analysis one must be careful not to give a patient the solution of a symptom or the translation of a wish until he is already so close to it that he has only one short step more to make in order to get hold of the explanation for himself. (Freud, 1913c, p. 140)

This implies that, for him, interpretation only meant putting into words what was already obvious in the patient's expressions, thus rejecting the idea, which has become widespread in the later development of psychoanalysis, that the analyst should look for the more subtle traces of the transference and interpret, or otherwise manage it, from the very beginning of the treatment, instead of waiting for the transference to gain momentum and become obvious.

There is, however, ample evidence that Freud was anything but passive in his clinical work. He commented, interpreted, told jokes, quoted literature, and made elaborate explanatory constructions in his attempt to account for the patient's neurosis, and counted on the latter's responses in order to check the accuracy of his constructions. Hence, he clearly conceived the psychoanalytic treatment as a dialogue.

How, then, did that peculiar phenomenon known as the "orthodox technique" come into being? In his letter to Ferenczi of 4 January 1928 (Falzeder & Brabant, 2000, pp. 331–332), Freud himself suggested an answer, in the following terms:

> My recommendations on technique which I gave back then were essentially negative. *I considered the most important thing to emphasize what one should not do, to demonstrate the temptations that work against analysis. Almost everything that is positive that one should do I left to "tact," which has been introduced by you. But what I achieved in so doing was that the obedient ones didn't take notice of the elasticity of these dissuasions and subjected themselves to them as if they were taboos.* That had to be revised at some time, without, of course, revoking the obligations. (p. 332, my italics)

Consequently, he obviously thought that positive technical measures should be based upon the analyst's criterion and sensitivity, rather than on the application of general rules. But the fact remains that there is such thing as a conception of what is considered to be "Freudian psychoanalysis" in terms of the patient carrying out a virtual monologue *vis-à-vis* an essentially silent and passive analyst.

At the other pole of the continuum of contemporary conceptions of technique, the Kleinian approach to the clinic emphasises the mutative role of interpretation, particularly of transference interpretations, as the main, or perhaps the only, instrument for change. In this, they follow the ideas of Strachey (1934), for whom the sort of intervention he calls "mutative interpretation" is "the ultimate operative factor in the therapeutic action of psycho-analysis" (p. 159) and, hence, "the ultimate instrument of psycho-analytic therapy" (p. 142). Such an interpretation should fulfil two requisites, which are its essential properties: (1) it should be *emotionally immediate*, which means that it should be directed to what Klein (1932, p. 51) called the "point of urgency"—that is, "the id-impulse which is actually in a state of cathexis" (Strachey, 1934, p. 149) and the anxiety it arouses—and (2) it "must be 'specific': that is to say, detailed and concrete" (p. 151). Such requirements can only be met by transference interpretations.

For Klein (1932) "not only a timely interpretation but a deep-going one is essential" (p. 52). Hence, the Kleinian technical approach requires that the analyst intervene with a transference interpretation, which should also be deep—that is, connected to its genetic sources in early infantile experiences—*as soon as this becomes obvious to the analyst*. As Greenson—who made a thorough study of Kleinian technique, which included taking supervisions with renowned Kleinian analysts, even though he had been trained in the ego-psychological tradition— puts it, "it appears that the Kleinians believe they can make deeply unconscious material instantly conscious, and simultaneously render it anxiety free, comprehensible and utilizable by the patient" (1974, p. 41). This is in sharp contrast with the Freudian practice of starting from the mental surface and then gradually working down to the deeper levels. Greenson considers this to be a consequence of the different theories of anxiety held by these two schools. It is worthwhile to read his discussion with Rosenfeld (1974; Greenson, 1975), who acted as the advocate for the Kleinian point of view.

Consequently, the Kleinian analyst is working under very strict demands, since he is supposed to fathom, minute by minute of each session, the unconscious phantasy and the corresponding anxiety that are active in the patient at that very moment, and interpret it before it is replaced by a new phantasy. I am using the Kleinian non-standard spelling "phantasy", in order to refer to their conception of imaginary primary contents of the unconscious, which represent the psychic dimension of instinctual drives (Isaacs, 1948).

Since unconscious phantasy is assumed to be in a constant state of flux and interpretation is required to be highly specific, in the sense of describing every concrete detail of the presently active phantasy, *just as it is*, without "introducing any similes, metaphors, or quotations to illustrate [the] point" (Klein, 1961, p. 18), it follows that the Kleinian analyst is bound to make many interpretations in the course of each session, and that they will tend to be lengthy, in order to capture the minutiae of the ever-flowing unconscious phantasy. Any other thing would be the equivalent of what Glover (1955) called an "inexact interpretation"—that is, an interpretation that replaces the former defensive displacement of repressed contents by another, perhaps less displaced, formulation, but which does not give its ultimate content its proper name. Of course, this implies the assumption that there actually is such thing as an "exact", "accurate", or "true" interpretation, which is far from being a generally accepted assertion, as we shall see when discussing the psychoanalytic concept of truth.

Obviously, the existence of two so very different conceptions of the interpretative technique poses a particular dilemma for the analyst: to interpret or not to interpret? This is not a minor matter, since it determines two distinct ways of conducting a psychoanalysis: one that relies on the patient's conscious co-operation and the use of his or her mental resources to advance the treatment, and another in which everything depends on the analyst's knowledge, skills, and *savoir-faire*. The result is that the patient obtains two quite different experiences of the treatment, its ambience, the analyst, him- or herself, and their mutual relationship. But what both approaches seem to share is the unquestioned belief in the existence of a single hidden "truth" that is there, waiting to be discovered, irrespective of whether the analyst feels that it is his or her job to unearth it, or that it is the patient who has to find the way to it, with the analyst's help.

Fortunately, this is not the only possible way to conceive our work. There is another possibility, one that seeks to strike a balance between creation and discovery in the interpretative process, as we shall now see.

Insight: discovery or creation?

We have already seen, when discussing the interpretative process, that there are different types of hermeneutics: there is a *univocal* conception of meaning, such as that of modernity, an *equivocal* conception, which is characteristic of our postmodern era, and an *analogical* way of approaching it. Each of them has its own view of interpretation. We have already seen that both the Kleinian and the orthodox Freudian theories of technique share a univocal conception of interpretation, meaning, and truth. Postmodern versions of psychoanalysis, such as Lacan's (1966) pose an equivocal hermeneutics. Mannoni (1969) has shown how the latter split the concept of the *sign* introduced by de Saussure (1916) in such a way that it lost its pre-established meaning and became an empty *signifier* that derived its ever-fluctuating meaning from its linguistic context. Univocal theories of meaning find a sign's meaning in its *reference*—that is, the non-semiotic reality that signs and texts are referring to. In Lacan's equivocal theory, language does not refer to anything but itself, and, hence, meaning emerges from the ever-changing drift of discourse, so that symbols lose any fixed meaning and can be used to represent anything, depending on the context and their position in the linguistic chain. As the unconscious is structured like a language, its contents are nothing but a suppressed discourse. Whereas the patient of a univocally-minded analyst has to discover the truth—either the historical truth of the origins of his neurosis or the inner truth of acknowledging one's impulses and fantasies—the patient of the linguistically equivocal analyst is expected to set free the unconscious discourse, thus encountering his own voice, which is the originator of meaning.

In Freud's writings there is an ambivalent tension between both epistemological and hermeneutical conceptions. On the one hand, the free association method opens the way for a polysemic and equivocal conception of meaning, leading to an endless search for new meanings, none of which is ever final, as can be seen in his image of the "dream navel" that I have already quoted (Freud, 1900a, p. 525). On the other, his limited concept of symbolism, in terms of an innate, immutable, and universal meaning (Freud, 1900a, pp. 350–404, 1916–1917, pp. 149–169), represents a univocal conception of meaning, in which it makes sense to ask what a certain symbol "really means". This duality of psychoanalytic knowledge is what demands an analogical theory of meaning, which does not forsake the search for psychological truth, but accepts and takes into account that there might be various versions of it, depending on the context and the nature of the ensuing dialogue.

Freud (1930a) was fond of comparing psychoanalysis with archaeology. The idea of unearthing the buried remnants of ancient civilisations appeared to be an apt metaphor for the exploration of the unconscious. But, to him, this was more than an analogy, but a concrete fact, as when he writes that:

> Since we overcame the error of supposing that the forgetting we are familiar with signified a destruction of the memory-trace – that is, its annihilation – we have been inclined to take the opposite view, that in mental life nothing which has once been formed can perish – that

everything is somehow preserved and that in suitable circumstances (when, for instance, regression goes back far enough) it can once more be brought to light. (p. 70)

But not only is the psychoanalytic digging as concrete and objective as that of the archaeologists, it is even better, since archaeological remnants can be damaged, destroyed, or lost, and none of this happens in the psychic sphere: "The fact remains that only in the mind is such a preservation of all the earlier stages alongside of the final form possible, and that we are not in a position to represent this phenomenon in pictorial terms" (p. 71).

If this position were to be taken literally, then it would be possible to reconstruct the patient's forgotten past in terms that are as objective as those of archaeology: "What we are in search of is a picture of the patient's forgotten years that shall be alike trustworthy and in all essential respects complete" (Freud, 1937d, p. 258). Indeed, for him, there is no essential difference between the reconstructive work of these two kinds of researchers, with the exception of a certain advantage for the analyst:

> The two processes are in fact identical, except that the analyst works under better conditions and has more material at his command to assist him, since what he is dealing with is not something destroyed but something that is still alive. (p. 259)

But this is precisely where the analogy is to find its limits, as all analogies do, since the very fact that the patient is a living being determines that there are no fixed perennial contents of the mind, but a fluid process of creation of meaning, which is modified by the subject being now part of a dialogue with another human being, intended to enquire into his mental processes and contents. So, the pair formed by the patient's free associations and other meaningful expressions and the analyst's interpretations or other interventions, is bound to be, at one and the same time, a *discovery* and a *creation* of meaning.

There has been much discussion on this. Classical psychoanalysis asserts that the analytic instrument allows us to discover a set of pre-existent meanings, ideas, and memories, as long as we take all the necessary measures to ensure that the patient's mental processes and productions are not contaminated by the analyst's prejudices, beliefs, or theories. Many revisionist authors reject such claims, on the grounds that it is utterly impossible to make "uncontaminated" observations of such mental processes, since the mind is intrinsically relational and any behavioural manifestation by the patient is necessarily a derivative and expression of the whole situation, which includes the patient, the analyst, their mutual relation, the setting, and the wider social context. Consequently, any verbal comment by the analyst has to be an attempt to put into her own words whatever she has perceived, felt, intuited, or thought about the patient or about what is happening to them both in the analytic situation.

The latter position implies that every interpretation is a creation of new meaning and, hence, more related to art than to science. This generates, of course, an intense opposition by the more scientific-minded colleagues, thus generating a chasm between two breeds of psychoanalysts: the artistic and the scientific, who sometimes, but not always, coincide with the humanistic and the medical professionals.

So, what is interpretation after all? Is it a discovery or a creation? It is most probably both. It is a discovery, in as much as it refers to some essential aspects of the patient's and the pair's experience that have remained unsaid, either as a consequence of some kind of interdiction or because of their nascent and inchoate nature, which has not yet undergone the organising power of words—what Donnel Stern (1983, 1997) calls the "unformulated experience". But it is also a creation, since the analytic dialogue must find new ways of conveying emotional truths and latent ideas. This is the dominion of metaphor, and metaphors are always created, being both an expression of the parties' and the pair's creativity and a reflection of an emotional and cognitive pattern that is there to be found and expressed (Bion's (1970, 1980) "thoughts in search of a thinker"), but there are many ways in which it may be said—as Aristotle wrote in his *Metaphysics* "Being is said in many ways"—and some of them are better than others (Tubert-Oklander, 1994, 2013a; Tubert-Oklander & Beuchot, 2008). A metaphor cannot be said to be either "true" or "false", but only more or less adequate for its aim, which is to identify, highlight, and point to a certain complex state of affairs; some of them are better, others not so good, some are poor, and yet others are outright bad, but in every case their validity depends on their aptness to convey the more significant aspects of that human experience or situation that is being referred to. Hence, my position on this matter is clearly at odds with Klein's (1961), who claimed that she did not use any sort of analogy in her interpreta-tions ("In my interpretations I tried, as always, to avoid (as I would with adults as well as with children) introducing any similes, meta-phors, or quotations to illustrate my point", pp. 17–18). The point of view that I am putting forward, on the contrary, is that *every interpreta-tion is a metaphor intended to give a meaning to an unconscious occurrence.* This means that, for any given clinical situation, there can be several alternative interpretations that highlight the same unconscious configuration. Although some of them might be equally apt, the fact that they are framed with diverse images gives them a different feel-ing and implications. It is something like playing the same melody with various instruments: the phrases are the same, but with different harmonics. For instance, a certain patient might feel that she is carry-ing the burden of a sign of her sins, but how different would be the feeling and connotations of the metaphor if either she or her analyst compared it with Hawthorne's *The Scarlet Letter*, with its implication of adulterous lust, or with the albatross that hangs from the neck of Coleridge's Ancient Mariner, which points at meaningless aggression and destructiveness. Of course, these harmonics might be the very reason why one metaphor is more adequate than another, but they might also set the general tone for an otherwise satisfactory interpre-tation. This is particularly important when the analyst employs a stan-dard symbolic language—such as Freud's, Klein's, or Jung's—for his or her understanding and formulating interpretations, since the use of such language determines the general climate of all the analyst's treat-ments.

So, to the question of "Discovery or creation?" the answer is, indeed, "Both". Interpretation must always keep an analogical dyna-mic balance and tension between imagination and rigour, science and poetry, which Luria (1968, 1972, 1979) used to call "Romantic Science". On this, he says,

> Scientific observation is not merely pure description of separate facts. Its main goal is to view an event from as many perspectives as possi-ble. The eye of science does not probe "a thing", an event isolated from other things or events. Its real object is to see and understand the way a thing or event relates to other things or events. (Luria, 1979, p. 120)

In other words, he was trying to do an interpretative neuropsychology, which is very similar to psychoanalysis. (It should be remembered that

Luria was a pioneer of psychoanalysis in the Soviet Union, until he had to abandon this field of research, which had become anathema under Communist rule.) And this brings us back to the problem of interpretation and insight.

Interpretation and insight

What is an interpretation? If we turn to *Websler's Unabridged Dictionary* (Merriam-Webster, 2002, see "Interpret"), we find that "to interpret" covers four spheres of meaning:

> 1: to explain or tell the meaning of: translate into intelligible or familiar language or terms: EXPOUND, ELUCIDATE, TRANSLATE.
>
> 2: to understand and appreciate in the light of individual belief, judgment, interest, or circumstance: CONSTRUE.
>
> 3: to apprehend and represent by means of art: show by illustrative representation: bring (a score or script) to active realization by performance.
>
> [4:] to act as an interpreter: TRANSLATE.

Hence, an *interpretation*, defined as "the act or the result of interpreting", corresponds to several operations: (a) an "explanation of what is not immediately plain or explicit . . . or unmistakable" (this is what hermeneuts do); (b) a "translation from one language into another— used of oral translation by interpreters" (translators and simultaneous interpreters); (c) an "explanation of actions, events, or statements by pointing out or suggesting inner relationships or motives or by relating particulars to general principles" (scientists, philosophers, and jurists); (d) a "representation in performance, delivery, or criticism of the thought and mood in a work of art or its producer especially as penetrated by the personality of the interpreter" (actors, musicians, and other artists, as well as art critics); (e) "a particular adaptation or application of a method or style or set of principles" (architects, designers, artisans, artists). And what does an analyst do? All of these: he looks for implicit meanings and creates a verbal expression of them, translates from one type of representation or symbolisation to another, explains and accounts for certain situations, events or expressions, personifies and incarnates abstract relations, values, and theories, and develops his own version of what psychoanalysis is. Each and every one of these functions is part of his active contribution to the interpretative process, a bundle of explicit and implicit communications, most of them unconscious, which have an effect on the patient and on the analytic relation, and fuel the spiral development of the process, whose aim is the development of insight.

And what is *insight*? In ordinary English, it is "the power or act of seeing into a situation or into oneself" or "the act or fact of apprehending the inner nature of things or of seeing intuitively: clear and immediate understanding" (Merriam-Webster, 2002, see "Insight"). In psychoanalysis, we use the term in a more restricted sense, to refer to a comprehension or awareness of the nature and unconscious meaning of a symptom, or any other expression, which usually explains it as a derivative of an unconscious emotional conflict and an attempt to solve the ensuing tension by means of a transaction.

Interpretation is expected to generate insight, and this is supposed to bring relief from anxiety and the disappearance or modification of the symptom. In the first days of psychoanalysis, it was assumed that it was *the information* provided by the interpretation that produced the change, but Freud (1914g) soon found out that knowledge was a necessary, but not sufficient, condition for therapeutic change. There was a need for some kind of work that paved the way for a new psychic development, and this led to the concept of *working through*. The analytic dialogue then became a form of exercise that developed the patient's *capacity for insight*. It was, therefore, indispensable that the patient should be an active party in such a dialogue, since merely listening to a string of interpretations would provide nothing but information about psychoanalytic theory, as applied to his own case.

The interpretative process starts from the conjunction of the patient's free flowing expressions, induced by the basic rule, the ongoing analytic relationship, and the analyst's interpretations, but sooner or later it turns into a dynamic dialogue in terms of mutual interpretation, since the patient is constantly interpreting, either explicitly or implicitly, the analyst's interpretations, as well as all of his verbal and non-verbal behaviour (Aron, 1991; Hoffman, 1983). As these conscious or unconscious comments also have to be identified, pointed out, described, interpreted, and accounted for by the analyst, the result is an ever-flowing process of reflection and creation of new meanings, in which the pair becomes increasingly more proficient in conversing about the patient's emotional experiences and mental processes, and their shared experience of their relationship (Tubert-Oklander, 2006a,b, 2013b). In the end, the patient develops her own capacity to reflect analytically and generate insights, as a result of the internalisation of the dialogue, which turns into an inner reflective dialogue—that is, thinking.

Now, to interpret is to assign a new meaning to a human expression, one that is not apparent in the interpreter's first contact with it. So, the emergence of new non-apparent meanings requires a certain effort, and this is the work of interpretation, which consists in placing the expression—or a part of it—in a new context or contexts, and see what new meanings emerge as a result of this operation (Beuchot, 1997; Tubert-Oklander, 1994, 2006a,b). These contexts may be spatial, temporal, situational, relational, socio-cultural, linguistic, political, mythical, or just associative. The best known of them is the classical transference interpretation, which places a certain event of the patient–analyst relationship in the context of a childhood situation with the patient's primary objects, thus substituting the here-now-with-me context by the there-then-with-others. The analogy between these two situations gives a new meaning, both to the present situation and to the old one.

Analysts have various ready-made theories to orientate their interpretations. We might say that these standard contexts represent different interpretative "languages", and they determine the whole perspective from which the patient's expressions are to be understood. Ferro (1996, 1999), studying this problem from a narratological perspective, describes several *interpretative models* or *listening vertices*, which generate different alternative narratives, constructed from the same original patient's expressions. This is a process of *translation*, from one language to another, and from one narrative to another (Tubert-Oklander, 2011a, 2013b).

The patient brings his own narrative, which features several characters and elements, placed in a specific relation to each other. Let us say that a man's narrative is that someone in his office never honours his word; he makes many promises that are never fulfilled. The patient expresses vehemently his feelings of offence, anger, and disbelief: how can anybody dare to make a promise if he has no intention of keeping it? This is a rotten world, everyone lies, you cannot trust anybody!

The first vertex for perceiving, understanding, and interpreting these expressions, thus constructing a new narrative from them, is to take each of the characters, elements, and situations in the story at face value, and assume that they refer to real people and events, albeit in a different spatial, temporal, and personal context. Hence, the analyst might interpret that the patient is talking about his disappointment with his father, who frequently did not fulfil the promises he had made to the small child. The intense anger expressed is an enactment, not only of his own anger *vis-à-vis* his father's unreliability, but also of his identification with the latter's violent reactions when the child retaliated by developing a pattern of frequent lying. The analyst who listens to his story would be the mother, to whom the patient used to complain bitterly, and so on. This is the Freudian interpretative style (Freud, 1912b, 1914g).

The second model understands the patient's narrative as an expression of the dynamics of his internal world. Then, the characters and their mutual relations would be understood as "parts of the patient, as projected internal images" (Ferro, 1996, p. 33). Then the lying character would be seen as a representation of the patient's mendacious internal father image, but also of his own dishonesty; the "I" in the story would be his inner child, abandoned and hurt, but also a stern superego, who ruthlessly attacks the lying child, and so on. This is the Kleinian way, as was clearly shown in Klein's (1961) analysis of Richard in her *Narrative of a Child Analysis*.

Yet, there is still a third model, one that retells the patient's story as an allegorical comment on the analytic relationship, "a story told from the patient's standpoint about the functioning of the analyst and of the patient in the consulting room" (Ferro, 1996, p. 33). From this perspective, which is clearly the one most favoured by the author, the analyst would immediately relate the patient's expression to the fact that he had been ill and had had to cancel two sessions the previous week, and had, therefore, failed to fulfil his promises to the patient (of giving him his regular sessions).

But the three models are equally strong, since "they are self-confirming owing to the stability of the listening vertices: each listening model validates itself from its own vertex and excludes the others" (Ferro, 1996, p. 33). In my own terms, they are different languages, and it cannot be said that a language is either "true" or "false", since each language has its own particular way of referring to the whole of human experience. This does not mean that they are all equivalent, since each narrative clearly depicts some aspects of the experience, while leaving out others; some things are better said in English than in Spanish, and vice versa, since each language has its assets and its drawbacks.

All orthodoxies insist in imposing what the Russian philosopher, Michael Bakhtin, called "monoglossia", the mandatory use of a single language, which stifles creativity. This is quite germane to the organisation of our profession, as pointed out by Pines (1989):

> When only one language is heard we are listening to dogma; creative growth comes from constructive dialogue, from the presence of diverse languages called by Michael Bakhtin "heteroglossia". . . . As a philosopher of language in Soviet Russia where a plurality of languages was not permitted by the ruling dogmatic ideology, Bakhtin regarded consciousness as the dialogue of "official language" whilst there is an "unofficial language" which is suppressed and repressed. This latter he regarded as the language of the unconscious. (p. 132)

If this is true, then a large portion of the unconscious derives from the interdiction, by the family and the social environment, of the child's development of her or his own language, feelings, wishes, and thoughts, and the analytic dialogue would be an invitation for the patient to find his own voice, instead of repeating the discourse of his introjected objects. But this cannot happen if the analyst insists that only her own theoretical language should be a valid presentation of truth in the analysis. The same is valid for the dealings of the psychoanalytic community, as Winnicott put forward in his letter to Melanie Klein of 17 November 1952:

> I personally think that it is very important that your work should be restated by people discovering in their own way and presenting what they discover in their own language. It is only in this way that the language will be kept alive. *If you make the stipulation that in future only your language shall be used for the statement of other people's discoveries then the language becomes a dead language, as it has already become in the Society.* You would be surprised at the sighs and groans that accompany every restatement of the internal object clichés by what I am going to call Kleinians. Your own statements are of course in quite a different category as the work is your own personal work and everyone is pleased that you have your own way of stating it. . . . I am

concerned with this set-up which might be called Kleinian which I believe to be the real danger to the diffusion of your work. *Your ideas will only live in so far as they are rediscovered and reformulated by original people in the psycho-analytic movement and outside it.* It is of course necessary for you to have a group in which you can feel at home. Every original worker requires a coterie in which there can be a resting place from controversy and in which one can feel cosy. The danger is, however, that the coterie develops a system based on the defence of the position gained by the original worker, in this case yourself. Freud, I believe, saw the danger of this. *You are the only one who can destroy this language called the Kleinian doctrine and Kleinism and all that with a constructive aim. If you do not destroy it then this artificially integrated phenomenon must be attacked destructively.* (Winnicott, 1952, pp. 34–35, my italics)

The very same thing happens with the psychoanalytic dialogue. The patient comes speaking his own dialect; the analyst responds by trying to say the same things as translated into a theoretical language; the patient comments on this, and either accepts, rejects, or corrects it, and gradually there develops a new dialect, which is the idiosyncratic language of the pair. But this cannot happen if the analyst is bent on keeping the purity of her own language, which is usually that of her professional group and tradition, since such a defensive attitude turns the analysis into a form of cultural colonialism. As Winnicott suggests, it is the analyst who has to destroy her own monolithic language, by concurring in the alternative use of several languages or dialects, and by accepting that the patient's idiolect has an impact on her analytic language. If she is not willing to do this, then "this artificially integrated phenomenon must be attacked destructively" by the patient. Hence, a significant part of what we consider to be a "negative transference" might well be a fundamental reaction to our self-assured and inflexible stance when interpreting. Of course, both the patient's destructive aggression *vis-à-vis* the analyst's omniscient attitude and the failure to express such negative feelings are transference reactions, which follow the relational patterns established in his early years, and should be duly analysed. But this cannot be done, unless the analyst acknowledges her own participation in the recreation of this enactment.

Bollas (2007) makes the same point when advocating a psychoanalytic pluralism. Theories are, for him, instruments for perception of analytic facts, and there is no virtue in sticking to a single tool when one can have several that offer a multi-dimensional view:

> It depends on how we understand theory. *Theories are views. Each theory sees something that other theories do not see.* What we gain from the eyes is different from what we take in from the ears. What we perceive of reality through the olfactory sense is different from what we take in from touch. Theory is a meta-sensual phenomenon. *Some theories are better than others,* just as it is possible to say that sight is probably more frequently used than smell in the perception of reality. So you can see that for me *pluralism is, in its core, a theory of perception,* and to say that one must become a Kleinian or a Lacanian, to the exclusion of the other theories, is as absurd as saying that one must become an advocate of the ear, or an eye-guy, or a touch person, or a sniffer.
>
> This issue becomes important when considering psychic transformations in psychoanalysis. . . . These theories reside in the psychoanalytic preconscious and will be activated by the analyst's need to see certain things at certain times. So if the analyst has been schooled in Freud, Klein, Bion, Winnicott, Lacan, Kohut and others then in my view he has more perceptual capability in his preconscious than an analyst who remains within only one vision. . . . I think many analysts would identify themselves with one group but they have in fact become pluralists without knowing it. (pp. 5–6, my italics)

Ferro (1996) presents a similar suggestion when, after describing the three interpretative models that we have already considered, he introduces a fourth model, which, unlike the others, is an open one:

> I should now like to present a contrasting fourth model, which is characterized by the instability of the *listening* vertices and therefore includes all the *possible stories* which become narratable on the basis of the patient's statement, and whose freedom of narrative combinations is positively exponential—because [any element in the patient's narrative] can be selected in model "a", "b" or "c". . . . Message decoding is no longer possible, but only the construction of a story—which will have the characteristic of being necessary to those two minds. This is because what will allow the narration to be organized in one sense rather than another will be the defences of both (or, as we might say, of the field).
>
> This will occur if the analyst allows the emotions arising in the room to pervade him and if, together with his patient, he selects from the

emotional noise a narrative harmony that confers order, rhythms and images on what was previously confused, chaotic and preverbal. (pp. 33–34, my italics)

Of course, the analyst is not always imbued with this openness, flexibility, and creativity. There are many moments in which she or he will work in terms of the pre-established models, and certainly most treatments start that way, before the development of the analytic relation and the evolution of the field set in motion an expanding analytic process. But the preordained models are nothing but the formalisation of some specific points of view that have been repeatedly found to be useful in understanding the clinical situations met by a particular analyst or group of analysts. It is this recurrent history of success that makes it possible to identify some points of view and requires that they be given a name. Then they can be taught, learnt, and used purposefully when one does not know what to do, this being the very function of technique. However, when the analyst is open-hearted, creative, and free from the burden of purposive thinking and acting, he is able to alternate between a very large and indefinite number of emerging models *in statu nascendi*, which have, as yet, no name or established identity. Some of them might later crystallise as alternative standard models, but no list of these may ever be comprehensive or definitive. Personally, I have found it necessary to include a fourth such model, which precedes Ferro's higher level integrative one. This interprets the patient's productions in terms of a mythical narrative derived from the social, cultural, and political context to which both analyst and patient belong (Tubert-Oklander, 2006a,b,c, 2010, 2013b), but the fact remains that the analyst's most creative moments happen when he sheds his well-known models and lets new, unexpected analogies emerge.

Of course, it is quite possible and desirable to enrich an analyst's listening and perceptive apparatus by studying the experiences, teachings, and practices of the various established schools of psychoanalysis, as Bollas (2007) suggests, in order that he be able to oscillate from one model to another, until one of them fits. However, these must be, sooner or later, left behind. Ferro (1996) depicts it by means of as schema, in which the continuum from Models (1), (2), (3), through Model (*n*), oscillates with truly creative work (C). "The analyst will be aware that the boundaries of C are fragile and constantly expanding, because what is C today will necessarily fall into M 1, M 2, M 3 . . . M (*n*), and may subsequently become a theory" (p. 34).

When the analyst opens up and lets herself flow, which is the equivalent to Freud's (1912e) "evenly-suspended attention", the unconscious connection with the patient determines the emergence of all kinds of ideas, feelings, impulses, and images. All of them are tried automatically as analogical models that act as tentative context for interpreting the patient's expressions, the analyst's inner experiences (Jacobs, 1993a,b; Wender, 1993), and the events that occur in the analytic situation, until some of them finally make the connection, and this becomes the basis for a verbal interpretation or a non-verbal equivalent.

Insight is considered to be the result of the interpretative activity in the analysis—whether through the analyst's responses to the patient's expressions or the interpretative dialogue that develops in the course of the analytic relationship—that determines a new understanding of already known facts. It is traditionally conceived as something that happens "within" the patient, but it has later been reformulated by the Barangers (2008, 2009), in terms of psychoanalytic field theory, as a reorganisation of the bipersonal field, one that puts an end to stereotypy and paralysis of thought, and frees both parties to communicate about the particular experience that they share—the analytic experience:

> When they find themselves communicating in the field and between themselves at the moment of insight, analyst and analysand feel that they communicate within themselves and enjoy a wider access to the various areas of their psychic life. This is a moderate inner communication that takes into account the differences between regions and functions—neither invasion nor confusion, but discriminated unification. *The observer ego, or the ego in an observation function, that in the patient had plunged into regression and had lost autonomy and that in the analyst had been reduced to the impotent contemplation of the bastion, re-emerges in both in full swing.* (Baranger & Baranger, 2009, pp. 13–14, my italics)

This description depicts a psychopathological situation in which the analytic pair has fallen prey to an unconscious pact between the two parties—what the authors call a "bastion"—to avoid becoming cognisant of a psychic situation that affects them both, and how the function of thinking and communicating may be recovered by means of an explicit verbal understanding of what is happening—that is, an interpretation. This will be further explored in the next chapter, when discussing the obstacles to the analytic process. But there are other instances of this articulation of interpretation and insight bringing about a reorganisation of the analytic field. This is what happens when, as Ferro (1996) describes, the analytic dialogue selects "from the emotional noise a narrative harmony that confers order, rhythms and images on what was previously confused, chaotic and preverbal" (p. 34): in other words, when what Donnel Stern (1983) called "unformulated experience" becomes organised and explicitly expressed in words, or when a new understanding substitutes for an older and until then unquestioned version, shedding new light on what had been previously believed to be true.

In any case, understanding insight as an evolution of the bipersonal field allows us to account better for what it brings about in each of the parties' minds, as well as in their mutual relation and dialogue.

Insight is not enough: the need for working through

The theory of the treatment evolved from its origins in the cathartic method, which bypassed the patient's opposition by means of hypnosis and promised an easy cure of symptoms by simply recovering the lost memories of trauma, through the first stages of psychoanalysis, in which there was still an emphasis on the patient's ignorance of himself, to be solved by the new information contained in interpretations, to a more mature form that recognised the need of ongoing work in order to overcome resistances. This new concept—*Durcharbeitung*, usually translated as "working through"—was introduced by Freud in 1914, in his paper "Remembering, repeating, working-though" (1914g), in which he emphasised the fact that the patient's resistances to making conscious the unconscious—and, hence, to the therapeutic process—are ever-present and pervading. Consequently, the analyst's job was no longer to infer the patient's unconscious contents and give him clear and explicit information about it, but to pinpoint and denounce the resistances that are active at that very moment, with the expectation that this would lead the patient to overcome them. This he describes in the following terms:

Finally, there was evolved the consistent technique used today, in which the analyst gives up the attempt to bring a particular moment or problem into focus. He contents himself with studying whatever is present for the time being on the surface of the patient's mind, and he employs the art of interpretation mainly for the purpose of recognizing the resistances which appear there, and making them conscious to the patient. *From this there results a new sort of division of labour: the doctor uncovers the resistances which are unknown to the patient; when these have been got the better of, the patient often relates the forgotten situations and connections without any difficulty.* The aim of these different techniques has, of course, remained the same. Descriptively speaking, it is to fill in gaps in memory; dynamically speaking, it is to overcome resistances due to repression. (1914g, pp. 147–148, my italics)

But things were not that easy. Analysts soon found out that it was hardly ever enough to inform the patient of his or her resistances for these to disappear. This was quite disappointing for beginners:

I have often been asked to advise upon cases in which the doctor complained that he had pointed out his resistance to the patient and that nevertheless no change had set in; indeed, the resistance had become all the stronger, and the whole situation was more obscure than ever. The treatment seemed to make no headway. This gloomy foreboding always proved mistaken. The treatment was as a rule progressing most satisfactorily. The analyst had merely forgotten that giving the resistance a name could not result in its immediate cessation. *One must allow the patient time to become more conversant with this resistance with which he has now become acquainted, to work through it, to overcome it, by continuing, in defiance of it, the analytic work according to the fundamental rule of analysis.* Only when the resistance is at its height can the analyst, *working in common with his patient,* discover the repressed instinctual impulses which are feeding the resistance; and it is this kind of experience which convinces the patient of the existence and power of such impulses. *The doctor has nothing else to do than to wait and let things take their course, a course which cannot be avoided nor always hastened.* If he holds fast to this conviction he will often be spared the illusion of having failed when in fact he is conducting the treatment on the right lines. (p. 155, my italics)

So, things are not just a question of information: there is work to be done, and this should be carried out *in common* by the analyst and the patient; thus, there is a need for conscious co-operation. Hence, the making conscious of the unconscious is not a revelation, and neither is it a technical intervention such as a surgical operation, but it is an educational process similar to that which doctors have to do in the treatment of chronic diseases, such as diabetes or coronary insuffi-ciency, which require a change in the patient's habits and lifestyle.

Freud (1916–1917) once compared this work with that of educa-tion—indeed, a re-education—as can be seen in the following passage:

> An analytic treatment demands from both doctor and patient the accomplishment of serious work, which is employed in lifting internal resistances. Through the overcoming of these resistances the patient's mental life is permanently changed, is raised to a high level of devel-opment and remains protected against fresh possibilities of falling ill. *This work of overcoming resistances is the essential function of analytic treat-ment; the patient has to accomplish it and the doctor makes this possible for him with the help of suggestion operating in an educative sense.* For that reason *psycho-analytic treatment has justly been described as a kind of after-education.* (p. 451, my italics)

So, it is the patient who has to carry out the work of overcoming her resistances, under the guidance of, and following the stimulus offered by, the doctor, and all of this is a learning process. But, although the analyst initiates and fosters the process, this cannot be controlled, since it follows its own course and at its own pace, irrespective of both parties' will and intention. Hence, "the doctor has nothing else to do than to wait and let things take their course, a course which cannot be avoided nor always hastened". This does not mean that he should remain passive and expectant; there are still quite a few therapeutic jobs that must be carried out: the evolution of the process has to be monitored and somehow modulated by the analyst's interventions, its accidents should be identified and, if possible, corrected before they harm either the parties or the process, its achievements have to be identified and acknowledged, and the whole sequence has to be commented on, but the fact remains that the process itself is dynamic, evolving, and largely autonomous, since it stems from unconscious sources.

None the less, this process requires a steady effort, and the bulk of it appertains to the patient. This was clearly Freud's stance on the matter, as shown in the following quotation from Kardiner's (1977) narrative of his analysis with the master:

At the end of the fifth month, March [that is, one month before terminating the analysis, since Freud had assigned only six months for the
treatment], he began saying, "Herr Doctor, ein bis[s]chen Durcharbeitung" ["a bit of working through"]. Now, this idea caused me a
good deal of bewilderment. I had no idea what he meant, and I begged
him to elucidate what he meant by *Durcharbeitung*. He said, "Well,
why don't you bring your childhood neurotic manifestations into your
current life?"

I did not know at the time that this was the main job of analysis, but
I did say to Freud, "I thought that was your job". However, at that
time [1922] Freud didn't consider it to be so. He thought that once you
had uncovered the Oedipus complex and understood your unconscious homosexuality, that once you knew the origins and sources of
all these reactions, something would happen that would enable you to
translate these insights into your current life and therefore alter it.

However, as for me, at the time his invitation that I should work
through this whole thing only left me bewildered. From that point on,
the analysis drifted. (pp. 62–63)

Apparently, Freud had it quite clear that the working through of the
resistances needed the patient to explore every present ramification
and manifestation of the childhood conflicts that had been exposed by
the analysis, but expected that the patient do it all by himself. This is
what baffled Kardiner. Nowadays, most analysts would agree with
him that starting this process was, at least partly, Freud's job. Present
analytic practice usually requires that the analyst should interpret
these current derivatives of past conflicts.

Klein (1961), in particular, emphasised the need for a systematic
interpretation of the manifold ramifications of infantile conflicts, as a
contribution to working through:

Working-through was one of the essential demands that Freud made
on an analysis. The necessity to work through is again and again
proved in our day-to-day experience: for instance, we see that
patients, who at some stage have gained insight, repudiate this very
insight in the following sessions and sometimes even seem to have
forgotten that they had ever accepted it. *It is only by drawing our conclusions from the material as it reappears in different contexts, and is interpreted
accordingly, that we gradually help the patient to acquire insight in a more
lasting way.* The process of adequately working-through includes

bringing about changes in the character and strength of the manifold splitting processes which we meet with even in neurotic patients, as well as the consistent analysis of paranoid and depressive anxieties. Ultimately this leads to greater integration. (p. 12, my italics)

Unfortunately, this led to a point of view that was precisely the opposite of Freud's, one that puts all the burden of working through on the analyst's operations and interventions, an approach that may foster passivity and submission in the patient, as a response to the repetitive interpretations. For Klein, the rationale for interpreting each one of the ramifications of the original conflict in the various contexts of the patient's existence was to reaffirm the insights generated by the analyst's previous interpretations, to avoid their being repudiated and forgotten. This assumes that such interpretations must necessarily be true, an assumption that might turn the analysis into a form of indoctrination. If, on the other hand, one adheres to the view that all interpretations are metaphorical and an attempt to approach one possible description of inner experience, then the exploration of the various contexts and points of view becomes an exercise of the insight-generating analytic function of the personality of both parties, and of the dyad. This requires that the analysis become a dialogue, in which the various points of view and perspectives, both of the analyst and the patient, may be explored, developed, and compared. The result is a further development of the capacity for insight and for the generation of new meanings and metaphors, in each of the parties and in the pair, as a part of their common co-operative work of enquiry.

But the process of working through is not limited to the cognitive functions. Resistances to change are derived from the organism's and the mind's conservative tendencies. Each time that we manage to carry out an action with some success, this makes it more likely that the next time we face a similar situation our reaction to it will be the same. This phenomenon is referred to in such terms as "habit", "procedure", "ritual", "tradition", "repetition", or "mental structure". In psychoanalysis, we used to speak of the "compulsion to repeat". For instance, if some mental operation ("defence") has proved to be successful in the past in avoiding the emergence of anxiety or some other unpleasant feeling, for example, guilt, shame, fear, or confusion, this makes it much more likely that the subject will automatically use it again when facing a similar situation. These automatic reactions tend to be self-validating and self-replicating, and consequently ana-chronistic, since they correspond to the old-time situation in which they originated and are not amenable to learning from experience. Hence, they need to be questioned and interfered with in their auto-matic functioning by the demand that they should be put into words, which are necessarily slower and clumsier than fluid action. This may remind us of the funny story of the caterpillar who was asked how on earth did it manage to co-ordinate the movement of so many legs, and, consequently, was never able to walk again! But this operation is no joke, since every new learning requires an unlearning of previous action schemas, as shown by Piaget (1954), and this generates a temporary disorganisation of behaviour and loss of previous know-ledge and skills.

Once the patient has become aware of his automatic repetitive reactions, he needs to start a conscious effort to act against this natural tendency to do everything in the same way in which it has always been done, not only by him, but also by his family, groups, institu-tions, and culture. This demands action in each of what Pichon-Rivière (1971) used to call the *three areas of behaviour*: mind, body, and *external world*. This means going back to what I have previously referred to as the *golden braid: cognition, emotion,* and *conation*. Hence, the working-through effort should aim at three distinct but interre-lated tasks: *cognitive transformation, affective mobilisation,* and *behav-ioural change*. The work intended to overcome the conservative and repetitive tendencies that act as resistances to new experiences and developments should, then, be fought on three fronts, or in any combination of them: *cognition* (thinking, perceiving, remembering, speaking new ideas that had been precluded before), *emotion* (daring to feel, express, acknowledge, and relate in terms of previously forbid-den feelings and impulses), and *action* (experimenting and developing new ways of dealing with physical, relational, and social reality, and interacting with other human beings, starting with the analyst).

The traditional defence mechanisms are a form of action, albeit one that takes place mainly in the internal arena, but defence usually also includes some sort of external action, which sometimes is a sort of ritual, aimed at modifying the emotional state of both the agent and others; it is a communicational manoeuvre, in the context of interper-sonal relations. Gear and Liendo (1977) have suggested that each psychopathological organisation revolves around one *basic acting-*

out—that is, a specific unconscious action that establishes, develops, and maintains the pathological personality structure—and that any rational therapeutic response to it should include a *counter-acting-out*, which is a conscious action designed to counteract and neutralise the pathological one. This, of course, appertains to the practice of psycho-analytic focal therapy (Balint, Ornstein, & Balint, 1972; Malan, 1963), but even in standard psychoanalysis a time comes when the patient has to face the necessity of starting on a new course of action, in order to change her own personal situation and relationships. Such a discov-ery might be made by the patient alone or the analyst might have to suggest it, and then analyse the transference implications of having suggested it.

This implies, of course, taking into account the patient's conscious co-operation and will. Some accounts of the psychoanalytic treatment, such as the Kleinian or the Lacanian versions of it, seem to have dispensed altogether with the participation of the patient's conscious ego, but the very concept of working through cannot make much sense without it. Besides, the patient's conscious wishes, thoughts, opinions, and values have to have a hearing and be duly analysed.

Rycroft (1966b) recognises that there are cases in which there are no particular difficulties in assuming that the patient's infantile wishes, which have been made unconscious by repression, are acting as veritable causes of his or her symptoms, and that this situation can be solved if the analyst manages to make the patient aware of these unconscious and infantile determinants. But this is not always so:

> Even today I frequently have clinical experiences which can be read-ily understood in this way. But, and it is a big but, these experiences only occur with a certain type of patient and under certain conditions. They occur with patients who are basically healthy and whose person-ality neither the therapist nor the patient feels inclined to call into question, and they occur only if both the patient and his nearest and nominally dearest wish him to lose its symptoms. In other words the patient loses his symptoms only if two conditions are fulfilled: firstly, that he understands their origin, and secondly, that his conscious wish to lose his symptoms is greater than his wish to retain the *status quo* in his personal relationships. For instance, if a married man is impo-tent or sexually perverted, his recovery depends not only on his understanding of the origins of his disability but also on whether his wife really and truly welcomes his recovery, and on whether, if she

doesn't, he feels prepared to overcome her reluctance or, if that seems impossible, to make alternative arrangements. Whether he does feel prepared to do either will depend on many more factors than the unconscious determinants of his symptoms: it will be influenced by his conscious values, his religious attitudes, his general feelings towards his wife, his assessment of her mental stability, etc. (pp. 9–10)

Of course, this means that the analysis has to take into account the patient's whole personality, including that conscious ego which happens to be the analyst's co-therapist, and that the patient's symptoms are not solely an individual matter, but, rather, depend on conscious and unconscious inter- and transpersonal events and factors, which must also be the object of insight and working through. But once the patient has made an analytically informed decision about what he really wants, there still remains the need to take action against the way things are and have always been, both in the intrapersonal and in the inter- and transpersonal arenas.

Such an effort to swim upstream, salmon-like, requires a conscious determination and an unconscious disposition, which may be nurtured, fostered, and facilitated by the analyst's intervention, but that in the end can only be based on the patient's willingness to believe that this might be possible and to engage in a protracted, painful, costly, and exhausting endeavour to make it happen. Without this most active participation on the part of the patient, all our therapeutic efforts are bound to fail.

During this stage of working through, the analytic dialogue oscillates between consideration of the conscious and the unconscious motives for, and resistances against, the wished-for change, as we shall see in the following chapter, on "The evolution of the analytic process".

CHAPTER TEN

The evolution of the analytic process (1): the beginning and the middle

Drawing on a stream

Any attempt to describe the evolution of a fluid process invokes the temptation, which stems from the way our minds work, of dividing it into stages. This is bound to prove to be as hopeless as drawing pictures on a stream, and yet the structure of Indo-European languages demands that we artificially divide any continuous evolution in order to be able to speak about it (Whorf, 1956). This might be a useful fiction, as long as we keep in mind that these bits and pieces of an organic whole do not really exist, but are only stylistic props to aid us in the description. So, I shall try to depict the evolution of an analytic process in terms that are ample enough to accommodate the inexhaustible variety of the analytic relationship and to avoid any attempt to use them as a blueprint for the conduction of treatments.

It would seem, of course, a truism to say that the analytic process has a beginning, a development, an end, and an aftermath. If analysis were a disease, we could speak of a preclinical stage, almost unknown to us, since it happens before we first meet the patient, in which the latter is incubating the very idea of entering analysis. Then would

213

come a clinical stage, going from the ill-defined prodromes, through a well-established status phase, to its denouement. This would be followed by period of convalescence. But the main liability of this analogy is that it seems to uphold the conception of a "natural history" of the analytic process, as suggested by Meltzer (1967), which leaves out the unpredictable and creative nature of human relations.

A much better analogy for the analytic treatment was introduced by Freud (1913c) in "On beginning the treatment", in which he compared it to "the noble game of chess", whose mid-game is so complex that it cannot be formalised:

> Anyone who hopes to learn the noble game of chess from books will soon discover that only the openings and end-games admit of an exhaustive systematic presentation and that the infinite variety of moves which develop after the opening defy any such description. This gap in instruction can only be filled by a diligent study of games fought out by masters. The rules which can be laid down for the practice of psycho-analytic treatment are subject to similar limitations. (p. 123)

The use of chess as a metaphor suits our purpose well, because this game implies an interaction between two thinking human beings, each trying to fathom (interpret) the other's intentions. This is precisely what makes their mutual behaviour unpredictable and prevents us from drawing any standard description of its course. So, I shall not attempt to map the evolution of the analytic process, but, rather, pose a few themes for reflection about our experience of it; this being in consonance with the spirit of this book, which aims at conveying a way of perceiving, thinking, feeling, and acting in our clinics, instead of describing specific operations or events. The minutiae of everyday practice can only be learnt, as Freud suggested, through the study and the discussion of well-conducted cases (the "games fought out by masters").

I shall follow, in my description, the scheme presented by Freud's metaphor, and divide the process into: (a) a *preamble*, (b) an *opening*, (c) a *mid-game*, (d) a *closure*, and (e) an *aftermath*. This is a useful fiction, which does not in any way deny the inevitable continuity of the phases.

The preamble

Although common sense tells us that a treatment must necessarily start with the first meeting between the analyst and the prospective patient, this is only true for our conscious secondary process mentation. At the unconscious level, the roots of the analytic relation come from long way back. By the time the patient decides to make a move in order to contact an analyst, she has been carrying out an inner debate, both conscious and unconscious, about the necessity, the dangers, and the advisability of seeking help. There is both a conscious expectation and an unconscious fantasy of what such help might imply, and a disposition to recreate previous experiences—both "good" (tender, pleasurable, intimate, soothing, healing) and "bad" (hurtful, violent, disappointing, sickening)—in this prospective new relationship. Every patient comes with a sometimes hidden hope of finding a truly responsive other, open to seeing, listening, feeling, and understanding her, and capable of reflecting some self-image that might heal deep emotional wounds and repair a damaged self-esteem. However, the fear of disappointment and the humiliation of being in need frequently lead the patient to declare explicitly an utter hopelessness and disbelief.

The analyst is also loaded with conscious and unconscious expectations and dispositions to transfer his own inner world on to the would-be patient. The deep motives that underlie his vocation, which have, one hopes, been identified, understood, and worked through partially during the training analysis, are as active as ever, and looking for a suitable object that may act as a stimulus for their recreation. This is compounded by the influence of the particular stage in the analyst's personal and professional life, his current interests, values, fears, and longings, as well as economic and career needs, and the general social climate. There is also the phenomenon of what Racker (1953, 1957) calls the "indirect countertransference"; that is, a countertransference derived from the relation to a third party (analyst, supervisor, colleague, the person who referred the patient, etc.) whose opinion about the patient's treatment is emotionally important for the analyst.

So, by the time the analyst picks up the phone or receives any other communication from a prospective patient, the scene is already set for the transference–countertransference to develop.

The opening

Everything starts with an interview. The analyst interviews the patient and the patient interviews the analyst. Both are trying to size up the other, discover what can be expected from each other. The analyst calls it "diagnosis" and it means trying to work out what sort of unsavoury situation has brought the patient to her office, what can be done about it, whether it belongs to her particular area of expertise or not, and what are the chances that their working together might be beneficial for the patient. This is arrived at by means of attentive empathic listening, a few questions, and perhaps some tentative interpretation, to see what sort of response it gets.

The patient is also trying, at least at a conscious level, to see who the analyst is and what sort of ware she is peddling. But at the unconscious level, he is always sizing up whether this is a person who will be able and willing to see, listen to, value, understand, share, accompany, and somehow aid him. This is so, even when the patient is actively denying the existence of any need or hope for help, since people who have suffered severe disappointments in the past are often wary of running the risk of trusting again. In the end, the patient's decision to enter treatment will depend partly on the analyst's ability to muster the patient's conscious co-operation, by means of conveying a reasonable understanding of the implications of being in psychoanalysis, but also mainly on her being able to reach this hidden part of the patient that stubbornly refuses to forsake all hope.

So, after these first moves of the dialogue and interaction between them, which might take one or several interviews, analyst and patient are ready to embark on their first negotiation. The analyst has to explain her view of what is happening to the patient, why analysis is an option as a way to deal with the present situation, and what are the requirements for carrying it out. The patient will probably ask some questions, which need to be answered, or, at least, an explanation as to why they cannot be answered is required. The conditions in which the analysis will take place are usually a matter for discussion, particularly the questions of frequency, duration, and time of the appointments, fees, holidays, and cancellation policies. This discussion and the final agreement reached are usually referred as the "analytic contract", as we have seen in Chapter Four.

The way in which the contract is negotiated and established already sets the tone for what the analytic interaction is going to be.

The fact that the analyst shows a preference for an *authoritarian, demagogic,* or *democratic contract* (Etchegoyen, 1986, pp. 64–68) says a lot about her personality, ideology, values, and conception of the treatment. The use of a *reflective contract,* which is not only democratic, but also includes the proposal of examining together the implications and consequences of the contract and its dispositions for their nascent relationship, is also a testimony to the uniqueness of a dialogue and a relationship that reflect upon themselves, thus becoming themselves an object of enquiry.

Given the patient's doubts and forebodings about needing, asking for, and receiving help, it is no wonder that many psychoanalytic treatments have to start with less than adequate conditions. Many patients can only enter treatment with a low frequency of sessions. This is usually rationalised in terms of the availability of money or time, but more often than not these realistic considerations are allied with a deep fear of needing and trusting another human being. However, if, in this circumstance, the analyst sticks to her guns, and tries to impose a standard analytic setting, this might deny the patient the only possible chance of having a treatment. It might be better to agree on a lower frequency that is acceptable to the patient, while interpreting the possible unconscious meaning of this restriction, and at the same time stating the analyst's belief that a higher frequency might be necessary in the future.

After the pair has reached a working agreement, the stage is set for the beginning of the analytic sessions. This has been traditionally seen as a radical change from the more relaxed climate of the interview, in which the parties are discussing the possibility and initiation of a treatment that has not yet actually begun, and the austere deprivation of psychoanalysis. When the analysis begins under such an assumption, the experience of the first sessions might be shocking, and even traumatic, for the patient, especially if the analyst remains silent throughout them and fails to answer the patient's questions without any explanation of this unusual behaviour. The same happens if the only response the patient receives to whatever he feels like saying is a transference interpretation, which seems to imply that his anxieties, fears, doubts, living conditions, or memories are a matter of no concern for the analyst, who is bent upon making the enquiry of the unconscious aspects of the analytic relation the main, or even the sole, aim of the analytic activity. Another such instance of unresponsiveness to the patient's conscious worries occurs when the analyst only seems to take notice of his resistances, thus introducing the assumption that the patient is intrinsically dishonest and that the analyst's task is to denounce his mendacity. This is a consequence of what Ricoeur (1965) called a "hermeneutics of suspicion"—that is, the assumption that everything a person says is a distortion, aimed at concealing some unsavoury truth. I believe such an approach to be anti-therapeutic and that it should be replaced by what Orange (2011) has named a "hermeneutics of trust", which means an attitude of confident hospi-tality towards the patient and his experiences and suffering.

None of this negates the significance of the analyst's disposition to listen silently, the interpretation of the transference, and the analysis of resistances, but only reminds us that the patient has a need to be seen, heard, understood, and believed in her own terms, for the analy-sis to take off. This has been emphasised by Kohut (1971, 1977, 1984) and self psychology, in terms of the human need for a positive mirror-ing, in order to develop a living and valuable feeling of self. This need persists during the whole life span, but it is in infancy and childhood, that is, during the period of the construction of the personality, that it is truly vital for the establishment of a healthy self (Kohut, 1982).

The same need for mirroring has been described by Winnicott (1967) as the mirror-role of the mother and the family in the child's development. When this experience is lacking in the patient's life, it behoves the analyst to fulfil this function, as we shall see in Chapter Twelve, on "The healing process". This is a later development of Ferenczi's concepts of "The adaptation of the family to the child" (1928a), "The elasticity of psycho-analytic technique" (1928b), and allowing the patient "properly speaking for the first time, to enjoy the irresponsibility of childhood" (1929, p. 129).

This is why I do not make any qualitative distinction between the diagnostic interviews and the first stages of the analysis, since the former should also be therapeutic, in as much as they are an initial res-ponse to the patient's needs, and the latter are still very much a matter of getting to know each other and aiding the patient in the most diffi-cult task of starting to get an inkling of what psychoanalysis is. The very first interpretations are not only an instrument to reduce and give a meaning to the patient's anxieties, but also an induction into the analysis. The patient is learning what psychoanalysis is and what to expect from the analyst, and the analyst is learning who the patient is

and how it feels to be in a room with her, doing analysis, while starting to develop an idea of what might happen between them, as the
treatment advances.

When the idea the patient gets of the analyst and the analysis
fosters the development of hope, this is what Freud (1913c) called
"establishing an effective transference"—that is, a positive transference—in which the patient starts to expect good things from the
analyst. As we have seen in previous chapters, getting to this point is
"the first aim of the treatment", and this kind of relation develops
spontaneously, if the analyst "exhibits a serious interest in [the
patient], carefully clears away the resistances that crop up at the
beginning" and maintains an analytic attitude. Then the patient will
develop an attachment with the analyst and "link the doctor up with
one of the imagos of the people by whom he was accustomed to be
treated with affection" (pp. 139–140). This sets the basis for any future
analytic work.

Winnicott (1962b) described this initiatory process in quite similar
terms, although emphasising the need to contain and work through
the early traumata experienced by the patient during infancy and
childhood. The analyst then provides an "ego-support that we give
simply by doing standard analysis and by doing it well", and which
"corresponds to the ego-support of the mother which . . . makes the
infant ego strong if and only if the mother is able to play her special
part at this time" (p. 168). Consequently, analysts "become modern
representatives of the parent figures of the patient's childhood and
infancy [without] displacing such figures". As this process evolves,
we finally "see growth and emotional development that had become
held up in the original situation" (p. 168).

So, Freud seems to have been interested in the revival of the good
experiences the patient had had with his or her primary care-givers,
while Winnicott addressed the importance of the analyst not repeating their failures in responding to the emotional needs of the child.
However, both were right in underscoring the need for the analyst to
be what we might term "a good object" for the patient, that is, another
human being who is able and willing to respond to her emotional
needs of being seen, understood, acknowledged, valued, and cared
for. When this happens, the analyst comes to occupy the role of the
people the patient had experienced or expected to "treat her or him
with affection". The result is that the patient sets now on a train of

development that strengthens her capabilities and frees them from previous encumbrances. This, Winnicott says, "gives the analyst plea-sure": we might say that it stimulates the development of his or her positive transference towards the patient. So, the establishment of a workable psychoanalytic situation depends on attaining a bond of mutual empathy and trust.

Of course, the way to such a desirable outcome is not as easy as it sounds in this description; the development of trust necessarily goes through the enactment, interpretation, and working through of mis-trust, and the way to affection and sympathy requires going through the experience and understanding of fear, hate, and envy. But this is the very stuff of analysis in its central period. The boundary between the opening and the mid-game is far from being neat and clear, but the fact remains that the pair needs to establish a firm positive bond that may act as sound basis to sustain it during the stormy developments that are to come. The initial phase of the analysis corresponds, at least conceptually, to the emergence and the construction of such a bond.

The mid-game

Once the firm, positive transference–countertransference relationship has been established and patient and analyst have reached a workable agreement on what it is that they are doing together, they are already playing the mid-game. This is multifarious and unpredictable, so that, as Freud (1913c) wrote, "the infinite variety of moves which develop after the opening defy any . . . description" (p. 123). This makes impracticable any attempt to describe it in terms of a particular sequence, such as Meltzer's (1967) "natural history" of the treatment. What French psychoanalysts call, after Bouvet (1955; Sparer, 2009), the "type cure" (*la cure type*) cannot be thought of as an objective descrip-tion of the stages in the conduct of the analysis, but, rather, as an exposition of the principles of the healing process. This is precisely what I intend to do in this section: discuss some of the basic problems and principles of the evolution of the analysis.

The obstacles to the evolution of the process

If the analytic process were to follow a straightforward continuous progress, things would be much easier for analysts and analysands alike, but Freud soon discovered that any advancement along this path would necessarily be hindered by various obstacles, which he grouped under the generic term "resistances". What is a *resistance*? Freud originally defined it as a violation of the "basic rule" of analysis: the patient, who had agreed to observe his mental processes and say everything that he perceived, without omitting anything for any reason, over and over again found some grounds for failing to do so, without realising that this is tantamount to sabotaging the analysis. Freud saw it as an expression of the very same forces that implemented repression in the first place. This is a metapsychological explanation of the phenomenon, which was later taken over by ego psychology, seeing it as an automatic mechanism, unleashed by impending anxiety and aiming at the maintenance of homeostasis. An alternative personological, object-relations orientated explanation conceives resistance as an expression of the negative transference.

Freud (1914d) always emphasised that the interpretation of resistance and transference is the very basis of his therapeutic and research technique. Indeed, he went as far as asserting that the acceptance and use of these two concepts is the litmus test that differentiates what is psychoanalysis from what is not.

However, the relation between resistance and transference is complex. On the one hand, resistance may be interpreted as an expression of mistrust towards the analyst—that is, a negative transference. On the other hand, Freud considered that the transference acts in the service of resistance, since it substitutes repetitive actions for verbalised remembrance. It is most probably not useful to ask whether resistance is the origin of the transference or the other way round, since their relation might be better considered as dynamic, rather than genetic. Hence, which of them one interprets as being primary depends on the perspective chosen in order to view a hypercomplex phenomenon, and the best approach would be to alternate between the various perspectives, in order to attain a multi-dimensional perception of what is actually happening.

But the concept of resistance is used for much more than the patient's failure to comply with the basic rule. Freud's (1900a) most sweeping definition identified it with everything done by the analysand that obstructs his gaining access to the unconscious. Hence, "Psychoanalysis is justly suspicious. One of its rules is that whatever interrupts the progress of analytic work is a resistance" (p. 517). Of course, such an absolute assertion demanded qualification, and this he did in a note to a later edition, in which he clarified that "it is of course only to be taken as a technical rule, as a warning to analysts" (p. 517, n1). In other words, external obstacles do exist, but they might also be appropriated by resistance in order to impede the analysis, and analysts should heed this possibility.

Here, everything depends, of course, on how one defines the final goal of the analysis. For Freud it was indubitably *to make conscious the unconscious,* but other conceptions of the therapeutic process might define it in terms of other goals, such as attaining intimacy in relations, individuation, the integration of the personality, creative thinking, intersubjectivity (understood in terms of recognising the other's subjectivity), authenticity, and so on. Nevertheless, the fact is that in of all these conceptions a resistance can be defined as anything that impedes the attainment of the goal of the analysis or hinders the progress towards it. Hence, one might speak about the patient having a resistance towards establishing a more intimate relationship with the analyst or towards thinking her own thoughts. Now, the question is, who defines this goal? Apparently it is always the analyst, in terms of his theory, or the theory shared by his professional community. So it seems that *resistance is anything said or done by the patient that opposes the analyst's goals,* but this is tantamount to turning psychoanalysis into a form of indoctrination.

Freud (1921c) was well aware of this danger, which he considered to be a form of suggestion, and tried to warn analysts of this:

> I can remember . . . feeling a muffled hostility to Bernheim's tyranny of suggestion. When a patient who showed himself unamenable was met with the shout: 'What are you doing? *Vous vous contre-suggestion-nez'* [original italics], *I said to myself that this was an evident injustice and an act of violence. For the man certainly had a right to counter-suggestions if people were trying to subdue him with suggestions.* (p. 89, my italics)

As we have seen in Chapters Three and Four, Freud's (1919a) solution to this problem was to keep a neutral stance *vis-à-vis* the patient's values, ideology, and general outlook on life, avoiding the narcissistic lure of re-creating another human being. He considered such an effort to orientate the patient's life towards better goals not to be

> in the least necessary for therapeutic purposes. For I have been able to help people with whom I had nothing in common – neither race,

education, social position nor outlook upon life in general – without affecting their individuality. (p. 165)

Of course, this referred only to the analyst's *conscious* influence on the patient, but nothing was said at the time about the *unconscious* influence that the analyst's beliefs, values, and aims, as well as the underlying assumptions on which his theories were based, had on the patient. Besides, many of these beliefs and values were not considered at all to be assumptions, but only "the way things are", as we have seen in Chapter Nine, when discussing the *Weltanschauung,* or "conception of the world" (Hernández de Tubert, 2004).

For instance, Freud's (1930a) rebuttal of one of Christianity's "ideal demands", "Thou shalt love thy neighbour as thyself", is clearly an affirmation of his own assumptions about the human being, fairness, and life in general, which might not have been shared by any given patient. His argument against it is full of ideological assumptions, such as: (i) love is a limited good that should be preserved and spent wisely (just like capital); (ii) it must be deserved, that is, it should not be given unless as a part of an exchange for other goods; (iii) giving love to someone who does not deserve it is doing an injustice to the deserving; (iv) since there is a limited amount of love available, giving it away freely can only bring about a dearth of love for oneself and for one's intimates. Is this not a direct consequence of Freud's bourgeois values, when applied to human relationships? (Hernández de Tubert, 2008b). And would it not be reasonable to assert that these underlying assumptions of Freud's thinking would be reflected in the content of his interpretations when dealing with a patient who believed that love is a function of the personality that increases with practice, and, hence, tried to follow the Christian injunction? For instance, an interpretation that his acts of generosity towards strangers were *nothing but* a masochistic expression of unconscious guilt would gloss over the existence of significant differences between patient and analyst in their beliefs and assumptions about human nature and the meaning of life, or lack of it. This would be compounded by the fact that a large part of the patient's assumptions are as unconscious as the analyst's, and, hence, require a work of interpretation in order to become explicit.

Nowadays, many of us would feel that it is an important part of the analyst's work to explore, and to invite the patient to explore, each other's underlying assumptions, in order to clarify their mutual coincidences and differences, their meaning, and their consequences for the analytic relationship. But this shared work first requires overcoming a reluctance, *in both patient and analyst*, to qualify and relativise one's cherished beliefs, which derive from early introjections of one's primary relations.

This brings us to another major point: while classical theory conceived resistance as a manifestation of the patient's internal defences, the various relational theories, starting with object-relations theory, have come to view it as a field phenomenon, derived from unconscious resonances and collusions between both parties. In 1933, Ferenczi had suggested that when the analysis came to a stalemate—what nowadays we would call an *impasse*—this could be due to a negative transference of hatred and rage towards the analyst. Although these feelings and the reasons for them were usually suppressed and hidden behind "a striking, almost helpless compliance and willingness to accept [his] interpretations" (p. 197), when they finally emerged—either spontaneously or as a result of his probing into their suppressed feelings and thoughts towards him, as we have seen in Chapter Five—they took the form of an unsparing criticism of him. They "called [him] insensitive, cold, even hard and cruel, when they reproached [him] with being selfish, heartless, conceited" (p. 197). At first, he felt unfairly treated and resorted to the easy way out of blaming the patient's psychopathology for this misrepresentation, but then he began to wonder whether there might be some truth in their accusations, listened to them attentively, enquired into his own suppressed feelings, and finally concluded that they were right in their criticism. At this point, he felt that the only valid option, consistent with the truth-seeking spirit of psychoanalysis, was to openly acknowledge this to the patient. Surprisingly, this recognition, far from destroying the patient's confidence in him as an analyst, strengthened the analytic bond and opened the way for a deepening of the analysis.

In 1958, Racker (1958b) published a paper titled "Counter-resistance and interpretation", in which he referred to the by no means unusual clinical situation in which the analyst can see and understand something that appears to be important in the patient, but fails to interpret it. There are usually various rationalisations that seem to justify this omission, such as feeling that the patient is not yet ready to receive the interpretation, and sometimes they appear to be valid, but this is not always the case; frequently they were "merely a rejection produced by subjective factors, a 'counterresistance' opposing the interpretation", and this "coincided with resistances in the patient that concern the same situation. *Sometimes it is as though there were a tacit agreement between analyst and patient, a secret understanding to keep quiet about a certain topic*" (p. 215, my italics).

Such situations are frequently felt by the analyst to be the most urgent one at the moment. Hence, they correspond to the patient's central conflict, but also, not unsurprisingly, to one of the analyst's central conflicts, as Ferenczi (1985) courageously explored in his *Clinical Diary*. This is what makes it so difficult to analyse these instances of unconscious defensive collusion between the two parties, but it is also what makes it mandatory to identify and interpret them as an essential part of the analytic enquiry.

The Barangers (2008, 2009) developed, from the early 1960s, the concept of the "bastion", defined as something that the patient considers vital to keep out of the analysis. This is based on a splitting process that does not necessarily imply repression: some of the split-off contents may be conscious or can easily become conscious, while "others, on the contrary, are repressed and correspond to more archaic splits that support the present splitting" (2009, p. 8). But the bastion crystallises only when the patient's manoeuvres to avoid knowing what has been split meet a similar wish of not knowing in the analyst. Then an unconscious collusion emerges, which can only be understood as a field phenomenon.

The bastion is constructed, not only from the conjunction of patient's and the analyst's pathological nuclei, but also from both parties' beliefs, values, and assumptions, including the analyst's theories and her conception of the treatment. Certain theories may contribute to, and rationalise for the therapist, the existence and maintenance of a bastion (Baranger, Baranger, & Mom, 1978). This does not in any way refute them, but only shows that any theoretical point of view may be unconsciously used for defensive purposes by both analyst and patient. Besides, the fact that the analyst has identified herself with a certain perspective in psychoanalysis also has unconscious determinants, as does the fact that the patient has sought to be, and chosen to remain, in analysis with a certain analyst belonging to a particular school of analytic thought and practice.

However, sooner or later, the analyst has to face the fact that the analysis is not working any more (this is what Baranger, Baranger, & Mom (1982) call a "non-process"). If she avoids falling into the trap of the easy way out of blaming it all on the patient's resistances, and strives—as Ferenczi (1933) did—to identify and understand her own unconscious contribution to this stalemate, there might be a new opening of the dialogue that revitalises the process. In this, the patient frequently gives some hints of understanding the situation, and the open discussion of the bastion they have built together determines that sort of restructuring of the field that we call "insight". Since "the analytic process can be conceived as the successive resolution of the impediments that time and again hinder communication and the mobility of the field" (Baranger & Baranger, 2009, p. 8), the identification, analysis, open discussion, and eventual resolution of the bastions that emerge during the treatment may be conceived as the gist of the analytic work.

Another related phenomenon that impedes the continuation of the work of analysis is what Puget and Wender (1982) called the "phenomenon of the overlapping worlds". Since analyst and patient are bound to share a significant part of their experiential worlds (the general cultural, social, and political context, institutional participation (e.g., in training analyses), common acquaintances, etc.), the patient's expressions frequently touch upon some of the analyst's personal concerns and anxieties. One such situation is the impact of social catastrophe (wars, both internal and external, crises, revolutions, terrorism, abrupt changes in government, political assassinations, and so on) on the analytic pair, with its consequent disturbance of the interpretative process, as described by Puget (1988) who points out that

> one of the difficulties in conceptualizing the state of social catastrophe and its psychoanalytic registration derives from the fact that the psychoanalyst is immersed in the same social context as his patients, and is affected by the same fears and difficulties in understanding actual events. (p. 86)

Hence, if the country is at war, a king dies, there is a general election, an earthquake, or an epidemic, or the psychoanalytic institution to which both parties belong is undergoing a crisis, it is very difficult, perhaps impossible, for an analyst to keep his analytic stance, instead of becoming submerged into the traumatic situation that both of them share, thus taking what the patient is saying not as an association, but as factual information about something that concerns them both. The same thing happens when the patient gets to know something about the personal life of the analyst, or when the patient's anxieties, experiences, and dilemmas are akin to his. In such cases, there is a silent tension that interferes with the progress of the analysis.

In this, although Puget and Wender would have the analyst use his self-analysing function to recover the capacity for analytic detachment, a relational approach would demand an open discussion of the present obstacle, as Ferenczi (1933) suggested, since they represent an unconscious field phenomenon that should be made explicit and duly interpreted. Besides, even though such phenomena have been identified from their emergence in extraordinary circumstances, there is reason to believe that they are a part of an unconscious ongoing process that underlies the psychoanalytic dialogue. (There is more about this in the next subsection, on "Enactment and transference".)

This field conception of the obstacles to the treatment and its dissolution might well be applied to the more severe disturbances of the process that Etchegoyen (1986) calls the "strategies of the ego". There are three of them: *acting out*, the *negative therapeutic reaction*, and the *reversible perspective*. Each of them hinders, distorts, or completely obstructs the psychoanalytic process in a particular way:

> What is common to all three is that they prevent insight from crystallizing. What distinguishes them is that each operates in its own special way. *Acting out* disturbs the analytic task, which is also the task of achieving insight. The *negative therapeutic reaction*, as its name indicates, does not impede the task, but it disturbs the achievement of insight, which are lost or not consolidated. In the *reversible perspective*, finally, insight is not achieved because the patient does not wish it so and in fact is looking for something else. In sum, acting out operates on the *task*, the negative therapeutic reaction on the *achievements* and the reversal of perspective on the *contract*. (pp. 700–701)

It is surprising that the author does not include resistance in his description of the obstacles to the process, but our bewilderment recedes when we notice that there is not a single chapter in his 876 page treatise *Fundamentals of Psychoanalytic Technique* on the subject of resistance. Of course, the whole book deals with resistance and its resolution by means of interpretation, but he does not consider it to be a separate phenomenon, but, rather, an expression of the negative transference. This Kleinian perspective is in sharp contrast with the ego-psychological view of Greenson (1967), whose book on technique deals mainly with the varieties of resistance.

Now, *acting out*, defined as an attack on the analytic task of verbalising, made by a patient who would rather repeat her experiences in action than express them in words (Freud, 1914g), can also be interpreted as a reaction to a failure, on the part of the analyst, to identify and respond to some of the patient's emotional needs or demands. Kohut (1984), for example, has studied extensively how the analyst's failure to respond to the patient's selfobject needs might determine an acting out, which seems to be especially designed in order to wake the analyst up from his empathic slumber.

Of course, this interpretation is based upon a theory that includes the assumption that the subject—both the baby during infancy and the patient in treatment—requires that the caring other identify, understand, and respond to her emotional and developmental needs, in order to spur the developmental, and, hence, the therapeutic, process. But even if one sticks to the classic psychoanalytic theory of drive–defence conflicts, it is conceivable that the analysand's need that her plight should be understood and interpreted by the analyst might seek another form of expression if the latter fails to respond in an analytically adequate way.

The *negative therapeutic reaction* was first described by Freud (1923b), in *The Ego and the Id*, as a particular mismatch between the parties, in which the analyst finds that there has been a significant progress in the treatment, but the patient disagrees, denies the analyst's positive evaluation, attributes it to other causes alien to the analytic work, and presents a symptomatic aggravation. Freud first considers this phenomenon in terms of the negative transference, but later discards this hypothesis, and states "not only that such people cannot endure any praise or appreciation, but that they react inversely to the progress of the treatment" (p. 49).

After discarding several alternative hypotheses, Freud reaches what he deems to be a "final" conclusion, that "the most powerful of all obstacles to recovery, more powerful than the familiar ones of narcissistic inaccessibility, a negative attitude towards the physician and clinging to the gain from illness" (p. 49) is an unconscious sense of guilt. This is his explanation for the negative therapeutic reaction. There have been other theoretical explanations, each of which provides a rationale for a way of handling this problem. Freud himself later attributed this reaction to the patient's primary masochism, thus replacing the expression "unconscious feeling of guilt" with that of "need for punishment" (in "The economic problem of masochism" (1924c)) and to the workings of the death instinct (in "Analysis terminable and interminable" (1937c)). Riviere (1936) takes exception at the idea that "the patient does not want to get well" or that he has a desire for suffering:

> If the patient desires to preserve things as they are and even sacrifices his cure for that reason, it is not really because he does not wish to get well. *The reason why he does not get well and tries to prevent any change is because, however he might wish for it, he has no faith in getting well.* What he really expects unconsciously is not a change for the better but a change for the worse, and what is more, one that will not affect himself only, but the analyst as well. *It is partly to save the analyst from the consequences of this that he refuses to move in any direction.* (p. 312, my italics)

Then, on the basis of the Kleinian concept of the "depressive position", she suggests that what the patient is unconsciously trying to do is to preserve and heal his internalised objects, both "good" and "bad", but felt to be damaged. This is akin to Fairbairn's (1952) explanation of the death instinct as an expression of the subject's love for the bad internal objects. For Riviere, the patient feels that getting well is a betrayal of his internal objects and that this is tantamount to damaging them, as well as the analyst in the transference.

Klein (1957), for her part, emphasised the role of envy in the negative therapeutic reaction: the patient is envious of the richness of an analyst who has so much that she can even give the patient the leftovers. She believes envy to be primary, as a direct expression of the death instinct. An alternative explanation, which she does not consider, is that destructive envy is a secondary phenomenon, an expression of narcissistic omnipotence in a patient who feels humiliated by having to need the help and care of another human being. This would be an instance of the dire pessimism about herself described by Riviere (Tubert-Oklander & Hernández de Tubert, 1997).

What is more remarkable about these explanations is they have usually been taken as mutually exclusive, and each has been hailed as being the ultimate cause of the negative therapeutic reaction. This univocal attitude breeds dogmatism. It is probably much better to adopt the analogical pluralistic stance suggested by Bollas (2007) of taking the various theories as several alternative intellectual instruments for the perception and understanding of any given clinical fact, and play with them until one fits. The other position of adhering stubbornly to a single interpretation, irrespective of the patient's expression and the total situation, might even be iatrogenic, as suggested by Riviere (1936), when she writes that "nothing will lead more surely to a negative therapeutic reaction in the patient than failure to recognize anything but the aggression in his material" (p. 311).

Here, the author is suggesting a relational explanation of the negative therapeutic reaction: the patient rejects the analyst's claims to therapeutic success because she feels misunderstood and unfairly treated. If we extend this in order to conceive such a reaction as a field phenomenon, we shall be able to take into account the possible differences—both conscious and unconscious—between the parties in their respective experiences and conceptions of the analytic process. It might well be that something that the analyst conceives as a progress is nothing of the kind from the patient's point of view, and that knowing what the analyst believes to have understood only makes the patient feel misunderstood, or even unheard and unseen. The only way out of this *cul-de-sac* is that the analyst must engage, as Ferenczi (1933) suggested, in self-criticism, invite the patient to openly voice her criticism of the analyst, and then listen to it! In any case, the mere fact that there is a discrepancy between the two as to the nature and value of something that has happened or is happening between them should be explicitly acknowledged and taken as an object of their shared analytic enquiry.

This brings us to Etchegoyen's third "strategy", which is the *reversible perspective* or, in a perhaps better English translation of his original Spanish text, the *reversal of perspective*. This is a situation in which the analyst suddenly discovers that the patient has been silently defining the treatment situation as something utterly different from psychoanalysis. Hence, patient and analyst have been working in quite different, or even opposite, directions, even though both have been following the external tasks that make up the visible aspect of an analysis: attendance, punctuality, payment, respect for the explicit rules, associating (for the patient) and interpreting (for the analyst). The result has been an impasse, in which things are apparently being done as they should, but nothing is being accomplished, from an analytic point of view.

This concept—originally introduced by Bion (1963) as a feature of the psychotic part of the personality, and reframed by Etchegoyen in clinical terms—became obvious in the analytic treatment of severe personality disorders. Etchegoyen (1986, pp. 768–771) presents to us the clinical case of a homeopathic doctor, who came to analysis when the homeopathic treatment of his asthma unleashed an unbearable state of anxiety. When both anxiety and asthma were alleviated, the patient began secretly to take pulsatilla (a homeopathic drug) in order to be able to keep thinking that he was actually curing himself, and not being cured by the analysis. In the end, the analyst found out that the patient had intended, from the very beginning, to use the analysis as an auxiliary method to ameliorate the anxiety that the homeopathic treatment produced, as a necessary therapeutic aggravation, so that he might tolerate it and cure himself with his own methods. When this was finally openly discussed, the analyst told his patient that he should opt for one of the two treatments, and the latter decided to leave the analysis and continue with a self-applied homeopathic therapy.

Such events are characteristic of patients with severe malignant narcissism, as in the case of perversion or psychopathy, in which there is a conscious dishonesty on the patient's part. Our method requires at least a conscious good faith, and capsizes when faced with conscious deception. The only thing we can do with lies is to denounce them and try to interpret their underlying motives, but this will only work if and when we manage to get in touch with a truthful part of the patient's personality that is able and willing to consider and analyse the workings of his mendacious part.

However, there are more benign instances of such reversion of perspective. These stem from unacknowledged and sometimes unconscious differences in the patient's and the analyst's assumptions. If there is no defensive need, in either of them, to deny the existence of such differences, their voicing might lead to solving a previous misunderstanding. For instance, a patient might finally come to understand that the analyst considers knowing and awareness of one's vital situation to be an unquestionable asset, and say: "Doctor, now that I understand your position and intention, I have to tell you that I truly believe there are things that it is better not to know." If both parties are able and willing to conceive, accept, and discuss these differences, one possible outcome might be that the patient could decide that she should seek some other kind of treatment, and the analyst might agree with this.

The very same thing occurs when there are differences in their conceptions of the goals of the treatment. For example, an analyst might be convinced that homosexuality is a disease and that the analysis should not be finished until the patient becomes heterosexual, while the latter considers it to be a valid option in life and is willing to terminate a treatment that has been successful, from her point of view, without changing her sexual orientation. In any case, the existence of such differences should become the focus of the analytic enquiry in their mutual dialogue.

None of these considerations negates, in any way, what we already know about defence mechanisms, resistances, strategies, and negative transference, from a one-person psychology point of view. What is being said is that, in parallel with all the intrapersonal manoeuvres that psychoanalysis has successfully explored, there is a whole dimension of bipersonal, interactive, field, and social phenomena that should be taken into account for the identification, understanding, interpretation, discussion, and eventual solution of the obstacles to the analytic process.

In this, we might well follow Freud's (1900a) example. When he wrote that "whatever interrupts the progress of analytic work is a resistance" (p. 517), he did not mean "one hundred per cent of the cases in which something interrupts the progress of analytic work are an expression of resistance", but, rather, "one should take any occurrence that interrupts the progress of analytic work as a resistance, until proved otherwise". This is the sort of aphorism used by physicians since the time of Hippocrates. Hence, we might well affirm that "every obstacle to the process is a field phenomenon", as long as we take care to add "until proved otherwise". Since the bipersonal and field dimension of clinical phenomena has been largely ignored for so long, it is an act of prudence, from a strategic point of view, to give it pre-eminence, lest it be unwillingly passed over, out of sheer intellectual habit. Since ignoring intrapersonal mechanisms is much less likely for any properly trained psychoanalyst or psychoanalytic therapist, as their study has been widely emphasised in her training, the sought result would be a more balanced view, which oscillates between an intrapersonal and a bipersonal and field perception and understanding of clinical events.

Enactment and transference

Much has been said, in the various chapters of this book, about transference and countertransference, so I shall restrict my present comments to a discussion of enactment and the dialectics of repetition and novelty.

The term "enactment" is relatively new in psychoanalytic literature. It is certainly not part of the classical language of psychoanalysis, and it has been in use only for the past twenty-five years. The first published articles on the subject were written by Jacobs (1986), and McLaughlin (1987).

An *enactment* is an unconscious scene that is being played by only two actors—the patient and the analyst—who are not at all conscious, at the beginning, of what is actually happening. The script that is being enacted stems from the confluence of both parties' unconscious experience, but the effect of the psychoanalytic device highlights the patient's contribution, while keeping most of the analyst's in the background, at the time of analysing the event. None the less, the analytic enquiry of these occurrences demands that the analyst's unconscious contribution be included, as a part of the field phenomenon. One such development is the discovery, analysis, and resolution of a bastion.

In these terms, an enactment is a discrete event, which might be going on for some time, which is finally identified and analysed. These are critical and highly significant episodes, sometimes intensely dramatic (Bateman, 1998), whose analysis frequently represents a turning point in the course of a treatment, but the term "enactment" also has a wider connotation. It refers to a continuous process of mutual unconscious influence between patient and analyst, mediated by their unwilling non-verbal communication (McLaughlin, 1987). From this point of view, since this unconscious communication is the vehicle for the unconscious fantasies that are the very stuff of the transference–countertransference field, the whole psychoanalytic treatment may be viewed as continuous enactment, which is to be enquired into and interpreted by the analysis. Of course, such a wide definition of the term makes it almost an equivalent of "interaction", but since this other term is usually taken to cover only the visible aspects of behaviour, the word enactment is kept as a reminder that we are talking about an *unconscious* communication and interaction that serves to express unconscious meanings.

In order to avoid the ambiguity of this expression, Bass (2003) has suggested that we use "enactment" with a lower-case "e" to refer to "ordinary, quotidian enactments that form the daily ebb and flow of ordinary analytic process" (p. 657) and "Enactment" with an upper-case "E" for "highly condensed precipitates of unconscious psychic elements in patient and in analyst that mobilize our full, heightened attention and define, and take hold of, analytic activity for periods of time". The idea is to call into question the concept of enactment as a discrete occurrence, which tends to obscure "our awareness that every interaction between analyst and patient may be usefully viewed as a transference–countertransference enactment even, as is often the case, if its meaning, or even its very existence, is recognized only retro-spectively" (p. 660). But still something is lost when we emphasise the continuous aspect of enactment, thus neglecting the fact that there actually are some special moments of the analytic interaction that show its existence in sharp relief and have a special relevance for the evolution of the process.

However, Aron (2003b) holds some reservations about these ter-minological distinctions, since he feels that "as soon as we designate a term like enactment to refer to these special and discrete events, we may too easily lose sight of the continuing place of interaction in clin-ical work" (p. 627). The term has been useful for creating a conceptual space that allows the introduction of interactional concepts into psychoanalytic theory, which is, thus, expanded. But the term also contains and delimits recognition of the interactional dimension of psychoanalysis: "By being given a limited place under the rubric of enactment, interaction is safely sealed off, limiting our recognition of its centrality, and hence setting limits on the interpersonalization of psychoanalysis" (p. 627). In other words, Aron believes that, even though clinical experience and discoveries are forcing psychoanalysts to find a place in their theories for the sort of unconscious interper-sonal phenomena that had previously been excluded from the field of Freudian psychoanalysis (although not from interpersonal psychoanalysis), its subversive impact on the generally accepted theory is kept at bay by creating a particular niche for them, a special isolated space—such as the treatment of severely disturbed patients or some unusual clinical circumstances—in which these unexpected things happen, while preserving a belief in the general validity of established theory, which is thus protected from any need to be thoroughly revised (Aron, 1996).

A similar criticism is directed at the contemporary extension of the Kleinian concept of *projective identification*, in order to include inter-personal occurrences. It was Bion (1980) who suggested that this defensive operation was something more than an omnipotent fantasy of the subject, but, rather, included an actual interpersonal occurrence that had an impact on another human being, when he said, "I think that the patient does something to the analyst and the analyst does something to the patient; it is not just an omnipotent phantasy" (p. 15).

The Argentine psychoanalyst Grinberg (1962, 1979) developed from some of Bion's early observations his own concept of "projective counter-identification", which is supposed to be an objective uncon-scious reaction generated in the analyst by the violence of the patient's projective identifications. Hence, it is an objective reaction to the patient's projections, which should be differentiated from the analyst's countertransference reactions that stem from his neurotic remnants that are reactivated by the patient's conflicts. However, this differentiation might be called into question, since it is based on two assumptions that are not at all obvious, and which I consider to be false: (i) that there might be a reaction to another human being's influence that does not involve the receiver's own emotional attitude, and (ii) that responding with one's own emotions to another's inter-personal actions is a pathological symptom that may be avoided by analysis.

Both Bion and Grinberg are obviously trying to overcome the limi-tations of a theory that treats mental processes as if they were a closed system. If theory-building starts from the assumption that only indi-viduals are "real" and that their experience and behaviour depends only on their inner organisation and dynamics, then the great mystery that demands explanation is how is it ever possible for human beings to communicate and relate. But these attempts to fill in the gap between individuals by means of concepts such as "enactment" and "projective identification", although useful and certainly better than the previous theory, strike us as only partial and too limited to provide a satisfactory solution. This is why it might be better to carry out a more thorough revision of our theory, by affirming, as Fairbairn (1952) did, that human beings are essentially social and have a primary need of relating to other human beings. But, if we start from the assumption that only relations are real and individuals are the nodal points in a multifarious network of communication and relations (Foulkes, 1964), then it is the existence of individual experience, thinking, and will that needs to be explained. Obviously, what we need is a dual point of view, which should oscillate between one-person, two-person, and multi-person psychologies, taking them as complementary views, with a figure–ground relationship, providing us with a deeper perception and understanding of human experience and behaviour (Tubert-Oklander, 2013b).

Now, even if we accept the proposition that the psychoanalytic treatment is a continuous mutual enactment that gives a basis to the transference–countertransference field and the analytic process, there is still something missing, which is conveyed by Bass's concept of Enactment. This is the existence of "especially challenging moments for the analyst [which] may be decisive turning points in the analysis". They are also "times of high risk and high gain for both patient and analyst" (Aron, 2003b, p. 625). There is a continuous unconscious interaction going on, and this is the very stuff of psychoanalysis, since "free association consists of action and interaction, not just words. The talking cure is not a flow of words but is inherently an interactional experience" (p. 624), but there are also some critical moments that need to be identified, named, and thought through.

The same thing happens with the transference–countertransference. There is, indeed, a continuous process of unconscious mutual projection and recreation of previous patterns of relational experience in the course of the treatment, but some aspects and moments of it stand out from the rest of the relationship as being true confusions between the past and the present, the inner and the outer world, and by their mechanical repetitiveness. In Piaget's (1967) terms, every new experience has to be interpreted in the light of schemas derived from previous experience (*assimilation*), but after that it should be modified in order to include whatever is novel in the new experience (*accommodation*). In other words, someone who sees a goose for the first time might say "What a strange duck!" but sooner or later he will have to incorporate the knowledge of the existence of geese, swans, and flamingos. Or an uninformed patient who comes to analysis will look at the therapist and say "What a strange doctor!" (or teacher, priest, adviser, mother, or friend), long before starting to conceive what an analyst is. From this point of view, the transference may be viewed as a predominance of assimilation (repetition) on accommodation (learning from experience, reality principle). Of course, this might be said of any dogmatic thinking or attitude, but in psychoanalysis we are dealing not only with the kind of action schemas studied by Piaget—which are the basis for cognitive and conative functions—but with emotional and relational schemas, which are the motivational substrate that Piaget consciously left out of his research.

So, when, in the unconscious dynamics of relationship, there is a fluid alternation of assimilation and accommodation, new relations begin as re-editions of previous ones, but they are soon modified by the impact of what is truly new in this novel experience. Hence, there is learning from experience (Bion, 1962) and the personality and its relations evolve, grow, and mature; this is what we may consider to be health. But when assimilation prevails, everything is repeated as it has been before (or as it has been felt, experienced, or imagined to be); the spiral of life is substituted by the vicious circle of psychopathology and, instead of having a developing set of variations on the basic themes that define the subject's identity, we get the monotonous repetitiveness of a broken record. This is the traditional psychoanalytic concept of transference (Freud, 1912b).

The problem is that the transference was discovered from the impact of its pathology on the psychoanalytic treatment. Consequently, we tend to think of it in terms of the compulsion to repeat, which is a pathological phenomenon. (Indeed, pathology is defined by psychoanalysis in terms of its repetitiveness. There is nothing as predictable and dull as mental pathology, whereas health is characterised by its creativity, unpredictability, and joyfulness.) But this has hindered the study and theorisation of mental health. It is no wonder, then, that such an enquiry had to emerge from the investigation of infantile and child development and early relationships, and not from our clinics, which necessarily have a psychopathological bias.

Therefore, the systematic interpretation and working through of these repetitive stereotyped patterns of relationship, a scenario that is to be enacted conjointly by analyst and patient as the only actors (there is no one else in the room, at least in bipersonal psycho-analysis), opens the way for a more fluid and creative process of dialogue, relationship, and interaction between them (the spiral process). But interpretation is by no means limited to stereotypes: the emergence of new feelings, thoughts, and ways of relating also has to be acknowledged, named, thought through, and celebrated. The hermeneutic activity of analysis dwells on the fringe between the old and the new, repetition and innovation, inner and outer, mental and material, fantasy and reality. Just like Hermes, the messenger god who was the go-between for the communication between humans and the Olympians, the master of crossroads, boundaries, and thresholds, of dreams, interpretation, and oratory; patron of thieves, merchants, and travellers, psychoanalysis aids human beings in their transits and teaches them a way to articulate their experience of two worlds (Tubert-Oklander, 2013b). In the beginning, this is the analyst's role, but this responsibility is sooner or later taken over by a new form of dialogue that evolves in the pair and, when the twain finally part, it is expected that the former patient take away with him an internalised dialogue that will keep going on for the rest of his life; this is called thought. And so we come to the next stage, that of the ending, which is the subject of the next chapter.

CHAPTER ELEVEN

The evolution of the analytic process (2): the end

The meaning of the end

We have already seen the inception and the beginning of the process, as well as its prolonged middle term. It is now time to approach the subject of its end. But what do we mean by "ending an analysis"? Common sense tells us that a treatment ends when the patient and the analyst no longer meet on a regular basis, but in our discipline things do not usually follow this kind of logic. Freud (1937c) clearly stated this in "Analysis terminable and interminable", which represents his major effort at tackling this problem; there, he suggested that the end of the analysis comes when both parties no longer meet for analytic sessions, and that this happens when two conditions have been met: first, that all symptoms, inhibitions, and anxieties have disappeared, and second, that the analyst judges that "so much repressed material has been made conscious, so much that was unintelligible has been explained, and so much internal resistance conquered, that there is no need to fear a repetition of the pathological processes concerned" (p. 219). But there is still another possible meaning of terminating an analysis: that the patient has reached a level of absolute psychic normality and there is every reason to expect that this state will endure. This, he felt, happens in some favourable cases.

Nowadays, we would not be so positive about this. Every termination of an analysis is bound to be a partial disappointment for patient and analyst alike. But this is a disappointment of the magical and ideal expectations that both of us are bound to harbour, more or less consciously, at the beginning of the treatment, and which are to be contrasted with the more realistic expectations that might have been truly fulfilled. Besides, the achievements of an analysis frequently include some changes that had neither been expected nor imagined by either party. So, each of us has found in our work together, at one and the same time, more and less than our original expectations.

In addition, the extension of the process does not correspond to the formal limits of the treatment. An analytic process begins, for analyst and patient alike, long before they ever meet and continues developing after the interruption of regular sessions. Indeed, there is reason to believe that a major part of the therapeutic process happens *after the termination*. We do not know much about the patient's post-analytic process, since it happens, by definition, without our presence, but we know even less about the corresponding process in the analyst, since some former patients have been much more candid than analysts in publishing these intimate experiences. Besides, the living consequences of an analysis are bound to continue for a lifetime; that is the assumption behind the often-repeated declaration that the full termination of an analysis comes when the patient is able to continue the analysis by himself. This is equivalent to what Freud called "interminable analysis".

Leaving aside this interminability of a successful psychoanalytic process, I shall describe, for the sake of clarity, the last two phases of an analytic treatment, in its ordinary sense: the *closure* or *termination phase*, and the *aftermath* or *post-analysis*.

The closure

Much has been written on the termination of analysis, but most of the literature has focused on the criteria for deciding it. Each of the authors has posed a list of indicators, which is regularly a direct expression of their theoretical conception of what makes a healthy human being. Hence, we have criteria such as attaining a genital primacy, reaching the depressive position, the dissolution of the superego, the strengthening of the ego, the amelioration of defences, and so on. The basic psychiatric criterion of the disappearance of the symptoms that led the patient to seek treatment in the first place is usually suspect, but in the end it is frequently used in practice, because it is clear-cut and easy to apply to a given case.

In the beginnings of psychoanalysis, being cured was equated with symptomatic alleviation. This was consistent with the medical origin of our discipline. But soon Freud (1916–1917) realised that a deeper change was required, in order to avoid relapses.

So, a true cure would have meant the disappearance of the capacity to form new symptoms, and that implied attaining some change in the structure and dynamics of the patient's mind. But what is a symptom? Freud defined symptoms as "acts detrimental, or at least useless, to the subject's life as a whole, often complained of by him as unwelcome and bringing unpleasure or suffering to him" (1916–1917, p. 358). These are undesirable on account of the expenditure of energy they bring about, thus restricting the patient's capabilities:

> Since this outcome depends mainly on the quantity of the energy which is thus absorbed, you will easily see that "being ill" is in its essence a practical concept. But if you take up a theoretical point of view and disregard this matter of quantity, you may quite well say that we are all ill – that is, neurotic – since the preconditions for the formation of symptoms can also be observed in normal people. (p. 358)

Here, we are dealing with two different approaches: the medical view, for which there is such a thing as health, which is lost as a result of the disease and recovered through the treatment, and an existential view that sees the patient's suffering as part of the unavoidable human condition.

> You had formed a different picture of the return to health of a neurotic patient – that, after submitting to the tedious labours of a psycho-analysis, he would become another man; but the total result, so it seems, is that he has rather less that is unconscious and rather more that is conscious in him than he had before. The fact is that you are

probably under-estimating the importance of an internal change of this kind. *The neurotic who is cured has really become another man, though at bottom, of course, he has remained the same; that is to say, he has become what he might have become at best under the most favourable conditions.* But that is a very great deal. (Freud, 1916–1917, p. 435)

In 1927, Ferenczi wrote, in "The problem of the termination of the analysis", that a symptomatic cure is never enough, since it leaves untouched the underlying neurotic character structure, which is the cause of the disposition to develop a symptomatic neurosis, when having to face new demanding circumstances. Hence, a full treatment should always include character analysis: "Theoretically, no symptom analysis can be regarded as ended unless it is a complete character analysis into the bargain" (p. 80). This is even more urgent in the case of prospective psychoanalysts, so he suggested that a training analysis should be mandatory, and that it should be stricter and deeper than ordinary treatments. This is an issue that worried him during his final years, as he wrote in his last paper (Ferenczi, 1933) that "Above all, we ourselves must have been really well analysed, right down to 'rock bottom'" (p. 226). This means that analysts must have faced and recognised in themselves all those unpleasant character traits that they strive to uncover in their patients. The then common practice of having short training analyses, since these analysands were "normal", was detrimental, since it brought about the impossible situation that patients were having better analyses than their analysts, a fact they sensed, but tried to suppress or hide in order not to damage their analysts.

From these observations emerged the idea that a "full analysis" should bring about a state of absolute mental health and preclude the emergence of any further neurotic symptom. This was what Balint (1952) called "supertherapy". Freud (1937c), was very sceptical about the possibility of such a treatment.

Now, all these considerations are made *from the analyst's point of view*, who wonders whether the present conditions are such that he may decide to discharge the patient, *in terms of his own theories and values*. In Spanish, when a patient is discharged from a hospital or any other medical treatment, he is said to have been *"dado de alta"*—literally, "sent up"—in contrast to soldiers, who are *"dados de baja"*—"sent down". Such expressions show that the very idea of termination or discharge implies an authoritarian stance, in which the analyst is taken to be "the one who knows". If, as Lacan (1973) suggested, this is the very basis of the transference, then one would expect such an assumption to have been dissolved, or, at least, somehow modified, in the course of the treatment.

And what about the patient's point of view? In 1932, Balint observed, in "Character analysis and new beginning", that it was not unusual for patients who had already attained a symptomatic cure to still wish to continue the analysis:

> What keeps them at their analytic work is their wish, often unconscious, *to be able to love free from anxiety, to lose their fear of complete surrender*. . . . The marked neurotic symptoms disappeared through the treatment in a relatively short time, but there still remained *a complete incapacity or only a very qualified capacity for love* . . .
>
> Moreover, we are quite often sought by people who at the very first consultation present just this picture. It is difficult to place them under any diagnostic heading. *Their chief complaint is that they cannot find their place in life. Nothing is actually wrong with them* or, at most, they have some quite insignificant neurotic symptoms, *but they take no pleasure in anything*. (Balint, 1952, p. 151, my italics)

Apparently, Balint was talking about the sort of clinical problems that Fairbairn (1952) called "schizoid factors in the personality" and Kohut "narcissistic personality disorders" or "disorders of the self" (Kohut & Wolf, 1978). The therapeutic response that Balint (1932, 1968) proposed for such problems is pretty much the same that Ferenczi (1929, 1930, 1931, 1933) had suggested and that Winnicott (1955, 1956) espoused, which is that the patient should undergo a regression to infantile dependency towards the analyst and be able to experience a "new beginning", free from anxiety—that is, to enjoy the benefits of a normal childhood under the analyst's devoted care.

In the same vein, Guntrip (1963) suggested a sequence of three levels of psychotherapy. The first one is that of the *Oedipal conflict*, in which the analysis and working through of such conflict brings about a symptomatic cure, this being the domain of classical psychoanalysis. This is a moment in which the analysis may be terminated, but sometimes this "cure" might "turn out to be far more some degree of schizoid compromise, a half-in-and-half-out relationship to life in which the patient is not really satisfied" (p. 280). This is, of course, the situation that made Balint's patients wish to continue with their treatments. But if the patient leaves, she might do relatively well in life, having had a treatment that transformed, as Freud (1895d) wrote, "[neurotic] misery into common unhappiness" (p. 305). Then she would be living a *schizoid compromise*. But, if this later turns not to be enough for the former patient, or if the hardships of life determine a relapse or the appearance of a new form of pathology, then she might come back for further treatment, with the same analyst or with another. But this second analysis would need to be quite different from the first, being carried out in terms of *regression and regrowth*, this being the third and deepest level of psychotherapy. Guntrip's (1975) own analytical experiences, with Fairbairn and Winnicott, followed this pattern, and the same was true for Little's (1985) analyses with Ella Freeman Sharpe and Winnicott.

But if we are to consider common unhappiness as an indication for psychoanalytic treatment, this is a far cry from the usual psychiatric conception of psychopathology, and psychoanalysis would then no longer be considered as something akin to a medical treatment, but as an effort to aid some people in their search for the Good Life. In this, the analysand's point of view is essential, since only she can say whether her life is worth living and if she is willing to do something to improve it. It is not for the analyst to judge whether this evaluation is "right" or "wrong", although she will certainly have an opinion about it, which should be shared, discussed, and analysed with the patient.

Let us consider what sort of criteria analysts have used in the past to tackle this problem. In 1940, Edward Glover and Marjorie Brierley sent a questionnaire on a number of issues on psychoanalytic technique to all the members of the British Psychoanalytical Society. The first question on the subject of termination was as follows: "CRITERIA FOR TERMINATION. *What are your criteria (a) Symptomatic, (b) psycho-sexual, (c) social? Are your criteria mostly intuitive?*" (Glover, 1955, p. 327). One third of the contributors failed to answer this question, and all who answered said that they used all three of them, although emphasising the symptomatic criterion, on account of its practical importance. But most of them also remarked that their decisions were mainly based on intuition, "a feeling, or impression, that the 'end' is approaching" (p. 327), which some considered should be thoroughly tested.

Of course, Glover, ever a staunch advocate of rationality and science, felt this as a major lack. But there is a possible alternative reading of these data. Perhaps the respondents were reacting to a dimly felt impression that their preferred theories were too sketchy and limited to do justice to the enormous complexity of the analytic experience, particularly in as much as they considered only the patient's mental state in making a decision that affected two people, not one.

As carrying out a thorough revision of the highly complex and variegated literature on the termination of analysis and discussing the technical issues it poses exceeds by far the scope of this presentation, I shall sketch only a few reflections on it, from the point of view proposed by this book.

Most contemporary analysts would agree that terminating a treatment cannot be done as a merely administrative measure, but that it should involve a *termination phase* in which the very fact that the analysis is about to end should be analytically enquired into. The termination phase is *that period in which the theme that the analysis is bound to have an end becomes meaningful for the analytic dialogue.* This is initiated by the appearance, in either the patient or the analyst, of the idea of termination. It might be the patient who brings it as an explicit reference, or as an unconscious meaning that emerges from the analysis of the associations, a narrative, a dream, or a symptomatic action. On the other hand, it may be the analyst who suddenly finds himself having an idea that refers to the end of this particular treatment, or experiences a dream or a symptom that is later found to imply and express such an idea. It might also emerge from the analysis of a mutual enactment. In any case, the parties more or less suddenly find themselves talking about the possibility or the inevitability of the termination, and analysing its implications.

This termination period may take anything from six months to two years. This does not mean that the analytic dialogue is constantly referring to the subject; rather, it emerges repeatedly, every now and then, but is always there in the background. Eventually, one of them suggests that they should begin to think of a date. This is not easy, since quite frequently there is a reappearance of previous symptoms that had already disappeared, as soon as the date is set. It seems that somehow the pair is bound to live through a recapitulation of all their relationship, including the transference–countertransference conflicts.

Sometimes, this determines a need for a postponement, but finally a definitive date is set, and this also has a particular meaning. The patient might wish to end the treatment on his birthday, or some other significant date, just before the holidays, on the anniversary of the beginning of the treatment, and so on.

Much has been written about mourning during this terminal phase, but I believe this to be severely biased. There is, of course, a feeling of loss when facing an impending separation, and in some patients this can be particularly intense and needs protracted working through, but there are also feelings of achievement of a well-done task and joy at the prospects for a fuller life. The whole situation is much more similar to that of a child who has come of age and is about to leave his parents' house, than to bereavement. And, if a patient has a catastrophic feeling of being orphaned, one might wonder if the time has really come for terminating this treatment.

In this, the analyst's theoretical and philosophical assumptions play a major part. If she is convinced of the basically tragic nature of life, she would expect that the patient go through a great suffering when facing termination and interpret any positive feelings about it as a form of manic denial. But, when the patients of such an analyst display precisely the type of suffering the therapist expects from them, is this a spontaneous occurrence or a response to the analyst's *Lebenschauung* (conception of life) and the corresponding technical interventions?

For instance, Meltzer (1984) tells us about the enormous distress suffered by his patients when he terminated the treatment according to his "process" conception, which saw its evolution in terms of a "natural history" of the evolution of transference. This included a "weaning process", which came as a pre-determined denouement that the analyst only needed to recognise, acknowledge, and respect, without any consideration for either party's hopes or expectations. This led to a striking discordance between the analyst's evaluation that the termination was satisfactory from the process point of view and what was actually happening to the two people involved:

> Symptoms might have gone, external circumstances might have improved—often the patient would have to admit that every reasonable requirement for happiness was now at hand—but the patient still felt ill, perhaps in an indefinable way. The consequence was a deep

reluctance to finish, and a focus of distrust that stood painfully in conflict with better feelings towards the analyst. I noticed that I too often felt troubled, uncertain, worried, inclined to procrastinate. *This was particularly true when the weaning process set in earlier than usual, according to my training and prior experience, after two and a half or three years in some cases, or under the pressure of external events such as a pregnancy or a job opportunity abroad.* (p. 171, my italics)

Obviously, something was wrong. None the less, Meltzer decided to adhere to his theoretical assumptions and finish the treatments, but insisted on establishing a more formalised follow-up period, in order to understand better what had happened. His observations, which we shall discuss further in the next subsection, on the post-analytic process, finally confirmed for him his theoretical point of view, which emphasised the unavoidable pain involved in the weaning process.

Now, Meltzer's two personal analytic experiences did not include a proper termination, since his first analysis was interrupted by military service, and his second analysis, with Melanie Klein, was cut off by her unexpected death during the termination process. This is how he tells us about it:

I remember that when I returned from service to see my first analyst to tell him that I was going abroad to complete my training, I could hardly speak but wept for half an hour and had to leave. *I had assumed this to be a manifestation of guilt for my treachery until we met socially some years later and he helped me to see it differently.* I had also assumed that the acute misery, feeling of dying and loneliness after Melanie Klein's death were peculiar to the circumstances rather than to the process. But I have come to think differently about this too as *I have watched patient after patient re-experience the suffering of the baby during weaning.* (p. 173, my italics)

Meltzer's candid and poignant narrative helps us to attain a better understanding of his observations. This seems to be an instance of a generalisation and theorisation of a personal experience that has not been properly worked through. His first analyst did something to alleviate his remorse, years later and in a non-clinical setting, but Klein had no opportunity to do so. However, she would not have done it, since she was as convinced as her analysand that weaning must, perforce, be agonisingly painful, and that the end of an analysis is a revival of this experience (Klein, 1950).

Of course, "weaning" is a metaphor that may be used to convey the feelings generated by an irreversible change in life, one that implies both gains and losses. At least, this is a point of view that I share with many other analysts, although it should be remembered that, for Klein and her students and followers, this is no metaphor, but an accurate and precise description of what is happening in the patient's unconscious. Patients, however, seem to be well aware of the metaphoric nature of such images, and often contribute with alternative analogies, which they feel convey quite adequately their feelings towards the termination. This was recorded by Payne (1950) in the following terms:

> I have found the end compared with the anxieties of growing up, leaving school, leaving the university, rebirth, weaning, the end of mourning, all being critical times involving a re-organization of ego and libidinal interests. (p. 205)

Balint (1950) also recorded more of these patients' metaphors, as we shall see below.

Leaving aside the question of whether weaning might be a suitable metaphor for the end of the analysis (as I noted before, I prefer that of "leaving the parents' house"), there is still the fact that the actual weaning of a baby is not necessarily traumatic. This only happens when the interruption of breast-feeding is imposed abruptly, as a one-sided decision by the mother (or the paediatrician), and without taking into account the child's degree of maturity and feelings. It is certainly not traumatic when it comes at the right moment, in conjunction with the introduction of new feeding experiences and ways of maintaining an intimate contact with mother, and with an adequate negotiation between mother and child in order to bring about the desired changes.

The same thing happens with the analysis. Many analysts, including Melanie Klein, believe that the analytic attitude and technique should be kept unmodified until the last minute of the final session. But this does not take into account the evolution of the relationship, and neither does it help the patient in the transition between being in analysis and the post-analytic period. For instance, when one reads Klein's (1961) *Narrative of a Child Analysis*, one is impressed by the obvious fact that Richard (the patient) was trying, with all his resources, to say goodbye to her and to have her say goodbye to him. But she kept interpreting until the very end, in the same symbolic terms that referred to the inner world and not to their actual relationship. This clearly disheartened him:

> Richard had become very silent towards the end, but he said that he had decided to continue to work with Mrs K. at some time in the future. Mrs K. went with Richard to the village, but there he quickly took leave of her and said he would rather she did not see him get on the bus. (p. 464)

Ending an analysis is a major transition in a person's life, and one would expect that the analyst help the patient to go through this. This requires a change in the analytic relationship, which becomes more fluid and realistic, and the dialogue more mutual. Frequently, the patient needs to sit up, if she had been lying on the couch, in order to develop a face-to-face relationship, as a part of a re-individuation process. But one of the more important processes is what Mexican psychoanalyst Solís Garza (1981) called "detransferenciation", by which the patient relocates on to other people in his life certain aspects of his own self and relationships that had previously been deposited in the analyst.

The very idea of detransferenciation contradicts a certain psychoanalytic ideology that equates mental health with the development of a full autonomy. According to this view, a "fully analysed" person should have overcome any wish for dependency and act as a completely rational and autonomous individual. This I deem to be not only impossible, but undesirable. The human being always exists in terms of the others. Fairbairn (1952) recognised this, when he concluded that "the development of object-relationships is essentially *a process whereby infantile dependence upon the object gradually gives place to mature dependence upon the object*" (p. 34). Hence, for him, the evolution was from absolute (infantile) dependence to mature (relative) dependence. Winnicott (1963) follows a similar trend of thought, although he does not relinquish the ideal of "full maturity" in terms of independence, albeit an unattainable one. Kohut (1984), on the other hand, considered that the need for an empathic response from selfobjects continues during the whole life cycle, although it certainly evolves in the maturational process.

During the termination phase of an analysis, the patient has to withdraw the various relational components that had been concentrated on the analyst and take them to other present relations in everyday life. This is a natural and necessary process, which needs to be fostered, or at least acknowledged, by the analyst. Unfortunately, there are analysts who would interpret this as a manic denial of the pain of separation, thus giving the patient the message that he or she is not supposed to find help or joy in other relationships, apart from the transference. None the less, most patients nowadays suffer not from extreme dependency, but from an inability to rely on others, on account of a deep feeling of mistrust. Hence, they need the experience of the analytic relationship in order to learn how to depend on another human being. It is to be expected that a patient should be able to take this new ability to the actual relationships in his life, and this should not be interfered with by the analyst, because, if this task is not fulfilled during the termination phase, the patient is left to do it all by himself during post-analysis, and this might be more difficult and painful to accomplish.

It is interesting to see that Klein (1961) saw and interpreted this process with Richard, during his last session with her, although in such a way that seemed to imply a defensive function:

Richard said thoughtfully: "The Bear is the dark-blue Daddy", but added that his real Daddy was a light-blue Daddy. This was the first time that he used the words "light blue" about his father—it had always been reserved for the ideal Mummy or Mrs K.

Mrs K. interpreted that he now used light blue for Daddy and seemed to express his love for him in this way. It was also a consolation because he was losing Mrs K. to have Daddy as somebody nearly as good as Mummy.

Richard went into the kitchen and drank from the tap.

Mrs K. interpreted that if he could not have the good breast, he wanted now to take in the good penis of the father. (p. 462, my italics)

If Richard had learnt from his analyst to repair the relationship with his father, which had been strongly paranoid at the beginning of the treatment, what was the point of presenting this as a kind of consolation prize? Father was an essential and necessary object in Richard's life, and it was Klein who was replaceable. And why define Father as "nearly as good as Mummy"? Anyway, the mere fact that the analyst recognised the revaluation of the father's figure and that this might help the child to overcome the loss of Mrs Klein might have helped Richard with the transition, in spite of the lack of a true farewell. Besides, at the very end of the session, the child clearly expressed his wish "to continue to work with Mrs K. at some time in the future".

In the last few sessions, I believe it is necessary for analyst and patient to do some kind of evaluation of the work they have done together, what has happened, what they attained, what stayed lacking, what were the main fractures of their relationship and how they were solved, what was enough and what more than enough. This recapitulation is the first step in the process of translating their shared experience into the past tense.

When the last session finally comes, it is up to the two parties to bid farewell in their own way. This usually carries a bittersweet feeling, as summarised by Balint (1950):

> If this process can develop in an undisturbed way a surprisingly uniform experience dominates the very last period of the treatment. The patient feels that he is going through a kind of re-birth into a new life, that he has arrived at the end of a dark tunnel, that he sees light again after a long journey, that he has been given a new life, he experiences a sense of great freedom as if a heavy burden had dropped from him, etc. *It is a deeply moving experience; the general atmosphere is of taking leave for ever of something very dear, very precious — with all the corresponding grief and mourning — but this sincere and deeply felt grief is mitigated by the feeling of security, originating from the newly-won possibilities for real happiness.* Usually the patient leaves after the last session happy but with tears in his eyes and,—I think I may admit—the analyst is in a very similar mood. (p. 197, my italics)

This is the end of the regular sessions, but it is not the end of the story, as we shall now see.

The aftermath

Nowadays, there is a certain agreement, among psychoanalysts, that the analytic process continues and evolves after the discontinuation of the sessions. This is called "post-analysis". After the analyst effectively disappears from the scene, the patient is left alone to tackle a series of therapeutic tasks that are a part of the healing process. If the analysis were to be compared to a surgical intervention, then we might say that the patient is going through a period of "convalescence". In this, he can no longer count on the analyst's help to take the process to its completion (in as much as it can be said that there is such thing).

The immediate task for the patient, as soon as she terminates the analysis, is to reorganise her life, now that the analyst is no longer an active part of it. Starting from the more concrete aspects, it is obvious that there will be a rearrangement of schedules and economy. Suddenly, the patient finds that she has much more time available—both that of the sessions and of the necessary travel, which could be quite a lot in large cities. Besides, she is unexpectedly richer! These are welcome side effects, although the free time might sometimes be more difficult to occupy, but it is to be expected, if the analysis has increased—as it should—the patient's initiative and capacity for enjoyment, that there will be more than a few new activities and projects to fill in the gap.

Then, there is the need for a new distribution of emotional bonds. The relationship with the analyst had occupied for long a very important place in the analysand's emotional life—frequently much to the chagrin of his intimates—and now there is the need for a change. At first, it is the empty space that attracts the former patient's feelings. This has been the focus of most of the literature on the subject, which centred on the mourning for the loss of the analyst. But, as I have already mentioned, the end of an analysis is not a bereavement, but something more akin to a graduation: there is a separation and an end of a previous status, which generate feelings of loss, but they are combined with joy, relief, and pride at the achievement. However, there is still work to be done in order to dissolve the analytic bond, and this implies two tasks, one inner and one outer (Tubert-Oklander, 1989, 1997).

The inner task is the disassembling of the analyst's internal image, so that some aspects of the inner relationship with her may be transformed and assimilated into the self, so as to become personal capacities and properties. This is true for both emotions and cognitive and conative capabilities. For instance, for some time the former patient might think, when faced with some problem or decision, "What would my analyst say?" and find an answer from an inner voice, which is identified with that of the analyst. But sooner or later he will find out that this is really his inner voice, and forsake the need for such an explicit dialogue. This is the way in which capacities and skills are normally acquired: first the internalised relationship with the parent, teacher, or coach is conscious and explicit, and later it fades into the background and becomes unconscious or, more frequently, preconscious. Thus, Pichon-Rivière (1971, 1979) used to say that thinking was really a dialogue in the inner group.

The outer task is the displacement and relocation of certain aspects of the previous analytic bond on to other persons, groups, or institutions in the person's present environment. This covers not only emotional bonds, but also functional relationships. On the emotional side, the person's life is enriched by being able to have intimate and affectionate relations with spouse, family, and friends, a experience that had for some time been centred on the analyst. In functional terms, someone who has learnt to talk with his analyst about various matters, both personal and public, now finds out how pleasant it is to share conversation with others. Having learnt to rely on the analyst for help, he is now able and willing to relate with others who can be relied on.

This dismantling of the analyst's image and withdrawal of the parts of the self that had been previously deposited on her is partly experienced by the former patient as an intrinsically aggressive act and a destruction of the analyst. This is akin to the dynamics described by Winnicott (1971) in adolescent development, in which "growing up means taking the parent's place. *It really does.* In the unconscious fantasy, growing up is inherently an aggressive act. And the child is now no longer child-size" (p. 144).

For Winnicott, the parent's contribution to this process is that she has to accept being destroyed, *but survive*. It is not quite clear what he means by "survive". In Winnicott's writing, this term means more than continuing to exist, but continuing to fulfil her role (parent or analyst). A parent survives because he is still acting as a father or mother, in spite of the youngster's murderous attacks, and during the treatment an analyst survives because she goes on being an analyst, listening, trying to understand, and interpreting, instead of retaliating or cutting short the treatment. It is this survival that establishes the parent or analyst as a real external object that may be used (Winnicott, 1969).

But what happens during the post-analysis in which the analyst is no longer there to survive? Of course, there is always the possibility of calling or visiting the analyst, in order to check that he is still alive and well, but one would expect that a patient who has reached and accomplished the termination phase would be strong enough and realistic enough to contain within himself such an anxiety, while still trusting that the analyst survives somewhere. After some time, the anxiety subsides, as do the painful feelings of separation and loss.

This process has been poignantly described by one of the patients of Argentine psychoanalyst Guiard (1979), who wrote him, just one month after the end of her analysis, the following letter:

> It grieves me to recognise that all this process is somehow a work of destruction of your image within me, and then a reconstruction. But I know that you know and that you even expected this to happen. You could not stay within me as you were, since you were too indispensable and overshadowed myself. It's funny that during the first few days I thought, with great anxiety, that *I could not see you* (as if you had died) and then I realised that you were again alive, and now I do not feel that *I can't* go and see you, but something much more final, that *I must not* do it, just like I should not ask for help before having tried by myself to see whether I can do something or not. (pp. 177–178, translated for this edition)

This is, of course, true, but there is more to it. The post-analytic process is less dramatic if there has been work done, during the termination phase, in order to dismantle the asymmetrical roles of analyst and patient, and open the possibility of a more mutual dialogue. This requires analysing the effect that the peculiar therapeutic situation and the analytic device have on their relationship. Because what has to be destroyed is neither the analyst as a person, nor the real human relationship between the two, but that particular place that has been created as an artifice of our technique. If this task is not carried out during the termination phase and the analyst carries on as usual until the very last minute, the responsibility for the whole work of disassembly lies on the patient's shoulders. The result is the emergence of destructive hate, consuming guilt, and agonising pain. But is this really necessary, or is it an artifice?

Of course, there are some patients who have no option but to go through this, on account of their particular history and dynamics, but this is not true for everyone. Guiard's patient was helped through this difficult period by her knowledge of the analyst as a real person. She was quite sure that he knew what was going to happen and that he would welcome her impending independence. This echoes Kohut's (1982) depiction of the healthy parent's mirroring response to the child's independent development during the Oedipal stage "with pride, with self-expanding empathy, with joyful mirroring, to the next generation, thus affirming the younger generation's right to unfold and to be different" (p. 402).

One possible criticism of Kohut's version is that it poses an idealised view of the parent–child relationship, one that denies the unavoidable conflicts between them. But the acceptance of ambivalence in both parties does not preclude a predominance of love, compassion, consideration, and mutuality in the relationship. It is the negotiation of ambivalence and interpersonal conflict that opens the way to maturity. The patient has to be able to love and be grateful to the analyst, while at the same time using his or her capacity for aggression in order to destroy the dependent relationship. The analyst has to enjoy the patient's development and individuation, as parents have to do, while dealing with the pain of being no longer necessary and knowing that his idealised and omnipotent image is being destroyed by the patient.

The truth is that the analytic relationship goes through the same vicissitudes as other relations, with the very important addition of a major dose of awareness of self and the other, so that each party might learn from the experience.

And what is the destiny of the analytic relation? I have found it useful (Tubert-Oklander, 1989, 1997) to think of this in terms of the three dimensions of the relation described in Chapter Five: the transference–countertransference, the working alliance, and the real relationship. Each of them can be thought of as having a different evolution, albeit always keeping in mind that this is only an artificial division, constructed for conceptual purposes.

The traditional point of view about the *transference* is that it should be dissolved by the end of the analysis. If "transference–countertransference" is the name for the unconscious aspect of the analytic relationship, it is obvious that it can never disappear, since both analyst and patient will always maintain some kind of unconscious object relation for the rest of their lives. What does change is the magnitude of the emotional investment in these parallel relationships—parallel because, in the absence of a present reinforcement by their actual interaction, the relation becomes fully internal and non-correctible by the other's behaviour—and their original stereotyped and repetitive nature, which has been mitigated and softened by the analysis. Consequently, there is a gradual extinction of the passionate aspect of the bond, as the feelings are once again assimilated into the self-image and become the dynamic source for other relationships.

The *working alliance*, being the conscious, rational, and pragmatic aspect of the relationship, is easier to dispose of. The analytic contract clearly comes to an end together with the regular sessions, but the working habits that made it possible for both parties to co-operate still remain. The analyst's functional meaning for the patient, which at the end of the treatment is virtually reduced to being an interlocutor who helps her to reflect upon personal and shared experience, is deper-sonified and transformed into an inner dialogue with ideal figures, but the particular kind of dialogue that was initiated with the analyst goes on indefinitely. In conscious memory, the analyst might still have his place in the former patient's inner life, side by side with parents, relatives, teachers, friends, preferred authors, public figures, and other ideal objects that compose the inner group.

And what about the *"real" (existential) relationship*, which is, of course, irreplaceable? This is the area in which there is truly a loss, which needs some sort of accommodation. This is not the only signif-icant relationship that faces a time limit; the very same thing happens with former teachers, schoolmates, or friends from the time one lived in another place. In the internal field, the analyst is bound to acquire her or his place in the patient's personal history, together with other significant figures from the past. In the outer field, each analytic pair has to discover if there is a space open for some kind of relationship, after some time. In ordinary analyses this is usually not an issue, but in training analyses, in which the former analyst and analysand con-tinue being members of the same professional community, which is frequently quite small, the problem of their future relationship has to be faced. This means that we analysts might not have ever gone through a standard termination phase in our own treatment, or with many of our patients.

When patient and analyst must go on having some other kind of relationship, after the termination, sometimes there remains an under-lying uncomfortable feeling, which mars what otherwise might have been a sincere friendship. Passion always leaves some trace, and the transference is, perforce, a passionate relationship. In ordinary analyses, however, this is hardly noticeable, on account of the fact that the former patient and analyst do not usually meet in social or professional situations.

In any case, as in every other aspect of their relationship, the analyst should allow the former patient to decide what sort of contact he is willing to have with that person who has been his analyst, overriding the analyst's personal wishes on the matter, since the former's ethical commitment continues beyond the formal limits of the treatment.

And what happens when a former patient comes back requesting "more analysis"? Some analysts refuse to respond to such demands, since they consider that the process has been closed and should not be reopened, and, at best, suggest a reanalysis with another analyst. This might be painful and noxious for some patients, who feel rejected— and rightly so. Meltzer (1984) devised a way of responding to such petitions without relinquishing his natural history view of the analytic process, by offering to supervise the former patient's self-analysis of his or her dreams. This was carried out in an informal setting, similar to that of psychoanalytic supervisions, and there were no commentaries on transference or countertransference phenomena. The idea was "to operate as a two-person work group" (p. 176).

Although I agree with Meltzer that this sort of treatment does not usually require a regressive transference analysis, and that it can and should be carried out in terms of a fluid reflective dialogue on whatever the patient brings to attention, I feel his approach to be too rigid, both in demanding that the enquiry be restricted to dream analysis and in the absolute exclusion of any reference to the mutual relationship. Indeed, I do not share this strict division between analytic and supervisory work, since I do believe that an analysis is, in the end, "a two-person work group", and I do not leave out, in a supervisory relationship, the consideration of the emotional substrate of all intellectual shared work. The difference is mainly quantitative and a question of focus: the subject of the analytic dialogue is the patient's life and experiences, while that of a supervision is the supervisee's experience of relating to her patient, but the dynamic process is rather similar and both cases require taking into account the emotional aspects of the working relationship, albeit in different ways.

In my experience, these patients who come back, sometimes after many years, fall into one of two categories: either their treatment was interrupted prematurely, in which case I would consider the possibility of reinitiating an analysis that was left incomplete, or they had finished their analysis with a termination phase. In this case, they usually come because they have somehow stalled in their vital evolution and need some help to overcome the present obstacle and resume their course. In this sense, the analytic dialogue might be seen as a supervision of their conduct of their lives. It is also frequently the expression of a need to talk over with the analyst the previous experience they had shared during the analysis, and a way of reframing the relationship. Such treatments are usually brief and non-intensive, and the results are satisfactory for both parties.

CHAPTER TWELVE

The healing process

Is there actually a cure?

The fact that psychoanalysis emerged from medicine determines that it is largely committed to the use of the medical metaphor. Thus, emotional suffering, conflicts, existential doubts, and other kinds of distress derived from life situations are called an "illness", the attempt to aid people to overcome such a situation a "treatment", and the wished-for outcome, which includes an alleviation of the initial malaise, a "cure". But is it a happy metaphor? Most psychoanalysts would agree that it is only sketchy and partial at best, but that it can hardly be avoided. Bion (1970) posed this problem in clear-cut terms:

> Psycho-analysis cannot escape ideas of cure, treatment, illness, in psycho-analysts and patients alike. Eissler warns against a structure that is too rigid and too limited to permit development. At the opposite extreme the Sufis have no rigid institution yet have endured; their solution would open the way for an "expanding universe" of psycho-analysis but it would not be long before members of the psycho-analytic movement could not understand each other. (p. 83)

It is interesting to consider Bion's comparison with the Sufis. These Muslim mystics have relinquished both any standard theory and writing and institutions, and are still able to communicate, on the basis that those who have had the mystical experience of Truth are bound to understand each other, beyond their words, metaphors, images, and procedures. We might perhaps say that the same is true for anyone who has had an experience of the unconscious, but the problem is that there is ample evidence that analysts belonging to the various schools of psychoanalytic thought might have had very different analytic experiences, as a consequence of their theoretical and technical differences.

So, it seems we shall have to remain with the medical metaphor, in spite of its insufficiencies, although a few colleagues have rejected it wholesale and denied that psychoanalysis has anything to do with "curing". Hence, if we are to speak of the "healing process", we need to define what we actually mean by this term.

The basic questions are (i) does psychoanalysis actually cure anything? And, if it does not, (ii) why do people keep going to analysis? The question about the "cure" might be reframed profitably as follows: does analysis improve in any way the quality of life of those who undergo this kind of treatment? Any of us who has experienced a satisfactory psychoanalytic treatment will hasten to give a positive reply; others will not. But this is equivalent to the truism of saying that those who find their analysis satisfactory are satisfied with its results, and this is obviously not enough for our present purposes.

Starting now from the other end, what happens with those analysts who claim that their practice is not therapeutic at all and has nothing to do with human wellbeing, and yet continue doing psychoanalysis? How do they account for this apparent inconsistency? This position is characteristic of Lacanian psychoanalysis. Pepeli (2003) points out that, for Lacan, even though there is no therapeutic aim in psychoanalysis, in analysis the cure comes as a bonus (*la guérison vient par surcroit*); it is a fringe benefit that might or might not come. What the analysis actually gives is a privileged knowledge, acquired from the analytic experience, both of self and of the human condition. Such thinkers also usually adhere to Freud's (1930a) dismal characterisation of existence, deny the possibility of happiness, and consider that the only alleviation that might be provided by the treatment is a subtle evolution of the unavoidable human suffering, from the misery of not

being able to attain happiness to the rational and courageous acceptance that there is no such thing to be attained, and the enjoyment of
"uncovering the 'horrific, unspeakable pleasure' (*jouissance*) behind
one's neurotic symptoms" (Pepeli, 2003).

I must say that such a view is quite alien to my own experience of
psychoanalysis, both as a patient and as an analyst. The quality of my
own life has been greatly improved by psychoanalysis, and I certainly
expect the same thing to be true for my patients. This is an essential
element in my choice of profession and the continuation of my practice. It is obvious from this that psychoanalysis cannot be value-free
and that each of us practises it in terms of his or her own *Weltanschauung* (conception of the world) and *Lebensanchauung* (conception
of life). In such issues, it is not productive to discuss them with people
whose thinking starts from disparate assumptions, but I feel I can
safely assume that anybody who has taken the trouble to read this
book up to this point will essentially share my belief that there is
bound to be something in the analytic experience that makes life
worth living, whether we call it a "cure" for the malaise of life or use
some other term for it.

Most analysts would agree that it is to be expected that the successful termination of a psychoanalytic treatment should provide the
analysand with an increased capacity for (a) enjoyment, (b) rational
thinking, (c) effective action, and (d) meaningful relationships. To
these, some would add (e) creativity and (f) authenticity, although
these are more difficult to define. In addition, most of us believe that
self-knowledge has *something* to do with this positive evolution.

What should be quite obvious by now is that the psychoanalytical
"cure" is quite different from, much more, and frequently less than,
a symptomatic cure. If what you wish for is the alleviation or disappearance of symptoms, there are quite a few other therapeutic
resources available, from psychotropic drugs to cognitive–behavioural therapy. Those who come to psychoanalysis with such expectations either leave in a hurry or manage to learn that something more
important is at stake. This was stated by Storr (1966), in the following
terms:

> In very many instances, patients rapidly lose interest in the symptoms
> for which they originally sought treatment, *whether or not these symp-
> toms are actually relieved*; and the process of analysis becomes an end in

itself, a journey of exploration which is undertaken for its own sake; *not so much a treatment, more a way of life.* (p. 53, my italics)

[However] the demand for psychoanalysis greatly exceeds its availability. . . . This is the more remarkable, since the evidence that psychoanalysis cures anybody of anything is so shaky as to be practically non-existent. (pp. 56–57)

However, even if we were to accept that psychoanalysis is not a treatment at all (and this would effectively dispose of any demands of evidence-based medicine, but pay the price of losing the support of public health systems and private insurance), it is still a professional intervention aimed at producing some kind of change in the analysand's life. Hence, we would still need to establish whether it actually attains this desired change and, if this is the case, how this is done. In other words, we need a theory of analytic change.

Being convinced from my own experience, as most of us are, that a psychoanalytic treatment can be beneficial for many patients, I shall leave out the discussion of how to evaluate our results in such a way as to convince people who had not had an analytic experience, and concentrate on the theoretical explanation of how and why it happens. You will notice, of course, that I have relapsed into the use of the language derived from the medical metaphor in order to tackle this problem. I do so because it is simpler than the other clumsier alternatives for expressing these matters and also more consistent with common usage, although keeping in mind the above-mentioned caveat.

There are as many explanations of the therapeutic effect of psychoanalysis as psychoanalytic theories of the mind and its malfunctions. Each analytic school has emphasised a particular explanation, and usually rejected all others, although, when we study their clinical practice and experience in detail, we usually find that there are various factors in action in their treatments, although their theoretical reconstruction of what they do might take into account only one or some of them, and not the others. None the less, it is not the case that we are all doing pretty much the same things, although we describe them differently, because the kind of theoretical conception held by the analyst has a deep influence in the general atmosphere of the treatment, the quality of the analytic experience, and the nature of its outcome.

I shall, therefore, review the main descriptions and explanations of the healing process that are to be found in our discussions of the matter. Some of them emphasise that the treatment is a *cure*, understood as an active procedure or agency intended to influence another human being in a beneficial way, while others would rather speak of *healing*, conceived as a spontaneous vital process, such as the healing of wounds, which is fostered, nurtured, and cared for by the therapist, who cannot in any way produce or control it. The psychoanalytic treatment most probably partakes of both characteristics in a dynamic equilibrium.

The therapeutic action of psychoanalysis

The problem of adequately accounting for the therapeutic action of psychoanalysis has been of great interest lately for our professional community. A search in the PEP-Web database, with the keywords "therapeutic action psychoanalysis" gave forty references as a result, thirty-two of them from 1980 to the present date and fifteen after 2000. The oldest one was, of course, Strachey's 1934 article, "The nature of the therapeutic action of psycho-analysis", which has had an impact on the thinking and practice of so many generations of psychoanalysts.

The theories that try to account for the positive evolution of many psychoanalytic treatments are quite varied. Each of them seems to have focused on some aspect of the analytic relation and process, and excluded others. However, these differences are not as clear-cut as their proponents claim them to be, since most of them include, often implicitly, some of the factors that have been studied by other theories. This has been noted by Etchegoyen (1986) when he writes that

> the diverse criteria of the cure proposed do not differ too much when they are examined calmly and dispassionately. The theoretical supports and the methods for their attainment vary; but if they are compared, one immediately realizes where they correspond. (p. 631)

This is partly true; indeed, it does seem that sometimes the various theories are speaking of the same phenomena, with a different terminology. But it is also true that some discrepancies determine radically different therapeutic climates. For instance, it is not the same to be in treatment with an analyst who believes that there is one, and only one, correct interpretation for any given material and that only the analyst can have an access to it, or with one who believes that all interpretations are relative and metaphorical and that the path to a better understanding of the unconscious aspects of the analytic experience always goes through dialogue. One and the other treatment feel very different and tend to generate disparate outcomes. Even if the content of the interpretations happened to be the same and the neurotic symptoms were in both cases solved, the effect of the analytic relationship on the analysand's personality would be quite dissimilar.

I shall not attempt to review the literature on the subject in detail, but only spell out the terms of the controversy, in order to open a discussion on how analysis actually works. The main theories that have been proposed for this issue refer to: (1) the *cognitive transformation* implied by "making conscious the unconscious"; (2) the *emotional transmutation* that results from a new and more benign relational experience with another human being; (3) the *recovery of a developmental process* that had been stalled or distorted; (4) the *structural and functional changes* that occur in the organisation of the mind (often described as the "psychic apparatus"); (5) the *reorganisation of the interpersonal field and process* in the analytic situation; (6) the *development of a greater linguistic and symbolic capacity* that allows both parties to converse about significant issues; (7) the *quest for authenticity*. Each of these has originated different orientations in psychoanalytic theory and practice. Let us take a brief look at them.

The cognitive transformation

Freud's (1900a) original theory of illness and the cure particularly stressed the importance of knowledge: the patient was sick as a consequence of ignoring the many things he had forgotten—both childhood experiences and unacceptable impulses or desires—and was cured once this amnesia caused by repression was overcome. The aim of the treatment was to help the patient to remember and this was aided by the analyst's interpretations. An interpretation was an inference, made by the analyst and communicated explicitly to the patient, about what the patient had forgotten. Such inferences were based on the fact that the patient's unconscious was always striving to manifest itself and, since it regularly met with the ego's resistance, in the form of the various defence manoeuvres, it could only be expressed in an indirect and symbolic way, as a transactional formation that both revealed and hid it, at one and the same time, just like symptoms do.

But soon he was to find out that things were not so easy; the defences had to be worked through (Freud, 1914g) and this was somehow related to the repetition of past relational experiences with the analyst, called *transference* (Freud, 1912b, 1914g, 1915a). But the analyst's main instrument was still interpretation, now not only of contents, but also of resistances and the transference. The wished-for patient's response was a cognitive transformation, a reorganisation of her view of herself, other people, past and present, and life in general; this was called *insight*.

The main requirement set by this theory of interpretation and insight was that the interpretation had to be *true*—that is, it should correspond, in every detail, with the contents, structures, and functional dynamics of the patient's unconscious. Only this would lead to a full and effective insight. An interpretation that was only approximately true—what Glover (1955) called an "inexact interpretation"— might have some therapeutic effect if it provided a less costly and more effective form of defence (one that required a lesser distortion of the repressed impulses, wishes, and contents), but this would be a far cry from a real cure, since the basic pathogenic conflicts would not be solved.

The staunchest advocate of the exact interpretation was Strachey (1934, 1937). For him, what he called a *mutative interpretation* had to be true, precise in its detail, and pertinent, in as much as it referred to an id wish that was active at that very instant. Hence, it had to be a *transference interpretation* that described and explained the instinctual wishes that the patient's id directed towards the other person present in the room—the analyst.

Of course, Strachey's theory was much more complex than the very simple schema of ignorance *vs.* insight, since it included structural considerations, in terms of Freud's (1923b) tripartite division of the psychic apparatus, and the object relation that ensues between analyst and patient, both in its imaginary and real dimensions.

Fundamentally, Strachey suggests that the analyst occupies, by means of the patient's identification as described by Freud (1921c), the place of an "auxiliary superego". But this is a quite different superego since, where the patient's primitive and punitive superego forbids the expression of unconscious wishes, fantasies, and thoughts, the analytic superego actively fosters it, through the imposition of the basic rule of saying everything and omitting nothing. This novel situation, which Racker (1954) called the "abolition of rejection", is what sets the transference going. In order to have the potential to induce a therapeutic change, an interpretation has to reveal an id impulse that is active at that very moment and directed towards the analyst. This is a true "transference interpretation", and not a mere "interpretation of transference" (Strachey, 1937). In other words, it deals with what Klein (1932) called the "point of urgency", instead of only informing the patient that the analyst thinks that he has felt such and such wishes, fears, or whatever towards her, at some time or other. In this, it is fundamental that the very object towards which the instinctual wish is being directed is also the very same person who puts it into words, with neither anxiety nor anger, and, since the analyst is now in the place of the superego and her behaviour is so different from that of the patient's original objects, this gives the latter a new experience that is bound to be mutative.

"Mutative", here, is used in the same sense in which we speak of a mutation in genetics, that is, a change in a preordained symbolic sequence that controls the development and behaviour of an organism (Etchegoyen, 1986). Hence, a mutative interpretation is one that produces structural changes, but, in order to have such an effect, it is essential that it should be *true*, in as much as it depicts the patient's mental processes *just as they are at that precise instant*. Hence, it must be *immediate* (that is, refer to the impulses and wishes that are presently active) and *specific* (that is, precise and concrete in all its details); consequently, this excludes the use of inexact interpretations, such as metaphors, models, or analogies.

Strachey's contribution is the basis of the Kleinian interpretative technique, in which the whole burden of interpretation is vested in the analyst and any self-analytic effort by the patient is seen as a resistance and a form of narcissistic negative transference, particularly an expression of envy that makes the patient deny her real unavoidable need of the analyst (Klein, 1957). Of course, there are cases of severe pathological narcissism in which this is certainly true, but this cannot be generalised, as Klein does. In any case, the Kleinian analyst works under an enormous demand, since she is supposed to interpret, almost minute by minute, the fluid evolution of the unconscious fantasies that are active at that very moment, and the interpretation is supposed to be accurate and precise in all its minute detail. Those analysts of a hermeneutic bent, who consider interpretations to be feasible metaphors for emotional experiences and that they emerge from a co-operative dialogue, certainly make things easier for themselves and, I believe, more stimulating and creative for their patients.

I know that there are many sensitive and experienced Kleinian analysts who would feel misunderstood and caricatured by this description. But what I am trying to do is to show what happens in the clinic if the Kleinian theory of interpretation is taken seriously and literally, as many people do. Theories are always sketchy, partial, incomplete, and misleading, unless mitigated and corrected by experience, intuition, and good judgement, and this is the case of every one of the theories that we shall discuss in this section.

It should be emphasised that Strachey's theory does not only deal with the subject of the cognitive transformation implied in the act of making conscious unconscious contents, but also tries to account for the theoretical problem of why and how an external occurrence, such as an interpretation, has an effect on psychic structure. His answer is that, having identified the analyst with the superego, in a similar way as Freud (1921c) suggests that the group members identify the leader with their ego ideal, his real and concrete behaviour might introduce changes in the patient's superego, which, after all, was created by the internalisation of the parents. This depends on the fact that the analyst's real behaviour is in sharp contrast with that of the internal object that has been projected on to him. Hence, Strachey is implying what those analysts of a relational bent have been saying all along: that the therapeutic change is a consequence of the internalisation of a radically new and more benign experience of a relation with another human being—Alexander and French's (1946) "corrective emotional experience". But, and this is a very big "but", for Strachey the analyst's benignity is restricted to a neutral attitude of sincere interest, attentive listening, rationality in understanding, and the capacity for saying the truth about the patient, however unsavoury, without fear, anger, blame, revenge, or punishment, and does not include treating the patient with any particular kindness or trying to respond to his emotional needs in any way other than providing a veritable and trustworthy information about himself.

The emotional transmutation

A second theory of the therapeutic effect of psychoanalysis, which has been with us from early on, asserts that since patients have been originally harmed by inadequate relationships during childhood, what they need is the experience of a more adequate relation with the analyst that might compensate for what was lacking in their upbringing. Such a theory underscores the importance of environmental provision, both in child development and pathogenesis, on the one hand, and in therapeutic rectification, on the other.

Ferenczi (1929) initiated this trend, when he described the pathogenic effects of a child having been an unwelcome guest in his or her own family, and suggested that the treatment should offer the patient an opportunity to behave as a child in her relationship with the analyst, be cared for by the latter, and hence enjoy, "properly speaking for the first time, . . . the irresponsibility of childhood" (p. 129). This experience would allow, through internalisation, the creation of new mental structures that had not been formed when they should have been.

Of course, it was never just a question of being kind to the patient, since one of the consequences of early disappointments and environmental failures is the development of a profound mistrust of other human beings, with the consequent defences against dependence. This negative transference has to be thoroughly interpreted and worked through before the patient dares to abandon his resistances to engaging in a deep, intimate, and committed relationship with the analyst. But when this finally happens and the patient enters a period of regression, the analyst's therapeutic behaviour must change from an interpretative stance to a caring attitude that resembles that of a good mother towards her child. Finally, after the regression has been spent, the process should be completed by a new period of analytic activity:

This is the theory of the *therapeutic regression*, which has been espoused and further developed by many other authors, of which I shall only mention a few. In 1946, Alexander and French presented their conception of the *corrective emotional experience*. The idea was that, in order to hasten the treatment, the analyst should play a role that was in sharp contrast with the transference paradigm that the patient had projected on to him; hence, if the patient were experiencing the analyst as an extremely critical parent, the latter should express an admiration for the patient's abilities and achievements. The resulting emotional experience would be corrective because, as some patients say, "Nobody has treated me like this before." This technique has been widely criticised as inauthentic and manipulative, but the principle holds that receiving a good treatment from the analyst might correct the ill effects of untoward previous experiences. In a sense, everyone subscribes to it, although orthodox analysts such as Strachey would limit the extent of the analyst's kindness to the analytic attitude of serious interest, understanding, tolerance, and neutrality.

Winnicott (1955, 1956) suggested that there is a group of patients who suffer from the relational and structural consequences of an early environmental failure. These have to undergo a *regression to dependence*, during which the analyst's effective contribution would no longer be interpretation, but *management*—in the very same sense that a mother manages her baby.

The original environmental failure was a lack of the necessary adaptation by the caring adults—what Ferenczi (1928a) called the "adaptation of the family to the child"—and the baby's drastic solution was to "freeze" the experience, which ever since had remained locked inside, as a kind of cyst, protected by an organised set of defences. The benignity of the analytic setting acts as an invitation to regress to a dependent stage and unfreeze the traumatic experience, in the hope that this time things might turn out differently. As Winnicott (1955) wrote, "It is as if there is an expectation that favourable conditions may arise justifying regression and offering a new chance for forward development, that which was rendered impossible or difficult initially by environmental failure" (p. 18).

This very same idea was formulated by Balint (1932, 1952, 1968), in his concept of a "new beginning", although his suggestions about the provision of actual care for the patient were much more cautious and limited than Winnicott's. On the other side of the Atlantic, Searles (1965), Boyer (1986), Loewald (1960), and Kohut (1984) have treated various aspects of therapeutic regressions in severely damaged patients, the analyst's concomitant regression, and the therapeutic effect of the patient's experience of a novel behaviour in a caring other.

This theory has been the object of much criticism. In the first place, it seems to assume that time can somehow go backwards, so that the regressive process may reach the point in which things went astray and start all over again, as a response to the now adequate "child care" provided by the analyst. But is this really so? There might be "critical phases" in child development—that is, specific periods during which an adequate stimulus will generate some mental structures in a way that becomes unavailable at any other time (Vives, 1988). Besides that, what is an adequate response to an infantile emotional need? A baby feels understood if it receives a feed right when it needs it, but an adult patient, however regressed, would not feel understood at all if he or she were offered a milk bottle. Perhaps the analytic attitude, followed by an empathic interpretation, might be all that the patient needs in terms of care, at his or her present age.

One answer to such questioning is that ordinary analytic care is certainly enough *for some patients*, specifically those who have developed during infancy and childhood an adequate mental structure (organisation) as a result of having received sufficient care from mother, other adults, and a flexible, empathic, and accepting family environment. In Winnicott's (1949a) terms, the analyst benefits from the "dirty work" already done by parents, which resulted in the integrity of the individual he is now treating,

But what happens when the parents and the family have not done their part, or have even partaken in behaviour that has been harmful for the child? This results in a traumatic distortion of the personality, which Freud (1937c) called an "alteration of the ego". A normal ego is indispensable in order that the patient may co-operate wit the treatment, "but a normal ego of this sort is, like normality in general, an ideal fiction. . . . Every normal person, in fact, is only normal on the average" (p. 235).

So, every "analysable neurotic" will perforce have some degree of structural damage ("alteration of the ego") and this is bound to emerge in certain moments of the treatment. A patient with a severe personality disturbance ("psychotic"), on the other hand, will deploy these functional deficiencies from the very beginning and most of the time. What matters for this discussion is that, if the theory of the therapeutic regression is at least partially right, then such moments would demand a significant change in the analytic attitude. Winnicott (1967), for one, did believe that this applied to every patient, who needs the analyst to reflect back on her an image of herself, pretty much as the mother's face has to reflect to the baby an image of itself:

This glimpse of the baby's and child's seeing the self in the mother's face, and afterwards in a mirror, gives a way of looking at analysis and at the psychotherapeutic task. *Psychotherapy is not making clever and apt interpretations; by and large it is a long-term giving the patient back what the patient brings.* It is a complex derivative of the face that reflects what is there to be seen. I like to think of my work this way, and to think that if I do this well enough the patient will find his or her own self, and will be able to exist and to feel real. Feeling real is more than existing; it is finding a way to exist as oneself, and to relate to objects as oneself, and to have a self into which to retreat for relaxation. (p. 117)

Of course, a sensitive and empathic interpretation might well be a way of "giving the patient back what the patient brings", but the point is that *it is not the only way*, and that it might not be adequate for patients who are regularly or temporarily unable to understand an interpretation as such: that is, whose minds are operating in what Balint (1968) called the "area of the basic fault":

Obviously working-through is possible only if, and in so far as, the patient is capable of taking the interpretation in, experiencing it as an interpretation, and allowing it to influence his mind. With the class of "deeply disturbed" patients this may or may not be the case. But, if the patient does not experience the analyst's interpretation as an interpretation, i.e. a sentence consisting of words with agreed meaning, no working-through can take place. Working-through can come into operation only if our words have approximately the same meaning for our patients as for ourselves. (p. 14)

In such cases and moments, the response that the patient needs is a concrete action that can convey to him the feeling that his experience and need have been adequately perceived and understood.

If this is true, the study of the treatments of severely disturbed patients, who had traditionally been considered "unanalysable", might help us to detect, understand, and respond better to similar clinical phenomena that appear momentarily in the more traditional treatments.

In any case, it seems that most analysts would agree that the novel aspects of the experience of the analytic relationship have something to do with inner structural change. The difference here lies in the extent to which this factor is assumed to participate in the healing process and whether this is considered, or not, to be a sufficient cause for an abandonment or modification of the traditional psychoanalytic attitude.

The recovery of a developmental process

This theoretical approach is closely related to the previous one. It postulates a pre-ordained sequence of development, with successive stages that should be travelled one by one, in order to arrive to a final state of maturity. The first such theory was Freud's (1905d) libido theory, later systematised by Abraham (1927), and its final wished-for stage, which Erikson (1950) called its "utopia", was called "genitality". Other theories have replaced the instinctual evolution of this original formulation by a development of the ego and object relations, such as, for instance, Klein's (1975) "depressive position", Mahler's (1968; Mahler, Pine, & Bergman, 1975) "separation–individuation", or Winnicott's (1963) "independence".

The underlying assumption is that pathology ensues whenever some of these stages has somehow got stuck, so that any further development lacks a solid foundation and the symptoms reflect, in some way, what Winnicott (1955) called the "frozen failure". The effect of the analytic process is to "unfreeze" this situation and allow the patient a second chance to traverse the environmental stage in which the problem started and reinstate the normal environmental process. This is supposed to occur spontaneously, without any further inducement by the analyst, as the unfolding of a vital process.

But is development really a one-way path, with a series of pre-established stations, something like a railway? If that were the case, the only possible way of recovering the correct course, after having taken a wrong turn, would be to go back on one's steps, until finding the exact point in which things went wrong, and then reinitiate the journey on the right track. But contemporary research on infant development and early relations, such as Daniel Stern's (1985) and Beebe and Lachmann's (1988; Beebe, Jaffe, & Lachmann, 1992), suggest a much more complex view of development, one that is based on the subtle interactions between the baby and its mother, which are bound to generate alternative courses of development.

Besides, any linear theory of development assumes a regular evolution from an immature to a fully mature state—usually adulthood—

which is taken as a standard of "what a human being should be". This is obviously an ideological proposition, since it omits the fact that there are various contradictory contemporaneous views on such an ideal, this being the basis of much political conflict, and that different cultures throughout history have been characterised by equally diverse conceptions of human nature and the ideal version of the human being. Hence, it would appear that such developmental theories may be used as rationalisations of a practice that tends to make the patient conform to a predetermined conception of the human being.

Mitchell (1984) has suggested that the deficiencies of most contemporary object relations theories are a consequence of what he calls the "developmental tilt". Classic Freudian theory is based on the drive/structure model, which considers instinctual drives as the only source of human motivation; hence, it is fundamentally a-social, and derives all mental dynamics from inner sources. Object relations theories, on the other hand, consider the human being to be essentially social, and that his or her primary motivation is the need for relationships with other human beings. Hence, they are based on the relational/structure model, which is derived from an utterly different conception of the human being—Aristotle, not Plato (Scharff & Birtles, 1997).

These two theories are incommensurate (Greenberg & Mitchell, 1983). However, given the basic relevance of the transference with Freud in the construction of the analytic identity (Tubert-Oklander, 2013), most object relations theorists have sought ways to preserve their identification with Freudian theory, while introducing new concepts that are logically, theoretically, and clinically incompatible with it. One such manoeuvre has been to restrict the application of the new concepts to the understanding and treatment of severe personality disturbances, previously considered to be unanalysable, while keeping the treatment of "classical neurosis" as the turf for the existence and use of the original drive theory. The problem with this is that, sooner or later, such clinicians were bound to diagnose more and more of their patients as "severely disturbed", until the diagnosis of "neurosis" became a *rara avis* indeed. This was a consequence of their failure to acknowledge that what they were proposing was really a radical change in theory. Such is the case, according to Mitchell (1984) of writers such as Balint, Winnicott, Mahler, and Kohut.

The second and more damaging strategy for avoiding the conflict with Freudian drive theory is the "developmental tilt". This is the term used by Mitchell to refer to the argument that says that "Freud was correct in understanding the mind in terms of conflicts among drives; object relations are also important, but earlier" (p. 476). The disturbing new ideas about a primary need for relationship have been restricted to the earliest stages of development, long before the child-hood phenomena rightly studied by Freud; the dust has been swept under the carpet, so to speak:

> When a theorist following this strategy wants to introduce various relational needs and processes as primary in their own right, as irre-ducible, as neither merely gratifiers nor defenders against drives, they are often introduced as operative before the tripartite structures of id, ego and superego have become separated and articulated. Theor-ists concerned with linear continuity necessarily preserve the classical theory of neurosis as centered around sexual and aggressive conflicts at the oedipal phase. *They set object relations formulations into pre-existing theory by arguing that they pertain to a developmental epoch prior to the differentiation of psychic structures, in the earliest relationship of the mother and infant. The traditional model is jacked up, and new relational concepts are slid in underneath.* (Mitchell, 1984, p. 477, my italics)

But there is a price to be paid for preserving our identification with an ideal object: whenever a patient expresses his need for another person's response, including the analyst's, this is rapidly interpreted as an infantile striving. The analyst is forced by her theoretical assumptions to project the patient's needs and feelings into an imagi-nary infancy or childhood, thus sending the implicit message that it is an anachronistic and inadequate sentiment that will have to be over-come as the treatment progresses.

Of course, children have these needs, but so do adults, and there are ways of expressing them that are characteristic of each age. When a patient expects the analyst to express some satisfaction or joy towards his accomplishments, which are also those of the treatment and, hence, of the analyst, this is not necessarily an infantile attitude and should not be characterised as such. It would seem that theory and practice are held hostage to the unwarranted belief that a fully mature adult—if there is such a thing—should neither experience an emotional need for others, nor act in order to obtain the responses she needs from them.

One final criticism of the clinical consequences of the developmental tilt is that it depicts the patient as essentially passive and dependent on an external provision in order to recover the right track. This ignores the fact that human beings, beginning in infancy, are active participants in all their relationships. So, it is much more appropriate to view their development—both during infancy and childhood and in the course of treatment—as a result of a negotiation with a caring other, as has been repeatedly shown by the contemporary research of the infant–mother interaction. In this, such empirical studies might well serve as a vivid metaphor of the patient–analyst interaction, but only as a heuristic analogy, not an identity. For instance, Stern and his co-workers (Stern et al., 1998) have used the dialectic integration of observational studies of early relationships and their reconstruction from clinical analysis in order to construct a theoretical model of "Non-interpretive mechanisms in psychoanalytic therapy: the 'something more' than interpretation".

The structural and functional changes

A *structure* may be defined as "something made up of more or less interdependent elements or parts", or as "the manner of construction: the way in which the parts of something are put together or organized" (Merriam-Webster, 2002). In psychoanalysis, structural concepts are used in order to account for the *functioning of the mind*—explained in terms of a "[psychic] apparatus to which we ascribe the characteristics of being extended in space and of being made up of several portions— which we imagine, that is, as resembling a telescope or microscope or something of the kind" (Freud, 1940a, p. 145)—as well as for the clinical fact of *conflict*, which implies that the mind is divided in parts that have a relation between them. Freud's (1923b) structural theory divides the mind into three functional structures: the motivational structure or id, which is the site of the biologically determined instinctual drives; the moral structure or superego, which represents the societal values, norms, and conventions, derived from the internalisation of parental figures, and the executive structure, or ego, which includes consciousness, cognitive functions, and defence operations, being also derived from the internalisation of previous relationships.

Structural concepts also serve to explain how past experience determines present functioning and behaviour. This is essential for a theory like psychoanalysis, which looks into past events in order to account for repetition, regularity, and persistence in thinking, feeling, and acting. Another kind of psychoanalytic structural theory is the theory of internal objects, which postulates that the unconscious mind is populated by personified functional structures, derived from the internalisation of the experience of relationship with significant others, particularly during infancy and childhood, and which engage in mutual relationships which are akin to those that develop between actual persons. For Klein (1932, 1975) these are relatively stable "phantasies", which express instinctual urges (Isaacs, 1948). Fairbairn (1952) criticised as follows the idea of viewing internal objects as unconscious fantasies:

> Melanie Klein has never satisfactorily explained how phantasies of incorporating objects orally can give rise to the establishment of internal objects as endopsychic structures—and, unless they are such structures, they cannot be properly spoken of as internal objects at all, since otherwise they will remain mere figments of phantasy. (p. 154)

His own explanation is that such objects, which he defines as "bad internal objects" are the remnants of traumatic experiences that split the originally unitary mind into living fragments, dynamic structures that include the various functions of the personality (emotion, cognition, and conation), thus acting as if they were a kind of subsidiary personalities. Pichon-Rivière (1971), strongly influenced by Fairbairn, saw the psychic apparatus as an "internal group", whose interactions underlay the functioning of the personality.

It is obvious that any theory of therapy must be an explanation of structural change, since in psychoanalysis psychopathology is usually defined in terms of stereotyped and repetitious behaviour, and healing as the emergence of new and more desirable patterns. If one thinks in terms of Freud's structural model, it is quite obvious that the superego, which was originally formed from the internalisation of parental figures and later modified by that of teachers, political leaders, ideal characters in the wider culture, and other authority figures (Freud, 1933a), is amenable to being transformed by the internalisation of the relationship with the analyst, as Strachey (1934) suggested. This process includes the identification with the analyst's interpretative activity, both in its contents and in its spirit of endless search. For those of us who conceive analysis as a dialogue, this would include the internalisation of the dialogic experience, which would transmute an authoritarian internal group into a democratic, rational, and reflective one, thus determining a radical change in the functioning of the personality.

The same considerations are valid for the case of the ego, which is also built from the internalisation of personal relations. The new relational experiences and the reflection on them provided by the interpretative process are bound to determine several structural and functional changes, such as: (a) a weakening and diminished function of that part of the ego that tends to avoid unpleasant emotional experiences by means of an intentional distortion of cognitive processes, that is the defence mechanisms; (b) a strengthening of those cognitive and conative functions, related to the secondary process, that provide a feasible and more elaborate alternative to the operation of defence mechanisms; consequently, (c) an increase in the capacity to tolerate, contain, and coexist with fear, anxiety, depression, guilt, and shame, without disorganisation or loss of secondary process function; (d) a greater capacity to synthesise and integrate the various mental processes (emotional, cognitive, and conative), tendencies, values, and relationships; (e) an increased knowledge and understanding of those aspects of the world that exist in spite of the ego—"reality"—both internal and external, that may then be used as a source of information for deliberation and decision making. From the analytic dialogue, the ego learns the art of negotiation, which is essential for mediating between the demands of instinctual wishes, moral values, and the limits imposed by reality.

In the Freudian structural theory, there is no space for considering that the experience of analysis might induce any changes in the id, since it is considered to be strictly biological and, hence, beyond the scope of any psychological influence ("For the psychical field, the biological field does in fact play the part of the underlying bedrock", Freud, 1937c, p. 252). However, many post-Freudian theoreticians have had to account for their feeling that somehow the analysis modifies unconscious instinctual wishes, in spite of the fact that drive theory forbids it. This has led to several modifications of the meaning of theoretical terms, in order to accommodate new ideas without having to renounce the use of the Freudian vocabulary that serves as our *lingua franca*.

For instance, Klein preserved in her theory the centrality of instinctual drives, while dropping Freud's biological definition and turning
them into psychological currents that impel the ego and rule the establishment of object relations. These end up by being indistinguishable
from love and hate, and they are only apparent in terms of their experiential representation in unconscious fantasy. Hence, the Kleinian
theory is really a theory of the iconic symbolisation of emotional experience, and this is certainly amenable to being transformed by interpretation and present relationship.

Such therapeutic transformation of id wishes is, of course, quite
consistent with theories such as Ferenczi's (1929), Fairbairn's (1952),
and Kohut's (1982), who conceive the Freudian instinctual drives as
psychopathological products of a fragmentation of the self, induced
by traumatic experiences. Indeed, for these theoreticians, the therapeutic relationship "is equivalent to the introduction of positive life-
impulses and motives for [the patient's] subsequent existence"
(Ferenczi, 1929, p. 129), thus neutralising the self-destructive wishes
("death instinct", in Ferenczi's clinical use of the term) derived from
an insufficient loving response from the primary objects.

Within the realm of ego psychology, thinkers such as Jacobson
(1964) and Kernberg (1976, 1988) have proposed a primary and primitive stage of development, previous to the subject-object, libido-
aggression, and tripartite structural differentiations, which would
antedate the establishment of a more sophisticated organisation that
makes sense out of concepts such as those of instinctual drives, id,
ego, and superego. Kernberg, in particular, conceives the patterns of
internalised object relations as an expression of basic emotions, as the
"building-blocks" of the tripartite structure and the instinctual drives
of Freudian metapsychology. This is, of course, a major example of
Mitchell's (1984) "developmental tilt", which manages to keep the
essentials of Freudian theory by means of introducing an earlier stage
in which the individual boundaries are blurred and the intrapsychic
system is open to external influence, thus making it possible to explain
the therapeutic influence of psychoanalysis as something that might
change unconscious instinctual wishes.

The objections to the structural theory are, in the first place, those
that are general objections to metapsychology, specifically, that it
attempts the impossible task of explaining a highly personal experience in terms of an impersonal causal theory, as Guntrip (1961)

expounded. But even if we concentrate on a clinical theory of conscious and unconscious experience of relationship, we are still bound to harbour a whole set of assumptions—conscious, preconscious, or unconscious—about the nature, structure, and functioning of the mind. It is the task of metapsychology to identify, reconstruct, and make them explicit, so that they may be critically discussed.

Of course, there might be other metapsychologies that differ from that of Freudian theory, and object relations theory has been developing its own, although not always explicitly. Since not all our clinical experiences and observations can be framed in the terms of the tripartite structural model, there have been other metapsychological approaches, such as Kernberg's, that have tried to go beyond its inherent limitations.

A more radical approach has been that of Kohut (1984) and his self psychology, that left aside the problem of the functional structures that underlie emotional and relational experience and tried to describe and theorise the organisation and meaning of this experience. The main structural concept has been that of the *self*, which depends for its development and maintenance on the empathic responses of its *selfobjects*—that is, other human beings on which the individual depends and who are experienced as being an extension of the self. If the original self–selfobject relations—with the mother or other primary care-giver—fail, there is a primary self defect, which is then protected by *defensive structures*. Later in development, usually during latency and through the relationship with the father, some *compensatory structures* might be formed; this does not heal the primary structural defect, but might ameliorate its noxious effects. Hence, working through, during a psychoanalytic treatment, might focus on the understanding and healing of the primary defect, by means of the relationship with the analyst as a selfobject, or on the creation of compensatory structures that reduce the symptomatic and characterological expressions of the primary defect. All of this is attained by a process of transmuting internalisation that turns the new corrective self–selfobject experience in the transference into depersonified self structures.

What seems obvious is that, just as structural concepts are necessary, in order to connect the past with the present and account for the existence of conflict, they are also indispensable for explaining how the experience of a psychoanalytic treatment can introduce changes

in patterns of behaviour, thought, and experience that have been operative for a lifetime, and what makes these changes durable.

The reorganisation of the interpersonal field and process

The fact that Freudian theory focuses on the internalised effects of
past experiences as the determinants of present behaviour and experience tends to make it oblivious to the corresponding effects of
present happenings. None the less, there is no denying that present
relationships do have an actual influence on human beings—if this
were not the case, what would be the point of undergoing or conducting treatments? On the other hand, other analytic theories place a
greater emphasis on present interactions.

Sullivan (1953), for instance, developed an interpersonal theory of
normal and pathological mental functioning, which revolves around
his concept of anxiety. This is not ordinary anxiety, but a devastating
and disorganising anguish. It is not just intrapsychic, but interpersonal, as Levenson (1992) reminds us:

> *Anxiety is interpersonal and contagious. Anxiety occurs in the infant and
> child because it is being provoked in the necessary Other; and, it is the
> empathically communicated anxiety of the Other which floods the dependent
> child*. The subject develops an instrumentality for detecting, avoiding
> and "inattending" those occasions which might precipitate anxiety.
> This is, of course, Sullivan's famous *self-system* [original italics]—not
> synonymous with the self, as self psychologists conceive it; but rather
> an early warning system. *Anxiety, then, is not caused by repression of
> forbidden impulse; but by fear of the Other (or, more accurately, fear of the
> other's fear). Intrapsychic fantasy is more the reflection of interpersonal
> events than the cause.* (p. 452, my italics)

This is, of course, another, utterly different way of looking at
things, when compared with our own tradition, one that highlights a
whole series of clinical phenomena that are usually overlooked by our
usual emphasis on the intrapsychic and the predominance of the past.
As such, it complements well our own discoveries and knowledge.
However, a unilateral attention paid to the interpersonal is as partial
and problematic as one that only takes into account intrapersonal
factors, as it tends to minimise or ignore the fact that personal history
does determine one's misperception of present events, which Sullivan

called the "parataxic distortion", a concept that partially overlaps with what we psychoanalysts call the "transference".

Another similar approach is that of group analysis. Foulkes (1948, 1964) applied his teacher Kurt Goldstein's conception of the nervous system as a network of connections, in which individual neurons were the nodal points, to the understanding of the human group as a network of communications and relations, in which the individuals are the nodal points. Hence, neurosis could be conceived as a disturbance of the communication network in which we are all embedded. This is what Foulkes called the *group matrix*, which he defined as

> the hypothetical web of communication and relationship in a given group. It is the common shared ground which ultimately determines the meaning and significance of all events and upon which all communications and interpretations, verbal and non verbal, rest. (Foulkes, 1964, p. 292)

This, of course, also applies to the bipersonal group generated by the analytic situation, which may then be viewed, as Bion (1961) suggested, as an isolated subgroup that segregates itself from the community, but which still belongs to and is determined by it.

But the group-analytic view, as introduced by Foulkes in London and Pichon-Rivière in Buenos Aires, is not merely interpersonal or sociological, but, rather, a dialectic integration of the intra-, inter-, and transpersonal processes. As such, it is also a profitable perspective for understanding what actually happens in the bipersonal situation of the analytic treatment. The patient usually comes with a distorted and stereotyped view of his or her relationships. The startling discovery that the analyst does not respond in kind, but, rather, tries to see, listen to, and treat him for what he is, and proposes a reflective and searching dialogue that aims at understanding whatever they are living together, is a truly revolutionary event in the patient's life, one that starts a whole new style of relating. As one of my patients, a young woman, said at the end of her treatment, "When I first came here, I was busy all the time trying to guess what was it that you really wanted from me. When it finally dawned on me that you actually did not want anything at all from me, I was flabbergasted. Then, I started to enjoy it, and this has changed my life."

Of course, at the beginning, the whole relationship reflects this pathological stereotyping, and this involves the analyst as much as the patient. Instead of a dynamic field and an evolving process, we have a frozen field and a circular, self-replicating non-evolving process (Baranger & Baranger, 2009). It is their shared effort, initiated by the analyst's stubborn commitment to relating, understanding, and communicating, which finally breaks the vicious circle of automatic repetition and generates the spiral dialectic process described by Pichon-Rivière (1971). This is the crucible for the generation of therapeutic change. Such events in the transitional space created between the analyst and the analysand—Winnicott's (1971) "third area", between subjective experience and objective reality—have a bearing on the inner organisation ("psychic structure") of both parties' minds. As the British psychoanalyst and group analyst Malcolm Pines (1989) wrote:

> Therapy takes place in the "in-between", not within the patient, though the inner work of reflection, connection and insight undoubtedly occurs, but in the room, our words and our patient's words, our ways of being together, live in the overlap of boundaries between us and, as the anthropologists have shown, when boundaries overlap there is an area of the mysterious, the magical and the sacred. It is from being together in this way, by creating and sharing this new space, that we have our power. (p. 141)

The development of the linguistic and symbolic capacity

In psychoanalysis, our main instrument is language; it was, from the very beginning, and still is, Anna O's "talking cure" (Freud (with Breuer), 1895d, p. 30). Of course, as we have been discussing throughout this book, much more than words happens during a psychoanalytic treatment, but, in our therapeutic tradition, we are never satisfied until occurrences and experiences have been finally turned into a subject for that peculiar type of conversation that we call "psychoanalysis". Such a dialogue develops, in both patient and analyst but especially in the former, the capacity for the use of language as a tool for expressing, discussing, and understanding human experience. A person who had come to analysis unable to talk or only able to speak in concrete and practical terms, now becomes proficient at the metaphorical use of language, in order to convey and reflect upon emotional experience. The analyst, who is expected to have a highly sophisticated capacity for verbal expression, finds herself, at the beginning of the analysis, suddenly bereft of such capacity, and irretrievably at a loss for words other than the most conventional ones. This is a phenomenon of identification, which overtakes the whole analytic field. It is the painstaking step-by-step work of recovering, for the sake of language, what had previously been submerged in wordlessness. To borrow a metaphor from Freud (1933a), this is "a work of culture – not unlike the draining of the Zuider Zee" (p. 80). But we should remember that this phrase was intended to qualify his previous apothegm "Where id was, there ego shall be". Hence, it might well be argued that the id is nothing but that part of human experience that has been left out of language (and, hence, excluded from intra- and interpersonal communication), either because it has never been verbalised before—the "primary unconscious" (Freud, 1915e)—or because it has been banished (the "repressed" (Freud, 1915d)). If this were so, this "recovering land from the sea" would be equivalent to the development of the symbolic function of language. Lacan's (1966) work and most of the contributions of contemporary French psychoanalysis have been a development of this perspective.

If one articulates this hypothesis with the other theories of therapeutic change, it is obvious that the development of linguistic and symbolic capacity implies a structural change: the id, considered as the repository of the ineffable and the unspeakable, is certainly reduced, and the "land recouped from the sea" strengthens and fosters the development of the ego, while the superego is mollified and reincorporated into the ego by the inherent need for rationality imposed by language. There is a new emotional and relational experience, since the analyst, unlike the stern patient's superego, fosters truth and dialogue, and accepts the patient as she is, as noted by Strachey (1934). This restores a halted process of development that had been cut short by untoward relational experiences. The new interpersonal experience of acceptance, interest, care, and dialogue determines a corresponding change in the patient's personal relationships, inner mental processes, and behaviour. Therefore, the inception of a new level and function of language is a true revolution in the patient's life, which determines a major part of the therapeutic action of psychoanalysis. Other forms of treatment also have a therapeutic effect, based on relational experiences and the development of certain ego skills, but the psychoanalytic emphasis on verbalisation gives the therapeutic experience a special flavour and determines a particular outcome that does not come about spontaneously or through other types of therapy, and which relates to the specificity of psycho-analysis, which we shall discuss before the end of this chapter.

Sometimes, this perspective that emphasises the central role of language in the psychoanalytic treatment is felt to be too rationalistic, as if it excluded the emotional dimension, but this is only so if language is used as a function of the split-off intellect. If language is taken only as a vehicle for the transmission of content, the informa-tion remains sterile and divorced from actual existence, but if language coalesces with relationship, then the content becomes mean-ingful and mutative, as we shall presently see.

The quest for authenticity

Winnicott (1960) introduced a new paradigm for thinking about psychopathology and healing, with his concepts of the *True Self* and *False Self*. Traditional psychoanalysis had had no room for the con-cepts of authenticity and falsehood, although Freud always opposed human true nature—which, for him, meant a person's natural organic strivings—to society's narcissistic and highly censored and retouched image of ourselves. Consequently, both the therapy of neurotic indi-viduals and the hygienic improvement of society would require the recognition and acceptance of such truth, in terms of "natural needs" (Freud, 1910d).

But the inner truth to which Winnicott refers is quite different from this affirmation of "natural needs". For him, the True Self is the expression of a person's intrinsic vitality and creativity, related to the automatic life functions, such as breathing, and finding expression in what he calls the "spontaneous gesture". Such a gesture is the equiv-alent of saying, "I am me and I am alive", and it requires an empathic and understanding response from the other, which acts as a mirror that reflects and validates the subject's existence. Since Winnicott tended to reduce such interactions to the baby's experience of the rela-tionship with mother (a good example of Mitchell's (1984) "develop-mental tilt"), most of his examples refer to the mother's response to the baby's spontaneous gesture. For instance, the mother's face and gaze give back to the baby an idea of what he actually is:

> What does the baby see when he or she looks at the mother's face? I am suggesting that, ordinarily, what the baby sees is himself or

herself. In other words the mother is looking at the baby and *what she looks like is related to what she sees there.* (Winnicott, 1967, p. 112)

However, his idea is that this occurs mainly during infancy, and that

naturally, as the child develops and the maturational processes become sophisticated, and identifications multiply, the child becomes less and less dependent on getting back the self from the mother's and the father's face and from the faces of others who are in parental or sibling relationships. (p. 118)

How does this relate to Winnicott's assertion that the analyst must be a mirror for the patient, just like the mother is to the baby and child? This is, of course, explained in terms of the patient's regression to dependence. Kohut (1984), on the other hand, does not have this theoretical problem, since he proposes the existence of a separate line of development of narcissism, which evolves in parallel with that of object relations. "Narcissism", here, refers not to a closure of libidinal ties that are turned back towards the self, but to a complex set of mental phenomena related with the self-image and self-esteem, as a function of the relation with empathic others, who reflect back an image of the self. In this sense, narcissistic needs persist throughout the whole life cycle and maturation no longer implies transcending narcissism in order to attain true object relations, but, rather, evolving from the more primitive and infantile forms of narcissism to its more mature and socially valuable ones. Consequently, Kohut may now consider the effect of the analyst's mirroring function on the restoration of a fragmented self, without necessarily resorting to the hypothesis of the therapeutic regression.

In any case, Winnicott's (1967) observation about the analyst's mirroring function still holds as a valuable contribution to our understanding of the therapeutic process.

This glimpse of the baby's and child's seeing the self in the mother's face, and afterwards in a mirror, gives a way of looking at analysis and at the psychotherapeutic task. *Psychotherapy is not making clever and apt interpretations; by and large it is a long-term giving the patient back what the patient brings.* It is a complex derivative of the face that reflects what is there to be seen. *I like to think of my work this way, and to think that if I do this well enough the patient will find his or her own self, and will be able to exist and to feel real.* Feeling real is more than existing; it is finding a way to exist as oneself, and to relate to objects as oneself, and to have a self into which to retreat for relaxation.

But I would not like to give the impression that I think this task of reflecting what the patient brings is easy. It is not easy, and it is emotionally exhausting. But we get our rewards. Even when our patients do not get cured they are grateful to us for seeing them as they are, and this gives us a satisfaction of a deep kind. (pp. 117–118, my italics)

Of course, "giving the patient back what the patient brings" may also be done by means of interpretation, but the point is that it is not just the *content* of an interpretation that works, but the confluence of a verbal depiction in which the patient recognises himself and a relation that is accepting, empathic, understanding, and validating, thus providing an evidence that he actually has been seen, heard, considered, and valued, and not merely explained away. Pines (1998), who has made an in-depth and thorough study of mirroring (1982, 1985), has developed this idea, in the following terms:

The ability to listen openly and attentively disappears in situations of danger, the danger of reproof, of judgement, rejection, shaming, of painful exposure. Perhaps most of all the fear of being "objectivised", of not being in relation. I believe we only listen, take in and respond to what a therapist says if we feel a personal relationship with the other, in a situation of dialogue, for our truths are personal, parts of ourselves, even if unwanted or painful and can only be shared under condition of trust and mutuality. . . . *This is an attitude of respect and mutuality, to give back to the person what they have brought, not as a rebuttal but as an acknowledgement that what had previously belonged to only one now belongs to both, shared in the "in-between".* (1989, p. 141, my italics)

So, verbalisation and interpretation become a form of sharing and mirroring that makes the patient feel alive and real, and this is the essence of the True Self. But what about the False Self? According to Winnicott (1960), this is a "false personality", a character, not a person, that develops as a consequence of the non-empathic responses of the primary care-givers, which he called "impingements". Then, instead of building upon the original spontaneous gestures, which gives the later developments, based on learning, a feeling of reality, vitality, and truth, a merely compliant response takes the place of the spontaneous gesture. This is the beginning of an inauthentic form of existence, generating conducts that are only adequate responses to another person's wishes, needs, and expectations, instead of expressing one's own. The subject comes to forget what it felt like to have a personal wish, and takes the False Self to be the "real me". Such a situation, which might often be quite successful in social life, can only be solved in a psychoanalytic treatment if the analyst manages to identify and respond empathically to the scarce manifestations of the True Self that are left.

But who is to judge what is "true" and what is "false" in the patient's existence? In some passages of Winnicott's writings there is a feeling that the True Self is an ontological reality, an essence that lies dormant, like the Sleeping Beauty, waiting to be awakened by the loving arrival of the Prince. The idea that one's true being is some-where latent, hidden, and forgotten, waiting to be rediscovered (remembered) seems to be very attractive for most of us. So is the belief that we all have a certain preordained path to follow, and that it is only a question of finding it in order to attain happiness. In psychoanalysis, Bollas (1989) has suggested that the True Self has to accomplish its "destiny", which seems to be the full development of one's potentialities. Kohut (Kohut & Wolf, 1978) proposed, in a simi-lar vein, that the self is characterised by its "programme", which it is bound to develop in life. "The pursuit of the [patient's] action-poised programme arched in the energic field that established itself between his nuclear ambitions and ideals, will make it possible for him to lead a fulfilling, creative-productive life" (p. 424). But this process is not a product of the self; rather, *it is the self.*

But this point of view is not without problems. The main one is that it has reintroduced surreptitiously the spatial metaphor of a hidden "core", lying somewhere, waiting to be discovered, and this is tantamount to negating the creative aspects of the analytic interaction. In this version, the True Self is actually there, somewhere in the deep and sometime in the past, something to be recovered, not to be created and re-created by present experience.

Mitchell (1992) has criticised this essentialist use of the True Self concept. For him, there is no such thing as an organised "True Self", awaiting discovery, but authentic and inauthentic *experiences* of the self. The baby's self is a set of potentialities that may only develop as a function of the care-givers' responses. Some of these responses are adequate and respectful of the baby's temperament, thus giving her an acceptable and stimulating image of herself (and I avoid here the usual "it" to refer to the baby, since the recognition of gender is one of the main features of the response), others are inadequate and intrusive, in as much as they substitute the parents' projections for the perception and experience of the baby as a separate human being. The former foster the development of an authentic way of living, one that is experienced as a confluence and continuity of the subject's present and past, and of his or her programme for the future. The latter generate that sort of inauthentic experience that gives a meaning to the concept of the False Self.

The danger implicit in the concept of "authenticity" is that it might be used ideologically to impose on the patient the therapist's conception of what life should be. This would be an impingement. But the patient might also be applying a similarly colonising attitude towards his or her own experience, as an expression of a tyrannical superego, derived from the internalisation of past impingements. As Mitchell (1992) points out:

> By using the terms "authentic" and "inauthentic", are we not measuring our experience against some implicit standard, some preconceived idea of what is "me"? Do these terms also imply a "core" or "true" or "real" me that exists somewhere (smuggling back the spatial metaphor)? No. One has a sense of one's experience over time. One can measure a new experience in terms of continuity or discontinuity with the past and present, a new experience can represent and express one's history and current state or deny and betray one's history and current state. Speaking of authenticity versus inauthenticity or true versus false *experience* frees us from the spatial metaphor in a way that speaking of a true or false *self* or a "core" or "real" *self* does not. (p. 9)

The True and False Selves are not "things", but experiences; they should not be reified. And authenticity and inauthenticity are not absolute, but relative to the circumstances and context: today's truth might become tomorrow's falsehood. Hence, there are no definitive answers to be found in the analysis, but only a dialogic process of critical reflection and appraisal of each vital situation in terms of its degree of authenticity. So, we have an endless supply of questions and no final answers, an ongoing process, not a solution.

However, even the subtlest thinkers fall prey to the seductions of reified concepts, every now and then, even if it conflicts with the rest of their thought. Kohut, for example, proposes that the programme included in the nuclear self acts as an innate "blueprint" of the self that reveals its structure, nature, and destiny. This programme is a manifestation of the *bipolar self*, the tension arc between the person's ambitions and ideals, which is established during childhood (Kohut & Wolf, 1978). Hence, this nuclear self cannot be formed anew as a consequence of later relational experiences, including the analysis; a person's destiny is, therefore, a consequence of childhood experiences.

This taking the programme as a pre-existent algorithm for development instead of a kind of "work in progress" of the construction of a life impoverishes the creative potential of the analytic dialogue.

In this case, just as we saw while discussing the Kleinian theory of interpretation, the more rigid aspects of the theory fail to do justice to the subtlety of the practice of the more gifted clinicians who adhere to that point of view. Rubin (1998), who has written a critical analysis of the clinical consequences of Winnicott's False Self and Kohut's Bipolar Self concepts, acknowledges this discordance as follows:

> In viewing the blueprint for one's life residing within the nuclear program as a "pre-existing potential" . . . Kohut's theory may unwittingly create a teleological conception of subjectivity that places too much explanatory weight on the past and perhaps neglects—at least in *theory*—how self-experience is deeply shaped by later intersubjective contexts in which it is embedded, as well as subsequent developmental experiences. No self psychologist would recognize his or her own therapeutic work in my description, since fostering the spontaneous emergence of selfobject transferences and working through them in the *present* is an indispensable facet of self-psychologically informed clinical practice. But if Kohut's theoretical remarks about the nuclear program are taken literally, there is an agenda predisposing a return to the patient's *past*. (pp. 120–121)

So, the search for authenticity might lose its way, *just like all the other theories of the cure*, when its principles are taken literally, as if they were *the* truth, and not as alternative perspectives for thinking about the healing process. None the less, it is a valuable perspective that highlights some aspects of the therapeutic process that would not be identified otherwise.

This is, perhaps, the conclusion we may draw from this brief review of the various theories of the therapeutic action of psychoanalysis. Each of them has identified, described, and explained some aspect of this hyper-complex process, and is, hence, partially true, but it becomes rigid, and consequently false, when taken literally to the exclusion of the other points of view.

The specificity of psychoanalysis

I would like to finish this analysis of the healing process with some brief comments on the specificity of psychoanalysis. Psychoanalysis was the first systematic psychotherapy and, for many years, it was the only serious psychotherapeutic option. But, nowadays, there are numerous forms of psychotherapy and many of them can attain at least symptomatic cures. Yet, we all feel that there is something special about our type of treatment, something that goes beyond medical efficiency and creates a new kind of experience that did not exist before Freud invented his therapeutic and research device. However, it is quite difficult to pinpoint exactly what it is that differentiates psychoanalysis from other human endeavours.

The question about the specificity of psychoanalysis is an attempt to answer a question that haunts most of us: when am I doing psychoanalysis and when am I doing something that is not? Winnicott (1962b) dismissed this question in "The aims of psycho-analytical treatment" by saying,

> If our aim continues to be to verbalize the nascent conscious in terms of the transference, then we are practising analysis; if not, then we are analysts practising something else that we deem to be appropriate to the occasion. And why not?" (p. 170).

But what he was actually doing was to replace what seems to be a technical question by an existential one: am I still being a psychoanalyst, even though I am doing something else that I deem appropriate to the occasion (namely, psychotherapy)? Obviously, such questioning has everything to do with our identity as psychoanalysts. That is why it turns out to be so important for us.

A very common distortion of this problematic is its (mis)use for political purposes. Almost every political group in our professional

institution is set on declaring that its own view of therapy and practice *is* psychoanalysis, and that every other view "is not psychoanalysis"—implying that it is actually worthless and something that
should not be. But leaving out such aberrations, there is also the
need to feel that one belongs to one's own group, by partaking of its
values, beliefs, practices, and traditions. This corresponds to that
aspect of our identity that draws from our belonging to a community
that extends in time and space beyond the limits of our physical and
temporal existence.

But there is still another meaning to this question. I have
frequently experienced, and believe that many other colleagues do,
intense doubts about the value of what I am doing: is this the thing I
really value about psychoanalysis, the reason why I have chosen, and
still persist in, this impossible profession? Or have I just become an
interpretation-monger who repeats mechanically what he has been
taught, or even what he has at some time thought by himself, but that
has long since ceased to be a living expression and been turned into a
mechanical repetition? This has everything to do with that other inner
source of our identity that stems from our vital creativity.

There are some precious moments in life, in which our own existence and everything that happens and surrounds us becomes imbued
with a magical light that turns the experience into something other
than everyday life. Many artists have managed to capture and depict
such moments; Vincent van Gogh's painting, *Starry Night*, is one
instance of such an attainment, as is Coleridge's *Kubla Khan*, Shelley's
Ozymandias, or the Spanish poetry of Federico García Lorca or Saint
John of the Cross. Apparently, these moments of transfiguration and
bliss are more frequent during a happy childhood, and tend to be lost
in the course of human development and maturation. This view was
poignantly put forward by William Wordsworth in his *Ode:
Intimations of Immortality from Recollections of Early Childhood*:

> There was a time when meadow, grove, and stream,
> The earth, and every common sight,
> To me did seem
> Apparelled in celestial light,
> The glory and the freshness of a dream.
> It is not now as it hath been of yore;—
> Turn wheresoe'er I may,

>   By night or day,
>   The things which I have seen I now can see no more.
>
>   (pp.282–283)

And then:

>   Though nothing can bring back the hour
>   Of splendour in the grass, of glory in the flower;
>   We will grieve not, rather find
>   Strength in what remains behind;
>   In the primal sympathy
>   Which having been must ever be;
>   In the soothing thoughts that spring
>   Out of human suffering;
>   In the faith that looks through death,
>   In years that bring the philosophic mind.
>
>   (p. 287)

Is this not the very depiction of an analysis? It is, indeed, very similar to Winnicott's (1986) comment about happiness in marriage, in his discussion on creating living:

> Between the two extremes—those who feel they retain creative living in marriage and those who are hampered in this respect by marriage—there is surely some kind of borderline; and in this borderline very many of us happen to be situated. We are *happy enough*, and can be creative, but we do realize that there is inherently some kind of a clash between the personal impulse and the compromises that belong to any kind of relationship that has reliable features. . . . Someone said (only, I am afraid, facetiously): "There are two kinds of marriage; in one the girl knows she has married the wrong man on the way up to the altar, and in the other she knows it on the way back." But there is no reason to be funny about it really. The trouble is when we set out to give young people the idea that marriage is a prolonged love affair. But I would hate to do the opposite and to sell disillusionment to young people, to make it a business to see that young people know everything and have no illusions. If one *has been happy*, one can bear distress. It is the same when we say that a baby cannot be weaned unless he or she has had the breast, or breast equivalent. There is no disillusionment (acceptance of the Reality Principle) except on a basis of illusion. (pp. 46–47)

So, it is neither the case that there might conceivably be a state of permanent happiness, nor that happiness does not exist, except as an omnipotent fantasy, and that we shall have to make do with "common unhappiness". Happiness occurs in those moments of illusion in which we manage to "live creatively", and our actual relationship with another human being overlaps and is indistinguishable from our ideal fantasy. There are some such moments in life, and there have been in our infancy and childhood, although most of us have managed to forget them, in order to avoid the pains of disillusion (he or she who has had nothing cannot have lost anything). It takes a good analytic experience to recover these magical moments and once again be able to hope and love, but this can only happen when the analysis itself becomes an opportunity to experience these moments of happiness and hope.

In the psychoanalytic treatment, there are also such magical moments of transmutation—I have called them the "analytic moments" (Tubert-Oklander, 2000)—which bring with them "Intimations of Immortality". These are those moments in which a new experience and a new meaning emerge, and everything that we thought we knew is transformed, as we look at it afresh. We cannot produce them at will, although we may create the conditions that we know make more likely their occurrence, but, as far as I am concerned, they are the main reason for me to be a psychoanalyst and continue practising psychoanalysis.

It is quite possible that, just as the child's magical experience of the world is usually lost with growth and adulthood, the intimations received in our first experience of psychoanalysis might become unavailable as we are reshaped by decades of professional practice. But this need not be so, as Freud beautifully expressed in his letter to Lou Andreas-Salomé of 25 May 1916:

> I am always especially impressed when I read your comment on one of my papers. I know that in writing I have to blind myself artificially in order to focus all the light on one dark spot, renouncing cohesion, harmony, edifying effects and everything which you call the symbolic element, frightened as I am by the experience that any such claim, such expectation, carries within it the danger of distorting the truth, even though it may embellish it. Then you come along and add what is missing, build upon it, putting what has been isolated back into its proper context. I cannot always follow you, for my eyes, adapted as

they are to the dark, probably can't stand strong light or an extensive range of vision. But I haven't become so much of a mole as to be incapable of enjoying the suggestion of something brighter and more comprehensive, or even to deny its existence. (Freud, E. L., 1961, p. 312)

Personally, I have long ceased to be young, but I am not so old as to have forsaken the hope of once more witnessing and being a part of the miracle of the transmogrification of human experience that happens, every now and then, during an analysis. There is still for me—and I hope and wish there is for those readers who have shown the kindness, persistence, and patience to abide with me up to this point—the opportunity for ". . . bringing back the hour / Of splendour in the grass, of glory in the flower", and so it should be for our patients.

REFERENCES

Abraham, K. (1927). *Selected papers on Psycho-Analysis*, D. Bryan & A. Strachey (Trans.). London: Hogarth [reprinted, London: Karnac, 1979].

Alexander, F., & French, T. M. (1946). *Psychoanalytic Therapy: Principles and Application*. New York: Ronald.

Álvarez de Toledo, L. G. de (1996). The analysis of "associating", "interpreting" and "words": Use of this analysis to bring unconscious fantasies into the present and to achieve greater ego integration. *International Journal of Psychoanalysis, 77*: 291–317.

Aron, L. (1991). The patient's experience of the analyst's subjectivity. *Psychoanalytic Dialogues, 1*: 29–51. Reprinted in: S. A. Mitchell & L. Aron (Eds.), *Relational Psychoanalysis: The Emergence of a Tradition* (pp. 245–265). Hillsdale, NJ: Analytic Press, 1999.

Aron, L. (1996). *A Meeting of Minds: Mutuality in Psychoanalysis*. Hillsdale, NJ: Analytic Press.

Aron, L. (2003a). Presentation during the Winter 2003 Meeting of the American Psychoanalytic Association, New York, January.

Aron, L. (2003b). The paradoxical place of enactment in psychoanalysis: Introduction. *Psychoanalytic Dialogues, 13*: 623–631.

Aron, L., & Harris, A. (Eds.) (1993). *The Legacy of Sándor Ferenczi*. Hillsdale, NJ: Analytic Press.

Atwood, G. E., & Stolorow, R. D. (1984). *Structures of Subjectivity: Explorations in Psychoanalytic Phenomenology*. Hillsdale, NJ: Analytic Press.

Balint, M. (1932). Character analysis and new beginning. In: *Primary Love and Psycho-Analytic Technique* (2nd edn) (pp. 151–164). New York: Liveright, 1965.

Balint, M. (1950). On the termination of analysis. *International Journal of Psychoanalysis, 31*: 196–199. Reprinted in: *Primay Love and Psycho-Analytic Technique* (2nd edn) (pp. 223–229). New York: Liveright, 1965.

Balint, M. (1952). *Primary Love and Psycho-Analytic Technique* (2nd edn). New York: Liveright, 1965.

Balint, M. (1968). *The Basic Fault: Therapeutic Aspects of Regression* (2nd edn). London: Tavistock, 1979.

Balint, M., Ornstein, P. H., & Balint, E. (1972). *Focal Psychotherapy: An Example of Applied Psychoanalysis*. London: Tavistock.

Baranger, M., & Baranger, W. (2008)[1961–1962]. The analytic situation as a dynamic field. *International Journal of Psychoanalysis, 89*: 795–826.

Baranger, M., & Baranger, W. (2009). *The Work of Confluence: Listening and Interpreting in the Psychoanalytic Field*, L. Glocer Fiorini (Ed.). London: International Psychoanalytic Association/Karnac.

Baranger, M., Baranger, W., & Mom, J. M. (1978). Patología de la transferencia y contratransferencia en el psicoanálisis actual; el campo perverso [Pathology of transference and countertransference in present-day psychoanalysis: the perverse field]. *Revista de Psicoanálisis, 35*: 1101–1106.

Baranger, M., Baranger, W., & Mom, J. M. (1983). Process and non-process in analytic work. *International Journal of Psychoanalysis, 64*: 1–15. Reprinted in Baranger, M. & Baranger, W. (2009), *The Work of Confluence: Listening and Interpreting in the Psychoanalytic Field* (pp. 63–88), L. Glocer Fiorini (Ed.). London: International Psychoanalytic Association/Karnac.

Baranger, W. (1979). "Proceso en espiral" y "campo dinámico" ["Spiral process" and "dynamic field"]. *Revista Uruguaya de Psicoanálisis, 59*: 17–32. English translation in Baranger M., & Baranger W. (2009), *The Work of Confluence: Listening and Interpreting in the Psychoanalytic Field* (pp. 45–61), L. Glocer Fiorini (Ed.). London: International Psychoanalytic Association/Karnac.

Baranger, W. (1992). De la necesaria imprecisión en la nosografía psicoanalítica [On the necessary indeterminacy of the psychoanalytic nosography]. *Revista de Psicoanálisis, 1992, Número Especial Internacional* [Special International Issue], pp. 83–97.

Baranger, W., & Baranger, M. (1969). *Problemas del campo psicoanalítico.* [Problems of the psychoanalytic field.] Buenos Aires: Kargieman.

Bass, A. (2003). "E" enactments in psychoanalysis: another medium, another message. *Psychoanalytic Dialogues, 13*: 657–675.

Bateman, A. W. (1998). Thick- and thin-skinned organisations and enactment in borderline and narcissistic disorders. *International Journal of Psychoanalysis, 79*: 13–25.

Bateson, G. (1972). *Steps to an Ecology of Mind.* New York: Ballantine.

Beebe, B., & Lachmann, F. M. (1988). The contribution of mother–infant mutual influence to the origins of self- and object representations. *Psychoanalytic Psychology, 5*: 305–337. Reprinted in: N. J. Skolnick & S. C. Warshaw (Eds.), *Relational Perspectives in Psychoanalysis* (pp. 83–117). Hillsdale, NJ: Analytic Press.

Beebe, B., Jaffe, J., & Lachmann, F. M. (1992). A dyadic systems view of communication. In: N. J. Skolnick & S. C. Warshaw (Eds), *Relational Perspectives in Psychoanalysis* (pp. 61–81). Hillsdale, NJ: Analytic Press.

Benjamin, J. (1990). An outline of intersubjectivity: the development of recognition. *Psychoanalytic Psychology, 7*(Suppl.): 33–46. Reprinted in: *Like Subjects, Love Objects: Essays on Recognition and Sexual Difference* (pp. 27–48). New Haven, CT: Yale University Press, 1995.

Benjamin, J. (1995). *Like Subjects, Love Objects: Essays on Recognition and Sexual Difference.* New Haven, CT: Yale University Press.

Benjamin, J. (1998). *Shadow of the Other: Intersubjectivity and Gender in Psychoanalysis.* New York: Routledge.

Beuchot, M. (1997). *Tratado de hermenéutica analógica. Hacia un nuevo modelo de interpretación* [Treatise of analogical hermeneutics: towards a new model of interpretation] (4th edn). Mexico City: UNAM/Itaca, 2009.

Bibring, E. (1937). Contribution to the Symposium on the Theory of the Therapeutic Results of Psycho-Analysis. *International Journal of Psycho-analysis, 18*: 170–189.

Bion, W. R. (1961). *Experiences in Groups and Other Papers.* London: Tavistock.

Bion, W. R. (1962). *Learning from Experience.* London: Heinemann.

Bion, W. R. (1963). *Elements of Psycho-Analysis.* London: Heinemann.

Bion, W. R. (1967). Notes on memory and desire. *Psychoanalytic Forum, 2*: 271–280.

Bion, W. R. (1970). *Attention and Interpretation.* London: Tavistock.

Bion, W. R. (1974–1975). *Brazilian Lectures: 1973, São Paulo; 1974, Rio De Janeiro/São Paulo.* London: Karnac, 1992.

Bion, W. R. (1980). *Bion in New York and São Paulo,* F. Bion (Ed.). Strathtay, Perthshire: Clunie Press.

Bion, W. R. (1985). *The Italian Seminars*, F. Bion (Ed.), P. Slotkin (Trans.). London: Karnac, 2005.

Bleger, J. (1967a). Psycho-analysis of the psycho-analytic frame. *International Journal of Psychoanalysis, 48*: 511–519.

Bleger, J. (1967b). *Simbiosis y ambigüedad. Estudio psicoanalítico* [*Symbiosis and Ambiguity: A Psychoanalytic Study*]. Buenos Aires: Paidós.

Bleger, J. (1971). El grupo como institución y el grupo en las instituciones [The group as an institution and the group in institutions]. In: *Temas de psicología. (Entrevista y grupos)* [Themes in psychology. (Interview and groups)] (pp. 87–104). Buenos Aires: Nueva Visión.

Bleger, J. (1974). Schizophrenia, autism, and symbiosis. *Contemporary Psychoanalysis, 10*: 19–25.

Bollas, C. (1989). *Forces of Destiny: Psychoanalysis and Human Idiom*. London: Free Association Books.

Bollas, C. (2007). *The Freudian Moment*. London: Karnac.

Bouvet, M. (1955). La cure-type [The type cure]. In: *Oeuvres psychanalytiques. Résistances, transfert*, vol. II. Paris: Payot, 1968.

Bowlby, J. (1985). On knowing what you are not supposed to know and feeling what you are not supposed to feel. In: *A Secure Base: Parent–Child Attachment and Healthy Human Development* (pp. 99–118). New York: Basic Books, 1988.

Boyer, L. B. (1978). Countertransference experiences with severely regressed patients. *Contemporary Psychoanalysis, 14*: 48–71.

Boyer, L. B. (1986). Technical aspects of treating the regressed patient. *Contemporary Psychoanalysis, 22*: 25–44.

Brierley, M. (1943). Theory, practice and public relations. *International Journal of Psycho-Analysis, 24*: 119–125.

Brierley, M. (1944). Notes on metapsychology as process theory. *International Journal of Psychoanalysis, 25*: 97–106.

Brierley, M. (1945). Further notes on the implications of psycho-analysis: metapsychology and personology. *International Journal of Psychoanalysis, 26*: 89–114. Reprinted in: *Trends in Psycho-Analysis* (pp. 124–179). London: Hogarth, 1951.

Calvo, L. (2008). Racial fantasies and the primal scene of miscegenation. *International Journal of Psychoanalysis, 89*: 55–70.

Clark, A. (2009). Perception, action, and experience: unraveling the golden braid. *Neuropsychologia, 47*: 1460–1468.

Civitarese, G. (2008). *The Intimate Room: Theory and Technique of the Analytic Field*, P. Slotkin (Trans.). London: Routledge.

de Maré, P., Piper, R., & Thompson, S. (1991). *Koinonia: From Hate, through Dialogue, to Culture in the Large Group*. London: Karnac.

de Racker, G. T. (1961). On the formulation of the interpretation. *International Journal of Psychoanalysis*, *42*: 49–54.

de Saussure, F. (1916). *Course in General Linguistics*, C. Bally & A. Sechehaye (Eds.), R. Harris (Trans.). La Salle, IL: Open Court, 2006.

Descartes, R. (1637). *Discourse on Method*, P. Kraus & F. Hunt (Eds.), R. Kennington (Trans.). Newburyport, MA: Focus, 2007.

Donne, J. (1624). XVII. Meditation. In: *Devotion Upon Emergent Occasions*. Ann Arbor, MI: University of Michigan Press, 1959.

Erikson, E. H. (1950). *Childhood and Society*. New York: Norton [reprinted: London: Paladin, 1987].

Etchegoyen, R. H. (1985). Identification and its vicissitudes. *International Journal of Psychoanalysis*, *66*: 3–18.

Etchegoyen, R. H. (1986). *Fundamentals of Psychoanalytic Technique* (2nd revised edn), P. Pitchon (Trans.). London: Karnac, 2005.

Fairbairn, W. R. D. (1952). *Psychoanalytic Studies of the Personality*. London: Tavistock.

Fairbairn, W. R. D. (1958). On the nature and aims of psycho-analytical treatment. *International Journal of Psychoanalysis*, *39*: 374–385.

Falzeder, E., & Brabant, E. (Eds.) (2000). *The Correspondence of Sigmund Freud and Sándor Ferenczi, Volume 3, 1920–1933*. Cambridge, MA: Harvard University Press.

Fenichel, O. (1941). *Problems of Psychoanalytic Technique*. Albany, NY: Psychoanalytic Quarterly.

Ferenczi, S. (1919). Technical difficulties in the analysis of a case of hysteria. In: *Further Contributions to the Theory and Technique of Psycho-Analysis* (pp. 189–197), J. Rickman (Comp.), J. I. Suttie & others (Trans.). New York: Brunner/Mazel, 1980. [Original publication, London: Hogarth. Reprinted, London: Karnac, 2012.]

Ferenczi, S. (1921). The further development of an active therapy in psycho-analysis. In: *Further Contributions to the Theory and Technique of Psycho-Analysis* (pp. 198–217), J. Rickman (Comp.), J. I. Suttie & others (Trans.). New York: Brunner/Mazel, 1980. [Original publication, London: Hogarth. Reprinted, London: Karnac, 2012.]

Ferenczi, S. (1925). Contra-indications to the "active" psycho-analytical technique. In: *Further Contributions to the Theory and Technique of Psycho-Analysis* (pp. 217–230), J. Rickman (Comp.), J. I. Suttie & others (Trans.). New York: Brunner/Mazel, 1980. [Original publication, London: Hogarth. Reprinted, London: Karnac, 2012.]

Ferenczi, S. (1927). The problem of the termination of the analysis. In: *Final Contributions to the Problems and Methods of Psycho-Analysis* (pp. 77–86). New York: Brunner/Mazel, 1980 [reprinted, London: Karnac, 2011].

Ferenczi, S. (1928a). The adaptation of the family to the child. In: *Final Contributions to the Problems and Methods of Psycho-Analysis* (pp. 61–76). New York: Brunner/Mazel, 1980 [reprinted, London: Karnac, 2011].

Ferenczi, S. (1928b). The elasticity of psycho-analytic technique. In: *Final Contributions to the Problems and Methods of Psycho-Analysis* (pp. 87–101). New York: Brunner/Mazel, 1980 [reprinted, London: Karnac, 2011].

Ferenczi, S. (1929). The unwelcome child and his death-instinct. *International Journal of Psychoanalysis*, 10: 125–129. Reprinted in: *Final Contributions to the Problems and Methods of Psycho-Analysis* (pp. 102–107). New York: Brunner/Mazel, 1980 [reprinted, London: Karnac, 2011].

Ferenczi, S. (1930). The principle of relaxation and neocatharsis. *International Journal of Psychoanalysis*, 11: 428–443. Reprinted in: *Final Contributions to the Problems and Methods of Psycho-Analysis* (pp. 108–125). New York: Brunner/Mazel, 1980 [reprinted, London: Karnac, 2011].

Ferenczi, S. (1931). Child-analysis in the analysis of adults. *International Journal of Psychoanalysis*, 12: 468–482. Reprinted in: *Final Contributions to the Problems and Methods of Psycho-Analysis* (pp. 126–142). New York: Brunner/Mazel, 1980 [reprinted, London: Karnac, 2011].

Ferenczi, S. (1933). Confusion of the tongues between the adults and the child—(The language of tenderness and of passion). *International Journal of Psychoanalysis*, 1949, 30: 225–230. Also in *Contemporary Psychoanalysis*, 24: 196–206. Reprinted in: *Final Contributions to the Problems and Methods of Psycho-Analysis* (pp. 156–167). New York: Brunner/Mazel, 1980 [reprinted, London: Karnac, 2011].

Ferenczi, S. (1955). *Final Contributions to the Problems and Methods of Psycho-Analysis*. New York: Brunner/Mazel, 1980 [reprinted, London: Karnac, 2011].

Ferenczi, S. (1985). *The Clinical Diary of Sándor Ferenczi*, J. Dupont (Ed.), M. Balint & N. Z. Jackson (Trans.). Cambridge, MA: Harvard University Press, 1988.

Ferenczi, S., & Rank, O. (1924). *The Development of Psychoanalysis*, C. Newton (Trans.). Madison, WI: International Universities Press, 1986.

Ferro, A. (1996). *In the Analyst's Consulting Room*, P. Slotkin (Trans.). New York: Brunner-Routledge, 2002.

Ferro, A. (1999). *Psychoanalysis as Therapy and Storytelling*, P. Slotkin (Trans.). London: Routledge, 2006.

Ferro, A. (2002). *Seeds of Illness, Seeds of Recovery: The Genesis of Suffering and the Role of Psychoanalysis*, P. Slotkin (Trans.). New York: Brunner-Routledge, 2005.

Field, J. (Milner, M.) (1934). *A Life of One's Own*. London: Chatto & Windus [reprinted London: Routledge, 2011].

Fortune, C. (1993). The case of "R.N.": Sándor Ferenczi's radical experiments in psychoanalysis. In: L. Aron & A. Harris (Eds.), *The Legacy of Sándor Ferenczi* (pp. 101–120). Hillsdale, NJ: Analytic Press.

Fortune, C. (1994). Sándor Ferenczi's analysis of "R.N.": A critically important case in the history of psychoanalysis. *British Journal of Psychotherapy, 9*: 436–443.

Foulkes, S. H. (1948). *Introduction to Group-Analytic Psychotherapy: Studies in the Social Interaction of Individuals and Groups*. London: Heinemann [reprinted, London: Karnac, 1984].

Foulkes, S. H. (1964). *Therapeutic Group Analysis*. London: Allen & Unwin [reprinted, London: Karnac].

Foulkes, S. H. (1975). *Group-Analytic Psychotherapy: Method and Principles*. London: Gordon & Breach [reprinted, London: Karnac, 2012].

Foulkes, S. H. (1990). *Selected Papers: Psychoanalysis and Group Analysis*. London: Karnac.

Foulkes, S. H., & Anthony, E. J. (1965). *Group Psychotherapy: The Psychoanalytic Approach* (2nd edn). London: Penguin [reprinted, London: Karnac, 1984].

Freud A. (1927). Introduction to the technique of child analysis. In: *The Writings of Anna Freud, Volume I (1922–1935)*. New York: International Universities Press, 1973.

Freud, A. (1936). *The Ego and the Mechanisms of Defense: The Writings of Anna Freud, Volume II (1936)*, C. M. Baines (Trans.). New York: International Universities Press, 1973 [reprinted London: Karnac, 1999].

Freud A. (1954). The widening scope of indications for psychoanalysis—Discussion. *Journal of the American Psychoanalytical Association, 2*: 607–620.

Freud, E. L. (Ed.) (1961). *Letters of Sigmund Freud 1873–1939* (pp. 312–313), T. Stern & J. Stern (Trans.). London: Hogarth.

Freud, S. (1892–1893). A case of successful treatment by hypnotism. *S.E., 1*: 115–128. London: Hogarth.

Freud, S. (with Breuer, J.) (1895d). *Studies on Hysteria. S.E., 2*. London: Hogarth.

Freud, S. (1900a). *The Interpretation of Dreams. S.E., 4–5*. London: Hogarth.

Freud, S. (1904a). Freud's psycho-analytic procedure. *S.E., 7*: 247–254. London: Hogarth.

Freud, S. (1905d). *Three Essays on the Theory of Sexuality. S.E., 7*: 123–246. London: Hogarth.

Freud, S. (1909b). *Analysis of a Phobia in a Five-year-old Boy. S.E., 10*: 1–150. London: Hogarth.

Freud, S. (1909d). *Notes upon a Case of Obsessional Neurosis. S.E., 10*: 153–318. London: Hogarth.

Freud, S. (1910d). The future prospects of psycho-analytic therapy. *S.E., 11*: 139–152. London: Hogarth.

Freud, S. (1912b). The dynamics of transference. *S.E., 12*: 97–108. London: Hogarth.

Freud, S. (1912e). Recommendations to physicians practising psycho-analysis. *S.E., 12*: 109–120. London. Hogarth.

Freud, S. (1912g). A note on the unconscious in psycho-analysis. *S.E., 12*: 255–266. London: Hogarth.

Freud, S. (1913c). On beginning the treatment (Further recommendations on the technique of psychoanalysis I). *S.E., 12*: 121–144. London: Hogarth.

Freud, S. (1914c). On narcissism: an introduction. *S.E., 14*: 67–102. London: Hogarth.

Freud, S. (1914d). On the history of the psycho-analytic movement. *S.E., 14*: 1–66. London: Hogarth.

Freud, S. (1914g). Remembering, repeating, working-through (Further recommendations on the technique of psychoanalysis II). *S.E., 12*: 145–156. London: Hogarth.

Freud, S. (1915a). Observations on transference-love (Further recommendations on the technique of psychoanalysis III). *S.E., 12*: 157–171. London: Hogarth.

Freud, S. (1915c). Instincts and their vicissitudes. *S.E., 14*: 109–140. London: Hogarth.

Freud, S. (1915d). Repression. *S.E., 14*: 141–158. London: Hogarth.

Freud, S. (1915e). The unconscious. *S.E., 14*: 159–215. London: Hogarth.

Freud, S. (1916–1917). *Introductory Lectures on Psycho-Analysis. S.E., 15–16.* London: Hogarth.

Freud, S. (1917a). A difficulty in the path of psychoanalysis. *S.E., 17*: 135–144. London: Hogarth.

Freud, S. (1917e). Mourning and melancholia. *S.E., 14*: 237–258. London: Hogarth.

Freud, S. (1918b). *From the History of an Infantile Neurosis. S.E., 17*: 1–124. London: Hogarth.

Freud, S. (1919a). Lines of advance in psycho-analytic therapy. *S.E., 17*: 157–168. London: Hogarth.

Freud, S. (1920b). A note on the prehistory of the technique of analysis. *S.E., 18*: 261–265. London: Hogarth.

Freud, S. (1921c). *Group Psychology and the Analysis of the Ego. S.E., 18*: 65–144. London: Hogarth.

Freud, S. (1923b). *The Ego and the Id. S.E., 19*: 1–66. London: Hogarth.

Freud, S. (1924c). The economic problem of masochism. *S.E., 19*: 155–170. London: Hogarth.

Freud, S. (1927d). Humour. *S.E., 21*: 159–166. London: Hogarth.

Freud, S. (1930a). *Civilization and its Discontents. S.E., 21*: 64–145. London: Hogarth.

Freud, S. (1933a). *New Introductory Lectures on Psycho-Analysis, S.E., 22*: 1–182. London: Hogarth.

Freud, S. (1937c). Analysis terminable and interminable. *S.E., 23*: 209–254. London: Hogarth.

Freud, S. (1937d). Constructions in analysis. *S.E., 23*: 255–270. London: Hogarth.

Freud, S. (1940a). *An Outline of Psycho-Analysis. S.E., 23*: 139–208. London: Hogarth.

Freud, S. (1955a). Addendum: Original record of the case [of obsessional neurosis (the "Rat Man")]. *S.E., 10*: 251–318. London: Hogarth.

Fromm, E. (1941). *Escape From Freedom.* New York: Farrar & Rinehart [reprinted: New York: Holt, 1994].

Fromm, E. (1951). *The Forgotten Language: An Introduction to the Understanding of Dreams, Fairy Tales and Myths.* New York: Rinehart.

Fromm, E. (1979). *Greatness and Limitations of Freud's Thought.* London: Jonathan Cape, 1980 [reprinted: New York: Meridian, 1988].

Gadamer, H.-G. (1960). *Truth and Method* (2nd revised English edn, translated from the 5th German edn), W. Glen-Doepel (Trans.), J. Weinsheimer & D. G. Marshall (Revs.). London: Continuum, 2004.

Gear, M. C., & Liendo, E. C. (1977). *La acción psicoanalítica* [Psychoanalytic action]. Caracas: Monte Avila.

Ghent, E. (1990). Masochism, submission, surrender: masochism as a perversion of surrender. *Contemporary Psychoanalysis, 26*: 108–136. Reprinted in: S. A. Mitchell & L. Aron (Eds.), *Relational Psychoanalysis: The Emergence of a Tradition* (pp. 213–239). Hillsdale, NJ: Analytic Press, 1999.

Ghent, E. (2002). Introduction to the First IARPP Conference. *IARPP e-News, 1* (1): 7–9. In the web page of the International Association for Relational Psychoanalysis and Psychotherapy (accessed 17 December 2011) www.iarpp.net/resources/enews/enews1.pdf .

Giovacchini, P., & Boyer, L. B. (1975). The psychoanalytic impasse. *International Journal of Psychoanalytic Psychotherapy, 4*: 25–47

Glover, E. (1955). *The Technique of Psycho-Analysis*. New York: International Universities Press.

Goldstein, K. (1940). *Human Nature in the Light of Psychopathology*. Cambridge, MA: Harvard University Press.

Green, A. (1993). Two discussions of "The inner experiences of the analyst" and a response from Theodore Jacobs. *International Journal of Psychoanalysis, 74*: 1131–1136.

Greenberg, J. R., & Mitchell, S. A. (1983). *Object Relations in Psychoanalytic Theory*. Cambridge, MA: Harvard University Press.

Greenson, R. R. (1967). *The Technique and Practice of Psychoanalysis. Volume I*. New York: International Universities Press.

Greenson, R. R. (1974). Transference: Freud or Klein. *International Journal of Psychoanalysis, 55*: 37–48.

Greenson, R. R. (1975). Transference: Freud or Klein. A reply to the discussion by Herbert Rosenfeld. *International Journal of Psychoanalysis, 56*: 243–243.

Greenson, R. R., & Wexler, M. (1969). The non-transference relationship in the psychoanalytic situation. *International Journal of Psychoanalysis, 50*: 27–39.

Grinberg, L. (1962). On a specific aspect of countertransference due to the patient's projective identification. *International Journal of Psychoanalysis, 43*: 436–440.

Grinberg, L. (1979). Countertransference and projective counteridentification. *Contemporary Psychoanalysis, 15*: 226–247.

Grotstein, J. S. (1981). *Splitting and Projective Identification*. New York: Jason Aronson.

Guiard, F. E. (1979). Aportes al conocimiento del proceso postanalítico [Contributions to the knowledge of the post-analytic process]. *Psicoanálisis, 1*: 171–204.

Guntrip, H. (1961). *Personality Structure and Human Interaction: The Developing Synthesis of Psychodynamic Theory*. London: Hogarth [reprinted, London, Karnac, 2011].

Guntrip, H. (1963). Different levels of psychotherapy. In: *Psychoanalytic Theory, Therapy, and the Self* (pp. 276–287). New York: Basic Books.

Guntrip, H. (1971). *Psychoanalytic Theory, Therapy, and the Self*. New York: Basic Books.

Guntrip, H. (1975). My experience of analysis with Fairbairn and Winnicott—(How complete a result does psycho-analytic therapy achieve?). *International Review of Psycho-Analysis, 2*: 145–156. Also in *International Journal of Psycho-Analysis, 77*: 739–754.

Hamilton, E. (1942). *Mythology: Timeless Tales of Gods and Heroes*. New York: Little, Brown [reprinted, New York: Warner, 1999].

Heimann, P. (1950). On counter-transference. *International Journal of Psychoanalysis*, 31: 81–84. Reprinted in: *About Children and Children-No-Longer: Collected Papers 1942-80* (pp. 73–79), M. Tonnesman (Ed.). London: Routledge, 1989.

Heimann, P. (1978). On the necessity for the analyst to be natural with his patient. In: *About Children and Children-No-Longer: Collected Papers 1942–80* (pp. 311–323), M. Tonnesman (Ed.). London: Routledge, 1989.

Hernández de Tubert, R. (1999) La regressione: espressione psicopatologica o fattore terapeutico fondamentale? [Regression: Psychopathological expression or fundamental therapeutic factor?] In: F. Borgogno (Ed.), *La partecipazione affettiva dell' analista. Il contributo di Sándor Ferenczi al pensiero psicoanalitico contemporaneo* (pp. 186–209) [The analyst's affective participation: The contribution of Sándor Ferenczi to contemporary psychoanalytic thought]. Milan: Franco Angeli.

Hernández de Tubert, R. (2000). El principio de exclusión en el desarrollo del movimiento psicoanalítico [The principle of exclusion in the development of the psychoanalytic movement]. Read at the 8th International Meeting of the International Association for the History of Psychoanalysis, Versailles, France, July.

Hernández de Tubert, R. (2004). Inconsciente y concepción del mundo [The unconscious and the *Weltanschauung*]. In: M. Kolteniuk, J. Casillas, & J. de la Parra (Eds.), *El inconsciente freudiano* [The Freudian unconscious] (pp. 63–78). Mexico City: Editores de Textos Mexicanos.

Hernández de Tubert, R. (2005). Baluarte e ideología en la obra de Willy Baranger [The bastion and ideology in the work of Willy Baranger]. *Cuadernos de Psicoanálisis*, 38: 55–62.

Hernández de Tubert, R. (2006a). Los prejuicios de género en la interpretación de la teoría y la técnica psicoanalíticas. Su impacto en la transferencia-contratransferencia [Gender prejudices in the interpretation of psychoanalytic theory and practice: Their impact on the transference-countertransference]. *Cuadernos de Psicoanálisis*, 39(1–2): 26–36.

Hernández de Tubert, R. (2006b). Social trauma: the pathogenic effects of untoward social conditions. *International Forum of Psychoanalysis*, 15: 151–156.

Hernández-Tubert, R. (2008a). Contribution to the discussion. (Symposium on the Analytic Frame.) *Psychoanalytic Dialogues*, 18: 248–251.

Hernández de Tubert, R. (2008b). La antropología freudiana y la metasociología [Freudian anthropology and metasociology]. *Revista de Psicoanálisis*, 65(1): 29–56.

Hernández de Tubert, R., & Tubert-Oklander, J. (2005). Operative groups: a reply to Macario Giraldo. *Psychologist–Psychoanalyst*, 25(1): 3–7.

Hoffman, I. Z. (1983). The patient as interpreter of the analyst's experience. *Contemporary Psychoanalysis*, 19: 389–422. Reprinted in S. A. Mitchell & L. Aron (Eds.) *Relational Psychoanalysis: The Emergence of a Tradition* (pp. 41–72). Hillsdale, NJ: Analytic Press, 1999.

Hopper, E. (2003a). *The Social Unconscious*. London: Jessica Kingsley.

Hopper, E. (2003b). *Traumatic Experience in the Unconscious Life of Groups*. London: Jessica Kingsley.

Horney, K. (1939). *New Ways of Psychoanalysis*. London: Routledge & Kegan Paul [reprinted London: Routledge, 1999].

Horney, K. (1987). *Final Lectures*, D. H. Ingram (Ed.). New York: Norton.

Isaacs, S. (1948). The nature and function of phantasy. *International Journal of Psychoanalysis*, 29: 73–97.

Jacobs, T. J. (1986). On countertransference enactments. *Journal of the American Psychoanalytical Association*, 34: 289–307.

Jacobs, T. J. (1993a). The inner experiences of the analyst: their contribution to the analytic process. *International Journal of Psychoanalysis*, 74: 7–14.

Jacobs, T. J. (1993b). Response. *International Journal of Psychoanalysis*, 74: 1140–1145.

Jacobson, E. (1964). *The Self and the Object World*. New York: International Universities Press.

James, W. (1907). *Pragmatism: A New Name for Some Old Ways of Thinking*. Mineola, NY: Dover.

Jones, E. (1953). *Sigmund Freud Life and Work, Volume One: The Young Freud 1856–1900*. London: Hogarth, 1972.

Kardiner, A. (1977). *My Analysis with Freud: Reminiscences*. New York: Norton.

Kernberg, O. F. (1976). *Object Relations Theory and Clinical Psychoanalysis*. New York: Jason Aronson, 1995.

Kernberg, O. F. (1988). Psychic structure and structural change: an ego psychology-object relations theory viewpoint. *Journal American Psychoanalytic Association*, 36S: 315–337.

Keynes, G. (Ed.) (1972). *Complete Writings of William Blake*. Oxford: Oxford University Press.

Klein, G. S. (1973). Two theories or one? *Bulletin of the Menninger Clinic, 37*: 99–132.

Klein G. S. (1976). *Psychoanalytic Theory: An Exploration of Essentials*. New York: International Universities Press.

Klein, M. (1929). Personification in the play of children. *International Journal of Psychoanalysis, 10*: 193–204.

Klein, M. (1932). *The Psycho-Analysis of Children*. London: Hogarth.

Klein, M. (1950). On the criteria for the termination of a psycho-analysis. *International Journal of Psychoanalysis, 31*: 78–80. Reprinted in: *Envy and Gratitude and Other Works 1946–1963* (pp. 43–47). New York: Delta, 1975.

Klein, M. (1955). On identification. In: *Envy and Gratitude & Other Works 1946–1963* (pp. 141–175). New York: Delta, 1975.

Klein, M. (1957). Envy and gratitude. In: *Envy and Gratitude & Other Works 1946–1963* (pp. 176–235). New York: Delta, 1975.

Klein, M. (1961). *Narrative of a Child Analysis*. London: Hogarth.

Klein, M. (1975). *Envy and Gratitude & Other Works 1946–1963*. New York: Delta.

Klein, M., Heimann, P., Isaacs, S., & Riviere, J. (1952). *Developments in Psycho-Analysis*. London: Hogarth [reprinted London: Karnac, 2002).

Klimovsky, G. (2004). *Epistemología y psicoanálisis-Volumen I* [Epistemology and psychoanalysis-Volume I]. Buenos Aires: Biebel.

Kohut, H. (1959). Introspection, empathy, and psychoanalysis—an examination of the relationship between mode of observation and theory. *Journal of the American Psychoanalytic Association, 7*: 459–483.

Kohut, H. (1971). *The Analysis of the Self*. New York: International Universities Press.

Kohut, H. (1977). *The Restoration of the Self*. New York: International Universities Press.

Kohut, H. (1979). The two analyses of Mr. Z. *International Journal of Psychoanalysis, 60*: 3–28.

Kohut, H. (1982). Introspection, empathy, and the semicircle of mental health. *International Journal of Psychoanalysis, 63*: 395–407.

Kohut, H. (1984). *How Does Analysis Cure?* A. Goldberg (Ed.). Chicago, IL: University of Chicago Press.

Kohut, H., & Wolf, E. S. (1978). The disorders of the self and their treatment: an outline. *International Journal of Psychoanalysis, 59*: 413–425.

Kramer, S. (1986). Identification and its vicissitudes as observed in children: a developmental approach. *International Journal of Psychoanalysis, 67*: 161–172.

Kreeger, L. (Ed.) (1975). *The Large Group: Dynamics and Therapy*. London: Karnac.

Kris, E. (1936). The psychology of caricature. *International Journal of Psychoanalysis, 17*: 285–303.

Lacan, J. (1966). *Ecrits: The First Complete Edition in English*, B. Fink (Trans.). New York: Norton, 2006.

Lacan, J. (1973). *Seminar of Jacques Lacan: The Four Fundamental Concepts of Psychoanalysis—Book XI*, J.-A. Miller (Ed.), A. Sheridan (Trans.). New York: Norton, 1998.

Lacan, J. (1981). *Seminar of Jacques Lacan: The Psychoses 1955–1956—Book III*, J.-A. Miller (Ed.), R. Grieg (Trans.). New York: Norton, 1993.

Laing, R. D. (1959). *The Divided Self: An Existential Study in Sanity and Madness*. London: Tavistock [reprinted, Harmondsworth: Penguin, 1977].

Laplanche, J., & Pontalis, J.-B. (1967). *The Language of Psycho-Analysis*, D. Nicholson-Smith. (Trans.). London: Hogarth, 1973.

Lawrence, D. H. (1994). *The Complete Poems of D. H. Lawrence*. London: Wordsworth, 2002.

Levenson, E. A. (1992). Harry Stack Sullivan: from interpersonal psychiatry to interpersonal psychoanalysis. *Contemporary Psychoanalysis, 28*: 450–466.

Levenson, E. A. (1993). Shoot the messenger—interpersonal aspects of the analyst's interpretations. *Contemporary Psychoanalysis, 29*: 383–396.

Lewin, K. (1951). *Field Theory in Social Science*. New York: Harper.

Liberman, D. (1976a). *Comunicación y psicoanálisis* [Communication and psychoanalysis]. Buenos Aires: Alex.

Liberman, D. (1976b). *Lenguaje y técnica psicoanalítica* [Language and psychoanalytic technique]. Buenos Aires: Kargieman.

Little, M. (1951). Counter-transference and the patient's response to it. *International Journal of Psychoanalysis, 32*: 32–40. Reprinted in: *Transference Neurosis and Transference Psychosis: Toward Basic Unity* (pp. 33–50). New York: Jason Aronson, 1981.

Little, M. (1957). "R"—The analyst's total response to his patient's needs. *International Journal of Psychoanalysis, 38*: 240–254. Reprinted in: *Transference Neurosis and Transference Psychosis: Toward Basic Unity* (pp. 51-80). New York: Jason Aronson, 1981.

Little, M. I. (1981). *Transference Neurosis and Transference Psychosis: Toward Basic Unity*. New York: Jason Aronson.

Little, M. I. (1985). Winnicott working in areas where psychotic anxieties predominate: a personal record. *Free Associations, 1*: 9–42. Reprinted in: *Psychotic Anxieties and Containment: A Personal Record of an Analysis with Winnicott* (pp. 15–78). Northvale, NJ: Jason Aronson, 1990.

Loewald, H. W. (1951). Ego and reality. *International Journal of Psychoanalysis, 32*: 10–18. [Reprinted in: *Papers on Psychoanalysis*. New Haven, CT: Yale University Press, 1980, pp. 3–20.]

Loewald, H. W. (1960). On the therapeutic action of psycho-analysis. *International Journal of Psychoanalysis, 41*: 16–33. Reprinted in *Papers on Psychoanalysis* (pp. 221–256). New Haven, CT: Yale University Press, 1980.

Loewald, H. W. (1980). *Papers on Psychoanalysis*. New Haven, CT: Yale University Press.

Luria, A. M. (1968). *The Mind of a Mnemonist: A Little Book About A Vast Memory*, L. Solotaroff (Trans.). Cambridge, MA: Harvard University Press, 1987.

Luria, A. M. (1972). *The Man with a Shattered World: The History of a Brain Wound*, L. Solotaroff (Trans.). Cambridge, MA: Harvard University Press, 1987.

Luria, A. M. (1979). *The Making of a Mind*, M. Cole (Trans.). Cambridge, MA: Harvard University Press.

Macalpine, I. (1950). The development of transference. *Psychoanalytic Quarterly, 19*: 501–539.

Mahler, M. (1968). *On Human Symbiosis and the Vicissitudes of Individuation. Vol I: Infantile Psychosis*. New York: International Universities Press.

Mahler, M., Pine, F., & Bergman, A. (1975). *The Psychological Birth of the Human Infant: Symbiosis and Individuation*. New York: Basic Books,

Malan, D. H. (1963). *A Study of Brief Psychotherapy*. London: Tavistock [reprinted London: Routledge, 2001].

Mannoni, O. (1969). L'ellipse et la barre. In: *Clefs pour l'imaginaire ou L'autre scène*. Paris: Seuil.

Maroda, K. (2002). No place to hide: affectivity, the unconscious and the development of relational techniques. *Contemporary Psychoanalysis, 38*: 101–121.

Masson, J. M. (1984). *The Assault on Truth: Freud's Suppression of the Seduction Theory*. New York: Farrar, Straus & Giroux [reprinted London: Fontana, 1992].

Matte-Blanco, I. (1975). *The Unconscious as Infinite Sets: An Essay in Bi-Logic*. London: Duckworth [reprinted, London: Karnac, 1998].

Matte-Blanco, I. (1988). *Thinking, Feeling, and Being: Clinical Reflections on the Fundamental Antinomy of Human Beings and World*. London: Routledge.

McLaughlin, J. T. (1987). The play of transference: some reflections on enactment in the psychoanalytic situation. *Journal of the American Psychoanalytical Association, 35*: 557–582.

Mead, G. H. (1934). *Mind, Self and Society from the Standpoint of a Social Behaviorist*, C. W. Morris (Ed.). Chicago, IL: University of Chicago Press.

Meltzer, D. (1967). *The Psychoanalytical Process*. London: Heinemann [reprinted London: Karnac, 2008].

Meltzer, D. (1981). The Kleinian expansion of Freud's metapsychology. *International Journal of Psychoanalysis, 62*: 177–185.

Meltzer, D. (1984). *Dream-Life: A Re-examination of the Psycho-analytical Theory and Technique*. Strathtay, Perthshire: Clunie Press [reprinted London: Karnac, 2009].

Menninger, K. A. (1958). *Theory of Psychoanalytic Technique*. New York: Basic Books.

Merleau-Ponty, M. (1942). *The Structure of Behaviour*, A. L. Fischer (Trans.). London: Methuen, 1965.

Merleau-Ponty, M. (1945). *Phenomenology of Perception*, C. Smith (Trans.). London: Routledge, 1962.

Merriam-Webster (2002). *Webster's Third New International Dictionary, Unabridged*. Springfield, MA: Merriam-Webster.

Milner, M. (1952a). The framed gap. In: *The Suppressed Madness of Sane Men: Forty-four Years of Exploring Psychoanalysis* (pp. 79–82). London: Tavistock, 1987.

Milner, M. (1952b). The role of illusion in symbol formation. In: *The Suppressed Madness of Sane Men: Forty-four Years of Exploring Psychoanalysis* (pp. 83–113. London: Tavistock, 1987.

Mitchell, S. A. (1984). Object relations theories and the developmental tilt. *Contemporary Psychoanalysis, 20*: 473–499.

Mitchell, S. A. (1992). True self, false selves, and the ambiguity of authenticity. In: N. J. Skolnick & S. C. Warshaw (Eds.), *Relational Perspectives in Psychoanalysis* (pp. 1–20). Hillsdale, NJ: Analytic Press

Mitchell, S. A. (1993). *Hope and Dread in Psychoanalysis*. New York: Basic Books.

Mitchell, S. A. (2000). *Relationality: From Attachment to Intersubjectivity*. Hillsdale, NJ: Analytic Press.

Mitchell, S. A., & Aron, L. (Eds.) (1999). *Relational Psychoanalysis: The Emergence of a Tradition*. Hillsdale, NJ: Analytic Press.

Montevechio, B. (1999). *Las nuevas fronteras del psicoanálisis. Dionisio, Narciso, Edipo* [The new frontiers of psychoanalysis: Diosus, Narcissus, Oedipus]. Buenos Aires: Lumen.

Montevechio, B. (2002). *Más allá de Narciso. La problemática de las identidades* [Beyond Narcissus: the problematic of identities]. Buenos Aires: Lumen.

Nietzsche, F. (1872). *The Birth of Tragedy from the Spirit of Music*, D. Smith (Trans.). Oxford: Oxford University Press, 2008.

Ogden, T. H. (1989). On the concept of an autistic–contiguous position. *International Journal of Psychoanalysis, 70*: 127–140.

Ogden, T. H. (1991a). Analysing the matrix of transference. *International Journal of Psychoanalysis, 72*: 593–605. Reprinted in: *Subjects of Analysis* (pp. 137–165). Northvale, NJ: Jason Aronson, 1994 [reprinted London: Karnac, 2012].

Ogden, T. H. (1991b). An interview with Thomas Ogden. *Psychoanalytic Dialogues*, *1*: 361–376. Reprinted in: *Subjects of Analysis* (pp. 183–202). Northvale, NJ, Jason Aronson, 1994 [reprinted London: Karnac, 2012].

Ogden, T. H. (1994a). The analytic third: working with intersubjective clinical facts. *International Journal of Psychoanalysis*, *75*: 3–19. Reprinted in: *Subjects of Analysis* (pp. 61–95). Northvale, NJ: Jason Aronson, 1994 [reprinted London: Karnac, 2012].

Ogden, T. H. (1994b). *Subjects of Analysis*. Northvale, NJ: Jason Aronson [reprinted London: Karnac, 2012].

Orange, D. (2011). *The Suffering Stranger: Hermeneutics for Everyday Clinical Practice*. New York: Routledge.

O'Shaughnessy, E. (1986). A 3½-year-old boy's melancholic identification with an original object. *International Journal of Psychoanalysis*, *67*: 173–179.

Parsons, M. (1990). Marion Milner's "answering activity" and the question of psychoanalytic creativity. *International Journal of Psychoanalysis*, *17*: 413–424.

Paskauskas, R. A. (1993). *The Complete Correspondence of Sigmund Freud and Ernest Jones 1908–1939*. Cambridge, MA: Harvard University Press.

Payne, S. (1950). Short communication on criteria for terminating analysis. *International Journal of Psychoanalysis*, *31*: 205–205.

Pepeli, H. (2003). Psychoanalysis: a treatment, a cure . . . or much more than that? *Journal of the Centre for Freudian Analysis and Research*, *13*(autumn). www.jcfar.org (accessed 30 Apr 2012).

Piaget, J. (1954). *The Construction of Reality in the Child*. London: Routledge, 1999.

Piaget, J. (1967). *Biology and Knowledge: An Essay on the Relations between Organic Regulations and Cognitive Processes*. Edinburgh: University Press, 1971 [reprinted, Chicago, IL: University of Chicago Press, 1974.

Pichon-Rivière, E. (1971). *Del psicoanálisis a la psicología social* [From psychoanalysis to social psychology], in three volumes. Buenos Aires: Nueva Visión.

Pichon-Rivière, E. (1979). *Teoría del vínculo* [Theory of the bond]. Buenos Aires: Nueva Visión.

Pichon-Rivière, E., & de Quiroga, A. P. (1985). *Psicología de la vida cotidiana* [Psychology of everyday life]. Buenos Aires: Nueva Visión.

Pines, M. (1982). Reflections on mirroring. *Group Analysis*, *15*(2): S1–S26. Also in *International Review of Psychoanalysis*, 1984, *11*: 27–42. Reprinted in *Circular Reflections: Selected Papers on Group Analysis and Psychoanalysis* (pp. 17–37). London: Jessica Kingsley, 1998).

Pines, M. (1985). Mirroring and child development. *Psychoanalytic Inquiry*, 5: 211–231. Reprinted in: *Circular Reflections: Selected Papers on Group Analysis and Psychoanalysis* (pp. 41–58). London: Jessica Kingsley, 1998.

Pines, M. (1989). What should a psychotherapist know? In: *Circular Reflections: Selected Papers on Group Analysis and Psychoanalysis* (pp. 131–149). London: Jessica Kingsley, 1998.

Pines, M. (1998). *Circular Reflections: Selected Papers on Group Analysis and Psychoanalysis*. London: Jessica Kingsley.

Pirandello, L. (1921). *Six Characters in Search of an Author*, E. Storer (Trans.). New York: Dutton, 1922.

Pizer, S. (1992). The negotiation of paradox in the analytic process. *Psychoanalytic Dialogues*, 2: 215–240. Reprinted in: S. A. Mitchell & L. Aron (Eds.), *Relational Psychoanalysis: The Emergence of a Tradition* (pp. 337–364). Hillsdale, NJ: Analytic Press, 1999.

Ponsi, M. (1997). Interaction and transference. *International Journal of Psychoanalysis*, 78: 243–263.

Popper, K. R. (1958). Back to the Pre-Socratics. In: *Conjectures and Refutations: The Growth of Scientific Knowledge* (5th revised edition) (pp. 183–223). London: Routledge, 2002.

Puget, J. (1988). Social violence and psychoanalysis in Argentina: the unthinkable and the unthought. *Free Associations*, 1: 84–140.

Puget, J., & Wender, L. (1982). Analista y paciente en mundos super-puestos [Analyst and patient in overlapping worlds]. *Psicoanálisis*, 4: 503–536.

Racker, H. (1953). A contribution to the problem of counter-transference. *International Journal of Psychoanalysis*, 34: 313–324. Reprinted in: *Transference and Counter-Transference* (pp. 105–126). London: Hogarth, 1968).

Racker, H. (1954). Notes on the theory of transference. *Psychoanalytic Quarterly*, 23: 78-86. Reprinted in: *Transference and Counter-Transference* (pp. 71–78). London: Hogarth, 1968.

Racker, H. (1957). The meanings and uses of countertransference. *Psychoanalytic Quarterly*, 26: 303–357. Also in *Psychoanalytic Quarterly*, 2007, 76: 725–777. Reprinted in: *Transference and Counter-Transference* (pp.127–173). London: Hogarth, 1968.

Racker, H. (1958a). A study of some early conflicts through their return in the patient's relation with the interpretation. *International Journal of Psycho-Analysis*, 41: 47–58. Reprinted in: *Transference and Counter-Transference* (pp. 79–104). London: Hogarth, 1968.

Racker, H. (1958b). Counterresistance and interpretation. *Journal of the American Psychoanalytic Association*, 6: 215–221. Reprinted in: *Transference and Counter-Transference* (pp. 186–192). London: Hogarth, 1968.

Racker, H. (1960). *Transference and Counter-Transference*. London: Hogarth.

Ragen, T., & Aron, L. (1993). Abandoned workings: Ferenczi's mutual analysis. In: L. Aron & A. Harris (Eds.), *The Legacy of Sándor Ferenczi* (pp. 217–226). Hillsdale, NJ: Analytic Press.

Rapaport, D. (1951). The conceptual model of psychoanalysis. *Journal of Personality, 20*(1): 56–81. Reprinted in M. M. Gill (Ed.), *The Collected Papers of David Rapaport* (pp. 795–811). New York: Basic Books, 1967.

Renik, O. (1998). The analyst's subjectivity and the analyst's objectivity. *International Journal of Psychoanalysis, 79*: 487–497.

Ricoeur, P. (1965). *Freud and Philosophy: An Essay on Interpretation*, D. Savage (Trans.). New Haven, CT: Yale University Press, 1970.

Riviere, J. (1936). A contribution to the analysis of the negative therapeutic reaction. *International Journal of Psychoanalysis, 17*: 304–320.

Rosenfeld, H. (1974). A discussion of the paper by Ralph R. Greenson on "Transference: Freud or Klein". *International Journal of Psychoanalysis, 55*: 49–51

Roustang, F. (1976). *Dire Mastery: Discipleship from Freud to Lacan*, N. Lukacher (Trans.). Baltimore, MD: Johns Hopkins University Press, 1982.

Rubin, J. (1998). *A Psychoanalysis for Our Time: Exploring the Blindness of the Seeing I*. New York: New York University Press.

Rycroft, C. (1962). Beyond the reality principle. *International Journal of Psychoanalysis, 43*: 388–394. Reprinted in: *Imagination and Reality* (pp. 102–113). New York: International Universities Press, 1968.

Rycroft, C. (1966). Introduction: Causes and meaning. In: C. Rycroft (Ed.) *Psychoanalysis Observed* (pp. 7–21). Harmondsworth: Penguin. Reprinted in: P. Fuller (Ed.), *Psychoanalysis and Beyond* (pp. 41–51). Chicago, IL: University of Chicago Press, 1985.

Rycroft, C. (1968). *A Critical Dictionary of Psychoanalysis* (2nd edn). Harmondsworth: Penguin, 1995.

Sabato, E. (1941). Hombres y engranajes [Men and gears]. Buenos Aires: Emecé. Reprinted in *Hombres y engranajes. Heterodoxia*. [Men and gears—Heterodoxy] (pp. 7–94). Madrid: Alianza, 1973.

Sandler, J., & Sandler, A.-M. (2000). *Clinical and Observational Psychoanalytic Research: Roots of a Controversy: Andre Green & Daniel Stern*. London: Karnac.

Scharff, D. E., & Birtles, E. F. (1997). From instinct to self: the evolution and implications of W. R. D. Fairbairn's theory of object relations. *International Journal of Psychoanalysis, 78*: 1085–1103.

Schneider, S., & Weinberg, H. (Eds.) (2003). *The Large Group Revisited: The Herd, Primal Horde, Crowds and Masses*. London: Jessica Kingsley.

Schwaber, E. A. (1998). "Traveling affectively alone": a personal derailment in analytic listening. *Journal of the American Psychoanalytic Association, 46*: 1045–1065.

Searles, H. F. (1960). *The Nonhuman Environment: In Normal Development and Schizophrenia*. New York: International Universities Press.

Searles, H. F. (1965). *Collected Papers on Schizophrenia and Related Subjects*. New York: International Universities Press.

Searles, H. F. (1979). *Countertransference and Related Subjects*. New York: International Universities Press.

Shakespeare, W. (1975). *The Complete Works of William Shakespeare*. New York: Avenel.

Singer, I. (1971). The patient aids the analyst. In: B. Landis & E. Tauber (Eds.), *In the Name of Life* (pp. 181–192). New York: Grune & Stratton.

Smith, N. A. (1998). "Orpha reviving": toward an honorable recognition of Elizabeth Severn. *International Forum of Psychoanalysis, 7*: 241–246.

Smith, N. A. (1999). From Oedipus to Orpha: revisiting Ferenczi and Severn's landmark case. *American Journal of Psychoanalysis, 59*: 345–366.

Smuts, J. C. (1926). *Holism and Evolution*. London, Macmillan.

Solís Garza, H. (1981). Terminación de análisis [Termination of analysis]. *Cuadernos de Psicoanálisis, 14*: 65–141.

Sparer, E. A. (2009). *La cure psychanalytique classique* by Maurice Bouvet. *International Journal of Psychoanalysis, 60*: 422–426.

Spitz, R. (1965). *The First Year of Life*. New York: International Universities Press.

Sterba, R. (1934). The fate of the ego in analytic therapy. *International Journal of Psychoanalysis, 15*: 117–126.

Stern, D. B. (1983). Unformulated experience: from familiar chaos to creative disorder. *Contemporary Psychoanalysis, 19*: 71–99. Reprinted in: S. A. Mitchell & L. Aron (Eds.), *Relational Psychoanalysis: The Emergence of a Tradition* (pp. 79–105). Hillsdale, NJ: Analytic Press, 1999.

Stern D. B. (1997). *Unformulated Experience: From Dissociation to Imagination in Psychoanalysis*. Hillsdale, NJ: Analytic Press.

Stern, D. N. (1985). *The Interpersonal World of the Infant: A View from Psychoanalysis and Developmental Psychology*. New York: Basic Books.

Stern, D. N., Sander, L. W., Nahum, J. P., Harrison, A. M., Lyons-Ruth, K., Morgan, A. C., Bruschweilerstern, N., & Tronick, E. Z. (1998). Noninterpretive mechanisms in psychoanalytic therapy: The "something more" than interpretation *International Journal of Psychoanalysis, 79*: 903–921.

Stolorow, R. D., & Atwood, G. E. (1984). Psychoanalytic phenomenology: toward a science of human experience. *Psychoanalytic Inquiry, 4*: 87–105.

Stolorow, R. D., & Atwood, G. E. (1992). *Contexts of Being: The Intersubjective Foundations of Psychological Life*. Hillsdale, NJ: Analytic Press.

Stone, L. (1954). The widening scope of indications for psychoanalysis. *Journal of the American Psychoanalytic Association, 2*: 567–594.

Storr, A. (1966). The concept of cure. In: C. Rycroft (Ed.), *Psychoanalysis Observed* (pp. 50–82). Harmondsworth: Penguin.

Strachey, J. (1934). The nature of the therapeutic action of psycho-analysis. *International Journal of Psychoanalysis, 15*: 127–159.

Strachey, J. (1937). Contribution to the Symposium on the Theory of the Therapeutic Results of Psycho-Analysis. *International Journal of Psychoanalysis, 18*: 137–143.

Sullivan, H. S. (1940). *Conceptions of Modern Psychiatry*. New York: White Foundation, 1947.

Sullivan, H. S. (1953). *The Interpersonal Theory of Psychiatry*, H. S. Perry & M. L. Gawel (Eds.). New York: Norton.

Tubert-Oklander, J. (1988). Technical aspects of the analysis of an adolescent boy. *International Review of Psycho-Analysis, 15*: 207–224.

Tubert-Oklander, J. (1989). Los fenómenos postanalíticos: ¿qué es lo que ocurre después de que cae el telón? [Postanalytic phenomena: What happens after the curtain falls?] *Psicoanálisis, 11*: 473–487.

Tubert-Oklander, J. (1994). Las funciones de la interpretación [The functions of interpretation]. *Revista de Psicoanálisis, 51*: 515–544.

Tubert-Oklander, J. (1997). El postanálisis: una fase fundamental del proceso analítico [Post-analysis: An essential phase in the analytic process]. In: J. Vives Rocabert (Ed.), *El proceso psicoanalítico* [The psychoanalytic process] (pp. 305–320). Mexico City: Plaza y Valdés.

Tubert-Oklander, J. (1999). Sándor Ferenczi e la nascita della teoria delle relazioni oggettuali [Sándor Ferenczi and the birth of object-relations theory]. In: F. Borgogno (Ed.), *La partecipazione affettiva dell' analista. Il contributo di Sándor Ferenczi al pensiero psicoanalitico contemporaneo* [The analyst's affective participation: the contribution of Sándor Ferenczi to contemporary psychoanalytic thought] (pp. 261–287). Milan: Franco Angeli.

Tubert-Oklander, J. (2000). El psicoanálisis ante el nuevo milenio. Reflexiones sobre la epistemología del psicoanálisis [Psychoanalysis facing the new Millennium: reflections on the epistemology of psychoanalysis]. *Estudios sobre Psicosis y Retardo Mental, 5*: 275–295.

Tubert-Oklander, J. (2004a). "Le Journal Clinique de 1932" et la nouvelle clinique psychanalytique [The "Clinical Diary of 1932" and the new psychoanalytic clinic]. Le Coq-Héron, Paris, 178: 19–37.

Tubert-Oklander, J. (2004b). Il "Diario clinico" del 1932 e la sua influenza sulla prassi psicoanalitica [The "Clinical Diary" of 1932 and the new psychoanalytic clinic]. In F. Borgogno (Ed.) Ferenczi oggi [Ferenczi Today] (pp. 47–63). Turin: Bollati Boringhieri.

Tubert-Oklander, J. (2006a). I, thou, and us: relationality and the interpretive process in clinical practice. Psychoanalytic Dialogues, 16: 199–216.

Tubert-Oklander, J. (2006b). On the inherent relationality of the unconscious: reply to commentary. Psychoanalytic Dialogues, 16: 227–239.

Tubert-Oklander, J. (2006c). The individual, the group and society: their psychoanalytic inquiry. International Forum of Psychoanalysis, 15: 146–150.

Tubert-Oklander, J. (2007). The whole and the parts: working in the analytic field. Psychoanalytic Dialogues, 17: 115–132.

Tubert-Oklander, J. (2008). Contribution to the discussion. (Symposium on the Analytic Frame.) Psychoanalytic Dialogues, 18: 239–242.

Tubert-Oklander, J. (2009). Hermenéutica analógica y condición humana [Analogical hermeneutics and the human condition]. Analogía Filosófica, Special edition 24.

Tubert-Oklander, J. (2010). The matrix of despair: from despair to desire through dialogue. Group Analysis, 43: 127–140.

Tubert-Oklander, J. (2011a). Lost in translation: a contribution to intercultural understanding. Canadian Journal of Psychoanalysis, 19: 144–168.

Tubert-Oklander, J. (2011b). Enrique Pichon-Rivière: the social unconscious in the Latin-American tradition of group analysis. In: E. Hopper & H. Weinberg (Eds.), The Social Unconscious in Persons, Groups, and Societies—Volume I: Mainly Theory (pp. 45–67). London: Karnac.

Tubert-Oklander, J. (2013a). Field, process, and metaphor. In: M. Katz (Ed.), Metaphor and Fields: Common Ground, Common Language and the Future of Psychoanalysis (pp. 162–181). New York: Routledge.

Tubert-Oklander, J. (2013b). The One and the Many: Selected Papers on Relational Analysis and Group Analysis. London: Karnac.

Tubert-Oklander, J., & Beuchot Puente, M. (2008). Ciencia mestiza. Psicoanálisis y hermenéutica analógica [Hybrid science: Psychoanalysis and analogical hermeneutics]. Mexico City: Torres.

Tubert-Oklander, J., & Hernández de Tubert, R. (1997). Envidia y creatividad [Envy and creativity]. Cuadernos de Psicoanálisis, 31(1–2): 42–54.

Tubert-Oklander, J., & Hernández de Tubert, R. (2004). *Operative Groups: The Latin-American Approach to Group Analysis.* London: Jessica Kingsley.

Tustin, F. (1986). *Autistic Barriers in Neurotic Patients.* London: Karnac.

Tustin, F. (1990). *The Protective Shell in Children and Adults.* London: Karnac, 1992 [reprinted 2012].

Vives, R. J. (1988). Fases críticas en el desarrollo temprano [Critical phases in early development]. In: R. Parres (Ed.) *Psicoanálisis. Convergencia de teorías. Psicoanálisis y poder. Desarrollo temprano* [Psychoanalysis: Confluence of Theories—Psychoanalysis and Power—Early Development] (Volume I)] (pp. 319–325). Mexico City: FEPAL.

Watzlawick, P., Jackson, D. D., & Beavin, J. H. (1967). *Pragmatics of Human Communication.* New York: Norton.

Wender, L. (1993). Two discussions of "The inner experiences of the analyst" and a response from Theodore Jacobs. *International Journal of Psychoanalysis, 74:* 1136–1139.

Whorf, B. J. (1956). *Language, Thought, and Reality. Selected Writings of Benjamin Lee Whorf,* J. B. Carroll (Ed.). Cambridge, MA: MIT, 1967.

Winnicott, D. W. (1949a). Hate in the counter-transference. *International Journal of Psychoanalysis, 30:* 69–74. Reprinted in: *Through Paediatrics to Psycho-Analysis* (2nd edn) (pp. 267–279). London: Hogarth, 1975.

Winnicott, D. W. (1949b). Mind and its relation to the psyche-soma. In: *Through Paediatrics to Psycho-Analysis* (2nd edn) (pp. 243–254). London: Hogarth, 1975.

Winnicott, D. W. (1955). Metapsychological and clinical aspects of regression within the psycho-analytical set-up. *International Journal of Psychoanalysis, 36:*16–26. Reprinted in: *Through Paediatrics to Psycho-Analysis* (2nd edn) (pp. 278–294). London: Hogarth, 1975.

Winnicott, D. W. (1956). On transference. *International Journal of Psychoanalysis, 37:* 386–388. Reprinted in: *Through Paediatrics to Psycho-Analysis* (2nd edn) (pp. 295–299). London: Hogarth, 1975.

Winnicott, D. W. (1958a). *Through Paediatrics to Psycho-Analysis* (2nd edn). London: Hogarth, 1975.

Winnicott, D. W. (1958b). The capacity to be alone. *International Journal of Psychoanalysis, 39:* 416–420. Reprinted in: *The Maturational Processes and the Facilitating Environment* (pp. 29–36). London: Hogarth, 1965.

Winnicott, D. W. (1958c). Child analysis in the latency period. In: *The Maturational Processes and the Facilitating Environment* (pp. 115–123). London: Hogarth, 1965.

Winnicott, D. W. (1960). Ego distortion in terms of true and false self. In: *The Maturational Processes and the Facilitating Environment* (pp. 140–152). London: Hogarth, 1965.

Winnicott, D. W. (1962a). Ego integration in child development. In: *The Maturational Processes and the Facilitating Environment* (pp. 56–63). London: Hogarth, 1965.

Winnicott, D. W. (1962b). The aims of psycho-analytical treatment. In: *The Maturational Processes and the Facilitating Environment* (pp. 166–170). London: Hogarth, 1965.

Winnicott, D. W. (1963). From dependence towards independence in the development of the individual. In: In: *The Maturational Processes and the Facilitating Environment* (pp. 83–92). London: Hogarth, 1965.

Winnicott, D. W. (1965). *The Maturational Processes and the Facilitating Environment.* London: Hogarth.

Winnicott, D. W. (1967). Mirror-role of mother and family in child development. In: *Playing and Reality* (pp. 111–118). London: Tavistock, 1971.

Winnicott, D. W. (1969). The use of an object. *International Journal of Psychoanalysis, 50*: 711–716. Reprinted in: In: *Playing and Reality* (pp. 86–94). London: Tavistock, 1971.

Winnicott, D. W. (1971). *Playing and Reality.* London: Tavistock.

Winnicott, D. W. (1986). Living creatively. In: C. Winnicott, R. Shepherd, & M. Davis (Eds.), *Home is Where We Start From* (pp. 39–54). New York: Norton.

Wordsworth, W. (1807). *Ode: Intimations of Immortality from Recollections of Early Childhood.* In: A. Dore (Ed.), *The Premier Book of Major Poets* (pp. 282–288). New York: Fawcett.

Zac, J. (1968). Relación semana-fin de semana. Encuadre y acting out [The week–weekend relation: The setting and acting-out]. *Revista de Psicoanálisis, 25*(1): 27–91.

Zetzel, E. R. (1956). Current concepts of transference. *International Journal of Psychoanalysis, 37*: 369–375.

Zetzel, E. (1966). Additional notes upon a case of obsessional neurosis: Freud 1909. *International Journal of Psychoanalysis, 47*: 123–129.

INDEX